B

Social Archaeology

General Editor
Ian Hodder, Stanford University

Advisory Editors
Margaret Conkey, University of California at Berkeley
Mark Leone, University of Maryland
Alain Schnapp, U.E.R. d'Art et d'Archeologie, Paris
Stephen Shennan, University of Southampton
Bruce Trigger, McGill University, Montreal

Titles in Print

In preparation

TECHNOLOGY AND SOCIAL AGENCY

Outlining a Practice Framework for
Archaeology

Marcia-Anne Dobres

BLACKWELL
Publishers

First published 2000

2 4 6 8 10 9 7 5 3 1

Blackwell Publishers Ltd
108 Cowley Road
Oxford OX4 1JF
UK

Blackwell Publishers Inc.
350 Main Street
Malden, Massachusetts 02148
USA

British Library Cataloguing in Publication Data
A CIP catalogue record for this book is available from the British Library.

Library of Congress Cataloging-in-Publication Data
Library of Congress data is available for this book.

ISBN   1 57718 123 9 (hbk)
         1 57718 124 7

Typeset in 12 on 12.5 pt Garamond 3
by Best-set Typesetter Ltd., Hong Kong
Printed in Great Britain by MPG Books Ltd, Bodmin, Cornwall

This book is printed on acid-free paper

"Technology . . . the knack of so arranging the world that we don't have to experience it."

Max Frisch (1957: 165)

Contents

List of Figures

Preface

This book traverses a vast range of issues, explores many seemingly incompatible intellectual traditions, and negotiates some long-standing and contentious issues that swirl around the study of technology. While on the one hand I wrote it with the specific question of ancient technologies in mind, I try to present the argument in a way that is accessible and (hopefully) compelling to contemporary material culture and technology enthusiasts. Thus, both in inspiration and in identifying my audience it is unashamedly interdisciplinary. Because I take my ideas and insights from so many different arenas of scholarship, ranging from philosophy, sociology, and feminist politics to ethnoarchaeology and materials science, I have surely done some injustice to each. Any project daring such breadth cannot help suffering from what experts in each of the particular fields touched upon will likely consider superficial treatment. In advance, therefore, I apologize to readers who feel I have not fully (or fairly) treated their pet topics, theories, methodologies, or forms of logic with the depth and rigor they would wish. But I see this book as a step in what will, for me at least, remain an unfinished and ever-unfolding project. Thus, in giving it a name I have emphasized that it is outlin"ing" a practice framework for the study of technology and social agency, rather than presenting a fully developed outline. It is thus my sincere hope that it is read in the spirit in which it was written – to engage in an open and fruitful dialogue among researchers with differently vested interests in a common subject. I readily acknowledge, however, that such a conversation is necessarily fraught with ambiguity, contradiction, and negotiation, and may therefore read, to some, as more of an argument. It is not intended that way.

The initial idea for this book came from Ian Hodder, and I am indebted to him for his unwavering faith in the value of these ideas and my ability to articulate them. He made it possible to both jump-start and ensure the completion of this project by seeing to it that I had a contract in hand before I sought any external financial assistance. His support has opened worlds of opportunity to me.

The crux of ideas started to take shape back in 1993, in what has since developed into an extraordinary working, learning, and authoring relationship with Chris Hoffman. It was Chris who introduced me to the world of philosophy of technology. Chris has pushed me, held me back, given me guidance, and tolerated my fits of ranting, fussing, and fuming with remarkable patience and humor. Mike Schiffer has become one of my most supportive and most honest critics, and I cannot thank him enough for so openly engaging with me over the past three years, especially since we disagree about almost everything! Discussing our radically different views on a common and passionate topic of interest has been an enlightening experience. Mike closely read and made many useful and detailed comments on an earlier draft of the entire manuscript, and though I know much of what I wrote made him (and may still make him) cringe, this book is surely better and more tightly argued as a result. Through all of this, Meg Conkey has been an almost impossible-to-mimic role model of scholarly excellence, honesty, and stamina. She has been my staunchest and most nurturing source of intellectual stimulation for well over a decade, and I am a sincerely grateful for her friendship.

Over the past few years I have benefited from extended, often heated, but always useful conversations with a number of scholars. Special thanks go to Laura Ahearn (and the University of South Carolina "Interdisciplinary Agency Group"), Meredith Aronson, Peter Bleed, Joanna Casey, John Clark, Charles Cobb, Julie Cormack, Ruth Schwartz Cowan, Joan Gero, Olivier Gosselain, Jeremy Hackett, Michael Halberstram, Faye Harrison, Karl Heider, Tim Ingold, Matthew Johnson, Alice Kasakoff, Sue Kent, Ann Kingsolver, Bob Layton, Tom Leatherman, Heather Lechtman, Pierre Lemonnier, David Lewis-Williams, Kent Lightfoot, Thelma Lowe, Marie-Claude Mahias, Arwen Mohun, Henrietta Moore, Stephanie Moser, John Parkington (and his colleagues at the University of Cape Town), John Robb, Valentine Roux, Nerissa Russell, Ken Sassaman, Vern Scarborough, Jim Skibo, Olga Soffer, Anne Solomon, Ulrich Stodiek, Lucy Suchman, Ruth Tringham, Lyn Wadley, Roy Wagner, Rita Wright, and especially Alison Wylie.

In France, my research has been furthered by a number of friends and colleagues, notably André Alteirac, Françoise Audouze, Aline Averbough, Robert Bégouën, Anne Bertrand, the late Dominique Buisson, Jean Clottes, Jim Enloe, Jehanne Féblot-Augustins, Carole Fritz, Michèle Julien, Christiane Leroy-Prost, Michel Orliac, Geneviève Pinçon, Robert Simonnet, Georges Sauvet, Denis Vialou, Anne-Catherine Welté, and Yanick Leguillou. During my dissertation research, some of which is discussed in chapter 6, I was granted access to collections at the following museums and institutions: Musée d'Histoire Naturelle de Toulouse, Musée Départmental de l'Ariège,

Musée de Préhistoire Régionale de Menton, Musée du Mas d'Azil, Musée Bégouën, Musée de l'Homme (Paris), Musée des Antiquités Nationales (St. Germain-en-Laye), l'Institut de Paléontologie Humaine (Paris), the Centre Nationale de la Recherche Scientifique (Paris), Peabody Museum of Archaeology and Ethnology (Harvard University), and the Field Museum of Natural History (Chicago).

I began this project as a resident scholar at the School of American Research (1996–7). There I shared and developed my ideas with an extraordinary group of stimulating and knowledgeable researchers: Ned Blackhawk, Val Carnegie, Glen Conroy, Jackie Urla, and Brad Weiss. I earnestly thank Doug Schwartz, Duane Anderson, and everyone who ensured that my time at SAR was so productive. This book was also financially underwritten by a fellowship from the National Endowment for the Humanities, to whom I extend my gratitude as well. While revising and preparing the manuscript, I received facility support from the University of South Carolina, and in particular thank Leland Ferguson (Department of Anthropology) for providing me with an institutional base, and Carleton Giles (Instructional Support) for critical technical assistance. At Blackwell, my commissioning editors, John Davey and Tessa Harvey, have ably guided me through the complicated maze of publication. I extend my sincere appreciation to both, and especially to my editor, Louise Spencely, to Brian Johnson and Jason Pearce for seeing the manuscript through production, and to Bettina Wilkes for astute copy-editing. Together, they have helped make the final stages of this book's *chaîne opératoire* enjoyable and professional.

Finally, for teaching me just how much – and why – relationships matter, I dedicate this book to Sally, Bruce, Katie, and Matthew, and to the memory of my mother, Amalie Brenner Dobres.

Acknowledgments

The author and publishers are grateful for permission to reproduce the following published material:

Figure 1.1. courtesy of the Eli Whitney Museum, Hamden, Conn.;

Figure 1.2. from J. Gowlett (1984) *Ascent to Civilization*. New York: Alfred A. Knopf (p. 80; photo, Roxby Arch. Ltd., Peter Rauter);

Figure 1.3. from J. Augusta and Z. Burian (1960) *Prehistoric Man*. London: Paul Hamlyn (plate 36);

Figure 1.4. from R. Clairborne (1973) *The First Americans*. New York: Time-Life Series: Emergence of Man (p. 24; artist, Burt Silverman; background photo, ENTHEOS);

Figures 1.5 and 6.3. from C. Karlin, N. Pigeot, and S. Ploux (1992) "L'Ethnologie préhistorique." *La Recherche* 247: 1106–16 (pp. 1106–7 and 1110; artist, Giles Tosello);

Figure 1.7. from J. G. D. Clark (1953) "The Economic Approach to Prehistory." Albert Reckitt Memorial Lecture, British Academy (reprinted in *Contemporary Archaeology: A Guide to Theory and Contributions*, M. Leone (ed.). Carbondale, Ill.: Southern Illinois University Press, pp. 62–77, fig. 6, p. 75);

Figures 6.2a and b. from C. Karlin, P. Bodu, and J. Pelegrin (1991) "Processus techniques et chaînes opératoires: Comment les préhistoriens s'appropient un concept élaboré par les ethnologues," in *Observer l'action technique: Des chaînes opératoires, pour quoi faire?* H. Belfet (ed.). Paris: CNRS (pp. 101–17, fig. 2, p. 107, and fig. 3, p. 109);

Figures 6.4a and b. from N. Pigeot (1987) *Magdaléniens d'Etiolles: Débitage et organisation sociale*. Paris: CNRS, XXV Supplément à *Gallia Préhistoire* (plans 1 and 12);

Figure 6.4c. from M. Olive and N. Pigeot (1992) "Les tailleurs de silex Magdaléniens d'Etiolles: Vers l'identification d'une organisation sociale complexe?" in *La Pierre préhistorique*, M. Menu and P. Walter (eds.). Paris: Laboratoire de Recherche des Musées de France (pp. 173–85, fig. 2, p. 175; artist, Giles Tosello).

Introduction

This is a book about technology. It is, therefore, first and foremost a book about people. It is an argument about understanding past social relationships and how they were forged, mediated, and made meaningful during the everyday practice of material culture production and use. It is not a typical book about the archaeology of technology, because it is not about how artifacts were made and used, it is not about people–artifact relations, nor is it about the activities through which the object world was transformed. Rather, it is squarely and steadfastly centered on technology's subject matter – social relationships and mindful communities of practice. Rather than about their relationships with objects, this is a book concerned with people's relationships with each other and how they drew the making and remaking of the material world into their very being. This explicit focus on the subject of technology, which I will come to call social agency, calls for some pretty radical changes in the ontological, epistemological, analytical, and interpretive lenses currently employed in archaeology. In essence, it requires developing conceptual, methodological, and interpretive ways to look past objects, artifact patterns, and activities in order to bring into focus subjects, artifice, and agency.

As the reader will see, this is not a matter of semantics. I see a profound difference between saying that artifacts mediate social relationships, and saying that people mediate their social relationships through the production and use of artifacts. In developing my perspective I do my best to steer clear of the heated debates that have so often threatened to rip apart the archaeological community during the past twenty years or so. However, anyone with even a passing awareness of these controversies will recognize in these pages recurrent themes that cross-cut the continuum made up of positivist, processual, neo-Darwinian, selectionist, behavioral, feminist, marxist, postprocessual, and hermeneutic standpoints. I leave it to the reader to label my argument as they so please. I prefer to keep my eye on the prize: arguing the necessity of understanding the intertwined social and material constitution of technological practice in prehistory, and how these simultaneously tangible and intangible dynamics contributed, dialectically, to long-term cultural stability and change.

This is not an easy task, and I have not written this book to offer a cookbook of terms, theories, and analytic methodologies that can effect these goals, but to mark out some avenues worth exploring. While I sincerely believe most archaeologists are dedicated to elucidating important and meaningful aspects of ancient technologies in human terms, many of the core arguments and suggestions offered here are fundamentally incommensurate with mainstream perspectives. The words we all use in our work – technology, people, activities, interaction, meaning, and so forth – can have substantially different meanings depending on our ontologies and "where we're comin' from." Unfortunately, it has become painfully clear to me in the course of writing this book that there are fundamental differences in the ontologies, epistemological demands, working premises, and background intellectual persuasions that too often leave dedicated technologists talking past each other, even when they try doubly hard not to, and wondering why we don't simply build upon each other's ideas. I'm not so sure we can.

Thus, while I have tried to engage the relevant contemporary literature where I could, I have not dealt it on a point-by-point basis in order to detail the substantive differences (and few similarities) that exist. Instead, I have chosen another, hopefully more positive and constructive, route: outlining the contours of a practice framework that can help make human subjects central in technological research. But the ideas in this book are themselves only beginnings.

This book is a first attempt at outlining what a subject-centered approach to past technologies might become if given half a chance. It does not pretend to offer "a" theory of technology focused on the question of social agency; nor does it aspire to do so. Rather, it highlights a complex web of issues, dynamics, and questions I think we ought to be asking more explicitly in our materials research programs, and which I think can yield a more human understanding of ancient technologies – which most of us take as our goal.

Inspiration

This book gains inspiration not only from theoretical trends in archaeology and anthropology, but also from those sweeping across the humanities and even the soft and hard sciences. Since the "decentering of the subject" with the advent of post-modernism, new insights into the human condition have begun to take hold in fields as diverse and

seemingly disparate as molecular biology and literary theory. Among
them is the centrality of the body, understood not as a vessel or outer
skin containing hard wiring, genetic blueprints, and hormonal man-
dates, but as the subjective agent and context of its own making. For
example, the renowned evolutionary geneticist Richard Lewontin
recently spoke, passionately and convincingly, of the need to understand both the gene and the biological organism as "active subjects"
existing in (and not simply adapting to) an environment that is not
an external and objective reality, but one created through its ongoing
and processual interaction with them.[1] To understand "the organism
as subject and object of evolution," Lewontin stressed as a primary
factor the intersubjective and mediated context of dynamic interaction
– not that this "dialectic view" (Levins and Lewontin 1985) is likely
to find its way into high-school textbooks for quite some time. In
making his argument, Lewontin noted that evolutionary geneticists
have become "victims of their own metaphors," seeing the laws of
nature as omniscient, slavish, and judgmental, while falling prey to
epistemological and methodological reductionism that thwarts their
very *raison d'être*. Much like Fausto-Sterling,[2] Lewontin suggests that
to overcome these limitations we must recenter both the genetic and
organismic subject at the center of the evolutionary process (also Keller
1983). If this doesn't sound familiar, it will after reading this book.

At the opposite extreme, in philosophy, feminist, psychoanalytic,
and literary theory, for example, there has long been an interest in the
human body as simultaneously and decidedly social and mindful, as
well as physical and sensual (cf. Butler 1993; Csordas 1994a; Eagleton
1983; Grosz 1989; Moore 1994; Shilling 1993). In these unabashedly
humanistic disciplines, the constructed subject takes center-place, but
again there is an emphasis on situated context and interaction in the
making of agents and the structures in which they live. The reader will
see that similar ideas flow through this book, though as an archaeologist I find it necessary to deal with materiality far more substantively
than they typically do. On the other hand, contemporary culture
studies researchers, who have made an interest in constructed selves
their mantle, have begun to recognize what archaeologists have always
known from a number of paradigmatic vantage points: how very
central material culture is to everyday human life (cf. Miller 1987,
1998). As well, in sociology studies of scientific knowledge (known
colloquially as SSK) and in that interdisciplinary arena of science, technology, and society studies (STS) there has been increasing interest to
understand the situatedness of knowledge construction during explicitly material and fabricative endeavors. There is also curiosity regarding the formation of intersubjective communities of mindful,
embodied agent-practitioners (be they lab technicians, engineers,

computer "geeks," in vitro specialists, or potters) and how they understand the world as they do (notably Gooding 1990; Pickering 1995).[3]
Of course, sociocultural anthropologists have also had an interest in at
least some of these concerns, but until very recently (most notably,
Escobar 1994), without paying much attention to materiality in their
"thick descriptions" (as in Geertz 1973a).

Archaeologists, on the other hand, while always and rightfully
recognizing the centrality of material culture and technology in the
making and breaking of society, have not given "the body" its due.[4]
For too long archaeologists have shamelessly gazed on, or at least imagined, disembodied hands making and using the object world while
practically insensible to the body politic – describing technicians as
little more than efficient robots faithfully following some rigidly
choreographed template of motions and sequential fabricative operations dictated by a reified world view hovering in the superorganic
stratosphere, or by the unrelenting demands and limits of nature. To
correct such nightmarish visions of the past, this book argues that we
must refocus our conceptual and interpretive lens to recover the socially
grounded and mindful practices of the sensually engaged bodies of
technicians mediating social relationships in the technological arena.

As the argument in this book unfolds, the reader will see both direct
or oblique references to ideas, arguments, and insights from a range of
disciplines, some of which would appear (on the surface) to have little
bearing on prehistoric technology. But as archaeologists know especially well, surfaces are often misleading. Thus, one of the many sub-
texts of this book is to argue for the value of interdisciplinary dialogue,
and about the unnecessary limitations we place on ourselves when
academic xenophobia rears its ugly head.

Technology and Social Agency: All It Takes Is Practice

My focus in this book is on the embodied social practice of (ancient)
technology as an intersubjective arena of interaction and performance
unfolding in, but never simply dictated by, the material world. While
artifacts may have a fixed life history, technology is an ongoing and
unfinished process – a verb of action and interaction, if you will –
through which people, society, and materials together weave and
reweave the meaningful conditions of everyday life. In this, and not surprisingly, technology and society have much in common. This web is
made of a single social fabric and the individual threads that constitute
it have no integrity if disentangled from each other. Important main-
stays of culture, such as world views, social values, "inalienable posses-

sions," subjecthood, and collective rules of the socialized body, are expressed, reaffirmed, contested, and changed in the course of mundane and taken-for-granted routines of everyday artifact production and use. The "stocks of knowledge" engendered during habitual technical practices are simultaneously personal and social, just as they are both "of the moment" and deeply entrenched in history and symbolic representations. As well, the sorts of knowledge, understandings, and awarenesses that derive from one's encounters with their material world are neither neutral nor "merely" practical; they also reconfirm one's understanding of the world and how it should be worked. Technological knowledge, then, has both a transformative and political potential. Technology always has the possibility of being about relations of power.

In developing these ideas and exploring a few of their corollaries I emphasize the body. The human body is a medium through which artifacts get made and used; the phenomenological body is a thoughtful conduit linking the social and material together in practice; the corporeal body has both individuality and is socialized. As well, the body politic is made up of individuals, and in going through the motions the sentient body instantiates, engenders, and materializes knowledge that itself becomes a "body" of collective wisdom, rules, and proscriptions. This socialized, constructed, corporeal, and mindful body is nothing less than the essence of technological practice. Technological practice, in turn, is not simply the activities and physical actions of artifact production and use, but the unfolding of sensuous, engaged, mediated, meaningful, and materially grounded experience that makes individuals and collectives comprehend and act in the world as they do.

Organization of the Book

These are among the ideas I explore in outlining the contours of a practice framework for the study of technology and social agency in archaeology. But before articulating this view in chapters 3–5, it is essential that the reader understand what motivates this particular vision. Archaeology stakes its very existence on an old and rather tired cliché: to explain the present and hope to change things in the future, we must understand the past and how we came to be as we are. I take this truism to heart. Looking back to understand the present requires, unfortunately, a rather negative assessment of the state of technology studies in archaeology. There would be no reason for me to go out of my way (as I do) to argue that social agency is the heart and soul of ancient technology if I thought contemporary research had any hope of elucidating this insight on its own. As I take pains to argue in chapters 1 and 2, however, as things now stand I do not think this either likely or possible. In concert with the fundamental definitions, premises, and methodologies that underscore mainstream research, the historical legacy of archaeological studies of technology and their problematic ties to the very concept of modernity have promoted increasingly alienated, partitive, and essentialist understandings that have all but erased the phenomenological body of socialized technicians from our explanatory models. Simply put, the better we understand how modernity constrains our understandings of the premodern past, the better we can resist seductive simulacra and work to comprehend the past as different from the present.

Chapter 1 takes a broad view of technology studies in archaeology, identifying what I see as problematic, limiting, even off-the-mark questions, premises, theories, and methodologies that put interpretive blinders on what we make of ancient technologies. It argues that for more than a century we have unwittingly encased mindful and interactive communities of technician-agents in black boxes and have sealed the lid shut with a host of unwarranted epistemological and methodological claims. Chapter 2 further "deconstructs" the state of the art by exploring the historical and philosophical foundations so deeply entrenched in this anachronistically modern view of the premodern past. While some may find this appraisal little more than self-serving "navel-gazing" and an unnecessarily negative start to what purports to be a positive contribution to technology studies, it is not. Critical reflection can be liberatory, and chapters 1 and 2 serve as a wake-up call and a kind of corrective therapy for our collective "technological somnambulism" (Winner 1983). To reflect on the historical relationship between a body of scientific research and the intellectual paradigms and background sociopolitical conditions within which it has developed raises our awareness about what is lacking in, or missing from, these projects, and why. This, in turn, puts in motion the quest for alternatives. That, anyway, is my goal.

Chapter 3 begins constructing an alternative framework by introducing some of the manifold dynamics and phenomena that swirl around and within the corporeal body as it engages in technological practices. I keep the focus purposefully broad, and frame these issues in terms of what philosophers have to say on the subject of embodiment – which is plenty and fascinating. But the readers of this book know that philosophers tend not to appreciate the diversity, variability, and malleability of culture in the way that anthropologists and archaeologists do. Thus, in chapter 4, I bring this concern with the sensuality and mindfulness of technological practice into the realm of culture and society. Here, I explore the experiential, embodied, intersubjective, temporal, and performative nature of everyday technological practice as the link between engagement and meaning, artifice and artifacts, and between being-*in*-the-world and transforming it. This concern with technical performance, in turn, leads me in chapter 5 to identify and consider what I see as the heart and soul of technology, past and present – social agency – defined as the unfolding intersubjective experiences of "being" in a socially mediated and materially grounded world.

Because this book is dedicated to outlining a conceptual framework for understanding ancient technology as the experiential and situated practice of people engaging with each other while making and using material culture, and to comprehending how such meaningful material practices were tied to the body politic, it places special emphasis on the intertwined sociality and materiality of technology as an ongoing (temporally emergent) form of practice. In turn, a focus on social practice emphasizes relations of interdependency: between agents, structures, activities, meaning, cognition, knowledge, skill, material matters, identity, and power. Chapter 5 takes up these issues, especially considering how the *conceptual* framework of the *chaîne opératoire* can advance these interests. However, while the experiential basis of technique and gestures as an embodied and engaged form of mindful social practice has a strong material component, agency is not solely determined by material factors. On its own, however, a practice framework is only a partial corrective to the problems identified in chapters 1 and 2. We also need to rethink our research strategies and how they can be modified to better achieve these worthwhile ends. Thus, chapter 6 considers some methodological issues for putting a practice framework into practice.

While chapter 5 introduces the *conceptual* framework of the *chaîne opératoire*, particularly exploring the unfolding relationship between the corporeal and social body of technicians and the sequential processing and use of the material world, chapter 6 discusses and offers concrete examples to show the value of the *chaîne opératoire* as a materials research tool, or analytic methodology, especially useful for detailing artifact life-histories in order to think about the social agency underwriting those physical actions. As *both* an analytic methodology and a conceptual framework then, the study of sequential operational gestures, procedures, and judgments can bring to light material patterns capable of informing on social relations of production, meaningful interaction, and an agentive and embodied being-in-the-world that is the heart and soul of ancient technological practice.

In chapter 7, I revisit the three strands of thought that together inform this practice framework: the embodied and sensual experience of technological practice as a meaningful and uniquely human form of involvement in the world; the metaphorical and literal resonance between material production and social reproduction embodied during habitual routines of everyday practice; and the centrality of technicians and social agency in creating the structures that promote cultural stability and culture change. I then take one more stab at convincing the reader that these are worthwhile and legitimate subjects of study, by suggesting how they can be as relevant to understanding collective, even large-scale hierarchically organized technologies, as they can the individual and deceptively simple act of making an Oldowan chopper or Acheulean handaxe.

Conclusions

How the dialectic of agency and structure, of artifice and artifacts, and of subjects and objects unfolded in particular times and places is a question archaeologists interested in technology can address through rigorous materials research. Such dynamics are not beyond our means to comprehend, though the conceptual, analytic, and interpretive tools for doing so require serious revision. A relational and practice-centered view of human (even hominid) technologies requires, first, a rethinking of what constitutes technology, and second, a reconsidering of what one is studying through the medium of material patterns and empirical traces. This is no easy task, and this book can only begin to identify what I think is required to move such inquiry forward. It is also clear that there are no across-the-board answers to these questions, nor a formulaic package of methods and material correlates that can uniformly work to make sense of all the world's technologies.

Ultimately, this book is intended as an extended conceptual argument designed to promote substantive change in the way we think about technology, both those of the past as well as those practiced today and perhaps tomorrow. I believe such shifts in thinking must come before the necessary shifts in conducting research differently, though in chapter 6 I do offer some methodological techniques that have worked in my own materials research on European Palaeolithic technologies. Watson (1991) recently characterized the substantive difference between processual and postprocessual archaeology as between a "soulless method" (the former) and a "methodless soul" (the latter). In a small way, I hope the argument in this book is seen as trying to find some appropriate middle ground, taking the best concerns and ideas of each, while recognizing their limits and incompatibilities as well.

Given the variety of robust conceptual frameworks now at our disposal, some of which have been around for some time, the options for understanding (or explaining) past technologies are many. This book adds yet another set of ideas to the question concerning technology (apologies to Heidegger), explicitly focusing on social agency, practice, intersubjectivity, and the meaningful embodied experience of artifact making and use. Perhaps readers will see in my argument more of a connection with some of these other (existing) frameworks than I; and if there are ways to integrate them without over-essentializing my fundamental points nor claim concurrence simply to create a metatheory of technology (which makes me highly suspicious and nervous), then we will all be the better. After all, "every thinker puts some portion of an apparently stable world in peril and no one can predict what will emerge in its place" (Dewey 1960: 60 [orig. 1929]).

Technology is without question a complex social practice, no matter the time, place, or "kind" of society or material activities at hand. It would be presumptuous to suggest that any single framework was capable of comprehending its whole, and I certainly do not mean to suggest that in outlining a practice framework. What I do suggest, is that without embracing the dynamics of social agency and all that that entails, we can never comprehend the fullness of this quintessentially human experience.

1

Of Black Boxes and Matters Material: The State of Things

[T]he historian who is most conscious of his own situation is also most capable of transcending it. . . . Man's capacity to rise above his social and historical situation seems to be conditioned by the sensitivity with which he recognizes the extent of his involvement in it.

(E. H. Carr 1961: 53–4)

The study of prehistoric technology[1] has a long and privileged place in archaeology, and the study of techniques and innovations through time and across space is central to practically any understanding of the human career. While technology forms the centerpiece of most theories of human evolution and is central to defining cultural complexity, for well over a century archaeologists have worked with a largely implicit and taken-for-granted concept sorely in need of revision (Dobres and Hoffman 1994: 211–12; Ingold 1988a; Pfaffenberger 1992). Social science understandings of culture change over short and long expanses of time have been premised upon a particularly entrenched view privileging the instrumentality, practicality, and rationality of object making and use over the social, political, and symbolic nature of ancient material endeavors. The argument this chapter develops is that this Standard View (Pfaffenberger 1992) speaks more to a modern and technocentric vision of the world than it does about pasts understood in their own terms.

This decidedly modern view – that technology is a distinctive sphere of materially grounded pragmatic behaviors separate from, underlying, and impinging upon politics, social organization, beliefs, and value systems – is built on a materialist and rationalist edifice. As such, it squares well with the material, social, economic, and (especially) ideological conditions within which it has been shaped for more than a century (Habermas 1970; Marcuse 1968: 223; E. Wolf 1982: 8–18). But while an instrumentalist view of technology is endemic to the capitalist mode of production and the particular contours of modern industrialism, it is not necessarily appropriate for adequately grasping the technology-society "equation" for all times, places, and productive modes (Ingold 1988a, 1993a, 1995; Reynolds 1993). The following discussion argues that the particular technovision shaping the "machine age" has been projected backwards in time and retrofitted onto societies vastly different from our own, thereby producing simulacra *of* the past rather than models *for* the way it actually was (after Baudrillard 1983; Geertz 1966: 7–8).

Because "origins points" are necessarily false beginnings (Conkey 1986; Kus 1986) that imply unidirectional causality, where one starts such an analysis may give a false impression of what is a complex dialectic inseparably linking the subject matter of the past with archaeological practice conducted by researchers irrevocably situated in their own time, place, intellectual paradigms, and socioeconomic conditions. In terms of understanding the relationship between prehistoric technology and its being studied in the present, I hope to avoid any simpleminded misreading implying that one set of factors directly influenced the other. Instead, I want to emphasize the hermeneutic connecting the contemporary sociocultural conditions within which archeology is (and has been) undertaken with what archaeologists know about the past and how they produce such knowledge.

Why Start with the Sociopolitics of Research on Prehistoric Technology?

The above caveats notwithstanding, because archaeology is a contemporary practice that both reflects and contributes to present-day understandings of the human condition, it makes sense to start with a consideration of the sociopolitical and economic "times" in which the study of ancient technologies have been undertaken. In so doing, I do not mean to suggest that archaeologists are nothing more than puppets supporting dominant cultural ideologies. They need not be, and the history of archaeology is filled with examples of challenges to nationalist ideologies supported by self-serving claims about the past (particularly Parkington and Smith 1986; Schrire 1995).[2] Nonetheless, as shown by recent social science historiographies (Ross 1991), especially those in anthropology and archaeology (Fabian 1983; Stocking 1968, 1987, 1991; Trigger 1989; E. Wolf 1982; Wylie 1985a), preexisting sociopolitical interests and knowledge structures substantially impact intellectual inquiry (more generally, see Dickens 1983; Habermas 1970).

For the topic of technology, however, the dialectic of present and past has never been scrutinized in much detail. Although there are literally hundreds of books that analyze prehistoric technology and describe and explain technological change over time, none specifically concentrates on the concepts and conceptual paradigms within which such research has been undertaken. There are numerous excellent histories of archaeological method and theory written to draw out the prevailing cultural ontologies and sociopolitical interests within which they were developed (notably, Audouze and Leroi-Gourhan 1981; Kehoe 1998; Laming-Emperaire 1964; Trigger 1989). Yet none has privileged the study of technology. *Why* unpacking the concept of technology has been relatively neglected is as important to understand as the fact that the concept has remained relatively impervious to substantial revision by working archaeologists for more than a century.

One of the arguments running through this book is that social constructivist analyses (which some inappropriately disparage as "mere" deconstructive criticism) contribute to scientific inquiry in substantive ways, most especially by revealing unstated assumptions, inappropriate premises, and unquestioned methodologies underlying, and thus in part, structuring empirical research and resulting models (Latour 1987; Latour and Woolgar 1986; Lloyd 1996; Sabia and Wallulis 1983). To reflect on the relationship between a body of research and the intellectual paradigms and cultural world views within which it is embedded puts in motion the quest for alternatives that attempt better, more rigorous, and self-censoring research (Cutliffe 1995; Drygulski Wright 1987). This is central to the very notion of scientific progress (essays in Bleier 1988; Harding and Hintikka 1983; E. F. Keller 1982; T. Kuhn 1970, 1977). Thus, if archaeological research on technology is to improve its logical underpinnings as well as its analytic methodologies to effect better (specifically more humanistic) understandings, then it must confront its history and recognize what has been – and still is – overlooked, under-theorized, and over-determined. Only by such means can we imagine and pursue theoretical orientations and analytic methodologies that take up these issues explicitly, much in the same way as the New Archaeology attempted to "correct" the failings of Culture History.

The intent of this chapter, then, is to detail something of the history and contemporary contours of archaeological research on prehistoric technology, for it is the topic upon which the very foundations of the discipline were founded. My specific goals are: to explore how contemporary research on prehistoric technology defines its subject (or more correctly, object) matter; to identify the cultural premises and ontologies that have mediated this view; and to explore how this perspective has impacted specific analytic research methods and explanatory models developed to study and explain ancient technologies. In this chapter I restrict myself to laying out what Pfaffenberger (1992) calls the Standard View and exploring the insidious relationship between contemporary technocentrism and research on past technologies. Chapters 2 and 3 take up in more detail some of ontological, epistemological, historical, and philosophical foundations of this Standard View. To fulfill the objectives of this book, which are to outline the contours of a human-centered, specifically practice, framework and research methodology to further that end, I intentionally paint this Standard View in broad strokes rather than detail any specific ancient technology or explanatory model.[3]

This look in the mirror accomplishes three things: (1) it identifies topics and phenomena that have *not* been the focus of sustained theoretical or analytic attention (chapter 1); (2) it asks why they have been overlooked, ignored, or underplayed (chapters 2 and 3); and (3) it allows me to articulate an alternative conceptual framework (chapters 4 and 5) and propose the contours of an analytic methodology (chapter 6) with which they can be better brought into focus. The "technique" of grounding a search for alternative conceptual frameworks and analytic methodologies in a social constructivist historiography is intended to shift our attention from the study of artifacts and people–artifact relationships and refocus it on the social artifice and interpersonal relations of production by which they were made, used, and given value – without compromising rigorous analytic attention to the physical traces of prehistoric technologies extant in the archaeological record.

While I here concentrate primarily on the past three decades of research on ancient technologies and explore various concepts and premises embedded in what is, in fact, substantive research, I occasionally reach further back to archaeology's "origins" as a serious scholarly discipline in the mid to late 1800s, using Laming-Emperaire (1964), Trigger (1989), Kehoe (1998), and Willey and Sabloff (1974) as my guides. My reasons for juxtaposing archaeology's pasts and present are three-fold: first, because of the critical importance of discoveries pertaining to technological evolution made in the mid-nineteenth century; second, because through such discoveries archaeologists were able to demonstrate empirically the antiquity of humans and thereby carve out for themselves a legitimate place in the social sciences; and third, because these physical discoveries and the initial attempts to make sense of them came at the height of the industrial revolution. As I argue here and in the next chapter, this particular socioeconomic and political context, industrialism, had much to do with what early archaeologists studied, how they chose to study it, and their subsequent reconstructions and models of human (read: technological) evolution. But as I suggest here and explain in chapter 2, in recent times things have not changed as much as we would like to believe.

Contemporary Technovisions, or an Industrial Logic of Making and Using

Metaphors are helpful in expressing and materializing core ideals, attitudes, and epistemologies basic to everyday life (Lakoff 1987, 1989; Lakoff and Johnson 1980). Because the materiality of technology is a very real, lived human experience that helps give shape to our lives, communicating through the medium of technology and by way of techno-metaphors allows us express ourselves through shared idioms that, to employ a techno-metaphor myself, "hit the nail on the head." To "hammer" my point home consider the following: today we see in Technicolor®; ours is an industrial (or, according to some, a post-industrial) society; we live in the Computer Age. While the steam engine symbolizes the "machine age," stone "industries" exemplify the Palaeolithic. Culture has been likened to a thermostat, the body to a machine (we wonder what makes people "tick," fret when we're "wound up," and get "steaming" mad); and women's organs are still jokingly called "plumbing." Traffic "grinds" to a halt; societies are "built;" politicians "spearhead" campaigns and "cut" their opponents down during debates; parents "mold" children (the way bakers shape pastries?); and while both babies and objects are "produced," women and commodities are "exchanged." We call humans "resources," as if people and inert matter were interchangeable units of energy. And while we now "socialize" in Cyberspace and describe our future in terms of the cyborg, we also convince ourselves that Virtual Reality (and virtual sex) are "the real thing."

Contemporary values and attitudes about technology are often a means by which we evaluate the contributions different members of society make to its smooth functioning and/or to its transformation. Very often, people gain at least part of their economic, political, and social status by virtue of their association with particular technologies or tools. For example, gender value systems are inscribed onto the technological world of material resources and power at the same time that material technologies and technological activities become linked, in practice and belief, with particularly gendered individuals.[4] Even today, there are (still) few jobs that are not at least ideologically associated with either men or women, that do not differentially reward the players, and that do not also simultaneously conjure up normative idioms that reinforce these cultural proscriptions and practices. Gender is fundamental to the way technological work is organized and valued, just as technology is central to the social construction of gender (Asher 1987; Cowan 1979; Game and Pringle 1984; M. A. MacKenzie 1991; McGaw 1982). In terms of modern techno-metaphors, men are typically the ones said to "erect" machines (figure

Figure 1.1 The inseparable dialectic of technology and gendered sensibilities.
Source: Eli Whitney Museum, Hamden, Conn.

1.1), "mount" bridges, and wage daily war with "mother" nature. By virtue of their supposedly biologically endowed technological prowess with hard and mechanical things, men (in industrial societies, at least) are stereotypically seen as best suited to be the engineers who operate the machinery that makes industrial society run (see also Teilhart 1978). Reciprocally, technologies associated with the fabrication or use of hard and utilitarian *things*, such as cars, guns, and weapons of war, serve as powerful idioms of masculinity (Lechtman 1993: 409).

In contrast, women are ideologically and stereotypically associated with so-called soft, passive, and less-valued "domestic" technologies: sewing, vacuuming, having babies, and tending to the needs of the young, sick, and elderly. None of these are valued as high-tech activities, but they nonetheless help to define femininity with values such as nimble fingers (in both sewing and typing), the innate ability and desire to nurture, and the naturally endowed gift of patience. Historians such as Baker (1964), McGaw (1982), and Trescott (1979) have chronicled how and why material technologies, once ideologically (and in practice) valued as men's work, became "feminized" and subsequently downgraded both in social prestige and economic worth during women's exodus out of the "domestic sphere" and into factories and public workplaces early in the nineteenth century – for example, in cigar production (Baker 1964), the printing industry (Baron 1987; Cockburn 1985), and clerical work (Srole 1987). Similarly, the very idea that prehistoric hunting and lithic technologies were most likely a masculine domain, as rationalized in Brown (1970), reflects more on contemporary (western) gender ideologies and the political economy of archaeological practice than any inherent predispositions on the part of prehistoric males or females (Gero 1985, 1991a; for more on the gendered dimensions of "the hunt," see chapter 4).

More generally, Pacey (1983: 104) has noted that "nearly all women's work, indeed, falls within the usual definition of technology. What excludes it from recognition is not only the simplicity of the equipment used, but the fact that it implies a different concept of what technology is about." Indeed, feminist historians of science and medicine have shown that until mid-nineteenth-century developments in male-dominated reproductive technologies (such as the hard technics and objectified gaze of the speculum or more recently in-vitro fertilization), women's reproductive technologies were characteristically described as inherent, natural, and biological (Corea 1987; Laqueur 1990; Schiebinger 1993; Stanworth 1987). Even today, without the intervention of high-tech gadgets few would describe women's "natural" contraceptive and birthing practices or breast-feeding strategies as a technology *per se*. Clearly, the reasons certain technologies are so strongly associated with particular genders, even to the point where "hard" and "soft" technologies serve as code-words by which to acknowledge and differently value the abilities and contributions gendered individuals make to society, is not by virtue of fact or biology (Asher 1987). Rather, these particular ideas about gender and technology are shaped by the historical contours of the recent past – industrialism and the particular gendered divisions of labor driving and supporting it.

There is more to the meaning of technology than its acting as an organizing principle for metaphorically comprehending and living in the world; more, even, than how it is used to proscribe and evaluate the contributions different categories of individuals can (or should) make to society. For at least two centuries, social theorists (in particular, anthropologists and archaeologists) have evaluated and rated entire culture complexes, living and dead, in terms of their supposed evolutionary stage of technological complexity (as but one obvious example, see Oswalt 1976). From the very inception of archaeology as a systematic and scholarly discipline in the mid-1800s, archaeologists have catalogued human history according to (material) technological stages. The serial "fathers" of Old World archaeology (among them Thomsen, Jouannet, Boucher de Perthes, Montelius, Lartet, Pitt-Rivers, de Mortillet, and Petrie) all built their evolutionary scenarios on the basis of how tool forms and techniques of fabrication changed through time and across space, in linear and progressive fashion. For example, Pitt-Rivers (1875) demonstrated the evolutionary trajectory of weapons of war through his typological displays devoid of any cultural specificity; Tylor (1878) described the progressive evolution of world-wide fire-making technologies from use of the simple stick-and-groove, to the fire-drill, then flint, and finally to matches; and the Abbé Breuil (1912) relied heavily on technical attributes of stone and organic arti-facts to construct his typological schema for the French Palaeolithic. For him, the notched blade (*lame à coche*) and presence of split-based antler points were the index-fossils for the Aurignacian; a temporally unique lithic bifacial thinning technique pinpointed the Solutrean culture-phase in time and space; while a "revolution in the working of bone and horn" (ibid.: 216–17) became the hallmark of the Azilian (see also Piette 1895).

The mutual reinforcement of ideas and logic between archaeology and social anthropology at the turn of the century is well documented (Daniel 1963, 1967, 1975; M. Harris 1968; Trigger 1989; Willey and Sabloff 1974), and no better theorist with a hand in both fields can be considered in this regard than Emile Sollas. Building his case based on self-congratulatory, progressivist notions about cultural complexity premised on the primacy of western industrial technologies – then exemplified by steam locomotion (Petroski 1994) – Sollas (1911) main-tained that the paucity of their material technology made contempor-ary Australian Aborigines and Tasmanians exemplars, or "survivals," of the Neandertal stage of human evolution, while the living material and technical practices of southern African "Bushmen" showed they were still living an early Upper Palaeolithic (Aurignacian) way of life (also Lubbock 1865; discussion in Stocking 1987: 155–64).

As a well-established technique for constructing conceptual distance between subject and object, social scientists and folk culture alike privilege technology (and material culture, more generally) as the archetypal trait by which to measure and assess the evolutionary com-plexity of contemporary cultures. In so doing, they implicitly join char-acter to capacity as a way to evaluate worth against a western/industrial standard. Each culture has its place on the hierarchical and temporal ladder of Difference and Distance based, in large measure, on the mate-rial complexity of their technology. In this way the "coevalness" of Them and Us is denied (Fabian 1983). As Parkington and Smith note with regard to South Africa's history,

Archaeology and anthropology were born in colonially expanding periods of European history when capitalist enterprises were coming increasingly in contact and conflict with indigenous communities. The primitive, childlike or natural qualities of non-western peoples as expressed by anthropologists served to justify their political domina-tion and exploitation by more "civilized" peoples in the name of progress. Comparisons between the simple technology of isolated living groups and the archaeological record underlined the static nature of non-western communities. The contrast in technology and way of life between European society and the "natives" was such that large National Museums were required to display it. A hangover of this period with which we still have to grapple is the location of [the material record of] aboriginal people in Natural History museums in countries with a colonial past. European colonial materials are housed in Cultural History museums. (1986: 1)

Unfortunately, the use of archetypal techno-traits to evaluate and explain particular cultures is alive and well in contemporary anthropology. As but one example, Testart's (1982, 1986, 1988) explanatory model of mechanisms driving the (directional) evolution toward increasingly complex social formations is based on the claim that mobile hunter-gatherers are *unable* to develop material storage technologies because their lifeways are determined by the nature of their food resources (characterized by high patchiness and low reliability). According to Testart, environment determines mobility, which in turn either precludes or enables storage technologies, which in turn either precludes or enables hierarchically ordered social relations of production. Although by no means alone in conceptualizing *environment* → *technology* → *society* as a one-way street, Testart argues that social formations are constructed upon a technological edifice pragmatically and rationally responsive to the external environment (see below).[5] In his model, storage technology is the archetypal material trait by which to judge the overall technical system and character of contemporary Australian hunter-gatherers, whom he characterizes as "lacking," "blocked," "deficient," and existing as an "inferior backwater" (Testart 1988: 9–10; for a sustained critique of this view, see Ingold 1988b; also Halperin 1994).

On the other hand, the "imperialist nostalgia" embedded in the very concept of the ethnographic present is replete with mournful descriptions of the loss of "the old ways" by ethnographers, archaeologists, journalists, and travelers alike (Rosaldo 1989). For example, when first "discovered," the so-called Tasaday were romantically envisioned as the Last Stone Age Tribe (Nance 1975, 1982), living a pristine but noble life unfettered and untouched by the first-worldly materialism of industrial societies (also Diamond 1988). And, according to Toth et al., it was a mere 10,000 years ago that

all human societies used stone implements. In modern times, the relentless advance of more complex technologies has left but a few remnants of the primeval world, and even these will surely disappear before this century is out. Anthropologists must therefore hurry to study contemporary stone age craftsmen for clues they may provide about our early ancestors. (1992: 88)

This "pastoral view" of the Other is yet another trope common to western discourse (Williams 1973). Temporally displaced and nostalgic views of so-called primitive technologies (whether practiced in the good old days or miraculously surviving into the present) still loom large in contemporary research, whether it be based in ethnography, ethnoarchaeology, or replicative study.

Summary

Just as high-tech instruments are central to the daily practice of contemporary archaeological research (such as scanning-electron microscopes, x-ray and infrared spectroscopy, radiometric dating instruments, neutron-activation equipment, machines for chemical and petrologic analyses, and computers and satellites for GIS imaging), and just as technology is key to "tracking" human evolution and rating cultures through time and across space, technology is clearly one of the most powerful and symbolically charged tropes that give meaning to the modern world. Without actually challenging the basic claim that technology *is* central to human existence, I think it necessary to rethink what constitutes this phenomenon and tease apart the particular historical relationship between contemporary technocentrism and archaeological inquiry. It is imperative that we do so if we want to develop alternatives more in keeping with the stated goal of understanding the past as possibly unlike the present.

The point of these preliminary remarks is to outline in the most general terms something of the technocentric milieu within which so much of contemporary archaeology makes sense of ancient technologies (for more substantive considerations of the ideology underpinning modern technocentrism, see Habermas 1970; Marcuse 1964, 1968; Mitcham 1994; Pippin 1995; Winner 1977, 1986a). Because it is necessary to work back and forth between past and present over and over again to grasp fully the dialectic of presentism in the study of prehistoric technology, later in this chapter and again in the next I return to detail more substantively how contemporary ideologies and frames of reference too often resurface in models of prehistoric technologies.

Prehistory's Hero Story: Techno-logic Saves the Day

The modern take on human evolution in both scholarly texts and folk accounts is structured as an heroic epic (Keene 1993; Landau 1984,

1991; Terrell 1990; E. Wolf 1982: 5). As the story typically unfolds, it is against all odds that our hero fights valiantly, confronts the vagaries of a merciless and heartless (mother) Nature, and (in the end) bends Her to His will.[6] Once unquestioningly male, our contemporary techno-hero increasingly looks not unlike a late-twentieth-century liberated woman (see examples in Auel 1980; Fisher 1983; Pringle 1998; Tanner 1976; Tanner and Zihlman 1976). No matter – with guts, intellect, and technological prowess our hero/heroine beats the odds and evolves into what We are today: civilized, rational, and above all technical (Pfaffenberger 1992; Staudenmaier 1989: 145–8). This mythic tale often concludes with a sad postscript: we find that our technologically sophisticated and now fully civilized hero, "having accomplished great deeds, succumbs to pride or hubris and is destroyed" (Landau 1984: 265; also Terrell 1990: 12–15). In keeping with the ironic but clearly moralistic endings of the Frankenstein and Jekyll/Hyde epics, in this standard telling of our techno-evolutionary story, as *Technology Makyth Man* (Oakley 1959), so too, the unfeeling bureaucracy of the "megamachine" (Mumford 1967) will destroy Him (for its most recent retelling, see the excerpts from the Unabomber's Manifesto of 1996 on page 235).

Nowhere is the up-beat portion of this story told in a more compelling and dramatic fashion than in the visual format of the *Time-Life* "Emergence of Man" series (see, for example, Constable 1973; Edey 1972; Howell 1965; Prideaux 1973), in the pages of *National Geographic*'s illustrated series on human evolution, and in museum dioramas. Upon closer investigation, however, both pictorial and textual models of prehistoric technologies reveal a similarly structured hero-story, but with some telling details that attest quite clearly to its being articulated against the paradigmatic backdrop of industrial technovisions.

Visual reconstructions: popular media

The systematic analysis of pictorial reconstructions of ancient technologies found in popular journals and books, as well as those represented in three-dimensional dioramas on view (characteristically) in museums of natural history, points to a set of recurring themes and conventions that betrays a shared (albeit implicit) view of what technology was all about in our glorious past. Whether the material in question is stone, bone, metal, ceramics, or any of the common classes of resources utilized by prehistoric peoples, there are stock conventions to which most portrayals adhere. Typically since the 1960s, when the empirical study and replication of ancient manufacturing and use techniques became a major field of archaeological investigation, pictorial reconstructions have narrowed in on disembodied hands (figure 1.2). This perspective, hands severed from socially constituted bodies (which is but one among many visual conventions that could be employed), parallels the analytic attention the general archaeological community pays to questions of materials processing and the delineation of the sequential stages by which different artifact classes were fabricated, used, and repaired through time and across space, considered separate from their social milieu (see, for example, Bordes 1969; Camps-Fabrer 1989; Crabtree 1966, 1968; discussion below and in chapters 2 and 6).

As well, whether it is 2 million or merely 10,000 years ago, when humans (or hominids) are visually represented in their entirety, they are typically pictured slavishly toiling away on loess-swept bluffs or by lakeside shores without other members of the community anywhere in sight (figure 1.3). Even when work groups are pictured, these "paleo-visions" (Conkey 1996, and in press) implicitly convey the idea that prehistoric technicians had little meaningful engagement with one another (see critique in K. Gordon 1995). Instead, individuals are conventionally depicted looking down at their work, concentrating all their evolv(ing) skills and material prowess on surviving some harsh and unyielding environment through material/technical means (figure 1.4; also figure 6.4c). From these reconstructions one senses that the Protestant Work Ethic has always been part of the human condition! In reconstruction after reconstruction, this same structural pattern surfaces: technology is serious material business but not necessarily social or enjoyable.

The visual convention of depicting the serious and oddly *a*social character of ancient technological practice prevails in the popular media, even in pictorial representations supervised by professional archaeologists. Among the more influential of these visual reconstructions of technology over the last century commissioned specifically for popular audiences are Keith's and Boule's competing visions of Neandertal man in the *Illustrated London News*, 1909–11; Burian's evocative oil paintings (Augusta and Burian 1960; analysis in Stoczkowski 1997); *Time-Life*'s (1973) reconstructions in "The Neanderthals" (consultant: R. S. Solecki) and "Cro-Magnon Man" (consultants: P. E. L. Smith and R. Klein); Gowlett's (1984) still available *Ascent to Civilization*; and *National Geographic*'s extremely popular ongoing series on human evolution (for detailed analysis, see Moser 1998).

In these pages, prehistoric technicians are forever portrayed looking down at their work, concentrating serious and full attention on the material job at hand, seemingly unaware of and apparently not affected by each other's presence. The only exception to this general rule is that

Figure 1.2   The disembodied hand: the most ubiquitous visual convention for representing prehistoric technology.
Source: Gowlett 1984, p. 80; photo © by Peter Rauter, Roxby Arch. Ltd.

occasionally, in the background and out of the primary focal point, one can glimpse an adult female, presumably a mother, directly interacting with a small child (figure 1.5; Gifford-Gonzalez 1993a). Only rarely is a similar interactive relationship imagined between adult males and young children (ibid.; Gamble 1998). As I discuss below, graphically representing technology by disembodied hands holding fast to physical objects and picturing individual technicians divorced from the social body is a convention also found in the pictorial reconstructions that accompany both scientific reports and textbooks.

Moser (1993a, 1998) and Gifford-Gonzalez (1993a), in particular, have analyzed the dialectic of contemporary gender (and to a lesser extent racial and age) stereotypes and pictorial reconstructions of prehistory in the popular media.[7] For example, Gifford-Gonzalez's systematic study found that females are inevitably represented in more passive and submissive physical postures compared to males (for example, squatting, bending over, looking downward). As well, while through time males are characteristically shown actively engaged with the most up-to-date tools and fabrication and use techniques, females are (too often) depicted doing the same activity, scraping hides, in one particularly evocative and apparently timeless position, down on all fours.

Figure 1.3   The lone worker divorced from the body politic: a "peopled" reconstruction of prehistoric technology.
Source: Augusta and Burian 1960, plate 36; artist Zdenek Burian

Figure 1.4   The Protestant Work Ethic projected onto the premodern past: the serious business of prehistoric technology.
Source: Clairborne 1973, p. 24; artist: Burt Silverman; background photo: ENTHEOS (the image has been cropped for publication here)

Figure 1.5   The implicit projection of contemporary gender value systems onto prehistoric technological practices.
Source: Karlin et al. 1992, pp. 1106–7; artist: Gilles Tosello

The sexist conventions underwriting text-based reconstructions of the basic "Man the Hunter" version of the heroic techno-story, well-documented by now, focus almost exclusively on healthy adult males portrayed as the active inventors and agents of new material technologies and, by extension, culture change (Dahlberg 1981; Fedigan 1986; Hubbard 1982; Slocum 1975). Females, on the other hand, seem behaviorally tied to their biology; they are predisposed to tend the young while practicing innate and "soft" technologies such as hide-tanning, sewing, or bread-making. What makes the close scrutiny of pictorial reconstructions so compelling is that they do, in fact, reveal the strikingly similar use of conventional visual tropes in scholarly texts (Lynch and Woolgar 1990: 2–6; Molyneaux 1997; Moser 1992, 1993b, 1998; Rudwick 1976). More to the point, however, pictorial representations work recursively on the production of scientific knowledge, subtly influencing the scientific community from which these images originally derive (Baigire 1996; Rudwick 1992; Woolgar 1990: 149–50).

Figure 1.6   A striking resonance between the iconographic structure of peopled reconstructions of prehistoric technologies and the everyday practice of archaeological field and laboratory research.
Source: Author's photograph

After all, they're just pictures for the lay public

Of course, one might complain that the analysis of pictorial reconstructions is not an appropriate domain for scrutinizing archaeological technovisions. After all, for the most part these visual reconstructions are intended for popular culture and should not be taken to represent the level of scholarly sophistication evident in peer-reviewed texts. To this critique there are a number of replies. First, the old adage, "a picture is worth a thousands words," has merit for good reason. Piggott (1978: 53–5) understood this when considering the critical role of the visual in Pitt-Rivers' theories of technological evolution. In recent years, close readings of pictorial images, or what Rudwick (1976) calls the "visual language" of science, have developed into a solid historiographic technique for identifying and raising questions about implicit premises and under-theorized assumptions driving scientific research (Baigire 1996; Elkins 1996; Fyfe and Law 1988; Gilbert and Mulkay 1984; Haraway 1989; Law and Whittaker 1988; Lynch and Woolgar

1990; Myers 1990; Rudwick 1976, 1992; Schiebinger 1993). Systematic analyses of the most familiar and popular visual depictions of prehistoric times have begun to demonstrate the extent to which implicit (folk) paradigms have both materialized and shaped scientific discourse and the development of archaeological knowledge through the medium of visual iconography (as in Conkey 1997; Dobres 1992; Gamble 1998; Gifford-Gonzalez 1993a; Moser 1998; Moser and Gamble 1997; more generally, see Adkins and Adkins 1989). Moser (1992: 837–8; 1998) makes a compelling case that illustrative modes of scientific explanation in archaeology have long served as "self-contained theories," and not merely icing on the cake for the enjoyment of an untrained viewing public.

There is no doubt that devices for visualizing prehistory, whether in the pictorial forms found in popular media, in textbooks, or in serious scholarly contexts (discussed below), are *representations*. That is, they represent (namely, interpret) contemporary concerns, express present-day sensibilities, and employ conventions and metaphors in vogue at the time they are commissioned. Try as they might, they are not faithful replicas or unbiased depictions of the past as it was. One could suggest, in this regard, that today's overwhelming preference in the scholarly literature for depictions of the separate modification stages in fabricating (and using) artifacts, graphically displayed in the form of a disembodied hand holding and working a natural material, is but another attempt to limit pictorial representations to the objectively knowable dimensions of technology by purposefully excising the supposedly subjective and social "part" of the activity (discussed below, and again in chapter 6).

A second defense against the argument that analyses of visual modes of discourse in archaeology are an inappropriate source for deconstruction is the fact that, since the turn of the century at least, leading prehistorians have worked hand-in-hand not only with artists commissioned to produce reconstructions for popular media, but also in creating and detailing museum dioramas (discussion in Moser 1992). As chronicled by Daston and Galison (1992) and Laqueur (1990), there is an inescapable feedback between the development of natural history disciplines and the emergence and codification of their visual languages. In developing this line of inquiry, Rudwick (1976, 1992), in particular, has shown how visual discourse assisted the development and formalization of mid-eighteenth-century geology (the "parent" of Old World archaeology). Recent studies, especially by Moser (1992, 1993b, 1996, 1998), Molyneaux (1997), and Stoczkowski (1997), document the extent to which a similar relationship functioned in the development of early- to mid-nineteenth-century archaeological method and theory. This recursive relationship between visual modes of explanation and archaeological theory can be measured not only by the sheer increase in the number of such depictions during this time, but also in their standardization, conventionalization, and enormous popularity (more generally, see Daston and Galison 1992). More telling still is the striking resonance between the structured tropes found in these illustrations and how the very practice of archaeology in the field and lab is represented (figure 1.6).

Visual reconstructions: museum dioramas

Third, and perhaps most importantly, because visual representations of past lifeways are codified in museum displays, they serve as an exceptionally powerful and "stable" (Bann 1988) medium through which to communicate scientific understandings to the viewing public (Law and Whittaker 1988; Parkington and Smith 1986; J. Wright and A. Mazel 1987, 1991).[8] More than a century ago Pitt-Rivers (1891) recognized explicitly and made full use of the communicative power of museums by inventing what he christened "typological displays" of tool forms (such as spears), to demonstrate empirically the progressive and technological nature of human evolution as it was then understood.[9] As Bennett's (1995: 182–201) analysis shows, the "narrative machinery" of Pitt-Rivers' museum displays was understood and fully appreciated by prehistorians and the public alike. Pitt-Rivers' unabashedly political agenda in creating museum displays of contemporary archaeological theories was to educate the masses that the Law of Nature "makes no jumps" (Pitt-Rivers 1891: 116), and that by showing this graphically, to "make men cautious how they listen to scatter-brained revolutionary suggestions" (ibid.) such as those being voiced by the likes of Marx and Engels (Bowden 1991; W. Chapman 1985; Dobres 1992; Thompson 1977). Since that time, visual representations of archaeological theories of human evolution in public museums have served as an especially effective tool for translating into popular discourse (and with a minimum of bothersome text) prevailing scientific, ideological, and political ideas (Law and Whittaker 1988).[10]

What is too often forgotten when viewing objects and prehistoric reconstructions carefully arranged for our edification behind glass panels, is that, as much as museum displays make it possible to *see* theories and interpretations, "museums can make it hard to see" what has been excised, erased, and left out (Alpers 1991: 27; also Bann 1988; Berger 1973; Law and Whittaker 1988). That practically all dioramas of early human technologies are displayed in museums of natural history, including those depicting survival Stone Age technologies "still" practiced in modern-day Australia, New Guinea, and Africa, implicitly sends the same sort of ideological message intentionally conveyed by Pitt-Rivers a century ago: the primary body of "laws" to which technological evolution responds are natural, not cultural (Karp 1991:1ff; Parkington and Smith 1986; Price 1989).[11] Nor can there be much doubt that the ideological power these dioramic displays have on the public derives, in large measure, from archaeology's authority as the science of the human past (explicitly argued in Deetz 1972; Plog 1973; discussion in Trigger 1989).

It is certainly the case that contemporary museum dioramas often depict human/hominid work groups, in addition to their more traditional displays of tool forms evolving through time and disembodied hands holding onto or using artifacts. Nonetheless, even these three-dimensional and "peopled" displays employ iconographic conventions structurally similar to those found in artists' two-dimensional drawings: (1) technology is a serious (2) material matter (3) of survival against (4) natural elements, coupled with the apparent (5) lack of awareness of one another's presence. To this day, more often than not (6) males are depicted in the more active, upright and physically engaged poses, while (7) females are more typically found squatting, kneeling, or sitting, (8) looking down at the immediate task they are pursuing, though sometimes (9) also tending to children and babies.

It is unnecessary to belabor the point, but there is a curious irony at work here. The success of translating archaeological models of technological evolution to a non-scientific audience depends on the ability to objectify and (re)present them in idealized material form, such as dioramas and visual reconstructions. Paradoxically, this is an alternative way to think about prehistoric technology – as the concretization of culture-bound ideas and epistemologies about the world that include far more than the material making and use of things (chapters 4–7 develop this view in detail). It is precisely the power of the tangible to materialize intangible cultural principles, beliefs, and values that makes humans both materialists and symbolists simultaneously (Conkey 1993). Should it be any wonder, then, that the most fundamental (yet implicit) premises underlying scientific treatises on prehistoric technology are manifest in visual media, and that their analysis (while dismissed by some as visual "game-playing") can shed light on the most taken-for-granted but over-arching concepts and frameworks shared by both?

Visual reconstructions: scientific literature

Finally, peer-reviewed scholarly journals reporting the most up-to-date findings of rigorous empirical research on specific prehistoric technologies employ conventions similar to those found depicted in folk media. For example, in surveying scientific literature reporting research on late Pleistocene organic and lithic technologies published between 1960 and 1990, I found only a handful of visual reconstructions that depicted full-body images of humans/hominids or social groups of technicians at work (since 1990 this pattern has been shifting, clearly in response to the critiques outlined above).[12] What has predominated during the last thirty years has been hands: hands working antler, hands carving harpoons, hands preparing the platform of a stone nodule for blade removal, hands piercing leather with bone needles or awls, hands heat-treating unretouched blades before bifacial thinning, and so on.[13] It is painfully clear that the disembodied hand grasping a hard utilitarian object is *the* iconographic convention shared by popular media and scientific discourse and has been the single most powerful vision driving and materializing the concept of prehistoric technology for more than a century.

Of course, one could counter that the highly specialized audience for which these particular reports are intended has no need to see depictions of people and social groupings – no need, because the operative concept of prehistoric technology appears, on the face of it, to be about the making and use of things, rather than being simultaneously and inseparably about the social relations, divisions of labor, beliefs, values, contexts, and politics through which objects came into being. But for those who explicitly argue that technology is more than the physical transformation of hard matter from one state to another, these particular visual conventions, in both popular and academic media, attest to powerful but taken-for-granted and still lingering notions that demand scrutiny. Or, to put it more bluntly, "what masquerades as the academic is very often the popular in disguise, and we would do well to remember that this sophisticated veiling is merely one of the more commonplace methods for covering over what we do not wish to have revealed" (Moore 1994: 49–50).

Scientific text-based discourse

In addition to teasing apart the conceptual underpinnings shared by both popular and scientific forms of visual reconstructions, we need to investigate the structure of scholarly texts and ask whether they also share these idioms, and if so, why. Among the most common literary devices at work in the scientific literature that foreground the materiality of ancient techniques as distinct from their social constitution are descriptions lacking direct reference to the technical agents making and using technological things – that is, avoidance of third-person pronouns; Spector (1993) – and the overwhelming use of the passive tense to describe material fabrication and use techniques (for example, in phrases such as "pots were fired," "harpoons were repaired," and so on).[14] In comparison, in the early decades of the twentieth century, an era of scientific discourse untainted by "political correctness," professional archaeologists had no problem writing in proactive, albeit unabashedly gendered, terms (for example, in phrases such as "men hunted and made stone tools," "women gathered plants and stayed near the hearth tending their babies"; note here the active tenses and use of the third-person pronoun).

More often than not, today's treatises report that "animals were hunted with bifacially worked obsidian points," or that "nuts were gathered then processed on grinding stones." In contemporary archaeological writing, this anonymous and passive style of discourse "helps to objectify and limit technology to things and relations among things such that people often drop out of the picture altogether" (Dobres and Hoffman 1994: 230). Although this choice may in part be in response to the problematic gender attributions made by previous generations, this is not all there is to it. Explanations of technological change that highlight the mechanical properties of natural resources, economic principles of efficiency, functional requirements, environmental stimuli, and so forth still do not adequately or sufficiently account for *how* people understood, effected, and incorporated these material changes into their productive repertoires (Brumfiel 1991; Cross 1990: 2; Dobres 1995a; Dobres and Hoffman 1994: 231, 1999a; I consider this issue below and return to it again in chapters 4 and 5).

Although not necessarily quantifiable, perhaps the most striking aspect of the grammatical rules of scientific discourse to affect archaeology in recent years has been the conscious shift to writing in neutral and value-free terms. One of the many long-term goals of Anglo-American archaeological method, theory, and practice since at least the 1930s (and more recently advocated for French archaeology) has been to neuter earlier subject-centered and biased descriptions and analyses with a more standardized and technical language.[15] Among the many rhetorical tools employed toward this seemingly objective end are: (1) numerically based descriptions of artifacts, attributes, and assemblages; (2) the reliance on statistical methods to identify and summarize material patterns; as well as (3) the compilation in dictionary form of standardized terminologies for the description of artifact classes, attributes, and/or technologies (for example, Bordes 1981; Camps-Fabrer 1977; Camps-Fabrer et al. 1974; de Sonneville-Bordes and Perrot 1954–6; even earlier, see Colton and Hargrave 1937). The point here is not to discredit these particular strategies, for indeed the study of prehistoric technology has benefited greatly from the development of standardized terminologies and conventions. All the same, it is important to recognize what goes hand-in-hand with the use of a technical and seemingly neutral language: the erasure of explicit consideration of human technicians actively engaged with each other in their material and social reproduction of the world.

To comprehend better this shift toward neutral and seemingly objective descriptive techniques in the study of prehistoric technology, we need only look to the middle decades of this century. In order to advance further the strategic political claim that archaeology is the only authentic science of the past (R. Ford 1973), researchers embraced the use of mathematical equations to help articulate and formalize their definition of culture (for an explicit defense, see Meggers 1960). For example, in decidedly neutral and objective terms, L. White (1959: 20) created the expression $T(Sb \times Pr \times D)=S$ to represent his theory that technological factors determined the form of a social system; while $E \times T=P$ expressed his Law of Cultural Evolution, wherein energy harnessed in the form of material technology results in a cultural function (or product) to "serve the needs of man" (ibid.: 40).[16] The popularity of mathematical formulae, flow charts, Venn diagrams and other visual tools (especially statistical graphs) remains strong in the discipline precisely because these are seen as a formal and objective medium through which to depict the workings of the techno-economic sphere *vis-à-vis* other cultural sub-systems (figure 1.7, p. 44) (as rationalized in Steward 1955: 46; examples in Clarke 1968; M. Harris 1979: 52–4; Sabloff and Willey 1967; D. H. Thomas 1974).

Since the 1960s, if not earlier, visual diagrams have become an especially handy technique for graphically representing the complexity of feedback mechanisms theorized to have structured particular material technologies, ancient decision-making strategies, and technological change. Importantly, graphic strategies for modeling and explicating scientific theories do not act as mere decoration supplementing scholarly text (Adkins and Adkins 1989: 1–10; Daston and Galison 1992; Piggott 1978). Today, as earlier this century, they are "an essential part of an integrated visual-and-verbal mode of communication" (Rudwick 1976: 152). For the most part, however, these representations are sterilized of the active participation of people. Encased in their own sphere, or black box, technicians are connected only by the thinnest of straight black lines to related technoeconomic spheres, and labeled in the most dispassionate of terms, such as "divisions of labor," "sociopolitical organization," and the like (Brumfiel 1991; Hodder 1986; more generally Latour 1993; further discussion in chapter 6).

While these attempts to provide archaeological writing and visual models with analytic and descriptive rigor have undoubtedly proved useful, they have nonetheless promoted epistemological distance between knower and known (*sensu* Daston and Galison 1992: 81–3; Fabian 1983; Westkott 1979), not unlike the distance created when museum visitors view dioramas that freeze, displace, and objectify ethnographic subjects behind glass. Whether intended or not, these conventions have helped turn the subject matter of prehistoric technology into a neutral, quantifiable, and standardized object of study (the epistemological dimensions of this argument are explored in chapter 2). Daston and Galison (1992: 81) have reflected on the attitude the French physiologist E. J. Marey had about the promising hope of objectivity in scientific drawings of human anatomy being developed in the latter half of the nineteenth century (see also Jordanova 1993; Laqueur 1990; Schiebinger 1993). They point out that at this time the goal of producing objective graphic depictions was seen as a scientific *and* moral obligation (more generally, of course, see Weber 1946; further discussion in chapter 2). As they rightly note,

> modern objectivity mixes rather than integrates disparate components, which are historically and conceptually distinct. . . . This layering accounts for the hopelessly, but interestingly, confused present use of the term *objectivity*, which can be applied to everything from empirical reliability to procedural correctness to emotional detachment. (Daston and Galison 1992: 82, authors' emphasis)

My point here is not so much to critique contemporary discursive and graphic strategies of representation in the discipline as a prelude to proposing an alternative (but see Spector 1993). Rather, my intent is to unpack some of the taken-for-granted baggage that goes along with these strategies for, once the missing elements are identified, we are in a better position to ask if and how their oversight might be addressed.

The irony of the Standard View: retrofitting technological determinism into the deep past

To summarize to this point, what is missing from pictorial reconstructions in popular magazines, books, and museum dioramas – prehistoric technology understood as the active, historically constituted, symbolic, and socially charged engagement people have with their material world – is equally missing from scholarly texts. As Brumfiel (1991) has argued more generally, one of the characteristics of contemporary archaeological method and theory is the encasing of prehistoric agents in "black boxes," such that they seem inaccessible to rigorous, empirical, scientific research, and, by extension, of less importance to the behavioral processes in question (more generally, see Rosenberg 1985).[17] What pictorial idealizations of prehistoric technologies fail to depict are, similarly, what the scientific texts on which they are premised erase: technical agents strategically and meaningfully engaging with one another while materializing, through their face-to-face interactions, fundamental beliefs and cultural values – all the while "taking care of business."

This Standard View of ancient technology is, and has been from the outset, a series of simulacra projecting back to the very origins of the human lineage *contemporary* understandings of the technology–society "equation." In past and present alike, humans are defined, and define themselves, in similarly rational and objectified ways: by virtue of *what* they make, *how* they make, how they *use*, and the degree to which they *control* the natural world through material means. The commonly held belief is that, as humans "we envelope ourselves in technology" (Schick and Toth 1993: 16, 19).[18] By denying the explicit question of how humans (and earlier hominids) came to negotiate this particular relationship with the world, and by projecting the contemporary vision back to our primordial past, we have developed an ironically *a*temporal perspective that all but erases the last 3 million years of the human career – paradoxically the very thing archaeologists want to understand. Past and present alike, technology is an "it," a quantifiable, neutral, material thing that exists outside the body politic (Dobres 1995b) but in which we (have always) encase(d) ourselves.

In essence, this is a philosophical stance that reflects the alienated technological milieu in which archaeology is undertaken, as a capitalist, colonialist, and imperialist body of knowledge and practices (Trigger 1984; see chapter 2 for further elaboration). Precisely because it is understood as a fundamental pan-human trait, the historical processes that led to a separating of producers from their products, of technicians from their tools, and of social artifice from artifacts are erased from consideration and somehow taken for granted. For all time, tools and the ability to make them are definitionally reduced to material constructs (Kehoe 1992: 10; Lechtman 1993), essentialized as things detached from society, from expressions of individual and group agency, from history, context, and from culturally situated world views and values. Defined in this way, the complex whole from which human technologies derive is reduced to an essentialist and instrumentalist vision from which people are excised as active participants, and instead transformed into rational but passive respondents to external, asocial stimuli.

The ideological progressivism embedded in this view implies that those with the most materially complex ways of making, using, and controlling the natural world are similarly the most civilized and/or evolved (Ingold 1995), which is one of many reasons why Australian Aboriginal technologies have always been considered the most deficient on the face of the earth (Lubbock 1865; Pitt-Rivers 1875; Sollas 1911; Testart 1988; discussion in Oswalt 1976: 5–6). According to Oswalt (1976: 226), "counting the number of technounits [i.e., the individual parts that make up an artifact] is a rather exacting gauge to relative technological complexity."[19] Thus, in our heroic techno-epic one of the major evolutionary Rubicons humans crossed was when they invented composite tools of hafted artifacts and implements made up of multiple parts (sometime in the late Middle or early Upper Palaeolithic). Even before that, however, the shift from the unifacial flaking of (Oldowan) choppers to bifacially worked (Acheulean) handaxes was also a Rubicon of evolutionary import, although in this instance the technounits involve the number of flakes removed and from how many sides of the core. Retrodicting the contemporary notion that "more is better" onto the past as a way to measure cultural or technological complexity (although these two terms are often used synonymously) has led to the belief that the most partitive and materially "busy" of prehistoric technologies were also the most evolutionarily sophisticated. On the other hand, because of the difficulty in converting into energy measurements such dynamics as social arrangements, the interpersonal agency of engagement, and meaning and values, these factors are excised from calculation and consideration as either unknowable, something for future research, or worse, simply irrelevant to explaining culture and culture change.

I have purposefully avoided using the term until now, but describing society as enveloped in its material technologies is commonly known as "technological determinism."[20] Characterizing the essence of what it means to be evolved, human, and civilized by appeal to our increasingly technical and mechanized control over the world over the past few million years projects contemporary technological determinism back in time in order, ironically, to explain the present (J. Cohen 1955: 409; Ingold 1995). As Mumford (1967: 4) noted decades ago, "even the seemingly benign interpretation of Teilhard de Chardin reads back into the whole story of man the narrow technological rationalism of our own age"; an age in which humans see themselves at the mercy of machines, ever more dependent on impersonal material things to survive, and in which the very essence of human life is increasingly mechanized and de-humanized (see Winner 1977 for an insightful analysis of this stance).[21] Thus, at one and the same time we have two incommensurable ideas subsumed within technological determinism, each playing off the other: (1) that the essence of what it means to be human is encasing ourselves in material technologies and our ability (acquired through the neutral process of natural selection) to control nature by such means; while (2) "it" simultaneously de-humanizes us by increasingly taking over our lives.

Another way to comprehend contemporary technological determinism and its role in the study of ancient technologies is with the notion of "alienation" (Marx 1967 [orig. 1883]), by which was meant: (1) the alienation or separation of workers from the material fruits of their labor (producers separated from their products); (2) the alienation of workers from one another through the particular organizational "demands" that industrial technologies "require"; (3) the objectification of nature as separate from and increasingly subordinate to society's needs and desires (Merchant 1980); and perhaps most significantly, (4) the alienation of humans from their own humanity (namely, self-alienation; Petrovic 1983a, 1983b).[22] Alienation captures especially well the ideological presentism inherent in current thinking about prehistoric technology as it implicitly operates in scientific texts and visual modes of discourse.

Methodological Issues Promoting Alienation in Prehistory

Inverting analytic and ontological priorities

Present-day perspectives on the past underwritten by subtle forms of technological determinism have significantly impacted not only the concept of prehistoric technology, but also how "it" has been studied, limiting to primarily material and "natural" phenomena the range of likely causal factors (first) investigated, particularly those apparently related to resource procurement and modification, artifact design, artifact morphology, and tool function. In the past three decades (and on both sides of the Atlantic), there has been an veritable explosion of research working to delimit what is often called the "economic basis" of ancient material technologies and technological organization (although there are precedents much earlier this century, such as H. Martin 1910; the American literature is comprehensively reviewed in Nelson 1991; on craft specialization, see Costin 1991). Much of this work is explicitly guided by the general principles of Formalist economic and optimal foraging theories, themselves predicated on least-effort principles of optimization, maximization, and minimization (Halperin 1994: 22–3). According to the explicitly articulated premises of this body of research,

> technological organization is responsive to conditions of the environment including resource predictability, distribution, periodicity, productivity, mobility . . . size and patchiness of resource areas . . . and potential hazards. . . . Humans are viewed as decision makers within a

> variable environment; ecological structure is viewed as conditioning behavior to some degree. . . . Optimal or suitable choices among alternatives can be understood only within the context of environmental conditions and available technological capabilities. (Nelson 1991: 59–60)

Without question, such research has improved archaeological understandings and appreciation of the mechanical and/or chemical properties, as well as the performance characteristics (Schiffer and Skibo 1987), of natural resources and finished products. As well, we now can measure many of the (material) costs, risks, and benefits of procuring, using, transporting, and curating particular resources. Some of the most interesting findings in this regard stem from replicative studies, microscopic use-wear analyses, and ethnoarchaeology, all of which now dominate the field of prehistoric technology studies.

What is important here is not that these studies preclude the possibility that culturally bound beliefs and practices may also have played a part in delimiting the range of technical choices and strategies prehistoric technicians imagined and practiced. In fact, most researchers readily admit this is likely the case (for example, L. R. Binford 1962; McGuire and Schiffer 1983; Schiffer and Skibo 1987: 600; Skibo 1999). What is significant from a *methodological* standpoint, however, is that the several factors constituting cultural reason (*sensu* Sahlins 1976) are analytically considered only *after* material properties, optimal goal-oriented factors, and practical reason. In fact, to consider social factors first is thought by some to be the worst of humanistic (and hence unscientific) approaches. The analytical prioritizing of natural factors over cultural ones (no matter what is said to the contrary) is due, in part, to a supposedly epistemological quandary: archaeologists find it far more difficult to identify, much less measure, the material correlates of what are admittedly culturally and historically specific factors (J.-C. Gallay 1986: 126–57, 182; Schiffer and Skibo 1987: 601; Trigger 1989: 394–6; but for just such attempts, see C. Carr and J. E. Neitzel 1994; Schiffer 1992b).

Analytical prioritizing is justified and predicated on the (positivist) standpoint that in due course we will know and be able to control for the material determinants of technology found observable "in nature," and that once these first-level understandings are in hand will we be in the appropriate methodological position (and also have the necessary "anchors") with which to commence the far more difficult task of pinning down the material correlates, if any, of (the remaining) internally specific cultural factors (implied in Schiffer 1994, personal communication October 1996, January 1999; Skibo 1999: 5). According to this view, physical and objective factors, which can be reasoned in a rational, methodical, and replicable manner, should take analytic precedence over the socially conditioned, or "remote variables" (Schiffer and Skibo 1987: 600–1; also Nelson 1991: 81). The partitive and instrumentalist thinking that drives these arguments has been both projected back in time and given ontological status in the present. Not only does the hardware view of prehistoric technology structure the general contours of our explanatory models (making them self-congratulatory, moralistic hero stories); it equally guides the specific way we go about studying "it" (I return to this point in chapter 2).

Three rationalizations

Across the research community, there are three stock reasons given for privileging the methical study of the material side of ancient technology before turning to its messy social side. First, prevailing wisdom holds that it is simply good logic to control for and understand the (universal) natural phenomena and objective conditions structuring particular design features and technical choices before turning attention to the particularistic cultural elements involved. Indeed, these cultural factors will be all the more easily identified by default, as the leftover attributes not previously explained (defended in P. Bleed in press; Hayden 1993; Morrow 1987). Best exemplified by the "function v. style" debate of the past three decades, first-level dictates in choice of raw material, fabrication techniques, artifact form, function, and so forth are argued to reside in the physical nature of the materials worked, while culturally bound rules relating to design are secondary at best (cf. Allain and Rigaud 1986; Ashton 1985; Close 1978; a review of these positions can be found in Conkey 1990).[23]

Underlying this orthodoxy is a second-tier justification for analytically prioritizing the study of objective material matters before subjective social ones: the premise that nature precedes culture in determining what people can or cannot do. From this standpoint, nature is "out there" determining not only whole cultural systems, but especially technoeconomic responses that materially ensure survival (L. R. Binford 1965, 1968a: 272, 1973; P. Bleed and A. Bleed 1987: 189; Clarke 1968; Jochim 1981; Steward 1949, 1955). This is a layer-cake, or pyramidal, approach to understanding the multiple and overlapping influences of practical and cultural factors influencing artifact fabrication, morphology, and use. The base of the cake, which necessarily comes first, is that solid layer of tangible material realities comprehended through practical, methodical, objectified reason; the upper tiers are made of social relations and politics; the icing that decorates the whole thing (or system) includes those less-than-functional, less-than-technical, less-than-tangible (and non-quantitative) supplemental factors such as beliefs and the so-called noise of human agency (especially M. Harris 1979: 52–4).

The third set of claims supporting what many defend as simply the heuristic and "temporary" separation of multiple material and cultural factors, so as to control our understanding of each in its own right, is a complex epistemological position that is the subject of some detail in the following chapter. In brief, however, it turns on the argument that some things simply preserve better than others (which is, of course, true) and that we must necessarily work from the most to the least preservable traces of prehistory. Bailey (1983: 5) expressed this commonly held view most succinctly, when he argued that explanatory models in archaeology should devote special attention to the technological and economic aspects of prehistory, "since data on subsistence are more easily accessible to the archaeologist and more amenable to interpretation than the less tangible patterns of social organization and ideology" (also J.-C. Gallay 1986: 126–57, 182; Hawkes 1954; MacWhite 1956; M. A. Smith 1955). However, while differential material preservation of ancient lifeways is a fact, it does not follow that the principles structuring the form, function, and/or style of those traces were necessarily or even primarily dictated by practical reason, principles of optimization, and/or objective conditions found in nature.[24]

This partitive and prioritized approach to understanding the multiple overlapping (indeed inseparable) factors that together contribute to the structure and organization of prehistoric technologies is itself an historical product, rather than based on some tangible or epistemological reality. It is, paradoxically, structured by the contours of cultural (specifically industrial and capitalist) reasoning (following Habermas 1970; Marcuse 1964, 1968; Weber 1946; Winner 1977; overview in Pippin 1995). Simply put, divorcing practical from cultural reason, alienating the physical from the social, and privileging the tangible aspects of technoeconomic rationality over its supposedly intangible sociosymbolic dimensions for the sake of "methodological rigor" has limited significantly the range of factors we consider in explaining the contours of prehistoric technologies and ancient decision-making strategies. In this instance, an overly materialist theory of technology has directly affected research methodologies, which have in turn further structured (indeed limited) explanation. We need to ask *why* our theories about prehistoric technologies should be structured and limited by what are seemingly methodological weaknesses, rather than accept this as the holy grail.

Fetishizing nature, pacifying culture: natural and technological necessity (or, what determines who)

In addition to a hierarchically ordered list of prioritized factors considered more and less amenable to empirical study, instrumentalist views of technology generally favor the claim that each particular material technology associates with, indeed requires, a particular form of social organization. As the general argument goes, the technological (that is, material) ability to produce and manage a surplus (be it foodstuffs, beads, textiles, or pottery) must be in place *before* institutionalized social inequalities can develop (as in Hayden 1995a, 1998; Testart 1982; but compare to Bender 1985a, 1985b, who suggests the opposite). Each particular product apparently has its own material and technical requirements, and these in turn have their own "needs" in terms of an appropriate division of labor. In terms of cause and effect, the technology (cause) must exist (or be able to exist) before the appropriate social organization (effect) can develop (although at this point the reader should be able to identify inconsistencies in this line of argument). For example, if the technological goal is to erect a monument *x* stories high, then an appropriate number of "labor units" (people) organized in a particular way is necessary; if the intended goal is to capture as many salmon as possible during their seasonal upstream migratory run, then another kind of social organization is required; if subsistence centers on hunting gregarious herd animals such as reindeer or bison, then the hunters would not organize themselves as they would to hunt lone mountain goat or wild boar.

According to this line of reasoning, each form of social organization and associated suite of activities is a pragmatic and outwardly directed necessary response to meet (as well as possible) the needs of the material technology, be it storage, architecture, or hunting, and is clearly guided by the premises underwriting White's formulae: $T(Sb \times Pr \times D) = S$ and $E \times T = P$. Especially when theorizing the evolution of craft specialization and how social organization necessarily changed in response to this process, the monodirectionality of cause and effect requires that researchers work backward, garnering various measurements of technological outputs (products) as a way to infer the overall size and organizational nature of the production system that enabled it (such quantification is often aided by ethnoarchaeological research and lab-controlled replicative study) (examples include J. E. Clark 1986; Heizer 1966; Roux and Matarasso 1999; Torrence 1986; Tosi 1984; Velson and Clark 1975; see reviews in Costin 1991; Cross 1990, 1993; Rice 1981).

Given the fundamental part it plays in the techno-epic of human evolution, Pfaffenberger (1992: 495–7) has taken this "necessity is the mother of invention" view to task. "Necessity" takes two determinant forms: first, there are the demands of the natural environment necessitating particular material-technological-behavioral solutions; second, there are the demands of the technology itself, each requiring a particular division of labor. Ironically, in this paradigm the natural environment and material needs are conceptually transformed into animated (practically all-knowing) agents, while humans become passive "labor units" that respond pragmatically to such external stimuli (a view similar to what Hobbes suggested some 300 years ago, see Ferré 1995: 127). I see this as a gross perversion of agency: the inanimate world of nature is anthropomorphized as an acting, demanding structure, while human agents are conceptualized as little more than efficient robots responding to provocation by a needy material world (Dobres and Hoffman 1994: 227–30; Latour 1992; Pfaffenberger 1988; Winner 1986b: 3–18).

Two additional premises are also at work. It is assumed that: (1) first-order logical and rational responses dictated by external objective circumstances are, at their core, cross-cultural (or else that "remote" side of technology would need to be highlighted from the start); and (2) in responding to dispassionate external stimuli, humans re-act (at least to the best of their ability) in pragmatic, efficient, and optimal ways. As already noted, one indication of the extent to which this alienated and inversely anthropomorphized perspective has affected the study of prehistoric technology is the overwhelming use of passive tenses and the avoidance of third-person pronouns in the scientific literature describing, modeling, and explaining the human side of prehistoric technology and change, in tandem with the overwhelming use of the active verb tenses when describing, modeling, and explaining the material factors – as if the two were opposing, even competitive phenomena.[25]

Subjects as objects: human resources – just another variable

The very possibility of imagining human labor as a resource equivalent to inert energy and developing ways to measure and weigh its costs and benefits attests to the degree of alienation through which capitalist/industrial societies de-humanize industrial workers into partitive (and seemingly equivalent) labor units. Archaeologists have unwittingly retrofitted this way of thinking about human agents into the past precisely because it is the basis of their own world view. The net effect is that a prehistoric *Homo technologicus* looms large in the contemporary literature. In many respects, conceptualizing humans as alienated from their material products, from each other, from nature, and from themselves underlies much of the recent archaeological interest in developing mathematical formulae for reasonably inferring the number of people it would have required to undertake a particular technological activity. This is not intended as a criticism as much as it is to underscore how particular ways of understanding and describing society and technology in the present affect the kinds of questions we ask about society and technology in the past, and the research methodologies and (first-, second-, and third-order) analyses we think appropriate to the task. To ask about the number of labor/hours it would have required to produce a certain product, as if such demands were inherent in and determined by the material nature of the desired product, betrays the techno-deterministic underpinnings of such research (especially Winner 1986b: 121–37; also Lechtman 1977, 1993; Lemonnier 1989b, 1990; Morton 1988; Ridington 1982).

Homo technologicus: *a post-World War II phenomenon*

Trigger has argued convincingly that an explicit return to evolutionary thinking in the 1950s and 1960s served to rationalize and naturalize "the dominant economic and political situation in which America, and therefore American archaeologists, found themselves after World War II" (Trigger 1989: 289). Anglo-American archaeology was drawn to providing explanations for the position that their own state society held in the new world order, but did so in terms broad enough to constitute law-like regularities far removed from the vagaries of "great men" and the historical particularities of unique events. At this time, many anthropologists and archaeologists explicitly argued that science was the only basis of knowledge that could adequately assist this calling (R. Ford 1973; M. Harris 1968; for a devastating analysis of Americanist archaeology [still] in the service of the state, see Kehoe 1998). To seek out the nomothetic principles of cultural evolution driven by law-like regularities found in nature (as championed by White and his followers) was argued to be a democratic and *a*political basis for knowledge about the human career. On such a neutral footing archaeology, and especially its study of technology, could never again find itself in the service of self-legitimating colonialist, nationalist, and/or imperialist interests, because science was not biased.[26] While it is today a matter of heated debate whether the scientific method is inherently biased toward state (or other) interests, it is clear that the materialist and positivist demands archaeologists imposed upon their subject matter severely limited what was considered amenable to study and how such research should proceed (classic position statements in this regard include L. R. Binford 1981; Fritz and Plog 1970; Hawkes 1954; Leach 1973; Schiffer 1976; Watson et al. 1971; for an anachronistic example, see Barham 1992).

With the publication of *Silent Spring* (Carson 1962), the shift in understanding culture as actively adapted to its environment through the outwardly directed responses of its technology resonated with the developing awareness of ecological concerns in both popular and scientific discourse (Dobres 1995c: 86–91). Mid-twentieth-century recognition that significant population increases and rapid industrialization were taking a terrible toll on the earth's fragile ecosystem, and that uncontrolled technological expansion was to blame, led both the biological and social sciences, including archaeology, to focus concerted research effort on human ecology in order to understand better the conditions under which complex societies had survived or failed in the past and could, or would, survive in the future (Trigger 1989: 319–26; Winner 1986b: 121–37).[27] What better discipline than archaeology to provide lessons of the greatest time-depth (M. Harris 1968: 675)? In the 1970s, more than one theoretician argued that archaeology was the social science best suited to provide the necessary temporal scale for understanding the law-like relationship between culture and nature, especially through the study of prehistoric technology (notably, Butzer 1971: 610–11; R. Ford 1973; Fritz 1973; to understand the ideology underpinning these claims, see Kehoe 1998). And as had happened twice before, first with mid-nineteenth-century evolutionary theory, then with early-twentieth-century culture history, the study of technology again became a tool for interests beyond archaeology's purview, responding to and supporting a broad range of political and economic concerns (Dobres 1995c, 1995d).

With culture now defined as a thermodynamic system of integrated sub-systems, technology became society's "extrasomatic means of adaptation" (L. R. Binford 1968a: 272; J. G. D. Clark 1953; L. White 1959: 8, 49), and a battery of techno-metaphors once again provided the analogs for articulating and describing its internal and external workings. Culture was likened to a well-oiled perpetual motion machine, or thermostat "seeking" homeostasis through various mechanisms actively counterbalancing deviation amplifying events (D. L. Clarke 1968: 48–54). Along with the argument that culture is partitive and that its spheres differentially respond to external stimuli came yet another perversion of the society-technology dialectic. Now, what counted was the relationship *between* parts of the system (such as between society and technology), and between the system and the en-

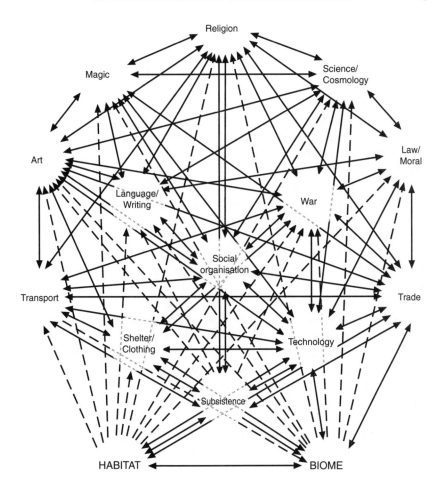

Figure 1.7   Graphic feedback model of a cultural system with sub-spheres connected by thin black lines.
Source: J. G. D. Clark 1953, p. 75, figure 6

vironment; not between and among the agents who invented, enacted, and gave meaning and value to their adaptive technological responses. No wonder it made sense to diagram visually this smoothly functioning system and work to connect the dots between neatly segmented spheres (figure 1.7). How the parts of the system fit together was clearly more important that what went on *inside* those separate domains (Latour 1993).[28]

With this line of reasoning in place, technology took center stage (again), though now it explained not only how cultures functioned and maintained their balance with nature, but also why they changed. Epistemologically, those parts of the system said to be most directly responsive to environmental stimuli were also argued to be most basic to cultural survival (and, conveniently for us, both knowable and quantifiable). Thus, for far more sophisticated reasons than those popular in the nineteenth century, technology (and its help-mate, subsistence) once again represented the cultural system, or at least its materialist core. In graphic representations, the seemingly remote parts of culture were often diagrammed as being "cushioned" from direct environmental stimuli by a buffer zone, commonly called the technoeconomic sphere (figure 1.7). In this "new" view, however, technology was still defined almost exclusively by imple-ments and their use, and now also by the level of efficiency with which they were extracted from natural resources (L. R. Binford 1968a: 272). And (as a century before), "it" was argued to evolve towards increasingly complex and more efficient forms that could be measured and quantified (as in Dunnell 1982; Foley 1987; Oswalt 1976; Torrence 1983).

Precisely because they were values and principles in vogue for making sense of the rapidly expanding capitalist marketplace and global industrialization, it made sense to working archaeologists to model culture as a materialist and economic enterprise adapting to external stimuli, to define cultural behavior in terms of energy expen-ditures, to measure complexity in technounits, to privilege subsistence practices and technology over social relations and symbols, and to take time and efficiency as cross-cultural principles structuring (material, adaptive) behavior. The influence of Parsonian Formalist economic theory on anthropological models of culture, along with the particular ways archaeologists simulated, theorized, and graphically depicted ancient cultures, were part and parcel of a discourse shared by econo-mists, social scientists, and popular culture alike during the industrial boom following 1945 (Halperin 1994; Mitcham 1994: 71; Winner 1986b: 121–37).

Archaeology's techno-paradigm: plus ça change, plus c'est la même chose

What is especially revealing in deconstructing the prevailing concept of prehistoric technology is that, in spite of the significantly different paradigms and analytic methodologies employed over the past century and a half, archaeologists have consistently treated the subject matter of technology as if it were an object. Nowhere is the position better stated than in J. Cohen's (1955: 409) ontological declaration that humans were "*Homo faber* before *Homo sapiens*," or the historian Basalla's

(1988: 30) more recent assertion in his book on the evolution of technology, that "the artifact – not scientific knowledge, nor the technical community, nor social and economic factors – is central to technology and technological change. . . . [T]he final product of innovative technological activity is typically an addition to the made world: a stone hammer, a clock, an electric motor."

While this instrumentalist concept is firmly embedded in the neo-evolutionary and adaptationist framework of contemporary anthropology and archaeology, it is strikingly similar to that suggested by the American culture-historian Wissler (1923: 89), who wrote that "tools are so universal that man has been defined as the tool-using animal, though it would be nearer the truth to say that he is a tool maker, for it is the devising and making of tools that sets man off so sharply from the animals" (also Osborn 1915). Wissler's essentializing of *Homo sapiens sapiens* to the heroic maker and user of tools *par excellence* is found over and over again in archaeological writings (both scientific and popular) between the early 1800s and the present.[29] Thus, it is no surprise that a similar, albeit less sophisticated, view guided the ideas and research of nineteenth-century French evolutionists Jouannet (1819), de Mortillet (1890), and Piette (1892); English prehistorians Lubbock (1865), Pitt-Rivers (1874, 1875), Dawson (1887), and the extremely influential ethnologist Tylor (1873, 1878); as well as Americans Squier and Davis (1848), and Abbott (1881).

Conclusions

For more a century and a half, then, what has consistently remained the object question in the study of prehistoric technology is hardware; an objective and measurable "thing" lying beyond the vagaries of interpersonal social engagement and meaning. This concept has persevered, ironically, regardless of whether one believed: (1) that cultures could be pigeon-holed on an evolutionary ladder of complexity based primarily on technological attributes measured against western standards; (2) that technology was a preeminent set of material traits useful for tracking culture histories through time and space; or (3), that a culture's survival and adaptation was a rational and pragmatic outward response to external stimuli (Dobres 1995c, 1995d). As Taylor (1989: 393–4) notes in pointing out the temporal irony of it all, "what is remarkable is that the basic moral and political standards by which we congratulate ourselves [today] were themselves powerful in the last century. Even more strikingly, the very picture of history as moral progress, as a 'going beyond' our forebears, which underlies our own sense of superiority, is very much a Victorian idea."

In this chapter I have argued that conceptualizing, describing, and explaining (any) past technology with the metaphors, abstractions, and methodologies of the present serves more to reaffirm the present with self-fulfilling prophecy than to understand the past on its own terms. As Leone (1982: 750) and Wallace (1986: 158–61) have argued for archaeology more generally, when we link contemporary conditions directly to some point in the past, the present serves as a prism casting an oddly familiar light on the questions we ask, the methods we use, and the answers we find acceptable (also Moore 1994). Those pasts then become little more than simulacra naturalizing the way things *are*, with the present as little more than the sum (evolutionary) total of rational responses to impersonal forces of nature, rather than the convoluted and decidedly human outcome of culturally reasoned and historically constituted social practices, strategies, and agendas. As a result, archaeology turns out to be far less explanatory, and far more teleological, ideological, and hegemonic, than it claims.

My purpose in uncovering some of the more problematic premises and assumptions buried under the weight of contemporary taken-for-granteds about (prehistoric) technology has not been to affix blame nor to suggest malicious agendas. Rather, my goal "attempts to infect the reader, so to speak, with a minor case of the ideology's persuasiveness in order to provide immunity against more pathological episodes" (Rosaldo 1989: 110; also E. H. Carr 1961). How can any past possibly be envisioned differently from the present, much less be studied with that possibility in mind, if both unwittingly depend on the same uncritical concept of technology? The remainder of this book outlines conceptual and methodological alternatives with which, hopefully, to begin curing some of the long dormant "pathologies" lying at the heart of our most worthwhile and important interest in technology.

2

Deconstructing the Black Box: Some Philosophical and Historical Reflections on the *Logos* of *Tekhnē*

The specialized social sciences, having abandoned a holistic perspective, thus come to resemble the Danae sisters of classical Greek legend, ever condemned to pour water into their separate bottomless containers.

(E. Wolf 1982: 11)

[D]isciplines, with their boundary-maintaining devices, institutional structures, accepted texts, methodologies, internal debates and circumscribed areas of study, tend by virtue of their very constitution, to be rather conservative in nature. Changes within them most frequently come about through borrowing ideas from outside.

(Miller and Tilley 1996: 5)

Why should a book outlining a practice framework for prehistoric technology concern itself with what philosophers have to say about contemporary technology and its conceptual underpinnings? Especially in light of the previous chapter, which examined the problematic relationship between industrial techno-think and the study of prehistoric technology, it is fair to ask if continued exploration of the present state of the art is the best way to go about reconceptualizing technology with archaeological interests in mind.

I offer three reasons for taking up the difficult project of reconceptualizing prehistoric technology with inspiration drawn from sources beyond the confines of archaeological discourse. First is *the similarity of what philosophers and archaeologists take as a special topic of merit, namely technology and society*. My guess is that a relatively small number of practicing archaeologists reading this book are aware of the rich body of literature in philosophy dedicated to a topic we all hold near and dear, let alone have actually waded through much of it (notable exceptions include Ingold 1988a, 1993a, 1999; Schiffer 1992a; Schiffer and Skibo 1987). Certainly few engineering students are taught that philosophers have something important to contribute to their education, and in general, most people tend to think of philosophers as "merely" concerned to contemplate ethics and metaphysics from their armchairs rather than tackle real-world issues. In comparison, archaeologists in the lab and the field daily confront the empirical and quantifiable remains of the past. Surely both fields have their share of speculation, but the former would seem to make it their *raison d'être*, while the latter takes pains to circumvent it wherever possible. Nonetheless, twentieth-century archaeology and philosophy share a special concern to understand the significance of technology in the history and "nature" of the human condition. Clearly, each goes about their calling differently, works with dissimilar databases, and employs differently phrased research questions (not to mention having different intellectual histories that shape inquiry and what constitutes a satisfactory answer). All this notwithstanding, it is precisely because of their decidedly different approaches to the compelling questions that concern technology and society that philosophers can provide archaeologists with insights that are not likely to develop independently.

Second, *philosophy and archaeology share a common interest in evaluating their insights through critically informed self-reflection.* Both disciplines worry as much about the social and political underpinnings of their theories and explanations as they do with their being perverted for ends for which they were never intended. Ethics and responsibility are concerns common to both philosophy and archaeology and serve as powerful checks and balances on the willingness of their practitioners to accept particular explanations and theories without examining the extent to which they may be structured by imperfectly articulated or altogether faulty logic, reasoning, and even wishful thinking. Epistemology is something with which both disciplines are profoundly concerned, although the ease with which their practitioners converse on this topic is surely not the same.

And finally (but by no means the last link between the two disciplines), *contemporary archaeology and philosophy share roots in intellectual currents beginning with the Age of Enlightenment and maturing during the height of the Industrial Age.* As such, both are not only products of western intellectualism sharing conceptual categories basic to western discourse, but also critically reflect on their underpinnings. What makes the linking of archaeological research on technology with contemporary philosophical reflections on western intellectualism so compelling is that philosophy contributes a valuable way of understanding the impact of this heritage on science and technology (Wylie 1985b). As the reader will see in this chapter and the next, these insights are profound and can be liberating. In concert with newly emerging perspectives on technology from contemporary social and material culture studies (chapter 4) and theories of social agency (chapter 5), philosophical insights on technology (which are further elaborated in the following chapter) can help create the intellectual room for archaeologists to develop interpretive frameworks, concepts, and research methodologies (chapter 6) that take the dynamics of prehistoric social agency to heart. My detour into a "poor person's" understanding of the philosophy of technology is intended to help archaeologists get better at peeking inside the black box currently encasing prehistoric technician-agents and in resituating them at the center of their technological practices and our theories about them (Dobres and Hoffman 1994, 1999a).

In this chapter, I discuss what I consider to be especially relevant arguments circulating among certain philosophers of technology that can help tease apart (or deconstruct) the several reasons why archaeologists have thought about and researched ancient technologies as they have (as characterized in chapter 1). Chapter 3 offers a more constructive discussion of philosophical insights on what technology *is* that, when combined with and modified by current trends in social theory and adapted to archaeological interests (chapters 4–7), can further our collective desire to understand the social dynamics of technology, past and present. Regrettably, philosophers of technology have practically no interaction with archaeologists (and very few anthropologists) and seem to care very little about (or even know the contours of) early hominid and human technologies, which is surely one of their limitations. Nor do they seem the least bit interested in helping correct archaeological blind spots, especially those contributing to the conceptual, methodological, and explanatory erasure of the ancient thinking, feeling, and interacting technician-agent. This does not mean that philosophy has nothing to offer archaeologists, for indeed it does, and I spell out what I think are some of these contributions in this and the next chapter.

I leave to chapter 4 a consideration of what I see as similarly oriented frameworks now developing in sociology, history, general material culture studies, and especially in the corners of sociocultural anthropology. There I discuss how, when these various insights are brought bear on the interests and goals of archaeology, they can jointly provide the contours of a human-centered framework for understanding ancient technology as social practice. As will be seen in chapter 5, because my version of a practice framework for the study and interpretation of ancient technologies is explicitly and broadly interdisciplinary, I am in full agreement with Miller and Tilley (1996: 13) that "being undisciplined can be highly productive."

Philosophical Reflections on that Historic Hybrid, *Tekhnē* + *Logos*

Why, in the industrial world, do we feel more comfortable conceptualizing separations rather than connections? Why do we talk of technology *and* society, artifacts *and* artifice, agency *and* structure? Why must we necessarily merge together separate words into awkward hybrids, such as "sociotechnical" or "ideotechnic," rather than their being simultaneously engendered in the single word "technology"? Why has the archaeological study of technology for so long concentrated on things and relations among things, in spite of the diversity of intellectual paradigms employed over the past century? What can possibly account for such a tenacious degree of artifact fetishism in a field of inquiry with such a volatile intellectual history and periods of critical and sophisticated introspection? Why are sociotechnical "webs" so hard to envision in the past? And most importantly, why is the black box encasing social agency, ideology, power, social relations, politics, and meaning nailed shut? Is this really an epistemological and methodological problem, as we're so often told, or are the reasons to be found elsewhere? To tease apart at least partial answers to these important questions we should start by considering the very word "technology," for as with most cultural constructs it has undergone significant change over time.

Historical reflections on "technology": the odd coupling of tekhnē *and* logos

Tekhnē

The very meaning of the word "technology" has been reconceptualized significantly over the past three centuries, and it is not mere coincidence that its redefinition came at the outset of the Industrial Revolution. As philosophers are quick to point out, the word "technology" is a recent hybridization of the Greek roots *tekhnē* and *logos*. According to *Webster's Third International Dictionary* (1968) and *The Oxford English Dictionary*, *tekhnē* (also sometimes *technē*) originally meant the instantiation through practice and application of an inseparable combination of art, skill and craft, principles and knowledge, methods, understanding and awareness.[1] As Ingold (1988a, 1990b, 1993b, 1999) has taken pains to argue, in the original sense of the word *tekhnē*, knowledgeable practice and practical knowledge were not so much different "sides" of a coin but inseparable aspects of the same phenomenon blended together *in practice* (more generally, see Dworkin 1986). In contrast, in contemporary parlance, practice and knowledge are treated as separate phenomena: technology equates with "science in action" and the application of abstract knowledge, principles, methods, and techniques to specific practical purposes; science equates with abstract or pure (elite) knowledge and principles that can be applied to the material world (Cowan 1996; Gosden 1994: 109). Yet, as the French anthropologist Mauss (1969a: 198–9 [orig. 1927]) noted, this "division between pure reason and practical reason seems scholastic, hardly authentic, hardly psychological, and even less sociological. We know, we see, we feel the profound links that unite them in their *raison d'être* and their history" (my translation).

The concern by some philosophers and historians of science and technology (for example, Basalla 1988; Bunge 1985) to distinguish between and among science, applied science, technology, and so-called pre-scientific (namely, technical) knowledge exemplifies this partitioning of what is, at best, a continuum of varying emphases. It is only when the original whole of *tekhnē* is conceptually divided into separate components – art, craft, skill, and methods *separate* from knowledge, principles, and understanding – that such distinctions matter and debates ensue. For example, Frazer (1890), Malinowski (1948), Mumford (1967), Nagel (1961), Pitt (1990), Rosenberg (1985), and Schiffer and Skibo (1987) are among many scholars variously trying to delineate the extent to which so-called pre-scientific knowledge is the practical application of preexisting abstract knowledge applied to "real" world problems, or whether abstract knowledge derives from the trial-and-error experiences of primitive (read: practical) technologies (analysis of this "scholar/craftsman" controversy can be found in Layton 1974; Mitcham 1994; Staudenmaier 1989). Underneath these debates lies the uneasy partitioning of *tekhnē* into its several constitutive elements.[2]

One all too familiar side of this debate claims that it is out of the practical craft of technology that more abstract understandings about the world develop, and that only after these are in hand can they be abstracted and (re)applied to other practical needs and interests (cf. Ihde 1983a; Janich 1978). Reconsider, for example, the aphorism "necessity is the mother of invention." This functional view depends upon the partitioning of practice/technology from knowledge/science, such that a "need" existing in nature motivates outwardly directed material responses and practical solutions (namely, technology) through trial-and-error (as discussed in chapter 1). The most pragmatic, rational, and efficient of these solutions, which take place in the so-called technoeconomic sphere, are then "selected for" based either on some version of Natural Selection or simple principles of cost/efficiency. And because they assist cultural survival, these necessary inventions diffuse upward into other spheres of social life. In this scenario, technology is little more than practical solutions embodied in craft and skill. Given time, however, the pre-scientific principles underlying them will become their own body of (pure) knowledge abstracted from their original practical source. With still more time, they will lead to "true" scientific knowledge, principles, theorems, and (ultimately) laws of causality.[3]

As one who well understands the fundamental role of (abstract) science in the design of (practical) technological inventions, Ferguson (1978: 460) is among many philosophers to attempt to reinsert the aesthetic back into the practicality of technical craft by arguing that, while "science will continue to influence technology, . . . it is art that will choose the specific shape of the future" (also Pye 1964). Whether we call this phenomenon scientific technology, technological science, technoscience, or something else, the question should be how knowledgeable practice and practical knowledge were simultaneously instantiated and reaffirmed through an inseparable mélange of everyday material practices conducted by social agents, and how (if at all) they came to be separated into more specialized forms of (abstract) knowledge and (technical) practices, thereby affording their practitioners different sorts of social, political, and economic prestige through the values and power variously attributed to them. For archaeologists and anthropologists, the point here is to work consciously against the partitive thinking that analytically separates art, skill and craft, abstract principles and practical knowledge, methods, understanding and awareness, such that "emphasis upon any of these constitutive items signifies that the others are emphasized along with it; this means that in any such case the whole phenomenon [technology] gets seen" (Heidegger 1962: 79; further discussion in chapter 3).

In contrast to these unidirectional debates, that either practical technology leads to abstract science or that abstract science enables practical technology, Heidegger (1977), Ihde (1983b, 1990), and Ortega y Gasset (in Mitcham 1994) suggest that the technologies we live by and through influence not just our explanations of the natural world (*sensu* science). Through their embodiment in daily practice, technologies influence both self-understandings and even what constitutes historical reality. To put it in other words, the sorts of awareness and understandings that result from technological practice conjure up the whole of *tekhnē* (Gosden 1994; Mitcham 1994: 97). The inseparability of abstract and practical knowledge intertwined with self and worldly awareness, all of which are engendered by social agents during their corporeal and social engagement with the physical making and using of material things, is a conceptual framework sociocultural anthropologists and archaeologists are just beginning to explore. This is the issue I develop in the remainder of this book.

It is significant in this regard that the ancient Greek term for technical (*technikos*) meant skill, art, and the practical, thus implying the whole of *tekhnē*. The Greek exemplar of the technical was both the carpenter *and* the knowledge and skills instantiated in their activities

(Bloom 1968: 443, n. 22). That is, "technical" originally and simultaneously meant the skilled and valued agent who does craft work as well as the knowledgeable activities and practical skills of crafting. In contrast, the contemporary value given to the knowledgeable skills and craft of the hands-on carpenter stand far below that of the thinking scientist (or engineer) who applies abstract knowledge to practical matters.

Today, the word "technical" is used colloquially to mean the narrowest (mechanical or practical) aspects of a (material) technology, thus conflating it with its legalistic sense of "attending to detail." As I can fight only one conceptual battle at a time, and my explicit concern here is with reclaiming the intersubjective and meaningful dimensions of technological practice in prehistory, in the remainder of this book I maintain this colloquial distinction between "technology" and "technical." For example, I use "technical gestures" and "technical strategies" when I am narrowly discussing detailed aspects of artifact making and use, while I use "technological practice" and "technological world views" to emphasize the social, embodied, and meaningful dimensions of such activities. My use of the term "technical agent" and "technical agency" is more fully explained in chapter 5. The key point here is that in their original meanings both *tekhnē* and *technikos* (namely, technology and technical) instantiated in the same instance art, skill, practical activities of material making and using, *alongside* knowledge, awareness, and the agent – which is precisely what I mean by the term "technology."[4]

Logos

But what of the second half of the modern word "technology," the *logos* of material making and use? It is the latter part of this hybrid term that, I believe, causes contemporary archaeologists most of their conceptual problems. The original meaning of *logos* (also *logike*) was not only reason but also the ontological structure of reality, as well as speech, and "giving an account."[5] In its modern usage, however, *logos* (or more recognizably, logic) has come to mean a very *specific* kind of reason that produces theory: the dispassionate, the objective, the computational. To situate in its historical context the contemporary meaning of *logos*, we need to start with the late seventeenth century – the Age of Reason – then consider developments in the eighteenth century, when Enlightenment philosophy and science came to embody the very essence of modernity we still hold near and dear (Latour 1993; C. Taylor 1989).

The modern conception of society . . . has frequently been understood as an outgrowth of the epistemological revolution of the 17th [*sic*] century. The rise of a modern self-defining subject which aspires to take control of its own social relationships, rather than leaving these structures that shape its everyday existence to the authority of tradition, is related by many different schools of European thinkers to the increasing confidence of man in his own ability to manipulate and control the natural world. (Halberstram 1999: 17)

In particular, it was Francis Bacon (1561–1626), along with Galileo (1564–1642) and especially Descartes (1596–1650), who explicitly and aggressively prefigured the Enlightenment agenda of modern science and its "handmaiden" technology – later canonized by Locke (1632–1704) and Newton (1642–1727), especially – general summaries in Cassirer (1951); Golinski (1991); C. Taylor (1989); Vickers (1991); Westfall (1991).

For Bacon, the modern scientific project was to be the application of technical skills (in medicine, chemistry, and related disciplines) and analytic methods (specifically rational, objective, and dispassionate investigative techniques) to lay bare the tantalizing secrets of life and death hidden from the human gaze by that temptress, Nature (extended discussion in E. F. Keller 1985).[6] Bacon envisioned this empiricist and inductive basis of science (specifically defined as pertaining to abstract knowledge and principles) and its handmaiden, technology (that is, practical craft and rational investigative methods) to be "in the service of Man."[7] According to the "father of experimental philosophy," as he was called by the Royal Society, using science to probe the depths of Nature and reveal Her innermost secrets had to be an exclusively male endeavor, because the relentless and dispassionate pursuit of objective knowledge could be in no way tainted by (female) empathy, feeling, or any sort of dialectic between observer and observed or between knower and known (also Westkott 1979). In his *Critique of Pure Reason*, Kant (1996: Bxii–xiii [orig. 1781 and 1787]) describes the Copernican Revolution that laid the foundation for Bacon's enlightened view about the relationship between subject and object:

When Galileo causes balls, the weights of which he had himself previously determined, to roll down an inclined place; or when Torricelli made the air carry a weight which he had calculated beforehand to be equal to that of a definite volume of water . . . What all these investigators of nature comprehended was that reason has insight only into what it itself produces according to its own plan; and reason must not allow nature by itself to keep it in leading strings, as it were, but reason must – using principles that underlie its judgments – proceed according to constant laws and compel nature to answer reason's own questions.

The goal of this New Science, thus, was nothing less than an "emancipation from meaning . . . to draw back from the world, and concentrate purely on our own processes of observation and thought about things" (C. Taylor 1989: 7).[8]

With this concerted effort to produce true knowledge, the value of a hermaphroditic coupling of mind and matter and the once sacred, mystical, and poetic aspects of ancient alchemy were, in Bacon's project, consciously and purposefully replaced by the craft, method, dispassionate, and rational study of tangible matter (E. F. Keller 1985: 21–32; Staudenmaier 1989: 163–4; on Descartes' view of "disengaged reason," see C. Taylor 1989: 143–58). As Cassirer (1951: 15) puts it: "The first step which the eighteenth century took in this direction was to seek a clear line of demarcation between the mathematical and the philosophical spirit." The new and self-consciously enlightened definition of reason and *logos*, along with the faith now being placed in the powers of the analytical mind (as in the work of Descartes and, later, Newton), was further privileged and reaffirmed through the material technologies and scientific research programs being pursued starting in the eighteenth century.

Thus, at the same time that the objectivity and *logos* of scientific reasoning was explicitly being divorced from and privileged over pre-modern (that is, empathetic and embodied) forms of knowing, the subject matter science had long been dedicated to unraveling was being redefined as passive, inert, elemental object matter. In both instances, then, as disengaged procedures of knowledge acquisition and as regards the thing being studied, instrumentalism loomed large (C. Taylor 1989: 151–5). Importantly, it is not simple coincidence that the modern and partitive definition of *tekhnē* was underway at much the same time. These were profound changes in western thinking and everyday practice, for "this change in the method of natural science involve[d] . . . a decisive transformation in pure ontology" (Cassirer 1951: 38). Significantly, this 300-year legacy (still) underwrites the very word "technology" (Ingold 1999). And as chapter 1 shows, it also stifles archaeological research and understandings about technologies practiced long before the modernity of enlightened reason.

Bacon's explicit goal in redefining science by these progressive and self-consciously modern terms, and in clarifying technology's new and subservient role as its handmaiden, was to be able to employ the resulting true, certain, and objective knowledge of nature toward ever more practical and rational (that is, technological) ends.[9] However, as L. White, Jr. (1967: 1203) explains, "the emergence in widespread practice of the Baconian creed that scientific knowledge means technological power over nature can scarcely be dated before about 1850, save in the chemical industries, where it is anticipated in the 18th [*sic*] century." That is, as with any wholesale paradigm shift, there was a substantial time-lag between the first explicit articulation of Bacon's vision and its widespread acceptance and practice as the prevailing ontological and epistemological basis for the acquisition of western knowledge.

Another important point that philosophers make in this regard is that scientific theories "and their associated ideas strongly influence our visions of the natural order (cosmology) and ourselves (psychology)" (Mitcham 1994: 95; also E. F. Keller 1992; Merchant 1980, 1983; Schiebinger 1993; a prelude to this point is discussed in chapter 1; it is further elaborated in chapters 3 and 4). That is, what counts *as* Nature or "natural" (as opposed to something else, such as the work of God or Culture) and how Nature is conceived (as benevolent, destructive, active, inert, competitive, constraining, enabling, or even a feminine deity) is irrevocably and historically bound to the cultural ontologies and sociopolitical circumstances in which it is conceptualized and studied (L. White, Jr. 1967).[10] In western intellectualism, Bacon was among the first to distinguish consciously between, then reconnect in a significantly new and different way, the practical "side" of knowledge production through material/technological means and abstract (scientific) knowledge of the material (natural) world applied to practical problems.

For Bacon (as well as Descartes, then Locke and Newton), the mastery of Nature through the technical mechanics and craft of empirical scientific research, calculus, and mechanistic concepts, was to produce a special kind of abstract, objective, and rational knowledge – and, therefore, power (Butts 1995; as described for example in Foucault 1977). As Mitcham (1994: 113) points out: "it was for this reason that Francis Bacon, at the dawn of the modern age, sought to turn people away from philosophical [abstract] questioning and toward more practical [technical] affairs." And as Mumford (1967: 280) notes (though suggesting a somewhat earlier timing for these changes), "with this shift from the contemplative life of the religious to the active life of merchants, sailors, financiers, industrial enterprisers [sic], these canons [of calculation, discipline, and reason] took on the form of moral imperatives" (also Cassirer 1951).

> The new model of rational mastery . . . presents it as a matter of instrumental control. To be free from the illusion which mingles mind with matter is to have an understanding of the latter which facilitates its control. Similarly, to free oneself from passions and obey reason is to get the passions under instrumental direction. The hegemony of reason is defined no longer as that of a dominant vision but rather in terms of a directing agency subordinating a functional domain. (C. Taylor 1989: 149)[11]

Tekhnē + logos = *epistemological salvation in the modern era*

With these reflections in mind, we can begin to locate a sort of "origins point" in western intellectualism for the historical partitioning of *tekhnē* into its separate components – art, skill, and craft; principles and knowledge; methods; understanding; and awareness – and the conflation of its material and practical dimensions with the objective (and masculinist) rationality of *logos*. Weber (1946) provides powerful insights into the momentous coupling of the Protestant Reformation with Enlightenment science by underscoring the moral and ethical imperative underwriting this call for rational and dispassionate reason in the production of knowledge (also Cassirer 1951; C. Taylor 1989: 230–3). Weber's famous essay (1946), "Religious Rejections of the World and Their Directions," sets out to explain how and why working scientists at this time supplanted once highly valued religious, philosophical, and empathetic understandings of the mysteries of the natural world with what he calls the "first-worldly" asceticism of rational scientific knowledge. "Most typically, it [the Enlightenment] took the form of a search for salvation through the reckoning method" (Stafford 1991: 1).[12] That is, salvation was now to be gained by a new and secular route: by acquiring pure and abstract knowledge, established by mathematical forms of reasoning, that only an objective and rational science could produce. As philosophers and historians have noted, applying this secularized, dispassionate, and abstract knowledge to the practical and material problems of the real world (through that handmaiden, technology) conveniently served the increasing computational and material "demands" of capitalism.

Thus, starting with Bacon and gaining popularity throughout the eighteenth century, we begin to see the modern (nineteenth- and twentieth-century) definition of technology take root: founded on notions of disengaged rational logic and abstract computational knowledge, applied to solve practical problems given in the objective material world, achieved through craft activities, and for utilitarian purposes. Significantly, by the time Newton was galvanizing modern science around an explicit concern with quantification and mathematical methods, this increasingly instrumental approach to the study (and control) of nature was going by the name *"technologia"* (C. Taylor 1989: 233). The craft and material practice of technology (once known as *tekhnē* but now alienated from any salient connection to aesthetics and meaning), depended on a special kind of knowledge acquired only through the rationality of *logos*, put in the service of an Enlightened science to meet the needs of the Enlightened Man. Ingold (1995: 208) argues the case most succinctly, by pointing out that the western "sense of modernity, founded as it is upon a commitment to the supremacy of reason, is built into the very project of contemporary science" (also Habermas 1970; Haraway 1989, 1991; Latour 1993; Marcuse 1964). In this way, Bacon's new vision of science and technology were foundational elements of modernity, which was itself explicitly and consciously designed to distance the enlightened, civilized West from the mystical and "pre-scientific" sorts of knowledge shrouding the primitive material technologies (still) practiced by indigenous peoples increasingly coming under colonial rule.

Among others, M. Harris (1968) and Trigger (1989) have considered in detail the impact Enlightenment ideals of practical reason, progress, and "man's" dispassionate, logical, and technological mastery of Nature and Society had on anthropology and archaeology. But, as I suggested in chapter 1, we can also see their influence on the very meaning of (pre-historic) technology, on what properly constitutes its object matter, and on the analytic and interpretive methodologies we have developed to study "it." For example, the very way we write about ancient technologies (in the passive voice) and methodologically privilege the study of material matters (over those more "remote" social ones) have worked implicitly, but irrevocably, to assist in separating the *subject* matter of technology – technicians, their social relationships, their values and beliefs, their agency – from its physical *object* matter.

The historical coupling of Enlightenment *logos* with an instrumental concept of *tekhnē* has allowed for this conceptual transformation of the subject matter of ancient technology into a quantifiable object for dispassionate study (Mumford 1952, 1967). Or, as Ingold (1988a: 174) puts it:

> Once human consciousness is admitted as a force of production, we have to conclude that "people, as much as or more than the machine [. . .] make history" (MacKenzie 1984: 477). Indeed, the burden of Marx's argument is that this history has involved a progressive *objectification* of the productive forces, reaching its apotheosis in the industrial automaton. It would be a great mistake to read back into history the modern identification of the forces with all that is *external* to the human subject, and imagine that the primitive precursors of the machine were the hand-axe and digging stick. . . . However much it may have influenced the general course of history, the development of the forces has transformed the entire system of relations between worker, tool, and raw material, replacing subject-centered knowledge and skills with objective principles of mechanical functioning. [Author's emphasis].

For the study of prehistoric technology, the net effect of this complicated history has been to conceptually, analytically, and interpretively separate the things being made and used from the technical agents engaging in these intersubjective labors, from their overlapping forms of practical and esoteric knowledge, from their social relationships, and from the values and beliefs on which the "system" depended. In this sense, *tekhnē* has been separated from itself, and it is no mere coincidence that this process is often called "alienation" in the marxist sense of the term (discussed below).

This brief chapter cannot consider in depth the nexus of gendered, political, ideological, economic, and material changes taking place in the industrializing centers of western Europe and America during the seventeenth, eighteenth, and nineteenth centuries. What is important to stress, however, is that the *practical* alienation Bacon advocated in functionally distinguishing between science and technology, and the concomitant *intellectual* alienation of subject and object, were part and parcel of this wholesale cultural transformation (C. Taylor 1989). Major social and ideological forces both structured and helped to make sense of the real material changes people were experiencing during this slow and painful "birth" of the Machine Age.[13] For example, by Bacon's time (at least), the *status quo* was being challenged by the "need" for an increasingly large and mobile urban workforce capable of producing (abstract) capital through the manufacture of new kinds of products. What Mumford (1967: 273) called that "nice balance" between rural and urban life was now threatened; long-accepted divisions of labor in traditional agropastoral pursuits, the sense of self-worth they engendered, and the social and economic prestige they afforded individuals and communities were no longer stable. As the "technopolis" (Cox 1965: 5) increasingly became the context in which new kinds of social interactions were created and a new sense of social alienation (Ryan 1981) developed, abstract quantification came to hold a new and preeminent place in defining, among other things, the value of people's labor and the worth of their products (also Petrovic 1983b: 411).

As Marx (and his many followers) have argued, there *was* something specific and unique in the means and forces of industrial production that "necessitated" significantly different social relations than previously experienced. Philosophers have picked up on this argument, showing how the inevitably sensual but impersonal experience of automation and mechanization promotes alienation (discussed in chapter 3 and throughout the remainder of this book). The specific kinds of material technologies in which industrial people engage (hand tools, electrical "power" tools, the assembly line, computer technologies, even cyberspace, and so on) are material and experiential ways of producing (self) awareness significantly *different* from other kinds of corporeal experiences (Illich 1973; Mumford 1934, 1964; also Mauss

1935; discussion in Mitcham 1994: 181–6; for an archaeological example, see Dobres in press-a). For archaeologists, in particular, this line of reasoning suggests that more attention needs to be paid to the materiality of specific prehistoric technologies, not to identify their invariant and cross-cultural physical properties, but in order to understand the personal, social, and experiential basis of an awareness of self and Other they helped instantiate (I take up this point in detail in chapters 5 and 6).

In sum, the very possibility of making sense of the archaeological record as reflecting a linear scheme of humanity's ever progressive control of nature through techno+logical means was closely tied to the ascendance of Enlightenment philosophy (M. Harris 1968; Kehoe 1992; Trigger 1989: 84–6). And by the mid- to late-nineteenth century, evolutionary theories proposed by archaeologists were serving, teleologically, to legitimate and help explain at least some of the more radical upheavals people were experiencing in their everyday lives (discussion and examples provided in chapter 1).

Changing concepts of technology

By way of putting some closure on these brief historical considerations, it is worth noting that the first use of the word "technology" in its modern sense was not until quite recently – 1728 – when it was defined by the German philosopher Christian Wolff as "the science of the arts and of the works of art" (Mitcham 1994: 131). By 1777, "technology" meant an explicit focus on the functional and material aspects of the productive process, but it was another fifty years before the word first appeared in English. Jacob Bigelow's *Elements of Technology* (1831) defined technology very much in its modern sense, as "the principles, processes, and nomenclatures of the more conspicuous arts, particularly those which involve applications of science" (quoted in Mitcham 1994: 131). It is more than curious that this first appearance of the word "technology" in an English publication was only thirty years before the initial publication of Lyell's *Principles of Geology*, and came only three decades after the published drawings of the Hoxne Acheulean handaxe found by Frere in 1797.[14] Importantly, "technology" did not appear as its own entry in the *Encyclopedia Britannica* until the 15th edition, published in 1975. According to this entry, technology is the science of the application of knowledge to a practical purpose as well as the totality of means employed by "a people" to provide themselves the objects of material culture.

Contrary to conventional wisdom, then, it is not the rational and instrumental practicality of technologism that lies at the very heart of what it is to be human (chapter 1). Rather, *defining the human career in technological terms is a recent phenomenon*. What I argue in the remainder of this book is that, more than anything else, technology is a continually unfolding process of social, meaningful, and sensuous engagement – a verb of action and interaction – engendered by social agents during their everyday activities of object making and use in historically and culturally circumscribed settings. Technology is, first, foremost, and centrally about the meaningful social relationships people forge, reaffirm, and contest while going about such activities. Importantly, I do not give equal weight to people and artifacts in the technology-society "equation," nor do I limit technology to the materiality of gadgets and gizmos (as in folk notions of the term), although the tangible plays an important role in instantiating meaning and social relationships (as I discuss in chapters 4–7). Tangible objects are only some of the means by which *in*tangible realities and experiences, such as meanings, values, identities, relationships, status, society, and power, are made and remade.

Moreover, as I show in chapter 4, there surely *is* a *logos* to all *tekhnē*; but reason and logic are cultural constructions that never exist outside the (social) body politic in which they are practiced. Contemporary (western) logocentrism, colloquially known as technological determinism, claims that technologies are autonomous (rational) phenomena "acting on" societies and individuals in negative and largely destructive (or at least restrictive) ways. But, technological determinism has a "flip-side" which Winner (1983, 1986b) calls "technological somnambulism" (discussed in the following chapter). And while it may be true that in the modern world we "sleepwalk past the very conditions of our own making," archaeologists must be careful not to assume this has always been the state of things, as the Ingold quote (above) cautions.

Another Fateful Split: As if Once was Not Enough

To this point I have only considered how the conceptual segmentation of *tekhnē* into its alienated parts, and the selective grafting of its craft and practical dimensions onto a particular kind of *logos*, historically narrowed the meaning of "technology" to its contemporary sense. How the different social sciences, humanities, and physical sciences have carved up this redefined phenomenon still further, each taking only some part of the whole as their subject or object matter for study, has also contributed to irrevocable divisions in understanding that have only augmented the conceptual and methodological problems outlined in this and the previous chapter.

Philosophy, anthropology, archaeology, sociology, history, political science, and the material sciences . . . each gets its piece of the cake

Philosophers of technology have concentrated much of their attention on comprehending the sources of abstract and practical techno-knowledge and understanding the impact of such knowledge on the general human experience of engaging with material phenomena (reviewed in chapter 3). In contrast, because technology in so-called primitive societies has long been considered pre-scientific craft and mere mechanical method, by the middle decades of the twentieth century sociocultural anthropologists felt it irrelevant to their interests in language, myth, kinship, and other (seemingly) non-material phenomena. Yet because western discourse has long held that (material) technologies were the foundation upon which cultures evolved, archaeologists have never wavered in their appreciation of human and pre-human technologies.

How these differentiated segments of technology have been subsequently carved up for study by the "appropriate" humanities, social, and material sciences has further alienated our understanding of the interrelationship of social relations of production, divisions of labor, values, politics, experiences, and symbolic aspects with the material and practical dimensions of object making and use. As a general rule, philosophers study the metaphysics and ethics of technology as well as the essence and nature of technological knowledge; anthropologists study its social organization, meanings, and values; archaeologists study the material origins of *Homo faber*, long-term change in ancient technologies, and the progressively civilizing and adaptive effect that the material control of Nature had on the evolution of Culture; sociologists, historians, and political scientists study the socioeconomic and political forces behind, and ramifications of, society's acceptance or rejection of particular inventions and technical practices;[15] while material scientists study the mechanical and chemical transformations involved in turning ore into metal, sand into glass, clay into ceramics, and minerals colorants into paint. Dividing up the various components of *tekhnē* and farming them out to the appropriate intellectual discipline has done little to create a holistic, or "unmutilated" (Gosden 1994: 180), understanding of its several "properties."

Thus another "fateful split" (E. Wolf 1982: 7–11) – that of the social sciences segmented into specialized divisions of intellectual labor – has also shaped our study and several understandings of technology, although this particular segmentation has not been the subject of much discussion (but see a brief consideration in Schiffer 1992b). Indeed, as a *hindrance* to learning what each other has to say, academic barriers and their different career tracks create unique vantage points "provided they remain separate" (Latour 1993: 5). According to E. Wolf (1982: 10–11), while

> ostensibly engaged in the study of human *behavior*, the various disciplines parcel out the subject among themselves. Each then proceeds to set up a model, seemingly a means to explain "hard" observable facts, yet actually an ideologically loaded scheme geared to a narrow definition of subject matter. Such schemes provide self-fulfilling answers, since phenomena other than those covered by the model are ruled out of the court of specialized discourse. (Author's emphasis)

It is not going too far to suggest, furthermore, that the social sciences in general (and perhaps most particularly archaeology) have a kind of science-envy rooted in the authority the so-called hard sciences have in contemporary society (E. F. Keller 1992: 97).[16] I believe this situation can be traced, in part, to the historical splitting of *tekhnē* into its several "elements": first was the *conceptual* split promoted by Bacon, which led to the privileging of science and the devaluing of technology as its handmaiden (discussed above); second was its *academic* partitioning in the nineteenth century. That is, first came the division between knowledge/science and practice/technology, then their reformulation within the maturing social sciences of sociology, anthropology, and archaeology in the mid- to late-nineteenth century. However, in the mid-seventeenth century,

> science was traditionally aristocratic, speculative, intellectual in intent; technology was lower-class, empirical, action-oriented. The quite sudden fusion of these two toward the middle of the 19th [*sic*] century is surely related to the slightly prior and contemporary democratic revolutions which, by reducing social barriers, tended to assert a functional unity of brain and hand. (L. White, Jr. 1967: 1204)[17]

To this day, materials research in technology studies are considered the technical end of archaeology – the real "science" done in the lab (for example, studies determining the chemical and petrological properties of raw materials and pigment compositions, research on firing techniques and their effects on clay or stone, replicative experiments to ascertain the bending pressures different organic materials can withstand). In contrast, more interpretive analyses (which are less often thought to have their own rigorous techniques and methodological rules) are still suspected of being little better than armchair speculation (for example, structural and stylistic analyses, inferences about social relations of production, even the view promoted in this book). Stoczkowski (1994: 246) puts it bluntly: "if certain theories seduce us, it is because they confirm our private naïve convictions, legitimized by means of some appearances of a scientific nature" (my translation). Because of ideas inherited from Bacon's time, coupled with the modern compartmentalization of academic research on technology and the privileged status of "hard" science within this system, the more science one claims in support their work on prehistoric technology, the better. But whether or not such science is the best, or only, means of understanding is debatable.

It is not my intent here to compare the explicit, much less implicit, values differently afforded "hard" scientific research undertaken in the laboratory with what is (still) taken to be the separate and subsequent interpretive enterprise. Nor is it necessary to explore further the particular brand of science-envy that archaeology has practiced for the last three decades. Surely the very term "social science" is itself worthy of attention in this regard, however. The range of disciplines constituting the "sciences of the social" bear the scars of the fateful split then reconstitution of the hybrids: Nature *and* Culture; science *and* technology; knowledge *and* practice. It is, however, worth reiterating at this juncture a point made in the previous chapter. Fabian's (1983) account of anthropology's (and by extension archaeology's) "denial of coevalness" shows clearly that the distinction between Us and Other, or between so-called etic and emic explanations, also bears witness to this fateful legacy. The deflection by which we conceptually turn contemporary geographic distance into evolutionary (a)temporal difference serves not only to conflate contemporary ethnographic societies with extinct ones, but also to create the conceptual space for claiming a neutral and objective distance between knower (Us; scientist) and known (Other; primitive; Westkott 1979). It is this same conceptual separation of hand, mind, space, and time that drives current debates as to the nature of "pre-scientific" knowledge in so-called primitive societies, be they of the present or the past. The very notion of a "pre"-scientific basis of knowledge bears the weight of nineteenth-century evolutionary (indeed, racist) ideas that see primitive technological craft, practice, and magic as the evolutionary precursors of civilized, abstract, pure, and lofty scientific knowledge.

Given the number of questionable premises and assumptions underwriting the analytic strategies of everyday technology research in archaeology, however, it is not at all clear why so much of the community still turns its analytic eye on the material dimensions of ancient technologies *before* admitting or being willing to grapple the cultural factors involved.[18] My admonition on this point is intended much in the same spirit as Morton's (1988) and Ingold's (1988b) challenges to Testart's (1988) unwillingness to consider the likelihood that complex cultural beliefs, values, and social relations significantly shape and are inseparable from the simple morphology and nature of Australian Aboriginal material technology. In this regard, Morton (1988: 20) deftly points out that "if hunter-gatherer experts spent as much time classifying modes of mythical consciousness and religious artefacts [sic] as they do technological items, the reconstruction of the past might be considerably enhanced."

These comments are not in any way suggesting that objective material realities do not affect the contours of human technologies and decision-making strategies. They most certainly do; and we must attend to them in our research and interpretive accounts (as I clearly advocate in chapters 5 and 6). My point here is the same as that argued in chapter 1: that we need to reflect critically on our analytic *priorities* and the premises on which they rest, priorities that place first emphasis on the empirical study of material and practical matters, and put off the more "remote" (social) side of technology for later consideration. We would also do well to reflect on the question of which intellectual disciplines are "best suited" to providing worthwhile understandings of technology and society: those in the humanities, or those in the social or material sciences.

The Fallacy of Misplaced Concreteness: Challenging Operative Premises

And at this juncture, it is helpful to shift attention away from these general historical considerations of what technology is and is not, to consider a particular methodological issue in the study of technologies, especially ancient ones. Another detour into the realm of philosophy can help us reassess what the material artifacts fortuitously preserved in the archaeological record actually "reflect."

The reader should now be aware that much of what they see *as* prehistoric technology (and here one typically conjures up images of stone tools, lithic waste, ceramic pots, or pottery wheels) is itself an artifact of western intellectualism. However, as with the changing meaning of the term "technology," even what constitutes archaeological "data" has changed significantly, especially over the past three or four decades. The reasons for this change in what counts *as* data are not as obvious as one might think, by which I mean they are neither practical, technical, nor necessarily material in origins. As I have argued at length elsewhere (Dobres 1995c, in press-b), the reasons why we today concentrate so much explicit attention on recovering and recording the patterning of spatially distributed artifacts on horizontal surfaces, and why we now painstakingly collect minute fragments of debitage (in addition to whole or near-complete pieces) is *not* because our techniques of recovery and laboratory analysis have improved since mid-century. Rather, these methodological and analytic changes in the everyday practice of field archaeology have come about through significant *conceptual* shifts: in the kinds of the questions we now about the past, and because of our epistemological "coming-of-age" (L. R. Binford 1964; Clarke 1973; Redman 1973, 1987).

One of the major hallmarks in the development of so-called Processual or "New" Archaeology commencing in the early 1960s was the demand that we pose well-conceived research questions before excavating, and consider in advance what particular sorts of material data would be likely to help answer those questions. As only one example, once the behavioral question of artifact function became a major focus of inquiry (L. R. Binford 1966, 1972; *contra* Bordes and de Sonneville-Bordes 1970), archaeologists quickly realized that once important whole and time-diagnostic *fossiles directeurs* were less informative than the breakage patterns and use-wear stigmata on discarded spalls. Thus, it was not that all of a sudden we invented new techniques to recover and study such evidence (though that, too, occurred); rather, it was that now we could imagine reasons why such material patterning could be informative in ways in which they were not previously.

My point in making this detour into the most obvious and heralded side of the recent history of archaeological method and theory is to make a critical distinction between the (static) material objects and physical patterns we study in the field and lab, and the (dynamic) albeit intangible processes we think explain them (issues of site formation processes aside). Surely the artifacts we excavate and their spatial arrangements are highly empirical, tangible, quantifiable, and (usually) directly observable. But as any good field archaeologist knows, it takes time, experience, knowledgeable practice, practical knowledge, skill, craft, art, and understanding to recognize archaeological data *as such*, and many a novice has been known to miss what the trained eye readily identifies as significant data. Nonetheless, it is one thing to have as our primary data the tangible remains of ancient technologies; it is quite another to be seduced into confusing what best preserves in the ground with the thing itself. That is, it is one thing to excavate broken harpoons, lithic debitage, grinding stone, hearths, and the like. But we must not confuse these material (archaeological) traces with the social (systemic) processes of which they were once a part (Schiffer 1972).

The seductiveness of the tangible – for example, in the physical remains of the archaeological record – leads to what the eminent philosopher Whitehead (1927) called the "fallacy of misplaced concreteness." By this term he meant confusing material things with the dynamic processes underwriting them, and especially in mistaking the material part of some phenomenon for the larger dynamic from which it derives. Nowhere is this intellectual conflation of thing and process (and, by extension, noun and verb) more clearly evident than in our general confusion with studying the materiality of technology as if it were the whole of ancient *tekhnē* (Dobres 1999a). Simply put: an Acheulean handaxe is not a prehistoric technology; the use-functions of harpoons and spear points are not, by themselves, a prehistoric technology; differential patterns in exhausted lithic cores, alone, are not a prehistoric technology; nor is the potter's wheel. These material entities constitute only the preserved part of ancient *tekhnē*, and it takes more than a handaxe, a utilitarian function, or a reduction strategy to make a technology.[19]

As much as archaeologists would like to believe that the reason they concentrate so intently on the materiality of technology (first) is simply because it is all they are left with (chapter 1), the reasons are far more insidious and problematic. Our Baconian legacy, the academic separation of science from interpretation in the study of technology, and the fallacy of misplaced concreteness combine to suggest less obvious reasons for taking the fortuitously preserved part of the past and confusing it with its once dynamic whole. To rationalize this elision of object with subject and (tangible) artifact with (intangible) artifice, we have created a battery of epistemological arguments of the sort once boldly asserted by Hawkes (1954), MacWhite (1956), and M. A. Smith (1955), and given ontological status by Leach (1973). As I discussed in chapter 1, our analytical prioritizing of the tangible and material aspects of prehistoric technology over its more cultural, albeit "remote," side has taken on a far more ontological status than it warrants.

It is the legacy of an Enlightened standpoint for understanding the world and the place of (western) self in it that makes it so difficult to comprehend people with other standpoints understanding their world differently.

The [Enlightenment] philosophy of disengagement and objectification has helped to create a picture of the human being, at its most extreme in certain forms of materialism, from which the last vestiges of subjectivity seem to have been expelled. It is a picture of the human being from a completely third-person perspective. The paradox is that this severe outlook is connected with, indeed based on, according a central place to the first-person stance [Descartes' "I think, therefore I am"]. Radical objectivity is only intelligible and accessible through radical subjectivity. (C. Taylor 1989: 175–6)

Because we have for so long unwittingly confused the material "side" of the *logos* of making and using with *tekhnē* itself, we have given little explicit attention to the necessary conceptual and methodological frameworks for considering *from the start tekhnē* as an indivisible whole. As I argue from this point on, it is likely that ancient *tekhnē* was structured *less* by some universal *logos* and as much (if not more) by culturally situated reason and embodied practice; by traditional notions about the "right" and "wrong" ways to make and use things; by personal and group interests having little directly to do with artifact making and use but which were advanced through technological practice; by socially constituted and contested codes of organization and task differentiation; by ontological world views dictating how the world worked and should be worked, and so forth.

If these less tangible factors impinge on technological practice and decisions more than we have been willing to concede thus far (and I strongly argue this proposition in the remainder of this book), then all the rigorous and eminently scientific analyses of the material "part" of that whole will never grasp them, *for they are not designed to do so.* Thus, we can assert all we want that until we fully understand all the material factors determining some practical technical choice the social side must wait, but such a claim is neither as legitimate nor as fruitful as it would appear. And on the face of it, the more we concentrate on this material side the more material problems we identify that require additional study, pushing back still further that worthy processual goal of studying statics to understand ancient dynamics.

Put another way, dismantling the whole of some ancient *tekhnē* into its supposedly constitutive elements (tangible and intangible), methodically prioritizing them for systematic study, then somewhere down the line expecting to put them back together into that original whole, is a misguided strategy at best. What such an analytic technique does, in fact, is *simulate* an altogether different sort of *tekhnē*; one that bears little resemblance to its original dynamic and human-centered whole but which resonates with what we call technology in the alienated modern world (after Baudrillard 1983). All said, in taking apart then trying to put Humpty Dumpty back together, sometimes an altogether different creature is created.

Conclusions

This chapter has briefly touched upon a number of ideas developed outside the realm of traditional archaeological interests in ancient technology. I hope they have allowed the reader the conceptual room in which to begin reconsidering our long taken-for-granted notions about the phenomenon we unquestioningly call technology. To accomplish this I have engaged in a bit of deconstruction showing, both historically and by foraging around the philosopher's territory, just how far the modern term is from its pre-modern sensibilities. While chapter 1 described the general nature of *what* I find problematic in the way archaeologists typically think about and undertake research on ancient technologies, here I have concentrated on unpacking some of the reasons *why* these ideas and approaches are favored. I see the deconstruction of taken-for-granted assumptions and working premises a useful means of prying the lid off the black box that has so effectively separated the thinking, feeling, and interacting technician (subject) from the thing (object) called technology.

In the next chapter I more systematically explore philosophical issues, not to continue deconstructing why archaeologists have historically conceptualized technology as they have, but for more constructive reasons: to introduce the reader to conceptual trends in the philosophy of technology that can promote the interests championed in this book. Chapters 4 and 5 go on to articulate a practice framework for thinking about technology as a sensual and meaningful form of social engagement with the world played out during materially grounded activities. Chapter 6 then discusses an analytic methodology eminently suitable to this reconceptualized project. After all, it simply makes no sense to change the conceptual framework, starting premises, and questions one asks about prehistoric technology, then go about research as usual.

3

Prying Open the Black Box: Philosophical Insights on Technology and Being

In this extension of the previous chapter I select and freely associate ideas from philosophy and related fields studying technology and argue their relevance for anthropological and archaeological concerns. In so doing, I do not pretend to offer a comprehensive review of ideas prevailing in the philosophy of technology,[1] nor to cover all the major intellectual camps. As with the writings of Marx, many philosophers of technology are obtuse and ambiguous to the degree that the lay reader, especially those with interests or intellectual backgrounds different from the philosopher, can find in their writings relevant ideas they never explicitly intended. I readily admit that this is my situation. This chapter is put together, therefore, as a *bricoleur* might approach the topic – taking bits and pieces of ideas from here and there and putting them together in ways that are suitable to other interests. While some might call this intellectual blasphemy, I see this as a properly "undisciplined" way to circumvent the limits of conventional reasoning and to further an unabashedly humanistic perspective on ancient technology (following Miller and Tilley 1996).

Philosophical Insights into Technology

Philosophers of technology are interested in five overlapping sets of questions: (1) the nature of humans *vis-à-vis* their technologies (this focus also relates to the philosophy of science); (2) the relationship between different sorts of technologies and the social, economic, and political structures in which they are practiced (this focus necessarily leads to two related interests: determinism and technology-as-ideology); (3) ethics and its necessary correlates, politics and power; (4) epistemology and problems of methodology (this focus attempts to redress the view that technology is merely applied science; it also explores the nature of technological knowledge); and (5) processes of technological change (though here they have much to learn from archaeologists, and not just in terms of chronologies). Though I do not maintain these rigid distinctions, in this and the following chapter I explore each of these emphases for what they have to offer archaeologists and anthropologists.

As well, researchers who apply philosophical arguments to their work on technology themselves distinguish three persuasions or emphases (Staudenmaier 1989: 5–8): (1) *external* views emphasize the influence of technology *on* social institutions (an archaeological example would be the evolutionary theories laid out in Leroi-Gourhan's [1943, 1945] two-volume work, *Evolution et techniques*); (2) *internal* perspectives seek to understand the place of technologies *in* society and to make sense of their interrelationship (a good example is Mumford's *Technics and Human Development*, or Weber's [1946] account of the interrelationship between capitalism, industrial technologies, and the development of modern scientific practice as discussed in chapter 2); and finally, (3) *contextual* standpoints see technology as a social construction requiring context-specific analyses of specific technologies in particular times and places (exemplified in Hughes' [1979, 1983] work on Edison's technology of electrification, or the various studies in Bijker et al. [1994] – an archaeologically inspired example would be Schiffer's [1991] study of the portable radio).

While applications of internal and external philosophical considerations often fail to be materially specific and concrete and sometimes over-emphasize certain factors as more deterministic than they are, contextual standpoints often fail to address fundamental issues of philosophy and do not necessarily appreciate the extent to which societies and technologies are constructed in concert with each other (Mitcham 1994: 116; Winner 1991). Yet a third way to categorize and organize philosophical writings on technology is by the general "ism" within which they develop. While I do my best not to use such off-putting labels, philosophers are generally defined by major intellectual schools of thought: phenomenology, existentialism, experientialism, realism, pragmatism, empiricism, metaphysics, and so forth. In what follows, I prefer simply to highlight some especially interesting things philosophers have to say about technology and leave it to the reader to pigeonhole them as they please.

Before proceeding, it is well to reiterate the main point thus far concerning the "tyranny of the obvious" in traditional archaeological studies of technology. To our detriment, the concept of (prehistoric) technology has remained relatively overlooked, under-theorized, and impervious to much critical evaluation *in spite of* the intellectual maturation of archaeology commencing in the 1960s, and the "second wave" of introspection starting in the mid-1980s. *As a concept,* technology has remained tenaciously self-evident even though our research questions, paradigms, and analytic techniques to study the past have changed considerably. I agree with Escobar (1994) that a review of philosophical insights can help address this blind spot. While chapters 1 and 2 began this exercise by identifying, then deconstructing certain taken-for-granted concepts and assumptions lurking below the surface of mainstream archaeological research, in this chapter I take a more *constructive* approach by exploring philosophical considerations for what they can offer a practice framework for archaeology.

Technology: an experience with "things-in-themselves"

Immanuel Kant (1724–1804)

Kant was primarily interested in questions about knowledge and judgment, their constitution, and their applications and limits. He was among the first to suggest there was a technical quality to the skills necessary for acquiring and using knowledge (for example, in both abstract scientific reasoning as well as in its practical dimensions as a basis for moral and ethical judgment). Kant considered the thinking process to be largely technical because it followed systematic, procedural rules and methods. He differentiated the procedural and pragmatic basis of (practical/technical) knowledge from the kind of abstract (scientific) knowledge one sought from their transcendental experience with objective phenomena. "Because these principles are necessary and discoverable, they defeat empiricism and skepticism, and because they are disclosed as simply conditions of orienting ourselves coherently within experience, they contrast with traditional rationalism and dogmatism" (Ameriks 1995: 398). Importantly, as Kant developed these ideas he came to argue that, contrary to what the Enlightened scientific community believed or hoped, the possibility of a direct, objective, and unmediated experience with "things-in-themselves" (*noumena*), and of such experiences producing true and abstract knowledge, was not possible (this theme was, of course, developed more fully by Nietzsche). Kant, though he always regarded himself as a philosopher of the Enlightenment (ibid.), nonetheless argued that "scientific knowledge is necessarily linked to the world of appearances (the phenomenal world); it can never make unmediated contact with 'things-in-themselves'" (Mitcham 1994: 31). This is a profoundly important idea for archaeology.

Kant went on to suggest, however, that with the development of critical reflection (including "transcendental deduction and empiricism") we could learn to delineate *a priori* forms (appearances) and, supported by this knowledge, to postulate the intangibles "behind" them.

With proper qualifications, Kant's doctrine of the transcendental ideality of space and time can be understood as a radicalization of the modern idea of primary and secondary qualities. Just as others had contended that sensible color and sound qualities, e.g., can be intersubjectively valid and even objectively based while existing only as relative to our sensibility and not as ascribable to objects in themselves, so Kant proposed that the same should be said of spatiotemporal predicates. (Ameriks 1995: 401)

According to Schopenhauer (1958: 418 [orig. 1818]), "Kant's greatest merit is in the distinction of the phenomenon from the thing-in-itself." To some extent, this argument is surprisingly reminiscent of L. R. Binford's (1968b: 22–3) suggestion that with critical thinking and the appropriate research methodologies archaeologists can infer the intangible dynamic processes accounting for the statics of the archaeological record (also Schiffer 1972, 1975a).

Kant's emphasis on sense-based ("sensible") experience and on differentiating between surface appearances and their intangible qualities has been noted and variously developed by a number of others. What many philosophers have argued, based on Kant's standpoint, is the general idea that human sensations are what link lived experience with appearances and, on a more abstract level, with the transcendental "thing" lying beyond direct observation or unmediated sensibility (for example, on Nietzsche, see Kaufmann 1974). In no way should this standpoint be confused with Collingwood's (1946) empathetic historical methodology, nor with the Enlightenment assertion that scientific reason and instrumental procedures can get the researcher beyond the problematic language of interpretation in order to describe things as they "really" are. Neither are Kant and his followers suggesting we can never know fundamental and worthwhile things about the object world. Indeed we can, but it is a matter of how that world is knowable and what the nature of that knowledge is.

As the reader will see, the linking of socially mediated experience with material technology (in the conventional sense of artifact making and using) becomes critical to arguments developed later in this chapter and in the remainder of the book.

Friedrich Dessauer (1881–1963)

Dessauer further elaborated Kant's ideas about experience, knowledge, and the nature of inner and outer phenomena, but came to a significantly different conclusion. Dessauer argued that the kinds of sensuous experiences humans have during their technological engagement with material culture making and use does, indeed, establish a true contact with "things-in-themselves." Importantly, he argued that the essence of technology is an *encounter*, an experience, that leads to sensed-based awareness and knowledge. In making this argument, Dessauer laid emphasis on the *act* of material creation and use, as well as the role of will, knowledge, skill, creativity, and imagination. It is in these several ideas that we begin to grasp at something akin to the original meaning of *tekhnē*.

It is likely that the reason Dessauer (more than Kant) understood that the sensual bodily experience of object making and use could be a source for knowledge of transcendent "things-in-themselves" (and awareness more generally) was that he was a working scientist who personally experienced the materiality of sensual object making and use. Dessauer earned his doctorate in applied physics at the age of 36, and during his life invented technical equipment for deep-penetration x-ray therapy.[2]

Dessauer went on to suggest that particular kinds of modern material technologies were "a new way for human beings to exist in the world" (Mitcham 1994: 31; also Heidegger 1977: 5; Illich 1973). This idea, that the specific material nature of computer and atomic technologies were shaping a different kind of human than had ever existed before, has been further developed under the rubric of artifactology (Ferré 1995: 65; Mitcham 1994: 182–91; but also Haraway 1991). In making this argument, Dessauer recognized the *power* of scientific and technological knowledge in its particular material forms. And as others have gone on to argue more explicitly, different kinds of material technologies (for example, the difference between so-called simple hand "crafts" and high-tech machinery and computers) imply significantly different sensory experiences with, and thus understandings of, the world and of oneself in it (notably in the writings of Bracca, Bunge, Ellul, García, Ihde, Illich, Mumford, Simondon, and Winner). Importantly, such material and experiential differences also suggest different sorts of knowledge and material bases of power, as expressly considered by Mumford (1934, 1964, 1967) and Illich (1973) (I return to this point in chapters 4 and 5).

Among the many interesting questions anthropologists and archaeologists of technology might ask themselves, based on this argument, is whether or not and to what extent there are different sorts of knowledge and "revealing" experiences to be had when humans engage with qualitatively different sorts of material resources and products. This is precisely the distinction Leroi-Gourhan (1964a: 63–5) made in claiming that an evolutionary Rubicon had been crossed by the "exteriorization of the organs of technology" – that is, from the hand used *as* a tool to the hand *holding* a tool. As I argue in the following chapter, however, while different sorts of corporeal experiences with material technologies do, indeed, contribute to different sorts of awarenesses, the physical human body is necessarily and forever tied to the social body. There are, thus, a number of mediating factors (especially socio-cultural and historical) standing between one's personal confrontation with things-in-themselves.

Another aspect of the Greek term *tekhnē* not yet considered means "bringing-forth" (Ferré 1995: 65–8), but not simply in terms of the literal and material transformation of (natural) resources into (cultural) products. This bringing forth (or engendering) through technological practice has to do with *how*, in the unfolding relation-ship created between humans and their material endeavors, the body acts as a thoughtful conduit linking the physical sensations of technological activity with human corporeality and sentience, and by extension, with awareness and understanding of the physical self and the world more generally (Dobres 1999b, in press-a). Nowhere has the particular linkage been more fully or insightfully explored than in the writings of Martin Heidegger (whom I discuss at length below and throughout the next four chapters). In understanding Dessauer's contributions to a philosophy of technology, then, it is important to stress that he conceptualized linkages between, first, human bodies, second, the material world, and third, the notion of *embodying,* as an ongoing and revealing process of self-awareness. These general ideas about the sensual and embodied nature of technology open important conceptual and interpretive avenues for anthropologists and archaeologists, as will be seen when I bring them together with the ideas of Marcel Mauss and contemporary practice theory (chapters 4 and 5).

It may be unnecessary to point out an obvious implication of Dessauer's emphasis on awareness and embodiment, but surely a fun-damental reason why contemporary capitalist societies do not think or explicitly talk about such material engagement as an arena for self/Other understandings and awareness – that is, the reason we con-ceptualize separations and distance from our material world rather than connections with it – is precisely because of the ideological alienation of producer (self and Us) from the material production process and product ("it") (on Locke's explicit promotion of disengagement and self-objectification, see C. Taylor 1989: 159–76). If Winner (1983, 1986a) is correct, that the very nature of contemporary industrial (alienated) society "requires" that we sleepwalk through the conditions of our own making (which he dubs "technological somnambulism"), then it should come as no surprise that we are (unconsciously) disci-plined in ways that make it impossible to "see" and sense how we are constituted by these particular sorts of embodied experiences. But it is also this very reasoning that, as archaeologists, we should take to heart when we try to make sense of the *tekhnē* of societies in other times and places practicing very different material technologies under very different ideological and contextual circumstances.

Finally, Dessauer made a significant contribution to the argument that technology brings *ideas* into physical being, and is itself "the material embodying of transcendent reality" (cited in Mitcham 1994: 32). This idea strikes a chord similar to what Childe (1956: 1) once suggested about artifacts: that they are "concrete expressions and embodiments of human thought and ideas." The *concrétization* of world views and perceptions in material form is something the French philosopher Simondon (1923–1989) also explored in detail (Simondon 1958; also Dumouchel 1995). The idea that it is in and through the immediacy of unfolding technological activities and their material outcomes that *in*tangible ideas and beliefs are given material expression is now receiving (renewed) interest in anthropological and archaeological studies of technology (and material culture more generally).[3]

But rather than being inspired by the writings of Dessauer and Simondon, the suggestion that technologies and material culture embody implicit (albeit normative) world views and cultural predilections gets much of its direct inspiration from one of Marx's more oft-quoted and ambiguous dictums: "As individuals express their life, so they are. What they are, therefore, coincides with their production, both with what they produce and with how they produce" (Marx and Engels 1970: 42). As will be seen, under anthropological tutelage, the combining of Dessauer's emphasis on the bodily experience of particular material technologies with the idea that technologies embody an essential material reality as they simultaneously express traditional cultural ontologies becomes a critical facet of the practice-centered approach to technology promoted in this book.

Technology: the thinking "man's" game

Lewis Mumford (1895–1988)

In contrast to Dessauer's emphasis on awareness through the corporeality of making and use, Mumford developed a decidedly outsider's view of human technologies. His major point was that human technologies, past and present, are the outward result of actions stemming from the mind and from aspirations for creative self-realization. In this, Mumford saw human technologies as decidedly different from any transformative material making and use found in the animal world, and he was explicit on this point. Of the several philosophers, historians, and sociologists of technology I touch on in this chapter, Mumford comes closest to an anthropological way of thinking about technology because of his special emphasis on the social nature of material culture production and use and because he is clearly the only one who actually read widely in the anthropological and archaeological literature of his day. But as clearly as Mumford was a romanticist in his perspective on the way humans should relate to their contemporary technologies, he was also devoutly anti-modernist (though no Luddite) in his railings against the deterministic and oppressive nature of what he called the megamachine.[4]

Precisely as Whitehead (1927) warned about the fallacy of misplaced concreteness (chapter 2), Mumford complained strenuously how, in trying to understand the place of technology in human evolution, the seductive appeal of the tangible had led to the "tendency to identify tools and machines with technology: to substitute the part for the whole" (Mumford 1967: 4). Contrary to the utilitarian basis of the conventional hero-story of human technological evolution, Mumford reasoned that "in treating tool-making as central to early man's survival, biologists and anthropologists for long underplayed, or neglected, a mass of activities in which many other species were for long more knowledgeable than man" (ibid.). That is, compared to the tool making and using activities of animals, Mumford maintained that it was language, symbols, aesthetics, and the social that had allowed humans to do something uniquely different with their material technical capabilities. (Without any reference to Mumford, see an even more eloquent and compelling version of this argument in Gosden 1994: 176–81.)

In other words, Mumford argued that animals (rather than humans) had the longest-standing tradition of tool making and use; what made humans unique among tool makers was of an altogether different order. Contrary to most of the writers of his time who were laying great emphasis on our evolutionary origins as *Homo faber*, Mumford countered this tyranny of the obvious by stressing the sentience of what it meant to be *Homo sapiens sapiens* – the twice-thinking animal. For Mumford, "it is not making but thinking, not the tool but the mind, that is the basis of humanity" (Mitcham 1994: 42; also Rothenberg 1993: 86–92). In fact, he argued that it was the evolution of language and symbolizing capabilities that were "incomparably more important to further human development than the chipping of a mountain of handaxes" (Mumford 1967: 8). In making this claim, Mumford inverted what is today perceived as a primarily unidirectional relationship between tool use, symbolic capabilities, and the origins of language. For him, however, *Homo sapiens sapiens* necessarily became *Homo faber* "not because he made fire [a] servant, but because he found it possible, by means of his symbols, to express fellowship and love, to enrich present life with vivid memories of the past and formative impulses toward the future, to expand and intensify those moments of life that had value and significance" (Mumford 1952: 35).

Mumford was certainly insightful in proposing an alternative view of what it is to be human, by laying emphasis on our unique "mind-making, self-mastering, and self-designing" qualities. However, the unrealistic ends to which he applied these arguments, which were "to initiate a radical reorientation of mental attitudes that would trans-form [contemporary] monotechnical civilization" (Mitcham 1994: 44), went far beyond what even the most sympathetic reader could be expected to tolerate. In addition, Mumford's overemphasis on the skill, art, and craft of *tekhnē* denied how the materiality of human technologies influenced the embodied experiences that made us twice-thinking. In his romanticized view, only self-powered and simple, craft-like tools could safely be in the service of humanity; the material technologies of the megamachine, especially in their contemporary industrial guise, were as inherently oppressive as the dictatorial and overly regulated social formation that made them possible (a view similarly expressed in the Unabomber's Manifesto; see page 235). Ironically, and in ways his philosophy never intended, Mumford's very separation of art (as the "inner life of the mind") from technology (defined as negative power-manipulation through external objects) unwittingly compartmentalized *tekhnē* into its constituent parts.

Technology: self, experience, and circumstances

José Ortega y Gasset (1883–1955)[5]

By emphasizing the simultaneity of corporeal experience and sentience in technological practice (that is, of knowing and awareness instantiated through the unfolding experience of "things-in-themselves"), Dessauer unlocked the door on what has since become an especially fruitful exploration of the meaningful ways people engage with each other and their material technologies. In taking up these ideas, José Ortega y Gasset (writing about the same time as Mumford) sought to understand the dialectic of self and experience in a material-phenomenal world. Because his is a more multifaceted and seemingly cultural view of humans than most philosophers employ, Mitcham (1994: 45) considers Ortega y Gasset's work "anthropological" in nature. As an anthropologist and archaeologist, however, I respectfully disagree.

Contrary to Malinowski's (1939) brand of functionalism, for Ortega y Gasset a person's instrumental life does not directly correspond to their organic ("real") needs. To make this distinction between pragmatic rational need and a technological stimulus, Ortega y Gasset suggests that first there is creative imagination, then its material realization. Taking the standpoint that technological knowledge is applied science, Ortega y Gasset builds an evolutionary trajectory similar to Mumford's: over time and through practice the primitive technology of craft and skill, which was inspired by creative imagination and the internal "drive" toward self-actualization, led to the technoscientific knowledge of the engineer, and ultimately, to the abstract forms of knowledge we today call science. On this, he and Mumford seem to agree. But in contrast to Mumford (and more in keeping with Dessauer), Ortega y Gasset recognizes that the materiality of technology is necessarily implicated in the human world. What makes these writings "anthropological" for Mitcham (1994: 45) is Ortega y Gasset's view that it is through their relationship with material and social circumstances that humans are self-knowing and active agents. On this critically valuable insight, characterized by his terse aphorism "I am I plus my circumstances," Ortega y Gasset prefigures something akin to the problematic now central in much of anthropological and sociological theory: the dialectic of agency and structure (discussed in chapter 5).

In trying to make sense of this recursive social, personal, sentient, and material relationship, Ortega y Gasset appears to gain inspiration from Marx (1963: 15 [orig. 1869]) and that other famous dictum: "men make their own history, but they do not make it just as they please; they do not make it under circumstances chosen by themselves, but under circumstances directly encountered, given and transmitted from the past." But Ortega y Gasset does not offer an anthropological perspective on these ideas. For example: he lacks an explicit concern with comprehending the dialectic of individual and society in culture-bound contexts, especially in non-western settings; it is not clear what constitutes the "structure," or conditions, in which technical agents constitute themselves as knowing agents; he does not explicate the relationship between these conditions and the dynamics of society and culture; nor does he propose how these interrelationships might change over time. As I set out in chapter 5, to make such insights useful for understanding and theorizing about technology as a sociomaterial dynamic of embodied engagement, and what is sorely needed in any philosophical consideration of the dynamic "I am I plus my circumstances," is *explicit* consideration of the recursive relationship of structure and agency from an anthropological point of view.

With these general remarks as a brief synthesis of some of the more insightful and potentially useful ideas philosophers of technology have on the particular ways that material technologies instantiate knowing, feeling, acting agents through corporeal engagement with artifact making and use, we can turn to the difficult but especially powerful ideas of Martin Heidegger.

Technology: the bodily engagement of being-in-the-world

Martin Heidegger (1889–1976)

Heidegger has recently become a source of insight for archaeology (i.e., Dobres 1995a; Dobres and Hoffman 1994; Gosden 1994; Karlsson 1997; J. Thomas 1993, 1996a, 1996b; Tilley 1994). He has also become the subject of some scrutiny, as well (for example, the 1996 volume of *Archaeological Dialogues* (3:1) entitled "Towards a Heideggerian Archaeology?"). But for all the proper concern to question both the intellectual and political underpinnings of his ideas, as well as the appropriateness of metaphysical notions about Being, awareness, and knowledge for the concrete problems of archaeological method and theory, we should not be too quick to dismiss his (or anyone's) ideas based solely on their political influences. As has been shown in the history of archaeology time and time again, all intellectual inspiration is grounded in external politics of one kind or another (but is perhaps most troubling when researchers profess too strenuously that they are *not* so influenced, after Wylie [1996: 1ff]; examples offered in chapter 1). Certainly in recent years there has been a move toward being explicit in this regard, and critical reflection on one's sources of inspiration is both welcome and necessary in practicing a more critically reflexive and self-censoring kind of archaeology. Nonetheless, as we have also learned from the explicit introduction of feminist political concerns into the archaeological arena, allowing outside influences to inform one's disciplinary interests can often lead to better and more critical research, and thus better science (Kelley and Hanen 1988; Wylie 1992a, 1992b, 1997; more generally, see Cutliffe 1995, and Lloyd 1996).[6]

On the more specific concern that Heidegger never wrote with archaeological interests in mind, Oudemans (1996: 32) points out that "Heidegger's thought has nothing to do either with method or with the foundation of an area of investigation like archaeology. The archaeologist had better stay away from it." But the history of archaeology is replete with examples of concepts, theories, methodologies, and research techniques imported from outside, adapted to the peculiarities of archaeological interests and data, and (with time and practice) developed into useful conceptual, methodological, and interpretive tools: the principles of Uniformitarianism; radiocarbon dating; systems theory; the neo-Darwinian synthesis; optimal foraging theory;

scanning electron microscopy; structuralism; gender theory; artificial intelligence; and GIS (to name a few). This book gains much of its inspiration from "undisciplined" ideas modified to archaeological interests. It should be clear, then, that I believe that importing into archaeology ideas formulated elsewhere should be evaluated on a case-by-case basis. In this instance, I believe that Heidegger's extraordinary work concerning technology and Being far outweigh what I find are tangential problems with his politics. And given the litany of conceptual and methodological problems the first two chapters of this book have identified with mainstream approaches to the study of prehistoric technology – in particular, the near total erasure of the thinking, feeling, interacting agent in our explanatory accounts – we should not overlook consideration of any promising avenue that a philosophy of technology might offer.

All these caveats aside, one of the most powerful concepts in Heidegger's writings about technology is his emphasis on the ongoing and sensual nature of technological practice as a self-centered form of bodily engagement with the material world. To counter the alienated paradigm of modernity promoted by Bacon and Descartes (discussed at length in chapter 2), Heidegger stresses the interconnections of matter, mind, knowledge, and practice. His emphasis on the gerund form of the verb *to be* (as in "Human Be-ing," or *Dasein*) is intended to comprehend the continually unfolding process of human existence *in* the everyday material world, rather than imagine Self as some reified and alienated entity reacting *to* it (Gosden 1994: 111; Petrovic 1983b; Polt 1999: 43). If technological somnambulism (Winner 1983) is the conceptual *erasure of the process* by which (industrialized, capitalist) people move through social and material conditions of their own making, and through those experiences become what they are, then Heidegger's emphasis on Being attempts to reclaim that dynamic for what it actually is.

Erasure effectively masks the recursivity of subjects and objects forever constituting and creating each other, such that "an overwhelming involvement in the material level tends to detract from metaphysical or spiritual reality" (Mitcham 1994: 54). This erasure of experience and involvement as the meaningful basis of human existence necessarily underwrites the particular scientific vision that has helped shape western industrialism and capitalism, perverting an understanding of the ongoingness of Be-ing into the ideologically static "Is" (Balbus 1994; Gosden 1994: 86; Habermas 1970; Marcuse 1964, 1968). To counter this erasure, Heidegger distinguishes between entities and being, where being is a meaningful presence (or awareness) created during human experience. He also emphasizes being-in-the-world as an unfolding (temporal) coming into existence of the agent through their particular material experiences (with technology, for example). Because awareness is continually engendered through these corporeal and unfolding experiences, they further augment, build on, and challenge preexisting sensibilities. Heidegger's distinction between entities and being "means that we will never understand human beings adequately if we treat them as things" (Polt 1999: 44).

To put this bluntly: the conceptual erasure of the process of becoming is what enables the conceptual transformation of human subjects and their technological practices into inert and reified objects of study (entities) by seemingly dispassionate, objective observers (be they materials scientists or archaeologists). Ironically, Heidegger's concept of being-in-the-world can be used to argue that even technological determinism, which altogether denies a meaningful connection between producers, production, and products, is (after all) just one of many ways of instantiating humans in the material world; it just happens to be an alienated, objectified, and rather perverted perception. It is Heidegger's emphasis on being, understood as one's *intelligible awareness of themselves in the world engendered through the unfolding of corporeal technological practice*, that not only resonates with ideas previously discussed but also goes to the heart of what I believe is lacking in contemporary research on prehistoric technology. This emphasis is intentionally poetic and humanistic as much as it is grounded in real world phenomena.

According to Heidegger, be-ing and do-ing are unfolding and intertwined corporeal experiences that link objects being produced with their sentient subject-producers (as Marx also recognized, see below). Through embodied (phenomenal) and mediated experiences with material things, technicians simultaneously produce both material objects and an awareness of themselves as knowing agents (Heidegger 1977). Heidegger calls this experience-based awareness (or "revealing") *Gestell*, and emphasizes that it both "sets up and challenges the world" (Mitcham 1994: 52). "In other words, there is at the heart of technical activity, if not *tekhnē* itself, an irreducible, nonlogical component. There is an aspect of *tekhnē* that necessarily cannot be brought into consciousness except through the immediacy of a singular, direct encounter" (ibid.: 127). I find this a singularly important, but altogether lacking understanding of what human technology is, or was. Importantly, while it emphasizes and acknowledges the centrality of the physical world in giving shape to the social experience of technological encounters, it simultaneously fights the desire to measure, weigh, or otherwise compute that contribution.

For Heidegger, then, object making and use is more than the material transformation of material things from one state to another; technical doing is more than the physical activity of object making and use; and being is more than a physical state of existence. While technology surely involves making and using things, it is not reducible to such activities (Polt 1999: 50; Zimmerman 1990). Through technological activities *both* people and objects become; through their use and re-use they continue to become; and even as they are "used up" they are still becoming. Such is the unfolding nature of technological being-in-the-world. Importantly, Heidegger's meaning of the term "machination" (*Machenschaft*), which he later comes to call "technology" (*Technik*) "is not just a human behavior, the act of manipulation: it is a *revelation of beings as a whole* as exploitable and manipulable objects" (Polt 1999: 142; emphasis in the original). Or, in terms that recall Mumford's concern with the megamachine and the alienated human condition of working with industrial technologies, quality is reduced to quantity and "mathematization of the world does away with all sacredness" (ibid.).

Discussion

Heidegger's weighty explorations into the "ing" condition of human being and producing during one's corporeal engagement with the world allows us to reconceptualize technology not as a noun or object, but more properly as *a verb of human action and interaction* (and not simply reaction) that is forever unfolding during the immediacy and contingency of such intersubjective encounters. An archaeological focus on technological activities too often misses the subtlety of this critically important distinction. An emphasis on verbs and gerunds also serves as a powerful corrective to the materialist claim that the physical nature of a society's technology (characterized in technounits or measures of energy input and output) represents a static (evolutionary) level of its cultural and/or evolutionary complexity (as in Oswalt 1973, 1976; Testart 1982, 1988; L. White 1959). As I show in chapters 4 and 5, when these ideas are developed with explicit appeal to anthropological theory and reformulated as part of a practice framework – that is, when we bring together Heidegger's standpoint on technology and being with the anthropological ideas of Mauss, Giddens, Bourdieu, and others – then the making and using of material things necessarily implicates the simultaneous making and remaking of social actors, society, and traditions, as well as their contestation and negotiation.

As far as Heidegger (1977: 318) is concerned, "technology is a way of revealing"; object making is key to producing an awareness of self and Other as well as for instantiating meanings that reach far beyond the immediacy of such practical activities (although it is necessarily through this immediacy and everydayness that such awareness is possible in the first place; Rothenberg 1993: 79–86). "*Gestell* is not another part of technology; it is that attitude toward the world that is the foundation for, yet wholly present in, technological activity" (Mitcham 1980: 320). Or, as Polt (1999: 171) puts it: "The techno-logical attitude involves much more than simply constructing and using complex machines; it is *a way of understanding beings as a whole*" (author's emphasis). Of course Heidegger's real interest is in explicat-ing modern technological conditions and alienated attitudes about Being in a capitalist, industrial world (Zimmermann 1990). In this particular regard he argues, similarly to Mumford and Marx (below), that "what is happening with technology is not some unqualified conquest of nature but the replacement of the natural milieu with the technical milieu" (Mitcham 1994: 60), where people and things have become virtually interchangeable.[7]

As with most philosophers, however, Heidegger uncritically uni-versalizes the alienating conditions that people in industrial societies experience and generalizes them to reflect the Human Condition.[8] As a result, some of these ideas are less applicable to anthropology and archaeology than his general argument about the sociomaterial consti-tution of being, making, producing, and doing, which are inclusive enough to be relevant for those of us who study people and technolo-gies of vastly different times, places, and social conditions. As I discuss at length in the next two chapters, anthropological research has shown all too clearly that not all human experiences with technology are as detached and objectified as they are perceived in industrial societies; not all societies divorce nature from culture; nor does everyone com-prehend technology as a mediator between the two. Philosophers of technology help us understand why social scientists "see" the subject matter of technology in objectified terms (as summarized in chapter 2). And while they can help with the difficult project of lifting the lid on that black box so that we may learn to see that dynamic differently (as discussed here), it is an anthropological perspective that can provide the broadest insights of all.

Heidegger's consequential and lasting contributions to understand-ing the dynamic of technology, society, and personhood rest with the weight he gives to everyday sensual experiences, or encounters, in the making of knowing and feeling subjects, and with suggestions as to how this unfolding phenomenological process contributes to larger societal phenomena (which, I suggest, prefigures central tenets of contemporary practice, or agency theory). As chapters 5 and 6 argue, understanding the contribution of everyday technological practice, as a particularly constituted form of being-in-the-world, to macro-scale sociocultural dynamics and long-term culture change – that is, com-prehending the relationship between agency and structure – is one of the most exciting and potentially rewarding areas in contemporary anthropology.

Related Philosophical Considerations

Ethics and social values

There are additional insights that philosophy can provide researchers interested in the technologies of other times, places, people, and circumstances. In particular, human technologies are inseparably caught up in webs of social values and social relations – which is what makes them qualitatively different from animal tool making and use activities. Because of this, technicians, technological acts, as well as end products are moral and ethical statements, especially about who should and should not make or use certain things, and about the "right" and "wrong" ways to accomplish such tasks (on Dewey's ideas in this regard, see J. Cohen 1955: 409–17; Hickman 1990). Simply put, technology is a particular kind of practice through which humans reflect on who and what they are. At the same time, technology materializes those beliefs and attitudes and reaffirms them in everyday practice (Lechtman 1977; Lemonnier 1989a, 1990; also Marx and Engels 1970: 42). For example, Ihde (1983b, 1986) considers how the institutional qualities of industrial technologies become our own (some would say perverted) experiential basis of meaning making: "We end up modeling ourselves on the very 'world' we project and interpret ourselves in terms of technology" (Ihde 1983: 22b); yet "the deeper question of technics and the human remains one about the *variable* possibilities of our seeing itself" (Ihde 1986: 90; my emphasis). According to Ihde, then, for all that has been said on the subject, our perceptions, experiences, and sense of self are not determined solely by the materiality of our technologies, and we can make and remake the world differently than it is.

According to Durbin (1978: 67–8), an ethical consideration of technology "amounts to a statement as to what one feels a good technological society *ought* to be like, plus some persuasive arguments aimed at getting influential others to agree" (Durbin's emphasis; also J. Cohen 1955). Through the prism of axiology, philosophers explore the ethical dimensions of modern technologies, technological power, and decision making, especially in the fields of engineering, nuclear energy, development, and medicine (among others, see: Durbin 1972, 1992; Ellul 1980, 1989; Illich 1973; Jonas 1984; Kranzberg 1980; Steiner 1971; synthesis in Mitcham 1994: 100–9). For example, Ferré (1995: 11) considers the covert links between science, technology, knowledge, and social values by extending Weber's sociological argument about the scientific and rational basis of a secular form of salvation in the modern world (chapter 2):

It would not be wrong, and it might be revealing, to say that technology is the offspring in *praxis* of the mating of knowledge and
value, epistemology with axiology. If the principal source of our most
reliable factual knowledge is science, and if the basic values of any
society constitute its actual functioning religion, then the technosphere
we inhabit is nothing less than the incarnation in social life of science
and religion.

While philosophers question the nature of modern techno-ethics, and
in some cases take it as an obligation to suggest standards and limits in
keeping with what they see as progressive human values (in particular,
Barbour 1980; Ferré 1995: 75–96; Winner 1986b), archaeologists can
refocus this line of inquiry and consider how an ancient society's material technologies and practices reflected back on and concretized their
values and ethics, and in this way "recover mind" (Leone 1982; also Ihde
1983b). The current surge of interest by sociocultural anthropologists
and some archaeologists in identifying the so-called world views
underlying and structuring ancient technological practice and choice
can be seen in this light (in particular, Lechtman 1977, 1984a, 1993;
Lemonnier 1986, 1989a; M. A. MacKenzie 1991; van der Leeuw et al.
1991; discussed in chapter 4). However, a major limitation in arguing
that ancient technologies materialized shared world views and sociopolitical attitudes about right and wrong is its undue emphasis on the
supposed *homogeneity* of these societies as cohesively bound collectivities
of people whose norms and ideals went unchallenged. While the technological arena is a social and material setting in which collective values
and world views are, indeed, reaffirmed, it is simultaneously an arena in
which they can be contested (chapter 5). This particular "side" of technology is something neither philosophers nor many sociocultural
anthropologists and archaeologists have considered sufficiently.

Politics and knowledge

Politics is perhaps the most obvious playing out of social values
and ethics that direct and structure particular technological choices
and delimit who is (and who is not) permitted to undertake such activities or have access to the necessary objects, resources, or knowledge
enabling material production or the use of products. By definition,
human technologies never stand outside the body politic, nor can they
exist without the socially constituted organization of productive labor.
Because of this, the particular uses to which technological activities,
knowledge and skill, proscribed rules of access, and end products are put
all become sources for social, material, economic, and political influence

and power.[9] And though this should not be confused with the notion of "blaming the hardware" (Winner 1986a: 20), Pippin (1995) insightfully argues that even when material technologies become autonomous and seem to take on a life of their own (as is often said of the modern condition), even they become political, by virtue of the physical ways they direct people to act or think (Ellul 1954; Ihde 1983b; Mumford 1934, 1964; Simondon 1958; Winner 1983, 1986b; also Foucault 1977). To put this in colloquial terms more familiar to archaeologists, once a technology is embedded with meanings, values, and a social history, it can persuasively "act back" on its makers and users (after Hodder 1982a, 1986; Tilley 1982): that is, technologies can be as "active" in shaping the human condition as material culture more generally. But this more active view of technology should not be confused with technological determinism.

We have seen the importance philosophers place on the way knowledge derives from the very act of corporeal engagement with "things-in-themselves." As such, "technology is not so much the *application* of knowledge as [it is] a *form* of knowledge, one persistently dependent on technical skill" (Mitcham 1994: 203, his emphases; also Ingold 1993a). Importantly, such knowledge (and its display through skill and competence) can be a means for earning, or better yet *making*, a place for oneself in the community: through the way "technical revealing" contributes to the development of ego; through the way technical know how and know to establishes one's reputation; or, through proscribed relationships between the skilled and unskilled and between those who know how and those who do not.[10] Technological knowledge, in all its practical and esoteric dimensions, can enable the exercise of social and material influence, power, and privilege for reasons that reach far beyond the practical ways so-called technoscience allows for the physical control and manipulation of material resources and products (*sensu* Schiffer and Skibo 1987; Testart 1982).

Summary

According to Mitcham (1994: 153), then, philosophers variously define technology as including everything from objects, machines, and artifacts to phenomenological, scientific, practical, and existential knowledge, and from volition (or "free will") to physical and cognitive activities of self and social transformations. Technologies are also simultaneously:

- social values and ethics;
- sensorimotor skills;

- applied science;
- rational and efficient action;
- the pursuit of technical efficiency;
- tactics for living and molding the environment to meet human needs;
- knowledgeable techniques for practical tasks;
- means to effect socially defined purposes;
- means for pursuing influence and power;
- means for realizing the "gestalt" of Self;
- self-initiated salvation;
- the invention and material realization of transcendent forms; and
- means of challenging and/or revealing nature.

However, precisely because they are instantiated in material practice and through particular forms of social relationships, it is not merely in the abstract that technologies give material expression to societal values, promote political interests (both in and of themselves and by how people employ them), and become a basis of "revealing." These claims speak to a very real human dynamic and can be reformulated to address the specific demands of archaeological research and the peculiarities of our data. For example, if we imagine a sort of epistemological continuum, with philosophers at one extreme, sociocultural anthropologists somewhere along that continuum, and archaeologists at the other extreme, then we realize that we are all asking similar questions about the ways humans materialize fundamental values, act in political ways, and create self/Other/worldly knowledge and awareness by and through their technological endeavors and the particular ways they interact with each other while doing so.

What makes the archaeologist's work significantly different, of course, is that we necessarily investigate these dynamics from a wholly different starting point than either philosophers or sociocultural anthropologists – that is, we necessarily work from material traces to social inferences. Nonetheless, for the very reasons stated above (that is, precisely *because* they were instantiated through the concrete forms of social relations and material practices in circumscribed contexts) the materiality of the archaeological record can be studied to infer something of the ancient values, politics, and forms of knowledge engendered through technology.[11]

On Materiality: Giving Back to Philosophy

What is glaringly missing from most philosophical discussions of technology, however, is concrete, context-specific, material grounding

(Borgmann 1995: 85; Gosden 1994: 114; Mitcham 1994: 141). Thus, it is not simply that archaeologists can gain insights from philosophers; the reverse is equally true. In several important ways, archaeologists can further develop the sorts of philosophical insights outlined above: by showing *how* the corporeal experience of material "things-in-themselves" engenders self-awareness and the making of technical agents as members of their communities, as well as by showing *how* such actions make society, concretize human values, knowledge, and power (Dobres and Hoffman 1999a; as elaborated in chapters 4 and 5). First, archaeology has long-term, hands-on experience with a vast array of analytic techniques for studying and comprehending in detail the physical nature of transformations in raw materials. Second, archaeologists and sociocultural anthropologists can broaden philosophical insights by highlighting the extraordinary diversity of non-industrial technologies practiced in the past and present. Third, the particular expertise archaeologists have developed through almost thirty years of hands-on replicative experiments and ethnoarchaeology can provide insights philosophers and engineers could not possibly imagine about "things-in-themselves." And fourth, archaeologists are the only social scientists to take time and exceptionally long-term social processes seriously in trying to understand not only the immediacy of ancient people's lives, but also temporal phenomena beyond their direct experience, awareness, or control (especially here, see Gosden 1994).

However, in order to make these contributions, archaeologists must recognize that the politically charged social and symbolic contexts in which ancient material technologies were practiced significantly influenced the being-in-the-world forms of knowledge, skill, and values expressed. To date, we have not done well in this regard. And while I do not advocate playing "dress-up" or acting out one's prehistoric fantasies while experimenting in the present, researchers whose main source of inference derives from replication and laboratory analyses must begin to consider how their own social context – the lab – delimits and structures an alienated understanding of the technology in question.[12]

Combining sensuality with the politics of production

Karl Marx (1818–1883)

It is difficult to know how best to introduce Marx's ideas into this attempt to reconceptualize technology starting with philosophical arguments. Along with the complexity and ambiguity of Marx's writings, the theoretical developments subsequent marxists make is too unwieldy (and in some ways tangential) to the concerns of this chapter. In what follows I do not presume to offer a complete or systematic discussion of marxist theories of production and their relationship to technology.[13] Nonetheless, it is worth touching on certain of his ideas that closely border on philosophical considerations in order to further develop the themes of this chapter. Compared to the ideas discussed thus far, it is clear that Marx was far more concrete, historically grounded, and materially specific than are most philosophers of technology. Thus, Marx's theories about the relationship between material production and society provide important insights precisely because they create a bridge between the generally ahistorical and acontextual ideas of philosophy and the materially and historically grounded work of contemporary sociologists, historians, anthropologists, and archaeologists.

Marx clearly took a sociological (rather than philosophical) approach to understanding the dialectic of social relations, forces of production, infrastructure, and superstructure, and to making sense of the historical and material conditions of the capitalist mode of production, in particular (Rothenberg 1993: 73–9). That is, rather than being motivated by a metaphysical interest in the human nature of (modern) *tekhnē*, his interest was to understand the causes and consequences of the capitalist condition in order to create a (revolutionary) alternative. That, among other things, makes Marx's views on technology different from those of philosophers.[14] Nonetheless, in what follows I consider some parallels, resonances, and advances that Marx's views provide for the philosophical themes previously outlined.

The first point of similarity is with philosophical explanations for the changing meaning of *tekhnē*. For Marx, the social nature of the productive process is not synonymous with specific material making and use activities, though each necessarily constitutes the other (Mitcham 1994: 81). For Marx, any mode of production consists of a dialectic woven from three inseparable phenomena: social relations; forces of production (materials and means – also called infrastructure); and beliefs/ideology (superstructure).[15] He argued that it is the alienation and commodity fetishism endemic to the capitalist mode of production that leads workers to comprehend the modern world as "an enormous collection of commodities," such that even human labor can be quantified (Ferré 1995: 55). In *Das Kapital*, Marx (1967) explained the historical and material conditions permitting these three phenomena to be ideologically reified as separate entities (discussion in Geras 1983; R. McGuire 1992: 50; Mitcham 1994: 81). His sketch of the historical process by which technology was (conceptually and socially) essentialized into commodity production recalls the changing meanings of *tekhnē* that philosophers and historians have traced: from that once complex whole of art, skill and craft, principles and knowledge, methods, understanding and awareness, to the rational and objectified technologism of capitalism.

Because of his interest in comprehending the dialectic of social relations, social reproduction, and material production, Marx spent much time developing the notion of *praxis* and what it meant in terms of human productive endeavors. Reminiscent of Dessauer's and Heidegger's emphases on the way technicians simultaneously produce self/Other/worldly knowledge and awareness through the embodied experience of working with the material world, Marx argued that human life and production are "sensuous activities" (*praxis*) rooted in the material world, though not reducible to it (Marx and Engels 1970; also Marx's *Theses on Feuerbach* [1845]). For example, in considering the importance alienation has on people's (negative) sense of themselves and the world around them, Fuller (1963) and Winner (1986b: 14–16) argue that Marx was more generally recognizing that the sensuality of embodied practical and material activity produced understandings, knowledge, and self-realization (also Gosden 1994: 68–73; Pálsson and Helgason 1999; on the link between this and Mauss's view of (em)bodied techniques, see chapters 4–6; also Bourdieu 1990; Schlanger 1998: 199).

Marx's particular concern, of course, was with modern *logos* and the impact of alienation on life in all its intertwined practical, material, personal, social, and ideological manifestations. This concern clearly resonates with Mumford's, Heidegger's, Ihde's, Simondon's, and Winner's emphases on how the particular institutional, bureaucratic, and authoritarian qualities of modern industrial technologies act as our own experiential basis of (disenfranchised, somnambulistic) self-awareness. As Feenberg (1995: 18) characterizes Marx's position (presented in Engels 1972 [orig. 1884]), there was a time in the past when "technology was associated with a way of life, with specific forms of personal development, virtues, etc. Only the success of capitalist de-skilling finally reduced these human dimensions of technique to marginal phenomena." It can be argued, on this basis, that Marx's concrete historical explanation for the causes and effects of capitalist commodity fetishism and alienation are the concrete extension of the general philosophical considerations previously discussed (also Carrier 1992). In other words, through his sociological concern to explain the material and historical development of capitalism and alienation, Marx provides philosophy with specific and concrete reasons why we sleepwalk through conditions of our own making (Winner 1983) while finding it logical and rational to "blame the hardware" (Feenberg 1995).

According to Mitcham (1994: 82) – and as Mumford tried to argue in overly romantic terms – for Marx "the instrument-aided creation of artifacts is intended to serve human purposes by transforming material into useful objects. The specifically human part of this transformation is that it takes place first in the mind, since [quoting Marx] 'at the end of every labor-process, we get a result that already exists in the imagination of the laborer at its commencement'" (on the relationship of imagination, technological inventions, and innovations, see Ferguson 1978; Layton 1974; Simondon 1958: 19). Equally, Marx and Engels' account of "the alienation and physical degradation of the laborer that ensue from [the] obsession with technology divorced from use-value as a way of enhancing profit" (Mitcham 1994: 82–3) is reminiscent of Mumford's argument regarding the necessity of having previously established a mechanized way of thinking and form of social organization before the material creation of the megamachine.

Finally, in terms of drawing parallels between philosophy and certain of Marx's ideas about social reproduction and material production, we can point to the obvious: technologies are decidedly political. For example, Vogel (1995) and Pippin (1995) argue that when marxists of the Frankfurt School point to the "misuse of technology" in contemporary capitalist society, they mean the hegemonic ways in which the *logos* and practical knowledge of modern technoscience is used to advance political interests, typically of the state or some dominant group, through material means (see especially, Feenberg 1995; Habermas 1970; Marcuse 1964, 1968; Mitcham 1994: 87; Murray 1982; also Haraway 1988b, 1991). This "take" on techno-politics stemming from marxist theory should be understood as a complement to, rather than a replacement of, the more traditional sense in which we often say that particular technologies have built-in political ramifications (as, for example, in Simondon's [1958] analysis of the way humans project negative values and judgments onto their material creations, such as robots or machines, then anthropomorphize them as inherently "bad"; see also Schiffer and Skibo 1987). In the next chapter, I briefly consider this same politically effective projection of values and judgments onto material technologies in terms of gender (and race) ideologies (see also chapter 1).

Once we accept that the problems caused by material technologies are not necessarily (or only) inherent in themselves, but are caused more by the social conditions in which people imagine, invent, use, and give value to them, then it is ludicrous to anthropomorphize (prehistoric) technology as an active agent with its own motivations and interests somehow able to exist outside of, but act back on, the body politic. Clay pots do not "need" to be made in a certain way any more than blade production "requires" prepared platforms of one sort or another. Those performance needs, those fabricative and use requirements (or production standards) rest with the makers and users. What may be considered acceptable levels of performance in the making or use of clay pots for one technological community may not be sufficient for another. The causes and consequences of material technologies begin and end in the human realm (Latour 1992). The field of artifactology, on the other hand, has developed in order to pursue Marx's insights on the negative aspects of the capitalist mode of production (Mitcham 1994: 181). With varying emphases, Illich (1973), Mumford (1964), Ellul (1954), and Winner (1977) evaluate the different causes, consequences, and degrees of intentionality with which particular industrial technologies lead not only to significant social inequalities but also to real material health and safety problems. For example, *contra* Simondon (1958), each argues that key to the negative aspects of modern industrial technologies is the fact that with mechanized, computer, and/or nuclear technologies power *does* reside in the product as well as in its production, and not exclusively in the social organization, values, or context of its use. This concern with the material power of industrial technologies and their negative impact on the well-being of society shows that not all philosophical explorations of technology are left in the abstract. Significantly, many philosophers, and especially those noted above, pay homage to Marx's explication of the negative conditions and consequences of capitalist production on *praxis* (Feenberg 1995).

Conclusions

There are many ways to draw out and summarize the several contributions philosophy makes to an understanding of technology. What resonates especially with anthropological and archaeological interests is the emphasis on how, through sensuous technological practice, the physical body acts as a thoughtful conduit for developing, expressing, and embodying self/Other/worldly knowledge.[16] Also appealing is the argument that the various sorts of knowledge arising from such physical and intersubjective engagement with the material world extend far beyond practical material matters. One of the pan-cultural and timeless truisms of all human technologies is that, in one way or another, all object making and use is done with and through the medium of the physical body, either acting alone or in concert with others. Importantly, individual bodies are socially and meaningfully constituted in time and space (something I discuss at length in chapters 5 and 6). Thus, while philosophers provide general insights on the sensuality of technological *praxis* as a uniquely human way of being-in-the-world, it is anthropologists and archaeologists who can bring these notions to bear on understanding specific cultures and their concrete social, material, and processual – that is, technological – practices.

It is through the socially constituted body of mindful practices that technology, knowledge, products, and people are engendered (Engeström and Middleton 1998). Among the fruits of such labor are commodities, self-awareness, expressions of self and group identity, the concretization and reaffirmation of shared world views and values, as well as their contestation. Although philosophers, sociocultural anthropologists, and archaeologists have similar interests in explicating the causes, consequences, and significances of technologies in time and space, each proceeds from different standpoints and appeals to different data and observations to make their claims. What connects archaeologists to these other disciplines is that we, too, have an observable link to the ancient embodiment of social, political, and symbolic experiences with *tekhnē*; it is called the variable patterning of the archaeological record.

Archaeologists have long argued that ancient material techniques of making and using were a form of pre-scientific knowledge about living in and manipulating the physical world that, with time and the right research methods, could be identified through empirical study. And this is where we have directed most of our energy over the past thirty years. But it needs to be said that this perspective on ancient *tekhnē* is not about the same sorts of instantiated, embodied, and mediated self/Other/worldly knowledge, know how, and comprehension of "things-in-themselves" described by Dessauer, Heidegger, and Marx. Precisely because contemporary technoscience is concerned with knowledge of the former kind, and because it is the sort of distanced and objectified knowledge in which a capitalist world view places faith (and out of which it creates value and authority), archaeologists have unwittingly projected only the practical *logos* of *tekhnē* back to our collective beginnings.

In contrast to this (and on a logical basis), because of the sensual and social nature of all human technology, links can be made between ancient practices of artifact making and use and philosophical arguments about embodied self/Other/worldly knowledge (and the ends to which it can be put). That is, through material and mindful engagement undertaken in structured social contexts, people make and remake themselves as they make and remake their material world. Of course, what archaeologists want to understand, as well, is not only how within concrete historical instances particular material technologies were made and used, but also how these embodied and mindful practices contributed to larger dynamics of sociocultural adaptation and evolution.

In spite of the multifaceted views of technology that philosophers have developed, *still* missing from their reflections is something so absolutely necessary, fundamental, and obvious it apparently "goes without saying": an explicit focus on people and their intersubjective relations in the course of activities of material production and use situated under particular social circumstances. Few philosophers take culture to be a meaningful structure in which societies and individuals are made and remade; few explicate how shared and/or contested symbols and meanings actually materialize through everyday technological practice to take on a "life of their own"; practically none refer to non-western technologies and practices in supporting their claim that technology is a form of social representation; nor do philosophers adequately account for why and how such world views do (or do not) change over time. But if, as Heidegger, Ihde, and other philosophers suggest, modern technologies have a qualitatively different character from so-called traditional technologies, then in order to account for this there must be more interdisciplinary dialogue among all those interested in technology. It is clear that anthropologists and archaeologists have much to learn from philosophers of technology; equally, if their universal claims are to be taken seriously, philosophers need to become aware of anthropological and archaeological insights about non-western and non-modern technologies.

The above criticisms notwithstanding, philosophical insights *are* liberating: they show us precisely how archaeology's "fallacy of misplaced concreteness," coupled with "a tyranny of the obvious," has inappropriately constrained the concept of (prehistoric) technology to conform to the functionalist technocracy of the present (after de Certeau 1984). From this emancipated vantage point, we place ourselves in a position to begin "seeing" prehistoric technology differently, precisely because our traditional definitions and constructs are no longer taken for granted. An emphasis on the embodied and sensual experience of "things-in-themselves" is but a start. Such experiences are socially and historically framed, situated within antecedent cultural and historical circumstances that are beyond the control or even the awareness of individual technicians. To try and interject these sorts of social factors into our definition of technology is the work of the rest of this book.

4

A Synoptic Approach to Technology: The Social Contours of a Practice Framework

Because black boxes encase the agency of technicians and their inter-subjective experiences and forms of engagement, in the preceding chapters I have gone to great lengths to deconstruct prevailing conceptual frameworks for the study of ancient technologies. These next two chapters involve the pro-active task of outlining an alternative framework, one designed to study and understand ancient technologies as if people mattered. The task of what I here call a practice framework is to provide concepts and methodologies for resituating agents at the center of their technologies and our accounts of them. In order to expand archaeological perspectives, I have tried to break down unnecessary intellectual barriers standing between archaeology and related social science disciplines also interested in technology, especially philosophy, sociocultural anthropology, sociology, history, and STS.[1] Similarly, in the synoptic view offered here (and elaborated with explicit reference to social agency in chapter 5), I resist the temptation to disconnect consideration of material, social, political, ideological, symbolic, and economic matters. Through concrete examples I argue that, although typically divided into heuristic spheres (such as social organization, belief systems, politics, science, economics, and even cosmology), *in practice* technology is a dynamic web weaving an unlimited number of factors, or threads, into a seamless whole.[2]

Technologies are always and everywhere socially constituted. They are forms of social and material transformation, each necessarily instantiating the other. To put this another way, technology is the social practice and the process-*ing* of the material world: it is an ever-unfolding and intersubjective dynamic that is *not* reducible to the activities of artifact making and use. To explore what these statements mean, I consider in detail three fundamental claims upon which they rest: (1) technologies are meaningful acts of social engagement with the material world that serve as a medium through which world views, values, and social judgments are expressed tangibly and reaffirmed or contested in practice; as an extension, (2) technological practice "produces" not only things, but also personal, practical, and cultural knowledge that can serve both discursive and non-discursive interests; and finally, (3) technologies are fundamentally about people, mindful communities of practice, and social relations of production. In this chapter, I consider the inseparable dialectic of the social and material "sides" of technology by exploring in detail the first two claims. The third, which concerns the agency "side" of technology, is the topic of chapter 5.

Technologies are Meaningful Acts of Social Engagement with the Material World

People give meaning to and transform their world through the immediacy of the direct and socially constituted experiences they have when working materials. This is a central point to philosophers of technology. As well, Conkey (1993) argues that what makes us human is the meaningful experience of existing in, making sense of, and placing value on the material world. What she stresses in this regard is that "humans are materialists and symbolists simultaneously" (ibid.). Similarly, Lemonnier (1990) and Hodder (1982a, 1982b, 1986) argue that the production of matter and the production of meaning are instantiated by each other, and that neither takes precedence in this relationship (also C. M. Keller and J. D. Keller 1996).[3] What necessarily glues together the material and symbolic into the holistic experience of being-in-the-world are the social relations and intersubjective contexts in which both materials and people are made and made sense of, over and over again.

While not considering the symbolic aspects of production as contemporary theorists do, Marx and Engels (1970: 42) understood the nature of this social-material dialectic some 100 years ago, when they argued that "as individuals express their life, so they are. What they are, therefore, coincides with their production, both with what they produce and with how they produce." Importantly, for Marx it is not just the physical nature of capitalist technical production that creates alienation and objectification in the industrial world (as Luddites would claim). It is also the nature of these material practices in concert with the particular way workers organize themselves that creates these perceptions and experiences. To extrapolate, technological experiences take on social, symbolic, political, and other sorts of significances and values not just by virtue of the material hardware employed. Direct hands-on experiences, whatever their nature, are necessarily made sense of within preexisting social and material conditions of production, use, and value.

While clearly gaining inspiration from Marx and Engels, V. Gordon Childe was among the first archaeologists to realize the symbolic underpinnings of the social and material aspects of ancient technology, suggesting that "even in prehistory" they were of a single whole cloth. He argued, for example, that ancient objects could be understood as "concrete expressions and embodiments of human thought and ideas" (Childe 1956: 1). Along similar lines, Ucko (1970) championed a "united approach" to the study of material culture, explicitly conjoining the social, symbolic, and technological into a single whole to grasp their interconnections. Taking this claim to heart has enabled archaeologists to infer the organizing principles, symbolic constructs, and cognitive structures of the ancient mind through the detailed study of artifact patterns and their underlying "grammars" (especially Adams 1971, 1973; Deetz 1977; Glassie 1975; Lechtman 1977, 1984a; Leone 1982; Leroi-Gourhan 1958, 1965; Renfrew and Zubrow 1994; Washburn 1977, 1994).[4] Because there is this inseparable relationship between meaning and the material world instantiated through social practice (such as technology), archaeologists can comprehend the intangible but meaningful world of the past through the study of its tangible traces.

A conceptual dead end: shredding the web to understand its inner workings

If one accepts this position, that technologies are meaningful acts of social engagement with the material world, then it is both artificial and inappropriate to tease apart "the social" from "the symbolic" from "the material" in an effort to identify the separate contribution each makes to that whole. If the "whole" of technology rests with the *simultaneously* symbolic, social, and material experience of being-in-the-world, then disengaging these dynamics from each other, even for heuristic convenience, does that whole a terrible disservice. As I have now argued, the conceptual and analytic act of ferreting out and affixing boundaries around the material, social, and symbolic "sides" of technology creates in its wake a false object of study: material things, separated from the agents who work and transform them, and each of these partitioned from the meaningful experiences such acts entail.

In finding fault with the current view of culture as a system of integrated sub-systems, theorists in anthropology and archaeology (notably, Brumfiel 1991; Haraway 1991), and culture studies more generally (Latour 1993), remark how artificial it is to compartmentalize the whole of culture into its "constituent" parts. In different ways, each points out how this view obscures the inherent tensions, ambiguities, and disequilibrium internal to "the system." Moreover, as Haraway and Latour argue explicitly, the very act of drawing feedback loops and arrows between separated sub-spheres creates an altogether different phenomenon from the one originally in question (also Heidegger 1967). Rather than a seamless whole, we are now studying an object divisible into neatly segregated components. In so doing, a black box swallows up credible and sustained consideration of the social agents and agency who make the system run (especially Brumfiel 1991).

Latour (1993: 35) provides historical grounding to explain this situation. He shows that the nineteenth-century modification of earlier views of culture and nature (treated as separate entities in Bacon's time) were once again blended, "and needed to be purified by carefully separating the part that belonged to things themselves and the part that could be attributed to the functioning of the economy, the unconscious, language, or symbols." It is problematic that this view continues to prevail. Though no doubt useful in their time, systemic models of culture draw thin (and straight) black lines to connect the technological sphere to social organization, and these to beliefs and ideology (figure 1.7). Unfortunately, this strategy creates at least three false assumptions about the whole it seeks to explain: (1) these spheres are conceptually distinct from one another; (2) they can be analyzed separately; (3) by identifying salient interconnections, the whole can be understood. In technology studies, specifically, we tend to separate the physical part belonging to things in themselves, from the part relating to economy, from the part relating to the meaning and symbols, and from the dynamic that instantiates them all – social agents and intersubjective relationships.

What ends up happening, however, is that the lines *themselves* become the focus of attention and explanation, as if they somehow represent the feedback process. But if lines are what connects the parts together, then where do we situate social agents? People are typically relegated to the sphere called social organization, and from a partitive view they cannot also be "in" the technological, symbolic, and political spheres. Clearly, then, partitioning culture into its components and drawing separate circles around technology, social organization, and beliefs creates an objectified understanding of a decidedly intersubjective dynamic. As well, dumping people and human agency into the black box called social organization does little to promote a holistic and human-centered account of the material and symbolic simultaneity of technology.

To me, a processual understanding of human technology, past or present, lies not in explicating the way its spheres integrate. Rather, it lies in comprehending how technical agents make sense of, and act in, the world they produce, reproduce, and transform. It is an altogether different project to consider technology, *from the outset*, as irreducibly material, social, and symbolic (Escobar 1994: 223; Pálsson and Helgason 1999), than it is to treat these dynamics separately (even if the explanatory goal is, ultimately, to understand their interrelationships). As well, it is an altogether different project to take intersubjective social relations and the negotiation of technical agency as the heart and soul of technology (chapter 5), than it is to the study the activities where such interactions takes place (for example, as championed by Schiffer 1992a, 1999; Schiffer with Miller 1999). The holistic and subject-oriented approach to technology advocated here, which foregrounds social relations and agency, is relatively untried in archaeology. For this reason, even developing a common and accessible language with which to talk about it is not easy. For example, Latour (1993) offers a "hybrid" view of technology, while Haraway (1991) speaks of "cyborgs." Regardless of what we call "it," the imperative is to start by asking: What difference does it make to treat technology as a "total social fact" (Mauss 1935) that weaves together materials, society, and beliefs? This is what I explore in the remainder of this chapter and all of the next.

Technologies are a medium for expressing, reaffirming, and contesting world views and social values

To elaborate my first claim, that technologies are meaningful acts of social engagement with the material world, we can consider how technologies both express and mediate social values, cultural ontologies, and attitudes about right and wrong. Since Childe (1936), there have been hundreds of studies to show that normative world views and mental templates were "reflected" in the physical structure and practices of ancient technologies or their end products. Perhaps none is more compelling, however, than Lechtman's (1977, 1984a, 1984b, 1993) work on pre-Hispanic (Moche) metallurgy in highland Peru (also Lechtman and Steinberg 1979). Her research is among the best and most materially rigorous in demonstrating how technological practices and end products materialized and expressed shared world views. More than this, she illustrates that the imagined range of technical options and design strategies technicians invented and practiced were delimited not so much by the physical and chemical properties of the materials being worked, as by cultural predilections and sensibilities. In so doing, Lechtman demonstrates for the past what Geertz (1973b) has argued for the present: in order to see what constitutes reality for a particular people we must look at the symbolic and rule-bound nature of their actions.

Materials analyses indicate that Moche technicians practiced an overly complicated annealing process to transform metal alloys [*tumbaga*] into products having the requisite gold appearance. From these data, Lechtman (1977: 10) argues that "what lay behind the technological style were attitudes of the artisans towards the materials they used, attitudes of cultural communities towards the nature of technological events themselves, and the objects resulting from them" (further developed in Lechtman 1984a, 1993). That is, throughout much of South America there was a long-standing preoccupation with incorporating essential characteristics into the very essence of objects (and persons) to "make" the surface appear faithful to its inner character (M. W. Helms, cited in Lechtman 1984a: 33–5). Because of the special economic, political, and ideological importance of certain metals and their colors in these societies, rather than simply coat a base metal object with a thin, cheap gold veneer, technicians found it *necessary* to introduce gold into the essence of the metal alloy and make it "bubble" to the surface during the annealing process. "Their desire to achieve culturally valued color effects was played out in the alloy systems they developed or invented" (ibid.: 21). Thus, it was a world view concerned with essences and surfaces that shaped the development of Moche fabricative techniques and design strategies, and Moche metallurgy resonated with culture-bound understandings of the way the world worked and should be worked.

What makes Lechtman's work compelling for archaeologists similarly interested in the cultural ontologies underlying ancient techniques of manufacture and use is that her hypothesis has been supported by the study of an unrelated technology: weaving. Certain Andean weaving technologies show a striking parallel to the underlying structure of Moche metallurgy though the materials have nothing in common. In this case, designs on the surface of cloth were found to have been structurally woven as part of the fabric itself and by such means appeared on the surface. Surface motifs were not embroidered onto a background fabric; rather, they came from interlacing warps and wefts in particular ways because "the visual message carried by Andean cloth . . . had to be contained in and to be generated by the very structure of the fabric itself" (Lechtman 1984a: 32). Thus, much like Moche metallurgy, "Andean weaving seems to have responded to notions that saw the achievement of a visual, surface message as emerging from underlying, invisible structural relations . . . [where] the visually apprehended aspect of an object . . . reveal[ed] its inner structure" (ibid.: 32–3).

At least two general lessons can be taken from Lechtman's groundbreaking work. First, not only is it possible to infer the intangible structures, causes, and emic significances of prehistoric technologies through the detailed study of their tangible remains; *it is also necessary,* in order to comprehend why particular techniques, design choices, and artifact morphologies were structured as they were. Without explicit attention to, and some comprehension of, the symbolic attitudes and fundamental belief systems through which Moche technical specialists perceived their material world and acted upon it, we cannot properly understand why they made the particular technical choices they did (also, Hosler 1996; van der Leeuw and Papousek 1992). As Lechtman's work shows especially well, to consider issues of practical reason, efficiency, artifact physics, and function separate from issues of cultural reason, meaning, and values (as if the latter were second-order phenomena) cannot help us understand how they were inseparably connected and manifest in practice. Moche metal working was a "total social fact," not divisible into material, social, and symbolic components. The second lesson can be derived from the particularities of pre-Hispanic Peruvian weaving and metal working. The structuring ideal, that the essence of an object lies in *how it becomes* and not simply its existence as an end result, serves as a reminder about the connection between the becoming of products and the becoming of meaning, awareness, and knowledge (chapter 3; I return to this point in chapter 5). This quality of becoming emphasizes the continually unfolding and experiential nature of technology that intertwines social reproduction and material production (Dobres 1999b).

A striking parallel to Lechtman's work on New World technologies can be found in Keightly's (1987) comparative study of east coast and northwest Neolithic Chinese pottery. In this instance, as well, he shows that the decidedly different mental templates underwriting regionally different material lifeways were not only expressed by the overall morphology of clay pots. They equally structured the specific choice of techniques by which they were produced. As he demonstrates, east coast pots were generally componential in form; legs, handles, spouts, and lids were added to the body of the vessel in separate technical stages. With appeal to other lines of evidence, Keightly argues that this "suggests a willingness to impose design rather than merely accept it as a given by the natural qualities of the clay" (ibid.: 97). By comparison, in the bulk of pots coming from the northwest, "such joinings were not integral to the design and visual impact of the pot; potters sought to conceal such joins so as to produce soft-cornered, harmonious, unified, globular shapes" (ibid.: 99). In other words, in the northwest the componential nature of clay pot production was subsequently erased through additional techniques that smoothed away such outward evidence.

Keightly then links these different regional technologies to other artifact patterns; for example, noting morphological and fabrication differences in terms of elevated designs and specialized functions (east coast) and those more "earth bound" and generalized (northwest). Extrapolating from the different rules found to govern technological production in the two regions, he suggests a significant difference in mentality, and by extension, social organization: east coast potters were "the makers of shapes," shapers of the world, and possibly craft specialists; northwest potters had a possibly less segmented view of the world, as expressed in the morphology and becoming of pots, and a less differentiated form of social organization.

The lesson that Keightly's (1987: 117) study provides is remarkably similar to Lechtman's, though there is no indication he was modeling his study on hers (or even knew about it):

> particular kinds of tools and products make a particular kind of man [sic]. In the case of China, where the contrast between the material remains of the northwest and East Coast cultures is, in certain techno-logical and aesthetic features, so striking, we may, I suggest, use the material culture . . . as a vital clue to the mental life, the tacit knowledge, the sensibility of the tool makers.

Through the technical and stylistic analysis of traditional archaeological data, he shows that shared world views, social relations of production, objective qualities of material resources, the structure of technical operations, as well as the morphology of end products acted *in concert* to give meaning and shape to the world.[5]

The world views that structure detailed ways in which people materially engage with and make their mark on the world are also embodied in origin myths, principles of social organization, and even proscribed rules for accessing the physical landscape and its resources. For example, in their very different studies of contemporary hunter-gatherer technologies, Ridington (1982, 1999), Ingold (1988b, 1993a), and H. S. Sharp (1991) show that mythology, gender ideologies, and kinship rules regulating access to sacred sites and material resources combine to play a significant role in structuring technical decisions about the right and wrong ways to manufacture and use tools (also Gould 1980; for horticulturalists, see Lemonnier 1986; M. A. MacKenzie 1991). Ridington's work, especially, shows that the basis of Dene (Athapaskan) hunting technology is a combination of practical and esoteric knowledge held "in the mind" rather than the hand. He argues that practical but non-material knowledge about the land (such as the location of desired resources, animal behavior, and so on) is itself a technology.

However, this particular technology, while eminently practical, is poetic in nature; it is expressed in origin myths rather than cartridge belts or snare traps (Ridington 1982, 1999). But what Ridington has observed among Subarctic Canadian hunter-gatherers is true for many societies where technology involves limited material hardware: "their means of production are mental as well as material. Their subsistence technology has emphasized the possession of [mindful] techniques rather than [material] artifacts" (Ridington 1988: 107). As his work shows, one cannot properly comprehend the material aspects of Dene technologies without appreciating the essential role played by esoteric knowledge, beliefs, and social organization. Combined, these poetic and practical technologies are what enable the Dene to cope with their ever-changing material, social, economic, political, and symbolic conditions, especially as part of the post-colonial world (Ridington 1983; I discuss Sharp and Ingold below).

From world views to social values

While a significant amount of attention has been paid to the general question of how world views, normative paradigms, and "mental templates" find expression in particular technical acts and strategies of material culture production and use, there is another aspect of this phenomenon less comfortably addressed in archaeology, but which fill the pages of contemporary material culture studies. At the same time that technologies materialize taken-for-granted (and often tacit) cultural ontologies for understanding and making sense of the world, in a very real sense they also express and reaffirm social values about the right and wrong ways things should or should not be done, and by whom. Technology thus becomes a question of social values, ethics, and by extension, politics and power. Social values and culturally sanctioned proscriptions about technical matters, however, are not limited to codified attitudes and explicit rules about the proper choice of material resources or the correct or best procedures for their transformation from one physical state to another. Sociotechnical values and attitudes extend beyond things-in-themselves, to involve makers and users being-in-the-world.

Among the sorts of communal values expressed in and through technological practices are opinions as to who may or may not make or use certain objects or practice particular technical procedures, as well as rules as to who is and is not permitted access to the "correct" material resources from which they should be made (for an early consideration, see McGhee 1977). How social attitudes encompass producers and consumers, and dictate, for both, the range of acceptable techniques of comportment, is most readily evident in studies of contemporary technologies, but there is no reason why these dynamics cannot be studied in prehistoric situations.

Technologies of "the hunt" and faunal processing

An early study by L. Sharp (1952) showed how traditional Yir Yoront (Australian) stone technology was inseparably bound up in a complicated mix of gender and age ideologies and kinship rules. Stone technology expressed and reaffirmed deeply held beliefs about Yir Yoront being-in-the-world: it dictated the correct way to make and use stone axes; defined who was permitted access to the appropriate raw materials, techniques, and technical knowledge; and laid out under what circumstances end products could be borrowed by others. In pre-colonial times, only adult men were sanctioned to make stone axes, while women and children were permitted to use them upon showing proper deference to the axe maker. Unfortunately, this arrangement was devastated when missionaries began providing women and younger individuals their own steel axes in the early 1940s. This action had the unintended consequence of disrupting not only the material basis of their lithic technology, but also kin, age, totemic, and gender-based rules of social hierarchy, precisely because each was so integral to the others. When the web weaving these seemingly separate cultural practices was torn apart, through the well-intentioned introduction of steel axes, each was shaken to their very foundations. But one should not think of this as some domino effect, for no thin black lines connected Yir Yoront lithic technology to their totemic social organization and gender/age ideologies. The picture is far more complicated.

Among contemporary Chipewya, the social value and prestige that comes with hunting land game resides not only in successfully spearing an animal (the western preoccupation), but equally in its subsequent technical processing (H. S. Sharp 1991; extended argument in Brumbach and Jarvenpa 1994, 1997; Jarvenpa and Brumbach 1995). Here is yet another example of how cosmologies and world views structure practical decisions about mundane technical matters, including the proper way to process and dry meat and who should be involved. They are also inseparable from the social and political value and statuses these processing activities afford the technicians – namely, men-hunters and women-processors. Similarly, among Iñupiat (Iñuit) whale hunters, it is the bodily comportment of the boat captain's wife on shore that determines the success or failure of the hunt (Bodenhorn 1990, 1993), and this is explicitly recognized by the actors in whale-hunting dramas. As a general rule, then, the technology of "hunting cannot be reduced to the catching and slaughtering of animals, but rather includes a whole set of activities, both technical and symbolic, in which the interpendence [*sic*] of women and men is fundamental" (Bodenhorn 1990: 55).

Using these brief examples we can ask a relatively under-theorized question: how does a researcher know where, when, and how to draw that imaginary line between the material and non-material components of technology (such as hunting), if *in practice* they are inseparably linked through the thoughts and value systems of technicians? For example, what is typically called the technology of faunal acquisition and processing, especially in prehistoric archaeology (but also in ethnoarchaeology and ethnography), often focuses narrowly on the material and hardware "side" of hunting and dismembering activities. In so doing, western sensibilities about what a technology of "the hunt" involves are reaffirmed, but this may bear little resemblance to the (emic) ethnographic or ancient situation (Brumbach and Jarvenpa 1994, 1997; Jarvenpa and Brumbach 1995). But Gifford-Gonzalez (1993b: 187–8) makes a strong case for a web of preexisting social conditions, beliefs, and historically defined value and proscriptions likely contribute to structuring physical decisions relating, for example, to which animal(s) to kill and how, which body parts to bring back to camp and which to leave behind, and so forth. In some instances these decisions might be sensitive to and bound up in culinary desires or to other needs and wishes dictated, not by the hunters (or rational efficiency), but by other members of the group and their interests (ibid.). They might also be responding to social and bodily proscriptions about when and how to respectfully and properly hunt a certain species, and who to blame if the hunt fails (Bodenhorn 1990, 1993). As well, decisions regarding when and how to hunt a particular animal may be a function of the proper ritual activities necessary to make the blood potent enough for subsequent mixing into pigment colors for seemingly "unrelated" activities such as rock art (Lewis-Williams 1995: 146–7). In each of these instances, technical decisions are brought forth and bound by rules and proscriptions about *who* should and should not be involved at various stages of the hunt and how such activities should proceed.

The social values differentially applied to technicians, their activities, their skills, the tools of the trade, their knowledge, and end products are not reducible only to gender distinctions (although gender differentiation certainly seems to be a major dynamic involved). They equally and necessarily turn on the overlapping ways that age, marital status, clan identities, and even individual personalities intersect with gender. In contexts where multiple kinds of status differentiation overlap (that is, ethnicity, race, class, religion, health, education, and so forth), the factors dictating the "who, what, where, when, how, and why" of a hunting technology are extremely complex. By *resisting* the temptation to heuristically separate the ways cultural ontologies, social values, and objective conditions overlap in practice, ethnographic studies, in particular, are beginning to provide insights into the social nature of (hunting) technologies, artifact design, and tool use. As well, there is now a solid base of empirical research on the extraordinary dialectic operating between the material complexities of colonial and contemporary African iron working, fertility symbolism, gender ideologies, and labor proscriptions (see note 5, page 243). Another fascinating ethnographic example can be found in Mahias (1989), who describes a remarkable resonance between the linguistic structure of Sanskrit texts, the material structure of dairy production, and fire-making technologies in India.

Netting technologies

An exemplary study demonstrating the issue under discussion is M. A. MacKenzie's (1991) work on the social and material "biography" of string bags in central New Guinea. She shows in extraordinary material detail that different looping techniques employed by the Telefol to fabricate *bilums* are structured by an inseparable combination of practical, social, and symbolic factors: one particular technique (*ding men*) is considered best for making the net bags people use to carry awkward or large loads to market and to cradle infants; another, with feathers (*uun kon men*), is used only by fully initiated adult men; a large open-looped bag (*men batbaat*) is made to be worn by widows "to mark their liminal status while mourning" (ibid.: 219); and wide bands of looped strings (*tijt*) is a technique practiced not only to make women's dancing regalia but also used by mothers to make their son's chest bands (*dagasaal men*). Interestingly, *dagasaal men*, which are worn at the commencement of the initiation cycle, are decorated with feathers collected by the young initiate's father.

To complicate things considerably, certain kinds of *bilums* and the particular looping techniques by which they are made serve an inseparable and non-hierarchical combination of functional, social, economic, political, and ideological ends: they carry subsistence goods; cradle babies; mark age, gender, initiation, and marital status; bind women and men together metaphorically, actually, and economically; signify who has access to certain kinds of practical and/or esoteric knowledge and skills; enable individuals to participate in important social and religious activities; differentiate ethnic communities from each other; serve as gifts; reaffirm shared community values of industry and skill; invoke ancestral spirits; protect the wearer; protect valued objects worn around the neck; and so forth. And by enacting these proper material and bodily codes of conduct during the everyday production and use of string bags, producers and consumers are not only reaffirming widely shared beliefs and a sense of ethnicity (Lemonnier 1986). Through such embodied experiences, they also create and re-create a sensual awareness of being-in-the-world *as* a Telefol (similarly, see Pálsson and Helgason 1999 on "skipperhood").

These rules of fabrication, use, meaning, and value instantiate each other such that none can be adequately understood if considered apart from the others. MacKenzie's study also demonstrates especially well that, by being "culturally competent" (*sensu* Bourdieu 1984) and knowing the traditional meanings, functions, and proper ways to make and use particular kinds of bags, community members are also able to challenge them (M. A. MacKenzie 1991: 164; also Moore 1986). But in spite of the fact that in some Telefol communities individuals or groups (mostly young people) are beginning to contest traditional values and proscriptions – for example, by knowingly breaking the rules of string bag production or by wearing or using them in the "wrong" ways – there is nonetheless a desire to express conformity and to project to neighboring groups a shared sense of community. In sum, then, the complex ways in which meaning and function intersect with social values, tradition, identity, and contestation show that seemingly mundane objects of everyday use and "simple" technologies of production are far more complex than their materiality might suggest.

Summary

As a general rule, the social, material, and historical contexts in which subsistence technologies and other economic activities are pursued implicate a host of related concerns having to do with cultural principles and rules of social and bodily comportment. Though from a western point of view these larger frames of reference do not link directly to the material technology in question, they are necessary for understanding why technical agents undertake these activities as they do (for additional examples, see especially Gosselain 1994, 1998; Hosler 1996; van der Leeuw et al. 1991). The immediate functional and objective factors structuring artifact manufacture and use, real as they are, are necessarily and always embedded in historically antecedent contexts of value, world views, proscriptions, and social intercourse (Cresswell 1993; Ingold 1993c). Because of this, practical matters should not be privileged *a priori* over the sociosymbolic "side" of what constitutes their very existence. Rather, it is the *interplay* of the tangible and intangible, of immediate contexts and antecedent history, of the seemingly inconsequential with matters of the greatest importance, that together shape technologies.

Technology Produces More than Things

Clearly, technologies and the products deriving from them serve practical economic needs and functions. And particularly at the macro-scale of human–land relationships, there is no doubt that a learned body of techniques for resource procurement, artifact manufacture, and use serve adaptive ends. It is at the relatively extrasocial scale of technological–ecological relationships that a significant body of archaeological research has been directed over the past three or more decades (Nelson 1991). Such research has shown how and to what extent technologies depend upon a widely shared and sound body of practical knowledge developed over time, through trial and error, experimentation, and innovation. What is often taken for granted, however, are the inner workings of the social community within which such knowledge is codified and reaffirmed through everyday practice and how such knowledge is passed on to successive generations.

In their research on blacksmithing activity systems, C. M. Keller and J. D. Keller (1996) explore in depth the "stocks of knowledge" that practical technologies engender. Similarly to Heidegger, they stress that an experiential corpus of technical knowledge "is dynamic, continually subject to growth and transformation in practice" (ibid.: 61), much like learning in general (ibid.: 176–9; also Lave and Wenger 1991; Pálsson and Helgason 1999).[6] Obviously, practical knowledge includes stocks of information about the viable range of physical sequences by which technicians can work metals into desired shapes having the requisite strength for their intended function; about the thermodynamic properties of different sorts of furnaces and combustible materials; and about the variety of tools and bodily gestures best suited for molding, hammering, and tempering the materials being worked – what Schiffer (1992a) and Schiffer and Skibo (1987) would include among their "performance characteristics." Among the products any technology produces, then, are a mental body of prescriptive facts about objective material matters learned through experience and (possibly) shared with others. This corpus of knowledge, derived from personal engagement with and transformation of the material world, is what Schiffer and Skibo (1987) call "techno-science."[7] It is also what we typically think of as rational and abstract scientific principles applied to craft activities (see especially Ingold 1988a: 154–9).

But as chapters 2 and 3 suggested, knowledge derived from embodied technical experience is meaningful in ways that reach far beyond the practical "know how" and "how to" of material culture transformation and use. In contemporary parlance, technological knowledge, even technoscientific knowledge, is often considered prescriptive, consisting of procedures (rules) that describe actions to be performed in order to achieve a practical end. Unfortunately, this prescriptive view, especially as researched in archaeology, tends to exclude knowledge that is more sense-based, intuited, and non-discursive, and thus seemingly not related directly to the productive activity at hand. Nonprescriptive kinds of technological knowledge also include phenomenological forms of awareness (of self and Other), as well as larger cultural epistemologies (as previously discussed). Importantly, these stocks of knowledge can, and often do, provide the basis for social and material power (Illich 1973; Mumford 1934, 1964, 1967; elaborated below and in chapters 3, 5, and 7). In anthropology and archaeology, Mauss (1935), Ridington (1982, 1988), Ingold (1988a, 1990b, 1993a), and Schiffer and Skibo (1987) are among many to show that the stocks of techno-knowledge people derive from their experiences working in and with the material world constitute a socially valued body of knowledge. Csikszentmihalyi and Rochberg-Halton (1981: 16) sum up the embodiment principle of technical knowledge as self/Other awareness especially well, suggesting that

> men and women make order in their selves . . . by first creating and then interacting with their material world. The nature of that transaction will determine, to a great extent, the kind of person that emerges. Thus the things that surround us are inseparable from who we are. The material objects we use are not just tools we can pick up and discard at our convenience; they constitute the framework of experiences that give order to our otherwise shapeless selves.

For example, C. M. Keller and J. D. Keller (1996) emphasize that it is through the particularly embodied experience of working metals that blacksmiths come to know themselves and their place in the social community. In this, their idea substantiates and grounds Heidegger's argument that being-in-the-world through technological practice is a path to self-awareness. This finding is similar to what M. A. MacKenzie's (1991) study of Telefol *bilums* shows as well (also P. Dickens 1996; Pálsson and Helgason 1999). The production of material culture produces experiential understandings made meaningful in sociosymbolic and political contexts that may have, on the surface, little to do with the business at hand. In fact, however, they have everything to do with the memories, values, and sensibilities of the technicians and communities undertaking these activities. As I explore at length in the following chapter, precisely because the technician's hand is connected to the collective body politic, technological acts done with the hand (or material extensions of it) engender a web of social, political, and symbolic meanings and functions from which they cannot be severed.

This idea can be substantiated by extending Schlanger's (1994, 1996) findings concerning how Levallois techniques of lithic flake preparation and removal are "a generative interplay between the mental and material activities" of ancient Neandertal knappers (Schlanger 1996: 231; see also chapter 6). This sophisticated study concentrates on cognition and decision-making strategies, but for Schlanger "the technician" is an abstract concept rather than an embodied agent. What is missing is explicit recognition that social context, antecedent structures, and values necessarily influenced how lithic knappers (Neandertal or otherwise) plied their trade. Although Schlanger's work is among the most thoughtful and critical in lithic studies today, he pays little attention to the social arena in which mental and material knapping activities necessarily worked together as a set of meaningful experiences which, in fact, provided those cognitive and practical stocks of knowledge in the first place. His insightful discussion creates a much-needed wedge between two relatively extrasocial theories: that Levallois was a predetermined mental plan applied to lithic cores (Bordes 1968, 1970, 1971); or, that it was a core rejuvenation and reduction strategy (Davidson and Noble 1993; Dibble 1989). But even Schlanger's nuanced study leaves us with a mental image of some lone Neandertal whacking away (albeit skillfully and with a full stock of practical knowledge in his or her head), detached and alienated from meaningful involvement with their social community.

The special emphasis that C. M. Keller and J. D. Keller (1996) place on the bodily and experiential basis of technical "know how" as a form of self/Other knowledge recalls a point I developed in chapter 2. As they put it:

> The mind–body dualism typical of Western science and philosophy has failed to account for the subjective experience of unity in productive activity. The separation of mind and body in research and the dissolution of activity systems in scholarly investigation also fails to provide accounts of the human realization of fulfillment in accomplishment. (1996: 174)

Cyril Stanley Smith (1970) has defined technology as the integrated work of the body's hand, mind, and eye. I am here emphasizing the *social* body from which the individual should not be severed. Since technoscientific stocks of knowledge can only exist within the body politic, how can practical knowledge be anything less than culturally reasoned? And, how can any scholarly attempt to extract an "underlying" *logos* from the whole of *tekhnē* possibly succeed?

Discussion

What the Kellers have taught us through their study of contemporary blacksmithing, what MacKenzie's analysis of Telefol *bilums* points to, what we can take from Keightly's work on Neolithic Chinese pottery, and what Lechtman's pioneering research on pre-Hispanic gold working provide, is a powerful vision of technology; the subjective and experiential basis of particular sorts of material encounters with the world serve as cultural epistemologies for knowing the way the world works, the way the world should be worked, and the place of the self and the group within it. As Lemonnier (1989a, 1990, 1992a) effectively shows in his cross-cultural studies of contemporary technologies, knowledge that is instantiated, learned, and reaffirmed through personal/collective bodily engagement with material things becomes a "system of representations" (after Lévi-Strauss 1963; Sperber 1985). As earlier recognized by Childe (1936, 1956) and Ucko (1970), technologies, technical acts, and technical things *are* "social representations" designating the cultural bodies of knowledge with which people make sense of and act in the world (Lemonnier 1986: 154; 1993a: 3). This is the same point that Conkey (1993) makes when reminding us that humans are materialists and symbolists simultaneously, and that Geertz (1973b) suggests in arguing that social reality is social action founded on symbolic constructs (also Bourdieu 1990).

Lemonnier's (1986, 1993b) study of Anga (New Guinea) horticultural practices, architecture, and pig traps, his work on the Concorde (1989a), and even Latour's (1991) novel study of hotel keys demonstrate (and with due attention to the materiality of those technologies) that the particular choice of design elements and techniques invented to solve practical problems are as much material expressions of "mental schemas" (Lemonnier 1993a: 3) as they are grounded in practical reason and objectivity. In fact, such strategies are one and the same. Practical reason in technological matters lies squarely within the realm of cultural reason precisely because it materializes within the context of preexisting world views and social attitudes about how things do and should work (Ingold 1990b: 7; 1993a). No matter how tacit and nondiscursive this awareness, no aspect of the material world is without signification, meaning, values, and functions that encompass far more than practical, efficient, objective knowledge (Rothenberg 1993: 73–86). Practical stocks of techno-knowledge necessarily implicate ongoing social and cognitive processes of differentiation and the concretization of collective and personal sensibilities (Pálsson and Helgason 1999); as such, they are never concerned "first" with objective reality, for that reality is necessarily perceived through the lens of cultural reason.

*From world views, knowledge, and social values to politics
and power*

The less than tangible aspects of technology stressed thus far, especially the link between practical and self/Other/worldly knowledge, intertwine to play an important role in structuring the physical making and use of material culture. Reciprocally, the various performance characteristics of material resources, technical acts, design features, and artifact functions substantiate and physically ground these knowledge-producing experiences. There is still more to this web than the dialectic of meaning and object, however. With the recognition that technologies necessarily implicate social values and culturally esteemed knowledge, it is but another step in logic, and another thread in the cloth, to ask: *Whose* values and judgments are being codified? *At whom* are they directed? And what other webs of relations and value are involved? In large measure, the question of social values and cultural symbols embedded in and expressed through the knowledgeable practice of everyday technologies is simultaneously a question of politics and power.[8]

Philosophers of contemporary technologies have much to say on the politics and ethical dimensions (or axiology) of modern technologies (briefly reviewed in chapter 2; see, Barbour 1980; Durbin 1972; Ellul 1989; Feenberg 1995; Habermas 1970; Kranzberg 1980; Law 1991; Pippin 1995; Winner 1977, 1986a, 1995; overview in Ferré 1995). And in recent years, sociocultural anthropologists and culture theorists have begun to consider these matters; for example, as regards the human genome project (Kevles and Hood 1992) and the politics of reproductive technologies (Corea 1987; O'Brien 1981; Wajcman 1996). What these studies explore are the complex, subtle, and even unintended ways that the political persuasions of particularly situated interest groups and differential networks of power structure the contexts and conditions within which some technical problems, at the expense of others, are deemed worthy of study. In turn, they question how such privileged research and their practical applications affect different segments of the public at large. While archaeologists concerned with times, societies, and technologies vastly different from these might doubt their usefulness for the question of prehistoric techno-politics, there is much to be learned from even a brief consideration of some of them.

Insights from STS:[9] techno-ideologies of class and gender

Political aspects of technology involve the actions, strategies, and capacities whereby groups and/or individuals influence the actions and/or beliefs of others, whether intended or not and regardless of their success or failure. At its simplest, the politics of technology concern the potential transformative effect that beliefs, attitudes, stocks of knowledge, and material practices have on what people think or do.[10] Winner (1986a: 28–9) draws an especially important conclusion from STS-oriented research over the past several decades:

> The things we call "technologies" are ways of building order in our world. Many technical devices and systems important in everyday life contain possibilities for many different ways of ordering human activity. Consciously or unconsciously, deliberately or inadvertently, societies choose structures for technologies that influence how people are going to work, communicate, travel, consume, and so forth over a very long time. In the processes by which structuring decisions are made, different people are situated differently and possess unequal degrees of power as well as unequal levels of awareness.

That is, regardless of time, place, or level of (material) technical sophistication, there are political "qualities" to design features and their implementation, to products, use-functions, and divisions of labor, as well as in the underlying cultural values that infuse these practices with meaning and structure. This is true not only in the ways technologies affect the individuals or collectivities making and/or using them, but equally in terms of the contexts within which they are invented. As Winner has shown for such diverse technologies as tomato-harvesting equipment, bridge construction, and nuclear reactors, even the most seemingly innocuous of practical design features are choices of "profound significance" (ibid.: 28) that have political qualities, whether intended or not. They are influential in the social, symbolic, economic, and even physical ways they direct the thoughts and actions of those making, using, or referring to them.

Similarly, many feminist historians study the intersection of gender ideologies, gendered divisions of labor, and the social values and proscriptions underwriting the invention, commodification, and rules of access to machines over the last two centuries. Of particular interest are studies highlighting the "consumption junction" (Cowan 1994) – that bundle of technical practices and social values tying together gender ideologies and consumer interests, tastes, and needs with matters of design and marketing strategies for creating and selling refrigerators, microwaves, typewriters, bicycles, the electric light, washing machines, automobiles, factory-made clothing, and the like. As these studies show, throughout the nineteenth and early twentieth centuries an ever more circumscribed range of material activities were being called "technology," and coming under the explicit symbolic and practical control of men. But we cannot "blame the hardware" for the political impact machines had on the devaluation of women's traditional (hand) labor. Rather, it was changing beliefs and social values (such as the Cult of Domesticity) coupled with biological notions about the kinds of work women and men were inherently suited to that fed these changes (Valenz 1995). As men's work was increasingly conflated with the very notion of technology, women's work was redefined and conceptually transformed into non-technological labor, but not because it was inherently so (Pacey 1983). Nor was this historical change some explicitly hatched political scheme conceived by all-knowing and overtly manipulative men.

Cultural sensibilities about work ethics and social propriety served as the structural frame within which particular sorts of technologies were invented, given value, and differentially practiced by women, men and (lower-class) children. McGaw's (1982, 1989, 1996) studies of the mechanization of the paper mill, household, and personal technologies (such as linen closets and the bra), as well as Cowan's (1979, 1983, 1985a, 1985b, 1994, 1996) work on the development of the cigar industry and how the refrigerator "got its hum," all highlight the interdependence of engendered social values, labor proscriptions, material objects, and techno-politics during the past two centuries.[11] Study after study now tracks the vicious downward spiral of (industrial) women's material, technical, symbolic, economic, and hence political disempowerment during the Industrial Revolution.[12] What these studies combine to suggest for the "deep past" is that it has probably *never* been the case that there were only two genders, men and women, nor that the former were the technological *savants* and the latter "merely" biologically predisposed to undertake non-technical activities such as tending hearth and home.

Insights from contemporary sociocultural studies

There is yet more to be said about the political dynamics of technologies than those already considered. What deserves more explicit consideration from archaeologists, especially those studying egalitarian social formations and so-called simple or utilitarian technologies, are the seemingly *innocuous* ways in which technical designs, implementation, stocks of knowledge, gestures, skills, and even tools are caught up in strategies of social differentiation, prestige, and status. Political ramifications must be contextualized in terms of the intersubjective agency and interests of the technicians involved, as well as within the larger framing circumstances such as prevailing (and contested) value systems. Because technologies are at once social, material, and symbolic they cannot help but become enmeshed in all the other "sides" of the human drama, especially that sphere we call politics. To overstate the obvious here, human technologies are always implicated in acts of influence. M. A. MacKenzie's (1991) study of string bags reminds us, especially, how human technologies, at least on a non-discursive level, instantiate significant and deeply embedded meanings, values, and political interests that people variously act upon in the course of their everyday lives.

For example, in the grand (evolutionary) scheme of things *bilums* rate as a relatively simple (material) technology not all that difficult for anyone (of any age or gender) to learn with a little training and practice. Nonetheless, *bilums* and the different looping techniques for making and remaking them are encapsulated within the politics of social differentiation, making them capable of conferring status and identity on those who are allowed to make and use them. As well, political statements can be made simply by looping in non-sanctioned ways, or using bags in ways that are just not "right." There is nothing either materially nor functionally unique about plant fibers, looping techniques, or the net bags themselves that make them especially suited to political manipulation. There is also nothing all that special about lithic knapping techniques, antler harpoons, clay pots, iron-working kilns, lassos, or bead-making strategies that makes them any more (or less) appropriate to political maneuvering than gold working, macaw feathers, obsidian blades, and other so-called prestige items (*contra* Hayden 1995a, 1998).

As the studies previously discussed show only too well, it is by virtue of their being mundane and seemingly innocuous everyday sorts of technical activities and items of the kind almost everyone is able to understand, fabricate, and use, that they are especially fertile ground for symbolic and political manipulation. Contrary to popular opinion, then, it is not only the rarity of resources employed, the level of its material complexity, nor how much surplus it can produce that makes a technology political. Rather, technologies can influence because they are materially grounded social practices that, through their very "becoming," differentiate individuals and collectivities and create arenas in which to display (or betray one's lack of) knowledge and skill and advance interests (Dobres 1995a, 1999b; Ingold 1993c; L. Sharp 1952).

The polysemic values embedded in technologies, and by extension conferred on technicians, involve more than rational knowledge about utilitarian and functional matters. Nor do they depend only on productivity, the exotic nature of the raw material, or rarity of the end product. One question archaeologists might explore more broadly than they have, is *how* prevailing value systems might have influenced how technicians went about their daily tasks. As phrased, I am emphasizing not so much the technician's discursive and aggrandizing agency in knowing and pushing at the boundaries of existing avenues for status and recognition through their technical prowess (but see chapter 5). Instead, I am highlighting the existing system of values, judgments, and tastes determining which kinds of technicians are entitled to particular kinds of social standing by virtue of the differently valued technologies they may or may not practice.[13] In reality, however, each depends upon the other: the value given to a particular technology is often defined by virtue of who is sanctioned to undertake it, just as (conversely) technicians achieve some of their social status by virtue of the value that set of practices and products holds for the community. In essence, political influence can play out within the conditions that obtain between how systems of social value give meaning to technologies while, recursively, technologies reaffirm and provide technicians with social standing.

Some implications for archaeology

My repeated emphasis on the dialectic of technology, knowledge, social values, and politics leads to an important conclusion: technologies are not only political when their manipulation is highly visible, such as when certain individuals or high-status groups (for example, "big men" or elites) possess or exercise some form of ideological or physical control "over" the means of production and/or unevenly distribute products through formalized prestige systems (examples in Hayden 1994, 1995a, 1995b, 1998; discussion in Robb 1999). Clearly, the values people give to their technologies and end products are always open to the possibility of political manipulation. To date, however, archaeologists have explicitly considered the politics of ancient technologies and techno-knowledge primarily in their studies of materially "complex" (and visible) prestige technologies and hierarchically organized (or at least middle-range) societies; those capable of surplus production or the manufacture of highly valued but access-restricted objects (for example, Brumfiel and Earle 1987; Costin 1991, 1996; Hayden 1995a, 1995b; Lechtman 1993; Manolakakis 1994; Rice 1981; Roux and Pelegrin 1989; Schiffer 1992b; Torrence 1986; Tosi 1984; Vidale 1989; R. P. Wright 1991; critique in J. E. Clark 1986). However, for the technologies of the sort practiced by so-called simple hunter-gatherers (past or present), subtle, non-discursive, tacit, and unintended political dynamics are rarely considered outright – by anthropologists, much less archaeologists (Cobb 1997; Dobres 1995c; Sassaman 1997).[14]

To take but one example, in Nelson's (1991) comprehensive review of archaeological research on "technological organization," neither politics nor social relations of production are addressed. Here, as with many examples I could offer (for it is not my intention to single out Nelson's review), the "organization of technology" concerns material but not social issues, as if technologies somehow organized themselves on the basis of practical reason and performance characteristics. It is only in the concluding paragraphs that Nelson tacks on the now standard addendum: that an "interest in how technological strategies facilitate social strategies of individualization, family integration, reciprocity, territorial interaction, and territorial flexibility would benefit our understandings of technological organization" (ibid.: 88). Note here that technology (*sans* people) "facilitates" the social rather than the other way around. Separating technology into its material and social sides is bad enough, but to imply that we can (someday) simply add understandings of social strategies and stir them into preexisting materialist models is both conceptually and analytically misguided.

For four chapters now I have been arguing that explicit consideration of the sociopolitical nature of technologies cannot be done *after* the material facts are settled; one cannot simply insert symbolism, questions of value, or the dynamics of social differentiation into a preexisting materialist pot that, by definition, discounts or downplays them as constitutive elements (Dobres 1995e). These intangible processes clearly play a structural role in shaping and changing technologies through time and space, and if we are to understand how they did so in the past, they must become *central* to our conceptual frameworks rather than added after the facts are in (Dobres and Hoffman 1994, 1999a). If the concept of technology is to reintegrate the cultural *logos* of ancient *tekhnē*, then our analytic methodologies must keep apace (Dobres 1995c, in press-b; as discussed in chapter 6).

It is time we took more seriously the likelihood that subtle, nondiscursive, tacit, and unintended sorts of political interests were practiced by even the most "primitive" technicians in the course of pursuing their most mundane and simplest (adaptive) technologies. And it is time to start asking such questions explicitly, and designing our research agendas with these questions in mind. Sillar (1996: 283) nicely sums up this basic point when he reminds us that

> Every technique is used in a cultural setting that affects the way it is understood in that society. Who performs the technique? What tools do they use? Where and when is the technique applied? What is its intended purpose? All of these questions affect how the technique is socially constituted (Dobres 1995) and how the technique itself becomes bound up with associations that affect how it is represented by society.

Similarly, in his innovative study of the techno-politics underwriting the procurement and exchange of lithic raw material among egalitarian hunter-gatherers in the southeastern United States, Sassaman (1997) suggests that when it comes to making sense of variability in the material practices of communally organized societies, "whether perceived as sacred or mundane, material evidence for social inequality most often causes archaeologists to revise social typology, rather than confront the complexities and dynamism of social power" (ibid.: 4). In other words, if in the technological practices of a simple society we find archaeological evidence for "politicking," then we tend to upgrade their form of social organization (that is, we move the definitional goal posts), perhaps calling them transegalitarian (Hayden 1998). We seem unwilling to accept the possibility that a non-hierarchical, essentially egalitarian social formation could have practiced a politicized, albeit "simple" technology.

Techno-politics in communal societies

While I discuss this more fully in the following chapter, it must be said at this point that there is always room for tacit and non-discursive attempts at personal and/or group influence: through technical activities; through the values and attitudes that underwrite them; or through established rules of conduct as to who should or should not engage in certain activities, work with particular resources, or have access to techniques, tool, or products (Heritage 1987: 243). In this most basic sense, subtle (even unintended) attempts to influence one's peers have their political "side," regardless of their success or failure and no matter how explicitly pursued (Giddens 1979: 256–7; see chapter 5). The politics of technology even go as far as to include how such attempts may be read, or misread, into the technical actions of others (Dobres 1995a, 1999b). Perhaps there is no better topic through which explore the politics of technology than the supposedly "least" political mode of production: communally organized societies.

As has now been demonstrated, in even the most egalitarian of social collectivities, the agency of individual technicians and work groups serves to influence others (Cobb 1993, 1997; Flanagan 1989; Keenan 1981; Keene 1991; Lee 1982; Miller and Tilley 1984; Saitta and Keene 1990; Sassaman 1997). Such expressions are political and operate within, while simultaneously straining at the edges of, widely shared beliefs in equality and reciprocity. For example, in his highly original and compelling study of an Israeli *kibbutz*, Keene (1991: 337) argues that within the communal mode, the social group as a whole – the commune – serves as the basis for all productive activity. Access to necessary factors of production is guaranteed to all members, and all members participate in determining the division between necessary and surplus labor. *This pattern still leaves room for internal variation and does not necessarily demand material equality or equal access to the means of production.* (my emphasis)

In principle, then, in even the most egalitarian and seemingly "simple" society people have the opportunity to achieve a certain amount of influence among, but not necessarily over, their peers. In particular, status and influence are often achieved by demonstrating skills and prowess in activities deemed important to the entire group (Dobres 1999b; examples can be found in Aldenderfer 1993; Hindess and Hirst 1975; King 1978; K. R. McGuire and Hildebrandt 1994; Ridington 1988; Shostak 1981). As I elaborate at length in the following chapter, it is precisely because of their overlapping social, symbolic, economic, material, practical, and political dimensions that the "simplest" technologies can express and reaffirm (at one and the same time) self, Other, cultural, practical, and worldly stocks of knowledge. At the same time, material production is an arena in which a technician's various stocks of knowledge and skill can be flaunted, suppressed, challenged, or otherwise negotiated. Thus the web of gestural, physical, and thoughtful acts woven into the very fabric of technology is, in every sense of the word, political. But making a reputation for oneself is not all that is involved here. As Leacock and Lee (1982: 9) noted more than fifteen years ago, communally organized societies are "fraught with contradictions" and problems that are not only about gaining status and prestige. They equally turn on more practical matters, such as the right and wrong ways to take care of everyday business without transgressing social rules and etiquette.

In addition to the range of political dynamics sketched above, there is the distinction between the "know how" of knowledgeable practice and the "know to" of practical knowledge (Ingold 1988a, 1991, 1993a, 1993b, 1993c; Pálsson 1994; Pálsson and Helgason 1999). There is more than a grain of truth in the Enlightenment adage, "Knowledge is power," because knowledge is never a value-free body of fact-based, objective observations unmediated by the social conditions in which they are made and given value. This critically important idea is not often taken up by archaeologists (but see Schiffer and Skibo 1987, 1997). Yet wherever there is knowledge there exists some political potential, especially in how technical stocks of practical and esoteric knowledge are developed and codified (Feenberg and Hannay 1995; Ingold 1990b: 10–11; 1993a; Sinclair in press).

For example, the knowledge underwriting technical practice can be overtly, subtly, or even unknowingly displayed by technicians during the most taken-for-granted of their production and use activities. When knowledge "held in the mind" is expressed outwardly, through varying levels of competence, skill, and "know how," it becomes a form of silent discourse communicating to one's neighbors the skill and wisdom (or lack thereof) certain individuals possess (Dobres 1995a, 1995c, 1999b; Graburn 1976: 21; Ingold 1993a: 438; 1993c). In having learned the right or best way to make and use objects, and by displaying this savoir-faire with confidence, skill, and flair, people create reputations among their peers. As I elaborate in chapters 5 and 7, however, it is rarely the case that technical knowledge and skills are shared equally among a community of technicians, nor that their public display guarantees social and/or material power, prestige, and/or status. For the past as well as the present, context is everything in trying to understand the politics of technological practice.

Non-discursive and discursive politics in the communal mode of production

Concrete examples can ground and further elaborate the politics of everyday technologies discussed in the abstract above. For example, as Lee (1982) and Silberbauer (1982: 29) show in their analyses of the Ju/'hoasni (!Kung) and G/wi, individuals in small-scale communally organized societies achieve their reputations and gain influence among their neighbors, in part, by demonstrating respected qualities for all to see. In such societies, possessing technical knowledge is a prominent basis for leadership (Honigmann 1981; Ingold 1993a, 1993b; Keene 1991; Lewis-Williams 1987, 1992; Ridington 1988). Not only esoteric or arcane knowledge, but even the most necessary, objective, and eminently adaptive stocks of practical "technoscience" can, and do, serve social, political and practical interests at one and the same time (Ridington 1982, 1988).

For example, in the earlier discussion of the Yir Yoront, we saw that technical knowledge, precisely because it engendered meaning and value, allowed only one segment of society the sanctioned authority to develop motor skills and a stock of practical knowledge necessary for making and using stone axes the "right" way. While non-discursive in their everyday expression, the politics underlying traditional proscriptions by which only adult, married Yir Yoront men were permitted to acquire the knowledge and technical competence to make stone axes are unmistakable (similar examples include Lechtman 1993; M. A. MacKenzie 1991).

Similarly, among Western Desert (Australian) Aborigines, the "right(eous)" raw material from which to make stone adzes is not the more readily available and better-quality white chert, but a non-local stone of clearly inferior functional properties. The reason for this seemingly inefficient and irrational choice in raw material is caught up in expressing and reaffirming custodial and affilial rights of access to the ancestral lands where such sources are found (Gould 1980: 146–59). These culturally reasoned technical decisions address non-technical matters (about righteous rocks and the Dreamtime), as they simultaneously display prized technical knowledge (about how to work inferior materials). Thus, the necessary practical knowledge and knowledgeable practice which enable basic resource exploitation not only enhance the technician's position within his community; in so doing they reaffirm traditional cultural values by materializing in practice the rules and privileges that come with patrilineal decent.

Ridington's (1988) work on the Dene shows especially well that technical knowledge held in the mind is not only culturally and personally efficacious; it also serves political interests. Among the Dene, social recognition and power is achieved not through overt self-aggrandizement, but through subtle displays of material and non-material technical knowledge and skill (also Christian and Gardner 1977). Similarly, Lapp reindeer herders earn their reputations, good and bad, through displays of the "know how" and "know to" of lassoing (Ingold 1993c). As Ingold (ibid.: 112) argues, different bodily techniques used to rope reindeer, as well the level of skill with which they are dispatched, are

> an arena in which technical competence is highly conspicuous and there the inept and clumsy are liable to find themselves the target of a torrent of (albeit good-natured) abuse. An owner who is not fully competent may find himself in the ignominious position of being unable to recover his property and having to rely on his friends or relatives to help out.

Technical (in)competence and the (in)ability to successfully effect the knowledge and skill of lasso throwing acts as "a subtle index – one among many – of the social relations, affiliation, and identities of the users" (ibid.: 124). Here is an excellent example of the covert and unintended ways technique, technical choice, competence, and knowledge "become" political.

As I more fully explore in the next chapter, the reputation one earns among one's neighbors, especially (but certainly not only) in egalitarian societies, derives in large measure from a combination of subtle and overt displays of "stocks of knowledge" and dexterity in everyday technological pursuits (Dobres 1995a, 1999b). Thus explicit control of the forces and relations of production are not the only index for measuring a technology's political effects. Under the proper circumstances, creating, possessing, and displaying technical knowledge can promote (or hinder) one's ability to influence others, especially because such displays are engendered by individuals already "pegged" in the social order by virtue of first-order identities: according to age, gender, clan or religious affiliation, marital status, and so forth. These arguments show that utilitarian and functional techniques and actions are necessarily framed against a background of sociopolitical interests. Nor must it be the case that only the most anomalous or "least rational" of technical practices are those likely to be underwritten by political interests (although these are certainly the most suggestive). Even the most widely shared and ubiquitous of techniques are part and parcel of the body politic.

Obviously, technical "know how" and "know to" expressed while making and using material culture is not only political at a non-discursive level. There is obviously a discursive level at which these dynamics can play out – for example, when technicians knowingly and overtly act on their own behalf and to achieve ends they see as advantageous to themselves or a group to which they belong (cf. Hayden 1994, 1995b, 1998). But in contrast to traditional ways of thinking, the preceding discussion demonstrates that sociopolitical and symbolic aspects of technology are not secondary to those called objective, practical, and rational. Neither are they a "side" issue complementing the utilitarian, functional, and material "core" of ancient *tekhnē-logos* nor restricted to only "some" kinds of societies or material practices. The main thrust of this book is to argue that a more holistic and practice-centered account of (ancient) technology can be achieved *only* by understanding how practical knowledge and knowledgeable practice instantiated each other through the experiences and meanings technicians gave to their interactions with each other and the material world, and how such knowledges and practices were guided by overlapping social, functional, rational, political, symbolic, and material factors.

More *implications for archaeology*

The more subtle dimensions of techno-politics I have been discussing have long been downplayed in many prehistoric contexts, especially for times and places where the advent of a "simple" (material) technology is argued to have provided humans (or hominids) an evolutionary (survival) advantage. Somehow or other, if a technology was evolutionarily adaptive and practical it could not also be political. What I find illogical in studies that highlight the rational, logical, and material basis of *Homo technologicus* is how primitive hominid technologies could have been invented and practiced in a social milieu, conferred some adaptive advantage on an entire species, yet remained politically neutral – all at the same time. Among the best-studied material-technical practices to have had no apparent political influence on human thought and action, while nonetheless conferring adaptive value on "the species" through their invention and dissemination, are the following: Oldowan and Acheulean "industries"; the Levallois technique; innovative uses of organic resources such as bone and antler; heat treating lithics; hafting techniques for composite artifacts; and, even watercraft![15] Although these technologies have always been considered Rubicons of evolutionary import, the primary explanatory accounts for their innovation and spread remain, for the most part, problematically *a*political (important exceptions include Arnold 1993, 1995; and Hayden 1995a, 1995b, 1998). Clearly each of these technical markers of human progress and cognitive development were central to the adaptive success of the human lineage, but the argument is that this is because of their material, functional, and economic advantages. All the while, they stand outside the body politic (whatever form it may have taken). I suggest that this lapse in logic is possible because we do not conceptualize these activities as simultaneously social and meaningful.

The general avoidance in considering the potential techno-politics of these (r)evolutionary technologies has much to do with lingering nineteenth-century notions that materially simple, egalitarian gatherer-hunters are *a*political precisely because politics, *a priori*, is the evolutionary domain of more hierarchically organized collectives, especially those "possessing" technologies capable of specialized material production and/or surplus (Engels 1972 [orig. 1884]; Hayden 1993, 1995a: 258; Testart 1982, 1988; critiques in Leacock and Lee 1982; Sassaman 1997; Wobst in press).[16] Yet as the preceding discussion argues, ancient technologies need not be large-scale, overly oppressive, enable material surplus, nor even require the conscious control of a labor force to have political qualities and ramifications (examples in Conkey 1991; Cross 1990; Dobres 1995a; Lechtman 1993; Roux and Matarasso 1999).

Given the concept of technology advanced here, politics is a processual quality of *all* socially constituted technologies, but not because of things-in-themselves nor because certain technologies can produce a material surplus to be controlled by only a few. As the case studies discussed in this chapter demonstrate, technologies are structured as much by the social, symbolic, and political attitudes and rules people have about the "proper" materials, designs, and forms to make and use as they are by the physical properties of the resources being worked. And because technologies are always in the process of becoming through the hands, skills, knowledge, values, practices, beliefs, social labor, and situated choices of technicians, it stands to reason that anywhere during that life-history they can enter into the political arena, no matter how democratically or hierarchically organized the society.

Conclusions

Throughout the preceding discussion I have repeatedly argued that technologies are means to overlapping ends, some of which are intended, successful, material, and utilitarian, while others are unintended, less than successful, intangible, yet meaningful all the same. Meanings, materials, agents, and society are created out of a web of seemingly unlimited threads that include the dynamism of differentially situated technicians, working in differently circumscribed contexts of object making and use, engaging with different material resources, and bringing to their activities personal predilections and shared ontologies, epistemologies, values, and histories. While clearly serving economic, practical, and often adaptive ends, at the scale of everyday intersubjective practice, the most mundane of technologies are surprisingly polysemic. And because they "exist" in so many domains simultaneously, technologies are physical, sensual, and meaningful experiences of being-in-the-world at multiple phenomenological scales: from that of individual technicians, to polities, to the species writ large. It follows, then, that conceptualizing technology as an object of study where material issues take explanatory and analytic precedence over cultural dimensions deflects us from understanding this whole.

The purpose of this chapter has been to start re-conceptualizing technology as a verb of action and interaction: between and among technicians, between individuals and the materials they work, and between these interactions and wider frames of meaning, action, history, and context. Technology is a process of combined social and material engagement situated within and structured by the interactions of technical agents with each other and their material world in historical contexts of time, space, and culture. Technologies are about transformations: the becoming of artifacts, the engendering of meaning, the creating of personal and group awareness and knowledge, the development of competence, skill, and identity – all through the sensuous experience of working with the material world on a daily basis. It is clear that seemingly epiphenomenal aspects of culture, such as beliefs, social relations, value systems, knowledge, rules of

comportment, and politics combine with the physical aspects of artifact production and use to structure how that becoming takes place.

Three intersecting claims underwrite this project, and two have been
considered here: (1) that technologies are meaningful acts of social
engagement with the material world that serve as a medium through
which world views, values, and social judgments are expressed tangibly
and reaffirmed or contested in daily practice; and (2) that technological
practice produces not only practical knowledge and material things, but
also personal and cultural understandings that can serve political ends.
The third claim, that technologies are fundamentally about people,
mindful communities of practice, and social relations of production, is
the subject of the following chapter, because thinking about ancient
technology as a process of combined social and material engagement
with the world requires that we begin to ask *how* practical knowledge
was learned, taught, valued, and differentially shared under certain historical conditions, and similarly, how knowledgeable practice served
multiple ends at one and the same time. These are not second-order questions in the study of ancient *tekhnē*. Rather, they are fundamental
to explaining the particular material choices, technical solutions, and
making and use activities that technicians practiced in the past, and to
understanding why they changed over time. But to comprehend them,
we must turn full attention to the *agents* undertaking these practices in
socially engaged communities.

5

Social Agency and Practice: The Heart and Soul of Technology

The fact is, human reason may carry you a little too far — over the hedge, in fact. It carried me a good way one time; but then I saw it would not do. I pulled up; I pulled up in time. But not too hard. I have always been in favour of a little theory: we must have thought; else we shall be landed back in the dark ages.

(Mr. Brooke to Mr. Casaubon, *Middlemarch*)

Technologies necessarily entail social relationships and always engender meaning. It is technical agents who are responsible for the production, use, and value given to material objects. Equally, it is agents and consumers who functionally and symbolically make and remake the world, in large measure, through technical means. However, more than any material limitations inherent in the mechanical and chemical properties of natural resources and/or ecological conditions, it is human agents and their webs of social relations and values that are central to the day-to-day (re)production of their material conditions. As argued in the preceding two chapters, people experience their technologies as materially grounded arenas wherein interactions of various sorts (social and material) occur while they take care of practical material matters. Thus, people and the material world simultaneously constitute, shape, and are shaped by each other. It is within this dialectic web of material production and social reproduction that the physicality of technical activities intersects with the lived and meaningful world of human agents.

As much as technologies are socially constituted endeavors in which material objects "become" and through such life-histories take on multiple meanings and functions, they are also arenas in which through their sensuous and bodily engagement with the world producers also "become" social products: men, women, skilled crafts people, engineers, novice potters, skippers, consumers, stone tool makers, apprentices, and so forth. And as archaeologists have long understood, it is often through technological practice that wholesale cultural transformations unfold.

Because of the recursive relationship that binds together people, products, artifice, artifacts, meaning, materials, change, and constancy, we cannot comprehend their interdependency using linear, partitive modeling. Instead, we must develop alternative concepts, frameworks, and methodologies that grapple with the whole of *tekhnē*, for agency and practice are no less than the heart and soul of human technology.

It is for these several reasons that I believe the emphasis in technology studies needs to focus on the dynamics of transformational processes, specifically on the intertwined relationship of material and social transformations. It is also why the material, social, and symbolic aspects of such transformations need to be considered in the same instance and not as separate, hierarchically ordered factors. As I have now stressed repeatedly, an especially important feature of the "human–technology equation" is the sensuous and bodily experience of making and using material culture, because the corporeal body is the mindful and social link between the making and use of things, the making and use of practical and cultural knowledge, the making and unmaking of subjects, the making and breaking of social relations, and the making and transformation of the body politic (Csordas 1994b; Pálsson 1994; Pálsson and Helgason 1999). Importantly, both as members of their collectivities and as producers and consumers of material culture, technicians are marked, and mark themselves, by virtue of these different sorts of experiences.

The fundamental premise on which these several claims rest bears repeating: just as technologies are material acts of transformation that unfold during the day-to-day involvement of technicians with their material world, they are simultaneously about the day-to-day enactment and transformation of individuals, social relationships, value systems, cultural epistemologies, and world views. The point of this chapter is to explore in some detail the *human link* responsible for weaving together the overlapping material, social, and symbolic dimensions of technologies.

As I argued in chapter 4, in its most commonsense expression one does not "possess" a technology. Rather, as part of the body politic people *enact* technologies through socially organized material practices (called activities). In so doing, they (re)produce and transform their social and material conditions. This is why I place so much emphasis on the idea that technology is best thought of as a verb of action and interaction rather than a noun of possession and object held in the hand. From this standpoint, even when single technicians work alone to fabricate, use, and repair material objects for some explicitly functional end, they are still part of their social community – a collectivity within which they develop their technical skills, learn to value them, and within which they display gestural competence and practical knowledge in acceptable or challenging ways. To say that individual bodies are necessarily tied to the body politic, even those engaged in the most mundane of technical activities, means they are woven into webs of preexisting social and material conditions, rules, values, hierarchies of knowledge, demands, and expectations that together weave the overarching structures, or forms of involvement (Gosden 1994: 86), within which their making and use activities unfold.

These are the ideas explored in this chapter, but already one can see how insights from diverse intellectual traditions converge on the claim that humans are socially constituted materialists who live in a symbolically perceived world in which personal and group interests and identities encounter ongoing material and social structures. It is in the technological arena, especially, that social traditions are at once reaffirmed and concretized while people simultaneously hammer out tensions and contradictions. Thus technology studies have much to offer in trying to understand the situated ways agency and structure both constitute and play off each other, and through this dialectic contribute to social tradition and cultural transformation.

In what follows, I return to the issues introduced in the previous chapter, this time considering them specifically in terms of the intersubjective sociopolitical dynamics of technological practice, or what I prefer to call *technical agency*. The first section explores the relevance of agency theory for archaeological concerns, highlighting those issues particularly useful for understanding the bodily experience of technological practice as a social and meaningful material activity. I then revisit the claims outlined in the previous chapter: that technologies are meaningful acts of social engagement with the material world that express and contest social values and judgments; and, that the experiential nature of technological practice produces knowledge, skills, and values that can be put to political and practical ends simultaneously. This time, however, I expand them by explicitly considering how artifice and social agency are implicated.

The third claim upon which my synoptic view of technology depends is the primary subject of this chapter: that technologies are fundamentally about people, mindful communities of practice, and social relations of production. Thus, in the first section I pause to make a critical conceptual distinction between the desire (and occasional ability) to identify the material traces of "real" individuals in the archaeological record, and the processual mandate of understanding the interpersonal dynamics of human technical agency as a social and micro-scale dynamic contributing to macro-scale phenomena, specifically social reproduction and culture change. To my way of thinking this is very much an issue of scale. Thus, I differentiate between the *conceptual* and *phenomenological* scales at which agentive processes play out and the *material* and *analytic* scales at which archaeological research can be pursued and material patterns interpreted.[1]

The second section of this chapter links this synoptic and agency perspective on technological practice to the *conceptual* framework known as *chaîne opératoire*. I introduce the concept of *chaîne opératoire* here, and not in the methodological chapter which follows, because it is first necessary to understand how the sequential and "processed" nature of technical gestures and acts of material transformation within the body politic forge structural and meaningful links between the artifice of technical agents and their material culture. In thus discussing the conceptual basis of *chaîne opératoire* I set the stage for chapter 6, which further develops this framework by concentrating on issues of analytic methodology.

Practice Theory and Technical Agency

Technical agency – why bother?

As I suggested in the previous chapter, technology can be thought of as a web that both metaphorically and literally weaves together people and their products. But the question remains: if they are not to be thought of as mere cultural dupes blindly faithful to mental templates, then how are technical agents implicated in all this recursive making and reaffirmation of their world views? And, more specifically, how do habitual and routinized sorts of everyday technological practices contribute to long-term culture change? Though I do not profess to have easy and straightforward answers to these questions, I do suggest that operationalizing the concept of agency and applying it to materials research explicitly focused on the question of technological practice can move us in the right direction.

Whereas many of the above-stated claims are now accepted components of the "technology equation," especially in ethnographic, ethno-archaeological, and contemporary material culture studies, there has been precious little explication of *how* ancient expressions of technical agency, especially at the scale of individuals and small-scale social collectives, structured and held such a complicated web of tangible and intangible elements together through mundane material practices (Dobres and Hoffman 1994, 1999a).[2] As discussed in the previous chapter, recent work demonstrating the extent to which symbolic world views and cultural ontologies underwrite technologies has begun to pry the lid off that black box encasing technical agents and mindful communities of practice. Such studies readily show the extent to which meanings and values shape practical material making and use activities. In doing so, however, they still beg the question of *how*, through their corporeal and everyday experiences of being-in-the-world, technical agents and communities of practice effect such cultural wizardry. After all, by their very nature, world views (just like artifacts) are of people's making, too.

Meaning does not miraculously hover above everyday material practices any more than it exists as some intangible substrate structuring action from below. Rich though they are, what is curiously missing from symbolic studies of technologies past and present is explicit discussion of how agents *make* meaning through their non-discursive, everyday technological practices enacted in particularly structured social settings (Dobres and Hoffman 1994). There is a disturbingly normative quality to this body of work that often leaves the reader with the sense that these world views float either above or below the practical consciousness of those faithfully adhering to them, and that technological practice is little more than the routinized, traditional, and thus patterned material behaviors of unconscious agents obliviously (but faithfully) going through the motions.

In place of this increasingly problematic and ironically asocial stance, agency theory demands interest in the central role that agents and mindful communities of practice had in weaving the material, social, and symbolic together into a meaningful and experienced whole through everyday technological endeavors. It further demands that we situate technical agents and their intersubjective relationships at the heart of their technologies, not outside them. This, then, is *a relational and phenomenological view of technology*; it interweaves people, their relationships, productive activities, meaning, and the material world into a single, indivisible whole. I take inspiration for this synoptic view, that technological practice is at one and the same time personal, social, material, meaningful, sensual, performative, practical, and political, from that body of contemporary social theory known as practice or agency theory.[3]

Much has been written on the topic of agency in archaeology in the past few years, and more is written every day.[4] However, with the advent of more subject-centered inquiry commencing in the mid-1980s, "peopling the past" has come to mean significantly different things, depending in large measure on the theoretical persuasions of the analyst and the epistemological limits that different perspectives suggest. This chapter is not the place to revisit the general history of agency in archaeology (see Dobres and Robb in press-b; Dobres and Hoffman 1994; Johnson 1989; Saitta 1994), nor is it necessary to tease apart subtle distinctions between and among these variously defined interests in prehistoric subjects. Rather, I here concentrate only on those aspects of agency theory I find useful and relevant to the question of (prehistoric) technology.

Agency and agents, structuration and structures

People and social collectives are the active agents of prehistory: not stone tools, pots, nor artifact physics; not the environment, efficiency, nor biological capacity; not rationality, functional need, nor practical reason. People and social collectives are also the active agents of their technologies. In concert with my view that people do not "possess" technology but enact it through knowledgeable practices, so too agents enact, but do not necessarily "possess," agency (Sztompka 1991: 99). In both cases, technology and agency, the focus is on dynamic, inter-subjective (intangible) relationships and practices, not just their material (measurable) outcomes. The question of agency in technology demands explicit concern with the social and meaningful "becoming" of artifacts through materially grounded activities conducted by technical agents and mindful communities of practice, rather than the more narrow and linear "biography" of material things and their subsequent use by people. Gosden (1994: 82, after Heidegger 1977) uses the term "mutuality" to emphasize the simultaneous becoming of agents and their artifacts.

To comprehend the relationship between agency and technology, as ongoing and dynamic processes not reducible to physical actions and outcomes, it is necessary to differentiate conceptually between the terms "agency," "agents," "structuration," and "structures," as they are not as self-evident as they seem (Dobres and Robb in press-b).[5] In keeping with my view of technology, I use the terms "agency" and "structuration" to highlight the dynamic unfolding *processes* by which people construct and express personhood, participate in social collectivities of various sorts, and through such means materially shape their lives. And as with "technology," "agency" and "structuration" are best thought of as verbs of engagement and interaction, such that individuals, work groups, and societies work through the ongoing process of "becoming" during their engagement with the conditions and structures framing them (Kegan Gardiner 1995; Giddens 1979: 55). As Rybicki (cited in Sztompka 1991: v) puts it: "society is never given in ready-made shape, but is permanently in the process of becoming." The same is true of agents.

This fluid and unfolding view of society and subjects forever "in the making" but never fully made is intended to counter the static and top-down concept of social structures and institutions (over)determining the actions of people, such that each "type" of social formation is differentiated from the others by its institutional structure (Ortner

1984: 146; Tilley 1982).[6] Instead, structuration is the ongoing production, maintenance, and transformation of societal institutions as well as the material, social, and symbolic conditions within which people exist and through which they reproduce and transform themselves. Sztompka (1991, 1994a) has given this forever unfinished project the acronym TSB, or *theory of social becoming*.

Central to this view of society are agents: people and social relationships of various sorts whose intersubjective practices and forms of engagement serve as the motor that keeps things in check, moving, and/or changing. Structuration thus depends on the agency of people, but in turn provides the structures within which agents exist. Rather than think of agents and structures as unequal opposites, where structures (particularly material conditions) impinge *on* people, and people in turn adapt *to* them, agency and structuration are interdigitating dynamics that constitute the "two-sided world" of social life (Abrams 1982: 2). In agency theory, then, societal institutions become structures through the agency of individuals and collectivities, at the same time that agents are structured by and exist within them (also Childe 1936; Marx 1963 [orig. 1869]; discussion in Gosden 1994). Another way to think of this is that people constitute their social collectives, yet the collective exists beyond the particular constitution or actions of any particular group of people.

On the other hand, agents and structures are the entities through and within which these processes unfold. Importantly, "agent" is a comprehensive term and includes "not only individuals but also concrete, bounded collectivities, groups, social movements etc." (Sztompka 1991: 99; 1994b; Sewell 1992: 21; Touraine 1984). As a term, then, "agent" is *not* synonymous with the individual (Kegan Gardiner 1995). For example, a community of practice (whether it be a hunting party, a group of technical laborers, or a network of design engineers) is as much "an agent" as each individual within that group (Aronson in press; Wenger 1998). At once, we can see that issues of scale are inherently important to questions of agency. Similarly, structures encompass many things, but specifically the conditions, contexts, rules, and resources (human and non-human) with whom individuals and communities engage during the practice of everyday life. Of course, not all structures have a physical dimension such as architecture, food production, or the environment. Indeed, some structures, such as ideology, politics, and symbols, have no corporeality, yet they shape, constrain, enable, and serve as the resources upon which people's actions and experiences are based.[7] What is important here is that both tangible and intangible structures are *perceived* and *experienced*, and through such means serve as the fluid parameters within which agents practice the everyday business of being-in-the-world.

If one recalls at this point the admittedly vague and purposefully broad definition of technology advanced in chapter 4, where material, social, and symbolic facets are woven into an inseparable whole affirmed in practice, then it is no easy matter to decide if technology is a tangible or intangible structure, a social or material practice, the outcome of agency, or a structure within which agency is enacted, a component of the unfolding structuration process or a fixed entity resulting from it! If this discussion has made the concept of technology a little less clear cut, and in so doing a little more seamlessly interwoven with social dynamics both macro and micro, then the reader can begin to see the value of raising the question of agency in the course of reconsidering technologies past and present.

As Giddens and Sztompka (cited above) argue, to conceptualize agency and structure (as well as agents and society) as oppositional and fixed entities, where at any given moment one more or less determines the others, is to create a false and modular distinction that hinders the possibility of understanding their interdependency (also Archer 1988). This is exactly the argument I am making about technology. To consider the inseparability of structure and agency as a "living socio-individual field in the process of becoming" (Sztompka 1991: 95) is to grapple with the complicated, indeed messy, process of culture in its overlapping material, social, and symbolic dimensions. Society, and hence structure, is an achieved strategy rather than a preexisting entity (J. Chapman in press; Chase 1989; Gosden 1994). At the risk of oversimplifying the above, however, there is another, albeit less nuanced way to think about this interplay: as agents move in and through the institutional structures that give material and meaningful shape to their lives and activities, they in turn give meaning to and transform those contexts and conditions. In this way, the recursive relationship between agents and structures becomes the unfolding (structuration) process that "makes" society. One might even say that structures exist only by virtue of the "argument" that unfolds between structures and agents during everyday practice (after Ledermann 1990).

Context and structuration

Importantly, for both individual and collective agents it is not so much their role or the rules and expectations that others have of them that counts in this dialectic; it is their *performance* that matters (Kopytoff 1990). One's place in the social collective does not determine how or even if one will act – only how one ought to act. Whether pro-active, as a form of resistance, a compromise for the "greater good," as complacent or willing acceptance, or as something else altogether, agency is contingent on context and not just proscriptions, rules, expectations, and structures (Scott 1990: 851). This, in turn, makes prediction rather more difficult. Rules may be the sum of generalized procedures drawn upon in everyday social reproduction, but *"there is no guarantee that agents will reproduce regularities as they previously have done* . . . agents may make mistakes . . . [and] actors who retain the competence and capacity to reproduce routine practices may refrain from doing so" (I. Cohen 1987: 300, author's emphasis).

It is also no sure bet that agents will act just because they can or should. In other words, *not* acting is still a form of agency (Kegan Gardiner 1995) – and context is the only means by which to understand these nuanced qualities of agency (see below). What this means for technology studies in particular, but archaeology more generally, is a new and different interest in the question of material patterns of variability juxtaposed against norms (Wobst 1997; see chapter 6 for a discussion of some of these implications).

Especially in technical matters, there is always more than one way to get a job done. Why technicians work their material resources in some ways and not others, therefore, becomes an important question. For Halperin (1994: 26), this means asking: "what kinds of structures are defining and driving what kinds of agents?" I would invert this question, however, and also ask: "what kinds of agents are defining and driving what kinds of structures?" If agents and structures are caught in mutually defining webs that constitute a two-sided world, then the particularly constituted material and social contexts in which these dynamics play out requires elucidation (I. Cohen 1987; Garfinkel 1984; Heritage 1987: 236). In sum, "the contexts within which people work are both complex and fluid. People move in and out of different structures in simultaneous and, often, overlapping patterns. The structures are critical however; without understanding these structures, a great deal of behavior can easily be misinterpreted" (Halperin 1994: 31). While the "fluidity of contexts" in which prehistoric agency was enacted is not something archaeologists have considered in those terms, research working to identify the social and material contexts of ancient lifeways is one of the several important contributions of both the processual and behavioral paradigms (notably, Schiffer 1972; also Hodder 1987a).

Of course, we do not all agree on what constitutes the relevant context(s) explaining artifact patterning, the ancient activities we infer from them, nor the causes of culture change. Some take macro-scale evolutionary history as the context structuring ancient behaviors, such as cognitive evolution and the evolution of symbolic behavior (for example, Mithen 1990, 1996); others see the environment and the availability of material resources as the informing/causal context (Jochim 1983; Winterhalder and Smith 1981). Still others, such as myself, prefer to think more intersubjectively, and consider locale-specific group

interaction as the context germane to understanding ancient technological practice and performance. Researchers, of course, work at a
variety of phenomenological and temporal scales situated between these
extremes. What we probably all agree on, however, is that context
(however defined) is a major piece in the explanatory puzzle, though
likely not a Rosetta Stone for deciphering the agency expressed therein
(Dietler and Herbich 1998: 234).

Through their socially constituted material actions, beliefs, and
interactions, then, individuals and communities enact agency. In so
doing, they promote agentive interests and through these means create
and transform themselves, their material conditions, and society at
large. This argument is particularly important for archaeologists, for
it suggests that to understand and explain the ebb and flow of cultures
over the *longue durée* we must pay attention to the *everyday* sorts of experiences, activities, meanings, and social interactions through which
change unfolded (Byers 1991; Chase 1989; Edmonds 1990: 58; Gosden
1994; Hodder in press). Practice and agency (though I am here specifically concerned with technological practice and the agency of technicians) exist at the intersection of a "two-sided world," itself constructed
out of the interplay of structure and action, of macro-scale and micro-
scale phenomena, over short and long expanses of time, and between
individuals and collectives (Archer 1988: xii–xxii; 1995; Sewell 1992;
Sztompka 1991: 91–9).

Simply put, then, agency is the arena in which the "riddle of social
becoming must be traced" (Sztompka 1991: 91). What is necessary and
helpful for archaeologists is that agency has material dimensions,
though as I argued above it is not reducible to them alone. As Gosden
(1994: 137) insightfully notes, "longer sweeps of recursiveness are
solidly material, as it is the enduring nature of material culture that
makes possible life on a scale greater than that of the individual."
Gosden makes clear, however, that these scales and phenomena are
not separate, but "interpenetrate" each other (for concrete examples
demonstrating and elaborating this point, see Barrett 1994, in press).
As with all archaeology, the inferential trick is in moving from a study
of these traces of technical practice differentially preserved in the
ground to an understanding of the agency of the prehistoric agents
involved, an issue I take up in chapter 6.

Habitus, *routines, and the everyday: the paradox of tradition and differentiation*

The subjective and experiential knowledge and awareness that derive
from material encounters with the world serve as personal and cultural

epistemologies for knowing the way the world works, the way the world should be worked, and the place of the self and the group within it (especially Csordas 1994b; Keightly 1987; C. M. Keller and J. D. Keller 1996; Lechtman 1977, 1984a; Lemonnier 1986, 1993b). In stressing this reflexivity, or "practical consciousness," however, Giddens (1979: 255) is quick to point out that such comprehension is but partial, only occasionally discursive, and most often "occluded" (Giddens 1984: xxx). In other words, while technicians are know-ledgeable and reflexive in creating and applying technoscientific knowledge to their routine technical activities, they are not omniscient masters and mistresses of the world; they do not have the "free will" to knowingly act as they choose; they do not always act according to plan; nor are agents necessarily correct in comprehending the world around them and understanding how best to act in it. In turn, these less-than-perfect and tacit understandings set the stage for a host of unintended consequences, many of which are beyond people's compre-hension or control. Thus, while agency is a form of involvement in the world (Gosden 1994: 86) expressed through material practices under-taken by collectivities of mindful and knowledgeable agents, not all of them possess the same skills, competence, stocks of knowledge, goals, control, awareness, or foresight about what they are doing (on the lack of omniscience and foresight, see Pauketat in press).

Thus, for all the reflexivity of the agent, there is a remarkable paradox in the way people go about their everyday lives, and it is called *habitus* (Bourdieu 1977). Everyday conventions embodied in normative techni-cal comportment dispose people to act in similarly routinized ways (something even Heidegger understood, see chapter 3). The "homo-geneity of *habitus*" (ibid.: 80) explains how normative and seemingly rule-bound aspects of everyday culture play out through "persistently-repeated forms of conduct" (I. Cohen 1987: 295). Importantly, the human body is the "nexus" of *habitus* (Gosden 1994: 119), because it serves as both source and medium for expressing (and contesting) every-day routines of social and physical action. Together, overlapping prac-tical, social, and esoteric knowledge and manual skills sharpened through the body's experience with things-in-themselves serve as every-day but largely non-discursive reminders that routinized habits "work" and one can trust them. Without question, the numerous studies dis-cussed in the previous chapter show that it is precisely because *habitus* underlies collective technological practice that habituated dispositions play such an essential role in materializing and reaffirming social repre-sentations of the world (Gosselain 1998; Goucher and Herbert 1996; Herbert 1993; Ingold 1993a, 1993b; Lemonnier 1986, 1989a; M. A. MacKenzie 1991). As a result, *habitus* has two important but unrelated effects. First, as the "unconscious harmonization of social life [that becomes one's] second nature" (Gosden 1994: 119), *habitus* gives agents "trust in the fabric of social activities and the object world that comprise the course and circumstances of their daily lives" (I. Cohen 1987: 302). At the same time, *habitus* helps explain why the material traces of archaeological cultures betray discernible, "traditional," isochrestic patterning.

Another point to make about *habitus* that is especially relevant for understanding technology is that "the production of social life is a skilled performance" (I. Cohen 1987: 286; also Ingold 1993c). This means that technical gestures, skill, competence, and knowledge which technicians bring to their work are "performed" in the context of traditions, normative values, and consensual expectations about how one should proceed. Thus, at the same time that practical consciousness guides agentive bodies during everyday technical routines, *habitus* compels them toward sameness. All the same, "when society is mainly analyzed in terms of values and [routinized] patterns of behavior, the impact of cultural elements is inevitably overestimated to the detriment of [an] interpretation of actual social relationships" (Crespi 1994: 126). In other words, while technological practices are widely shared and a primarily taken-for-granted part of people's daily routines, it does not follow that the intersubjective relationships upon which they rest are not important in their own right. Skilled technological performance also means that agents act with different levels of competence, knowledge, skill, and intention that, while meaningful, are tacit rather than fully discursive.

By "performance," however, I do not want to suggest that technicians are consciously "play acting" just to make an (aggrandizing) impression on their neighbors, though this is often what people mean when using the term "agency" (see critique in J. E. Clark in press). Rather, I intend the term "performance" to mean acting while interacting and experiencing the world. This sense of "performance," as unfolding in the moment of some intersubjective activity, is different from the way stage performers skillfully (and after much rehearsal) put into motion other people's agendas (namely, the author's and director's) in order to motivate an audience (which is intentionally watching them) to think and feel in certain ways. Technological performance, while it can surely lead observers to "peg" a technician in terms of their skill, competence, and so forth, is *more* than play acting (I return to this point below).

In sum, then, the kind of being-in-the-world awareness, reflexivity, and knowledge that is learned and mediated through a technician's corporeal engagement with material things in social settings is what makes mundane technical activities relevant to, and indeed the shaper of, larger cultural phenomena (Gosselain 1998 is but one case in point).

Both personhood and society come into being during the micro-politics of everyday life necessarily played out on and through the socially constituted bodies of agents undertaking mundane activities that express, advance, or hinder power and other interests (Foucault 1977; Lee Bartky 1995; Sawicki 1991). Among the many implications *habitus* has for the study of social life past or present, then, is the realization that routines (and their variations) are not meaningless and idiosyncratic noise filling up the black box of institutions and structures. Rather, the conventions tacitly and routinely performed in the everyday world of social tradition, and the variable expressions of agency enacted during them, are the "stuff" of wholesale cultural phenomena (Mauss 1935) as well as culture change (Boyd and Richerson 1985: 290; Chase 1989; Gosden 1994; Mithen 1990; Sassaman in press; Silverblatt 1988).

Practice theory takes culturally defined "stocks of knowledge" to be an important, albeit intangible, resource both for promoting agentive interests and for defining the parameters of appropriate social and material conduct. This emphasis on the role of agency in producing and acting out personal and culturally esteemed knowledge makes it necessary to understand how knowledge is articulated, codified, and displayed in taken-for-granted routines of everyday material production. Thus, it is especially through the unfolding and everyday *habitus* of artifact making and using for functional (and other) ends that technical activities become important means for expressing and materializing larger cultural epistemologies, ontologies, identities, and differences. The several case studies discussed in the previous chapter all allude to this process, even if they do not explain it as a consequence of *habitus*.

However, in spite of the basic security system provided by *habitus*, it does not follow that technicians and interactive communities of practice always work in harmony. As Dietler and Herbich (1998: 247) explain it:

> Rather than seeing practice as predetermined by a static set of cultural concepts or structures (e.g., some form of rigid mental template), the *habitus* is a dynamic relational phenomenon which is both an historical product and agent. This is because, as a set of learned dispositions that allow the solution of daily technical and social problems through a process of structured analogical reasoning, the solutions to these problems influence the development of dispositions. A certain *latitude in action* is thus possible as people respond to practical demands. (my emphasis)

That "latitude in action," in part, relates to differently situated and differently skilled cultural agents within a community, technically or otherwise engaged. Differences in experience, skill, knowledge, and one's awareness of being-in-the-world, as well as differences in explicitly articulated goals and how they should be accomplished, all become resources through which political interests materialize (for example, see Conkey 1991; Dobres 1995a, 1999b). And it is on this point that the harmony of *habitus* imperceptibly mixes with the agency of contestation and negotiation. Among the practically unlimited political interests one could mention, personhood is especially salient. For example, as Ingold (1993a: 438) convincingly argues, "techniques are active ingredients of personal and social identity . . . [and] the very practice of a technique is itself a statement about identity." Material resources also provide capital for advancing such interests, but it is worth reiterating that the material world provides the experiential basis that makes us who we are (Csikszentmihalyi and Rochberg-Halton 1981: 16; Csordas 1994b; C. M. Keller and J. D. Keller 1996).

My emphasis on the agent's sensual experience of being-in-the-(material)-world suggests, among other things, that no matter how "traditional" or conservative the rules of the community, and no matter how much *habitus* underlies conformity, not everyone shares the same experiences any more than they enjoy the same stocks of knowledge, skill, predilections, and attitudes about how best to proceed under the conditions in which they find themselves (an excellent example can be found in Pálsson and Helgason 1999). Less-than-uniform perceptions about what to do, when, where, and how, stemming from differently situated experiences, may also lead agents to perceive their conditions differently, leading to yet further differences in practice (Hartsock 1983; Longino 1993). As I elaborate in the following chapter, "situational novelty" (I. Cohen 1987: 291) and contingent possibilities, then, coupled with "the polymorphic diversity of human practices" (ibid.: 288), suggest the need for explicit attention not just to the average, but to more nuanced understandings of the subtle variability of ancient technological practices (Dobres in press-b). As well,

> the capacity to become an agent is potentially available to all people, but . . . such capacities are shaped in interpersonal and discursive fields or power that may inhibit or enable them. Each person's potential for activity will also be shaped throughout their life as behaviors are repressed, rewarded, learned, and transformed in the practice of organizations and institutions from the family to the state. (Kegan Gardiner 1995: 13)

Social relationships necessarily involve affiliation and differentiation. Who is interacting with whom, during what sorts of activities, in what sorts of materially grounded contexts of time and space; all these factors impinge on explaining why technical agents acted as they did in the past. As I argued in the previous chapter, recognizing that technological world views necessarily implicate social values and turn on culturally valued knowledge (practical or otherwise) compels one to ask: *whose* values and judgments are codified in technology? *At whom* are they directed? And, what other systems of value are implicated? The agency view of technology and decision making I am developing here, which is necessarily undertaken in socially circumscribed situations fraught with imprecision, contingency, and social negotiation, is substantively different from the premises and explanations of human behavior deriving from cultural materialism, culture ecology, optimal foraging theory, behavioralism, and evolutionary ecology (Dobres and Hoffman 1994: 223–4; compare, for example, to Bleed 1986; Hayden 1998; Mithen 1990; Nelson 1991; Schiffer 1992c; Shott 1986; Torrence 1986). It suggests, among other things, that even in the most cohesive of communities, where that homogeneity of *habitus* is said to be most pronounced (such as egalitarian hunter-gatherers), everyone will *not* necessarily and always agree on what must be done nor how to proceed (Conkey 1991; Dobres 1999b; Dobres and Hoffman 1994: 223–4; Keene 1991; Lee 1982). Life is a terrain full of ambiguity, ambivalence, and contestation; technology is both an arena where they come to the fore and an intersubjective site where they can be negotiated and worked through.

Thus, rather than privilege *either* institutional solidarity (Durkheim and Parson's "structure") *or* the methodological individualism of the all-knowing aggrandizer (Weber's "agent"), at stake in understanding the contours of technology as a form of intersubjective social practice are the cross-cutting axes of structure and agency caught, paradoxically, in an unending dialectic involving the persistence of tradition and processes of social differentiation (Sztompka 1994b: 30–5).

"Finding" agents in the archaeological record: agency is not physical traces of action

In studying past agency through the medium of material patterns, we must be careful, of course, not to conflate the process with the vestiges of ancient physical actions, be they use-wear stigmata, stylistic attributes, or spatial distribution patterns. As archaeology has come to recognize over the past thirty years, differentially preserved physical traces of prehistoric activities do not represent the intangible dynamics enacted while agents were taking care of business. The fear that one cannot "do" agency in archaeology unless one can securely delimit the physical traces of "real" prehistoric agents and track their actions materially, confuses the material remains of ancient activities with the human drama of the agency/structuration dialectic. Indeed, neither the processual, behavioral, nor post-processual position advocates delineating identity for its own sake. For example, informed by the epistemological and methodological principles of the processual paradigm, but without the benefit of contemporary agency theory, Redman (1977) championed an interest in studying what he called the "analytical individual" in prehistory. He was careful to warn, however, that "a preoccupation with identifying individuals will lead to debates over the validity of identification, displacing our primary concern – for the processes to be explicated with this information" (ibid.: 42). And contrary to popular opinion, there is nothing in the conceptual framework of agency theory that requires the identification of specific individuals, or necessitates explanations in terms of conscious and rational attempts at self-promotion (which is why the tenets of agency theory are not as self-evident as many believe).

Agency is an intersubjective quality and unfolding process of knowing, acting, and being-in-the-world. While often played out through material means, agency cannot be reduced to the physical consequences of its enactment (Barrett in press). Another way to say this is that while one can identify physical traces of ancient actions and activities in material remains, *one cannot excavate agency*.[8] Rather, and as has long been a centerpiece of the processual and behavioral paradigms, the static material remains of the archaeological record are the archaeologist's link for inferring the dynamic social processes accounting for them. The important distinction between agency and physical action means that, while material traces of past processes are not reflections of those processes, they can serve as material data with which to infer what those dynamics might have been (Dobres 1999b; chapter 6 considers the methodological implications of this argument).

As I have argued elsewhere in considering the goals of gender research in archaeology (Dobres 1995a: 42–3, 1995e: 53–4), attributing some identity to a past social dynamic (whatever kind of personhood is inferred) is not necessarily going to help us understand *how* such practices were part of social tradition, affiliation, and differentiation. To engender the past does not necessarily require knowledge of the names and addresses of those involved. It *does* require that we identify the contexts, structures, and intersubjective dynamics through which gendered agents (whether individual and collective) expressed themselves, consciously or otherwise. Thus neither the theoretical framework of agency, nor our desire to comprehend the dynamics of structuration in prehistory, are limited by matters of material fact (after Wylie 1989).

What limits reasonable attempts to infer the intangible dynamics of agency and structuration through the study of archaeological data are two-fold: first, unwillingness to accept that agency is an important cultural process worth studying; and second, the lack of a conceptual framework for understanding such dynamics across space and through time (Wylie 1986, 1989). Nor is this issue new to archaeology; both the processual and behavioral paradigms correctly argued that knowledge about the past was not limited to the material nature of archaeological patterning, but that conceptual, explanatory, and anthropological frameworks could and should be developed to make the intangible processes of the past comprehensible in the present (especially Binford 1968b; Schiffer 1975a, 1976).

Of course, archaeologists are not limited to mere speculation or best guesses in all of this. The use of multiple lines of evidence has long been employed to determine material and social contexts, delimit the numbers of people involved and the nature of their social interaction, identify their material activities, and so forth, and this is nothing less than the everyday craft of archaeology (Shanks and McGuire 1996). As I show by example in the next chapter, it is through detailed under-standing of these contexts that we can begin to nuance questions about agency. But, though we may not be able to specify with certainty who made and used what, it does not follow that we cannot theorize about the agency *process*. As we must not surrender to the fallacy of misplaced concreteness and mistake the materiality of physical actions for the agency producing them, neither should we succumb to the epistemo-logical quandaries raised by attempts to attribute specific agents to artifacts and technical strategies.

On the other hand, where the identification of agents and their moti-vations is possible (and this is always more likely in historic periods), the detail with which we can explicate past technical agency will, of course, improve. But just because in some instances we may be able to name names, this does not guarantee an adequate understanding of the agency involved. For even where we can know intimate details about who such agents were and the specifics of their individual life-histories, the contexts and conditions informing their actions, and even their explicit agendas – even in these rare cases we must still be explicit in using the principles of agency theory. Knowing who did, or made, or used what, without applying the concepts of agency, *habitus*, and structuration, does not insure an anthropological understanding of technology or any past human dynamic.

Agency, then, is only partly what agents do when they undertake all manner of physical and social activities. Activities are perhaps best understood as the overlapping social and material *arenas* within which agency and structuration play out. Or, as Sztompka (1991:

96–7) suggests, agency is "where structures (capacities for operation) and agents (capacities for action) meet, a synthetic product, a fusion of structural circumstances and agential endowment." Key here is the idea that *agency is actualized in practice*, but not reducible to physical action and activities. And this is why the study of activities is not the study of agency (see below). To anticipate any misreading on this crucial point, calls for a "middle-range theory of agency" or similar research agenda seeking to catalogue the material correlates of certain "kinds" of agency (defined as different types of activities and behaviors) completely miss the point of what agency is all about and how the material world is implicated and drawn into this drama (see also chapter 7). Concern needs to center on the intangible and intersubjective dynamics instantiated by different sorts of agents interacting with each other and the material world.

Scale

Conceptual, phenomenological, interpretive scales

At this point, a few explicit remarks on scale are in order. To think that one is "doing agency" only when one offers an explanation of culture change that turns on the self-aggrandizing actions of individual agents, "big men," or elites is to miss the subtlety of agency and structuration. Agency is a far more complicated and nuanced process: it can play out at the micro-scale (for example, at the phenomenological scale of face-to-face interaction), or the macro-scale (for instance, the agency of collectives "evolving" ranked forms of sociopolitical organization; excellent examples here include Joyce in press; Pauketat in press). Agency can unfold at scales anywhere along that continuum, or at multiple scales simultaneously. Agency is a multiscalar dynamic, and archaeologists can choose to focus attention on whatever phenomenological scales they think are relevant to their particular research question and to the specifics of the case they are studying. Importantly, concern with these issues must necessarily be raised before the recovery and analysis of archaeological data, not after.

The phenomenological scale(s) at which we theorize that agency "happened" in the past are not epistemological problems, limitations, or constraints inherent in the material nature of the archaeological record (after Wylie 1989). Improperly conflating phenomenological and interpretive/explanatory scales with material and analytic ones is what leads researchers to ask erroneous questions about agency, such as: "How can I find traces I can be sure reflect agency and not some other behavior?" "What if I can't specify who was involved?" "How can I explain the personal motivations of prehistoric agents if there is nothing that unequivocally reflects their beliefs?" Since agency is not necessarily synonymous with "the individual" it is not necessary to attribute a specific identity to the agent(s) in question. Agency can be a collective social movement. Thus, at a *phenomenological* scale, attempts to interpret past agency need not devolve into identifications of "real" past agents nor the individualized psychological and political motivations for their actions (for a counter-argument, see Cowgill in press). What is at issue are the multilayered human scales at which agency played out, the nature of those intersubjective processes, and how material culture was implicated.

Material and analytic scales

It is important not to conflate the conceptual and phenomenological scales at which agency plays out with the material and analytic scales of archaeological research. Analytic scales are heuristics that arbitrarily divide up the phenomenological continuum of social existence for the purpose of study. Thus, just as it is misguided to suggest that gender is merely an interpersonal household dynamic having little to do with class, power, or the state (a position thoroughly debunked in Costin 1991, 1996; Hastorf 1991; Silverblatt 1988), it would also be a mistake to think that agency resides or is expressed only in the physical actions of individual hands and that this phenomenological scale correlates with the most minute and discrete technical attributes on single artifacts. There is no one-to-one correspondence between a particular analytic or physical scale of materials research and a particular anthropological dynamic, agency or otherwise.

For example, intrahousehold spatial patterns and microscopic traces of artifact manufacture are studied in order to theorize the evolution of craft specialization and the state; detailed micro-wear research provides information on the course of cognitive evolution; macro-scale regional patterns of faunal exploitation are employed so as to contrast the everyday foodways of Neandertals and anatomically modern humans. Shall we only find the analytical individual in the most minute attributes related to the fabrication of a single ceramic pot? Or, do not empirical attributes of individually worked artifacts also speak to enduring traditions of form, technique, and design shared by whole "culture complexes"? Inversely, cannot the macro-morphological architectural features of household compounds, megaliths and temples, or burial mounds, which were surely built by collective effort, also help us understand how the individual was conceptualized and treated by the community?

The conceptual and interpretive scales at which we theorize about agency, and the phenomenological scales at which agency plays out in the real world, are not synonymous with the material and analytic scales at which archaeologists conduct research. While agency is enacted by individuals, collectives, and even "the state," we may choose to focus our interpretive lens anywhere along that continuum. Similarly, once we define the agency dynamic we wish to investigate, we can choose from a range of material and analytic scales those we think appropriate for that research question, as I show in chapter 6. We can choose to study microscopic use-wear stigmata, or we can compare and contrast interregional patterning of large-scale architectural features; we can span the globe, or focus on a single site; we can study a "moment" in time, or look at the *longue durée*. There is nothing inherent in archaeological data to suggest which material scales are tied to a particular phenomenological scale of agency. The analyst must make these choices based on factors specific to their research question, the nature of their material data, as well as their own predilections, rather than search for invariant correlations between different scales of social phenomena and material attributes (but for just such an attempt, see Carr 1994: 174–5, table 7.1; Carr and Maslowski 1994).

Summary

If we put agency theory into its historical frame, it is worth noting that it derives from Marx's mandate to understand the dialectic of institutional processes and the inner workings of society. Marx's (1963: 15 [orig. 1869]) famous dictum about the relationship between historical contingency, event, and structure in shaping social reproduction contains practically all the essential features of contemporary agency theory: "men make their own history, but they do not make it just as they please, they do not make it under circumstances chosen by themselves, but under circumstances directly encountered, given and transmitted from the past." This statement emphasizes that society is made of a plurality of individuals and collectivities; that sociocultural histories are produced rather than given (implying the processual nature of culture "in the making"); it explicitly denies the methodological individualism and "free will" ideologies popular at the time by arguing that people do not choose the conditions within which they live; and, these conditions have a material basis (further elaboration in Dobres and Robb in press-b). The above quotation also stresses that society derives from antecedent conditions, highlighting time and history as causal factors (Gosden 1994). Practice theory locates the reciprocal causality of agency and structure in time and space because they are both historically and materially constituted (Hodder 1987b). For archaeology, this means that our long-standing interest in how time, place, and material conditions shaped ancient lifeways and their transformations remains central and viable (Gosden 1994). It also means that archaeology has the potential to provide practice theory with more substantive grounding than it currently has, by giving it better material grounding and greater time depth (Dobres and Robb in press-b). Finally, Marx's emphasis on "men" implies an inter-subjective existence rather than a psychological, individualistic, or materialist one.

Marx's other theoretical contribution to understanding society and social change is only hinted at in the above quotation, but it concerns practice (*praxis*). Reminiscent of the philosophical ideas of Dessauer and Heidegger (discussed in chapter 3), *praxis* is a theory about know-ledge that concerns people's practical engagement with their world. In marxist theory, *praxis* emphasizes the process"ing" of practical activity as an unfolding dynamic that links material and sensual activity to thought, meaning, social relations, and structural change (Gosden 1994: 68–73; Kitching 1988: 26–32; R. McGuire 1992; Petrovic 1983c; Tilley 1982).[9] Thus, in his work Marx gave explicit attention to comprehending the dialectic of material conditions, institutions, and *praxis* – or what is in contemporary practice theory called the "duality" of structure and agency.

There is no better summation of the basic principles of agency theory appropriate to the question of prehistoric technology than the six onto-logical positions Sztompka (1991: 24) outlines:

first, that society is a process, undergoing constant change; second, that change is mostly endogenous, taking the form of self-transformation; third, that the ultimate motor of change is the agential power of human individuals or social collectivities; fourth, that the direction, goals and speed of change are contestable among multiple agents, and become an arena of conflict and struggle; fifth, that action occurs in the context of encountered structures, which it shapes in turn, result-ing in the dual quality of structures (as both shaping and shaped), and the dual quality of actors (as both producers and products); and sixth, that the interchange of action and structure occurs in time, by means of alternating phases of agential creativeness and structural determination.

The reason I emphasize the term "practice" as a shorthand for the multifaceted dialectic of agency, agents, structuration, and structures is that, for the question of technology in particular, these dynamics unfold in the course of everyday making and use activities (*sensu praxis*). Technological practice necessarily involves agents and structures, but it turns on agency and the entire structuration processes. For example, in chapter 4 I argued that technologies are meaningful acts of engagement with the world whereby technical strategies and design choices can materialize, reproduce, and transform social values and cultural predilections. I also stressed that the intersubjective, experiential, and embodied nature of technological practice produces self/Other/worldly/practical knowledge, skills, and values that can be put to political ends. The dialectic of agency, agents, structuration, and structures lies at the heart and soul of technology, and practice (especially technological) is an especially salient arena where they come together.

As socially, meaningfully, and materially constituted, then, agents (both individuals and collectives) are the medium through which technological practices materialize and work to maintain the traditional basis of society. Through technological practice, however, agents can challenge and contest cultural paradigms and tradition, and thus create the conditions that lead to change. Whether or not people get along while making and using material culture on a day-to-day basis; whether or not they share the same practical goals; whether or not they agree on the best or right way to do these activities; whether or not they contest who should or should not be involved at any stage in the endeavor; whether they have the same level of competence and skill – these are the very sorts of concerns that practice theory makes central for understanding both the reproduction of social structures and their transformation.

Once we have agents undertaking productive activities in meaningful, socially engaged ways; once we are able to think in terms of technical agency and artifice, rather than artifacts and performance characteristics; once we accept the intertwining of technology and social agency – we cannot help considering not only the normative, uncontested, and shared aspects of technical *habitus* but also its contested, challenged, and negotiated dimensions. I hope that, through this lengthy exploration of the principles and premises of agency theory, it is now a little easier to shift our gaze beyond the materiality of ancient technology and bring into view, at least conceptually, technological practice as the dynamic "becoming" of technicians, mindful communities of practice, and material culture through the sensual, lived, and engaged experience of working with the physical world in socially constituted arenas situated in time and space.

Technical Agency: Intertwining Social and Material Transformations

Embodied experience links habitus *and technique to the social body*

Chapters 3 and 4 stressed the unfolding nature of technology as a web of social, meaningful, and material transformations always in the act of becoming. This metaphor creates an especially dynamic way to think about the interplay of agents situated in fields of preexisting tangible and intangible structures, enacting technical agency while making and using artifacts. At every point in the sequential processing of objects, technical agents (and consumers, of course) learn how to become meaningful social agents, and through such experiences find their place(s) in the social collective (Mauss 1969a [orig. 1927]). These overlapping processes of individuation, personhood, and group affiliation, which continue over the course of one's life, are undertaken within structures and contexts that make up historical cultures. But the point to keep in mind is that this is a dynamic, meaningful, and continually unfolding enterprise. Over the course of their lives and as both individuals and members of the collective body politic, people live through a variety of experiences which transform their very existence, much as artifacts are transformed into cultural meaningful products and tools through their material "life history" (Appadurai 1986; Kopytoff 1986; Schiffer 1975b). Thus, there is a powerful resonance in the mutual becoming of people and products, in the creation of artifacts through human creativity, and in the simultaneous transformation of material resources and resourceful agents. The experiential basis of technical practice and the embodied being-in-the-world that continually unfolds as agents move in and through the social collective is intimately connected to everyday technological practice precisely because it is experienced and made meaningful through the hands, minds, and hearts of real physical bodies.

I stress corporeality here, because productive endeavors are partly meaningful in how people physically experience them (chapters 3 and 4). In concert with the particular social arrangements of artifact production and the "situatedness" of agents within these structures, particular sorts of technologies provide different kinds of experiential grounding for one's being-in-the-world (see especially, Mumford 1934, 1964). In stressing this link between the physicality of technological practice and the technician's body, I am not suggesting there is a universal experience to things-in-themselves that transcends the particularities of cultural context (also Dobres in press-a). Indeed, I am arguing quite the opposite. People give meaning to and take meaning from their material experiences only by virtue of the *specific* contexts in which they are situated; in turn, meaning becomes the basis for producing the stocks of knowledge, skills, and techniques on which technicians rely to make their way in the world (also Gosden 1994: 68–83). As argued by philosophers since the time of Kant, there is no essential meaning nor factual basis of knowledge that derives from the technician's direct and unmediated experience with things in themselves (Gosden 1994; Kaufmann 1974, summarizing Nietzsche); such knowledge only and necessarily derives from embedded and embodied engagement mediated through the lens of culture and traditional systems of meaning. Just as the physical body cannot be severed from the social body, understandings of the (physical) world cannot be separated from the sensual body and mindful practices through which they materialize (Pickering 1995).

For example, not everyone who makes and uses stone tools comprehends the experience in the same way, although those who undertake replicative experiments as a daily part of their research agenda might think otherwise. This is because lithic technology is not simply the manual and sequential modification of an inert mineral (stone) into a cultural artifact. The socially constituted body of a contemporary researcher undertaking lithic replication in the lab or under controlled field conditions is not, and can never be, the same as the prehistoric subject doing the same physical activity. How and why the modern researcher replicates an ancient lithic technique is situated not only within the historical contours of their archaeological inquiry, but also within wider epistemological and ontological contexts. That very situatedness is what allows the modern technician to conduct their research and learn from it, but it informs in ways different from the conditions informing the prehistoric worker. These informing and experiential contexts are an essential part of that technology and cannot be excised from consideration. No matter what archaeologists might say to the contrary, replicating lithic knapping techniques in a lab is *not* replicating a prehistoric lithic technology.

More specifically, technique is more than the suite of bodily gestures and physical actions producing material transformations. Technique is embodied (Mauss 1935) and acts as a platform for creating and expressing identity and differentiation, whether intended or not. As Lave and Wenger (1991: 115–16) argue especially:

> learning and a sense of identity are inseparable: [t]hey are aspects of the same phenomenon. . . . Shared participation is the stage on which the old and the new, the known and the unknown, the established and the hopeful, act out their differences and discover their commonalties,

manifest their fear of one another, and come to terms with their need for one another. . . . Conflict is experienced and worked out through a shared everyday practice in which differing viewpoints and common stakes are in interplay. . . . [I]dentity in relation with practice, and hence knowledge, are never unproblematic. This helps to account for the common observation that knowers come in a range of types, from clones to heretics.

Thus, while the embodied nature of techniques actualized in concrete material contexts of artifact production and use are grounded in the *habitus* and tacit routines of bodily comportment, their very constitution as shared intersubjective endeavors also creates an arena in which, for a number of reasons, people may not see eye to eye. It is for these reasons that the social agency that shrouds technique in meaning also creates the conditions by which technology can become a locus of social contestation and negotiation.

Importantly, a technician's body is not simply a surface (or stage) on which to perform manual skills so they can be "read" by others (*sensu* Ricoeur 1971). Neither is the technician's body an unproblematic and unfeeling vehicle that gets the job done (Gatens 1996). Personhood, in all its multiple layers, is internalized through the experience of technical practice. Thus, the corporeal body of the technical agent is a site, or interface, bringing together heuristic oppositions often incorrectly thought of as in conflict (mind:body; individual:society; self:other; agent:structure; subject:object; representation:reality; and especially *tekhnē:logos*) (Csordas 1994b; Dobres in press-a; Gosden 1994; Schlanger 1998). Our goal must be to theorize about and understand how the hands and body of the technician were, at one and the same time, a "surface" read by others, an entity encased in the *habitus* of the social body, as well as the corporeal medium for actualizing self-knowledge, ego, and agency. As Meskell (1998:159) puts it, though not about technicians in particular, "an embodied body represents, and is, a lived experience where the interplay of irreducible natural, social, cultural, and psychical phenomena are brought to fruition through each individual's resolution of external structures, embodied experience, and choice."[10]

In all of this, the material world that is experienced and made meaningful during people's engagement with it is not some neutral physical structure, or thing-in-itself. Rather, that world is mediated by cultural reason, symbolic sensibilities, and personal and collective history (Berger 1973; Cassirer 1970; Forge 1970; Kant 1996 [orig. 1781 and 1787]; Kemp 1990; Lewis-Williams 1984; Pollock 1987). Put differently, it is not the objective material world *per se* with which technicians engage; rather, that world (real and constraining though it may be) is mediated by value-laden and subjective understandings themselves instantiated through technological practice. This is not to say that there are not physical conditions and constraints that either can or cannot be circumvented by the cleverest of technicians. Rather, it is to suggest that technicians mediate their understanding of these through the lens of cultural reason and through the embodied knowledge and skill that derives from the *habitus* of technological practice (Mauss 1969b [orig. 1934]); for an extended discussion, see Schlanger 1998: 198). Through lived bodily experiences people navigate social conventions about the right and wrong ways to make and use material objects; they navigate the objective conditions (material and historic) which provide still another set of boundary conditions; they navigate their individual and collective ("situated") reflexivity; and they navigate identity, power, and so forth. In so doing, they maintain, reaffirm, and create the room within which to contest and challenge the social order.

Technical gestures: embodied knowledge and agency in practice

To a large extent, then, it is the agent's bodily engagement with the material and social conditions of their productive activities that grounds their talent and stocks of knowledge, just as that body is the basis of self-awareness and the means for establishing oneself within even wider streams of social relations. A key aspect of this physical engagement is *the gesture*. Gestures are not only the corporeal basis of an agent's embodied knowledge; gestures can also can be studied by archaeologists. The technical gestures of artifact production and use leave physical marks on the world, and archaeologists are now expert at identifying, studying, and replicating them with extraordinary precision. But technical gestures, just like techniques more generally, are an embodied, mediated, meaningful, and collective practice, even if done by one pair of hands.

Obviously, gestures are what make material production and artifact use possible: the way the hand and wrist are held firm but angled when shaving wood with a stone implement; how one twists their elbow up and down as they plait straw; the grip with which one holds an electric drill when screwing bolts to the underside of a steel plate; how the body rocks back and forth when rowing; how the neck is held rigid when the head bears a heavy weight. At the same time that gestures are part of the physical body of individual technical agents, however, they are also part of the body politic. If the corporeal body of the technical agent is the interface between internalized and externalized realities interpreted through practice, then the technical gestures practiced

by that corporeal body are also internalized (as experientially meaningful) as they are simultaneously witnessed (and interpreted) by
others. Understood this way, technical gestures, or what Mauss called
les techniques du corps, becomes yet another site, or interface, between
the materiality of technology, social agency, tradition, and large-scale
processes.

Chaîne opératoire: *a conceptual framework for the study of technical agency*

While Marcel Mauss is best known for his remarkable work on the
symbolic paradox of "giving while receiving" (Mauss 1924), his *Techniques du corps* (1935) has been recently rediscovered by those interested
in both contemporary and ancient technologies (cf. James and Allen
1998). As an ethnologist and sociologist trained by Durkheim, Mauss
saw technology as a "total social fact," and focused his attention
on understanding how bodily comportment reflects and is conditioned
by social tradition. With explicit use of the term *habitus* (in the sense
outlined above), Mauss demonstrated that the widely shared and
tradition-bound nature of technical routines and customs expressed
in "attitudes of the body" play a significant role in reaffirming the solidarity (and conservatism) of social traditions (also Lemonnier 1986).
He argued, insightfully, that the recursive relationship between the
corporeal body of individuals and the body politic unfolds during the
sequential processing and use of the material world as "traditionally
efficacious actions" (*actes traditionnels efficaces*).

In exploring this link between the corporeal and social body, Mauss
argued that even the most seemingly natural bodily actions are, in fact,
learned rather than strictly biological (also see Gatens 1996; Ingold
1995; for an excellent discussion of these several points in Mauss' work,
see Schlanger 1998). He showed that the simplest of physical activities
such as walking and running (even spitting) are choices made from
alternatives that in their very enactment, and whether intended or not,
express ethnic (or national), gender, age, and personal identities.
Importantly, these fundamental skills and the cultural attitudes they
reflect are taught: through explicit observation, unconscious mimick-
ing, subtle correction, outright manipulation, trial and error, and
above all, practice, practice, practice (Lave and Wenger 1991). For
example, Mauss compared the French person's "knock-kneed" gait to
the swinging and "ungainly" hips of Maori women, the walk of a girl
raised in a convent, and the different strides of British and French sol-
diers; he contrasted as socially conditioned the different planes along

which women and men throw objects; he noted that techniques for squatting on one's haunches is a world-wide phenomenon (except among westerners); and he even suggested that positions of sexual intercourse were also learned choices from among alternatives, full of meaning, and not as natural as they might seem.

Mauss' argument in all of this was that everyday sequential acts of bodily comportment, or what he called *enchaînements organiques*, are bound by, at the same time they give expression to, collective attitudes about the right and wrong ways to do things. Their daily repetition in unwavering sequences serves to keep members of the community "in check" in the most innocuous and non-discursive ways (see also chapter 7).[11] On the other hand, practice theory suggests that the "homogeneity of *habitus*" characterizing the normative basis of everyday technical gestures also involves a fair degree of conflict, mediation, and negotiation of different interests, situated reflexivity, skills, knowledge, and talents (Dobres and Hoffman 1994, 1999a). Thus, while Mauss stressed solidarity in trying to understand the socialization of the corporeal body, when it comes to the topic of technology and social agency, this normative emphasis must be balanced by a concern with difference and differentiation.

It was in the context of this interest in the sequential nature of bodily comportment, experienced as one goes about daily repetitive technological activities, that the term *chaîne opératoire* came into use, most prominently in the work of André Leroi-Gourhan (1943, 1945, 1964a, 1964b; discussion in Desrosiers 1991; Edmonds 1990; Lemonnier 1992b; Schlanger 1994). Unfortunately in recent years, *chaîne opératoire* has come to be more narrowly defined than its Maussian legacy warrants (Dobres 1999b). The bulk of the contemporary technology literature alluding to this term, especially in archaeological and ethnoarchaeological research, makes it practically synonymous with the American concept of artifact "life history" (as independently developed by Schiffer 1975b; Bleed 1991, n.d.; neither of which should be confused with artifact life-histories as described by Appadurai 1986; Kopytoff 1986). *Chaîne opératoire* is today most often defined as the technical chain of sequential material operations by which natural resources are acquired and physically transformed into cultural commodities (e.g., Cresswell 1983; Delaporte 1991; Sellett 1993).[12] As such, and as I elaborate in the following chapter, *chaîne opératoire* is an especially useful analytic methodology and research strategy for delimiting the material contours of ancient technologies and decision-making strategies, sequences, and practices (Pelegrin et al. 1988).

However, as the study of ancient materials processing has developed a rigorous scientific basis and analytic program, the "poetics" of technological practice, the sociality of bodily comportment, and the symbolic and political underpinnings of decision making have all but dropped from sight (Gosden 1994: 109; Heidegger 1977; Ridington 1982, 1999; as shown in chapters 1–3). Similarly, the current emphasis in *chaîne opératoire* research, on the material transformation of natural resources into cultural products through sequential physical actions, misses the "total social fact" that underwrites it. What is required if the term *chaîne opératoire* is to be of anthropological use in research on ancient technologies is the "re-insertion" of artifice, meaning, and sociality into descriptions of physical sequences of material transformations. It is for these reasons that before turning to the analytic methodology of *chaîne opératoire* research (chapter 6) it is first necessary to establish the appropriate *conceptual framework*, grounded in Mauss' total social fact but enlivened with a healthy dose of contemporary practice theory.

Agency and the "unfolding" of technique: technology by any other name

Strikingly similar to Heidegger's philosophical stance on being-in-the-world as knowledgeable awareness of self and Other instantiated through technological practice, Mauss argued that much of the cultural significance of objects and those who make and use them lies in the way technical acts and gestures materially "unfold" in a social milieu. Recognizing that the *enchaînement organique* of artifact production and use is processual establishes a powerful phenomenological link between the becoming of artifacts and the becoming of technical agents (Dobres 1999b). It is in this simultaneous processing of subjects, objects, agents, and artifacts that embodiment and experience make their mark.

The conceptual framework of *chaîne opératoire* is well suited to linking the tangible and intangible aspects of ancient embodied technological practice into a single whole for two reasons in particular. First, the conceptual framework of *chaîne opératoire* recognizes that technical gestures are performed in "public" domains. One of the critical factors that structures the ongoing dynamics of embodied technological practice is the fact that technicians engage in artifact production and use in socially constituted and materially grounded contexts, not in the abstract. Just as the corporeal body of individual technicians is part of the social body, so too, the technical activities of individuals typically take place in group settings, though these clearly vary across the social and physical landscape. Who is working alongside whom, what specific activities are going on, and where these activities are undertaken *vis-à-vis* others are among the proximate parameters within which individual and group knowledge, skill, and agency take shape. As I discuss more fully in the next chapter, much of this structuring context can be delineated through traditional archaeological research, and from these data the less tangible aspects of agency can be reasonably inferred. In principle, then, we can establish inferential links between the specifically delineated material sequences of prehistoric gestural acts of artifact production and use and the social arenas in which they unfolded (Dobres 1995a). As I try to show in chapter 6, it is on this point of delineating in as much detail as possible the (original) structuring context of artifact production and use that the concept of *chaîne opératoire* usefully merges with its value as a rigorous analytic research methodology.

The second reason the concept of *chaîne opératoire* is useful for linking the production of artifacts and agents together is because it highlights the sequential nature of both material and social production. For example, as only one salient social category that is cross-cut by others, gender is a series of identities "processed" over the course of one's life (Moore 1986; Ortner 1995: 184; M. Wolf 1974). When conflated with age, level of technical competence and knowledge, as well as the politics and ideology of value, we can differentiate as kinds of gendered people: the virgin girl prohibited from touching men's tools; the recently circumcised boy now apprenticed to a skilled craftsman; the menstruating or pregnant wife dangerous to the successful "birth" of objects produced by her husband; the grandmother teaching her mother's clay firing skills to her soon-to-be-married daughter; the grandfather imparting his lifetime of knowledge about animal behavior and hunting techniques to young initiates, and so forth. The production of social identities, such as those built upon a foundation of gender, are no less sequenced or "manufactured" than artifacts (de Lauretis 1987: 9). Agents are "processed" to become meaningful and functional members of society, and each of the many idealized personae that a technical agent embodies over the course of their life confers new and different statuses, rights, and obligations that can be put to political ends through powers of persuasion, displays of skill or knowledge valued by others, and so forth (after Ridington 1988).

These multiple layers of bodily, symbolic, cultural, and physical mediation also suggest that at every stage in the productive process there is the potential for technicians to break these rules and expectations, consciously or otherwise. This possibility, of altering the taken-for-granted habits and routines of rule-bound technical procedures, becomes a key locus for examining the agency of technological practice as something more than "either" practical or cultural reason, need, or overt politics. Importantly, it also allows us to make use of state-of-the-art research on the sequential processing of raw materials in order to consider their intangible determinants. This last point is crucial for archaeologists who, by necessity, work from the empirical traces of past material actions preserved in differently constituted archaeological assemblages, but wish to make reasonable inferences about the ancient artifice and agentive dynamics accounting for them.

The better we understand the variously peopled contexts of ancient artifact production and use, the more likely we are to understand the agency of these social, political, material, and ideological practices (example in chapter 6). And the more we recognize that creating and mediating social identities and technical agency were part and parcel of practical techniques and gestures of material culture production and use, the better we can weave the whole cloth of ancient technology into something meaningful in the present. Ancient technicians, having different talents and interests beyond the practical necessity of tool making and use, moved through streams of productive activities which provided them the practical and sensual experiences for their being-in-the-world. Contextualizing the sequencing of material transformations with these dynamics in mind makes it conceptually more difficult to divorce artifact production and use from social artifice, technical agency, and meaning making.

Some grounding

While this is not the place to rehearse my own research on the ancient technological practices of Late Pleistocene (Magdalenian) hunter-gatherers living in the French Midi-Pyrénées ca. 15,000–10,500 yBP, it is worthwhile to follow a case study to serve as an exemplar of how one can work to infuse theories of social agency and practice into archaeological research on technology. I discuss at length the methodological aspects of this research in the next chapter; here I want only to describe how I have inferred from the patterned material traces of ancient technical gestures something of the technical agency underwriting them.

To make sense of the social agency of Magdalenian technology requires attention to what I call the "technological character" of a site's composite assemblage, for at this physical scale (which highlights multiple overlapping activities) it is possible to conceptually link the actions of individual technicians to a particular social, material, and meaningful milieu. In my study of worked organic artifact assemblages recovered from eight broadly contemporaneous cave and rock shelter sites in the Ariège and Haute-Garonne (figure 6.7), I have found evidence that a wide range of material techniques and gestural strategies were practiced to make, use, repair, and recycle harpoons, spear points, sewing needles, punches, and the like (details in chapter 6). And even though these classic-looking artifact types were made, used, and repaired by the same community of technicians, sharing the same historical tradition, from exactly the same raw materials, and for the same practical purposes, they were not treated uniformly according to some regional or ethnic template ingrained from birth.

Across the region, the evidence shows that there was no one best or normative suite of technical strategies for making and repairing ubiquitous objects of everyday use; not in the treatment of antler harpoons specifically for hunting ibex, not in bone needles for sewing; not in spear points, not in half-rounded rods. Importantly, these data make it clear that the actual gestural sequences practiced were not constrained by the limitations of raw material nor by artifact function (full details in Dobres 1995c, 1996a). There was something *else* going on at each of these sites, beyond either the "homogeneity of *habitus*" or constraints of nature, that accounts for how and why these objects were so variably treated. The differently situated technicians occupying these sites and undertaking these activities clearly had at their disposal a range of known alternatives from which they were making site-specific choices that do not correlate with either function or material properties.

Instead of trying to explain this pattern by looking still deeper into the objective (physical) nature of the materials and activities in question (for the several reasons outlined in chapters 1 and 2), I have found it far more useful to pursue a practice framework. This means, in essence, working from the premise that the social context of site-specific production and use activities played a major role in structuring the choice of productive strategies actually practiced (Dobres in press-b). This focus on social context has led me to ask about the related, overlapping, and concomitant material activities in which these agents were engaging at each site. Specifically, I have found it necessary and useful to identify for each site the actual range of activities undertaken (artifact making?, use?, repair? blank production?, and so on), precisely how these were accomplished, and the intensity with which they took place. Knowing in some detail the range and intensity of technological activities pursued from site to site suggests the immediate boundary conditions in which social interaction and agency unfolded during these materially grounded, everyday activities. Thus, a practice framework, rather than being a "merely" theoretical stance, has required detailed attention to and use of the archaeological record.

A focus on technology and social agency necessitates paying rigorous attention to identifying, describing, and cataloguing site-specific material variability and norms in technical matters (Dobres in press-b). In my study, while there was clearly a normative "package" of every-day sorts of technological activities ubiquitously practiced around the region (artifact production, repair, gathering, hunting, faunal process-ing, fishing, lithic and other nonfood resource procurement, sewing, even some art), my findings show few similarities in how they were actually undertaken from site to site (figure 5.1). These data lead me to suggest that social interactions were unfolding differently at each site as well, and the patterning of material variability is the clue to delimiting these. But let me be clear here: these data are not the material correlates of agency. Rather, they are clues to the boundary conditions within which agency was being expressed. I submit that by knowing in detail these different intersubjective contexts, their ma-terial contours, and the actual choices individual workers were making from one site to another, I can ask how agency was implicated in their enactment. But in order to infer something of the nature of whatever those agency dynamics may have been, it is necessary to consider these

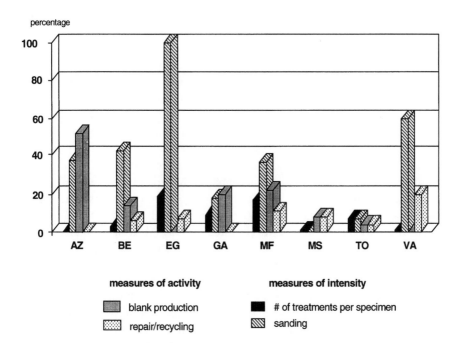

Figure 5.1   Graphic representation of diversity in Magdalenian organic technological activities and their variable intensity, as practiced in the Ariège and Haute-Garonne (AZ: Mas d'Azil; BE: Bédeilhac; EG: Les Eglises; GA: Spugo de Ganties; MF: Montfort; MS: Massat; TO: Tourasse; VA: La Vache).

activity patterns in terms of phenomenological and embodied social interaction mediated during the unfolding of technological practice (which, I reiterate, is not the same as considering these patterns reflections or correlates of such interaction).

When technical agents work in communal (that is, public) contexts, even if making and repairing their own arsenal of tools, they are at least tacitly aware of each other's bodies, actions, talents, and choices (Graburn 1976: 21; Ingold 1993c; Lave and Wenger 1991). They can see (and even hear, in the case of lithic knapping) different levels of skills, tricks of the trade, the practice of tradition, errors, and innovations going on around them. This intimate social context, which will vary significantly between small rock overhangs, larger open-air sites, and cavernous underground chambers, is a physically structured but meaningfully constituted arena in which technical agents can advance interests and express attitudes about how to get a job done. It is, simultaneously, a locale where neighbors can judge each other by group standards, join in or distance themselves from such activities, and thus go about the everyday strategies of social interaction. In such a socially mediated environment, even the most subtle and nondiscursive bodily actions become a communicative medium (Ingold 1993a: 438; Dobres 1999b).[13]

With these ideas in mind, I interpret the physical evidence of an extremely variable set of techniques and gestures practiced from site to site as an indication that *more* was going on than physical tool making, use, and repair. Magdalenian technicians were not merely interacting, but effectively mediating self and group interests, identities, and affiliations through the performative aspects of their bodily gestures and their material results. In making this claim, I take the material traces of embodied technical gestures involved in the most mundane and seemingly innocuous of Magdalenian technological activities as an indication of the dynamic nature of their social intercourse, one that in this particular case seems to have involved flexibility in basic social arrangements (Dobres 1995a). More specifically, these data suggest that within this generally egalitarian hunter-gatherer community there was latitude in how people expressed different categories of personhood, such as men, women, ibex hunters, plant gatherers, animal or plant processors, artisans, elders, children, and so forth. The subtle pursuit of different technical choices by individuals engaging in mindful communities of practice not only situated them in the community at large. Their choices were, I believe, a means of self-actualization: by earning the reputation required to be accepted as a skilled craftsperson and no longer a mere novice; by betraying the fact that they could no longer cut those finely detailed barbs on the shaft of a harpoon because, with advancing age, it was increasingly difficult to see or grasp a burin; by trying out a new technique to pierce the eye of a needle without the risk of looking like a "show off". . . .

The subtlety with which these dynamics were played out in the "technological sphere" suggests two things about the relationship of the corporeal body to the body politic in this particular instance: first, that identity and status were not rigidly fixed but could, within socially proscribed limits, be transcended through material means; and second, that everyday attempts at social "mobility" were subtle. Hayden's (1998) model of self-aggrandizing "prestige" technologies practiced by these so-called transegalitarian hunter-gatherers does not take into account the sorts of data presented here, nor does it consider that these mundane technological practices were part of that overall techno-system. It may well be that in other arenas of Magdalenian material culture production and consumption, such as wall and portable art, a different kind of social maneuvering was unfolding that was perhaps not as subtle as in the way these technicians treated their harpoons, points, and needles (for example, as explored in Dobres in press-a).

Ultimately, however, multiple classes of data that integrate mundane artifact production and use with more specialized classes of artifacts, such as portable and wall imagery, will need to be studied *in concert* if we are to understand when, where, how, and under what contextual conditions social maneuvering was and was not acceptable during the Magdalenian. Rather than take a narrow range of technological activities (such as visual imagery or items of personal adornment and burial treatment) and generalize to the workings of society at large (such as in Hayden 1995b, 1998; R. White 1989, 1992, 1993), our best bet is in considering a wider range of *concomitant* technological practices, mundane and unusual, in order to comprehend the variability of social practices they suggest.

Conclusions

In outlining this synoptic view of technology I have stressed the emergent dynamics of people being in the made (and remade) world, emphasizing in particular the paradox of social becoming within preexisting structures that are themselves continually subject to transformation. This is not only the structuration process, it is also the heart and soul of technology. People, especially in their personae as technical agents, become and augment who and what they are within social, symbolic, and material structures that unfold through lived time. In turn, this process of becoming, doing, feeling, and interacting feeds back on those structures. For these reasons, neither society nor social agents are ever finished products. In this chapter, I have especially concentrated on the experiential basis of technique and gestures as embodied practice, linking them with technical agency expressed in the course of artifact production and use. Given the importance of social agency to larger cultural phenomena, we need conceptual frameworks that can encompass the social, experiential, and meaningful nature of technological practice as a form of social intercourse linked to the material conditions of life. In this chapter I have offered one possibility, which I call a practice framework.

Technology, as embodied material practice, is a socially charged and materially grounded arena in which agents express and negotiate social relationships, establish and express value systems, and give meaning to the object world. I like to think of this as the "babble of technological voices." There is no single phenomenological scale at which this dynamic unfolds, though in my own work I have chosen to concentrate on face-to-face interaction in small-scale settings. But because agency is also a collective phenomenon, there is no reason why the same sort of practice framework cannot be applied to the question of evolutionary-scale technological complexity, as in the development of craft specialization, ranked societies, and so forth (for example, as explored in A. Joyce in press; J. E. Clark in press; Pauketat in press). Nor is the practice framework outlined here a call to identify the traces of the hands and actions of "real" individuals in the past. It is about investigating a cross-cultural process involving the mutual transformation of agents and artifacts through meaningful material practice. Thought of in this way, the sorts of material variability and implied social interactions that have so often been peripheralized as idiosyncratic noise of no anthropological merit, become the "stuff" of both culture and, most likely, culture change.

As Hodder (1986) and Brumfiel (1991) have eloquently argued, systemic approaches to the past sterilize culture of its humanity, leading Watson (1991) to recognize the "souless method" of mainstream research. The partitive approach to the study of ancient technology so long a cornerstone of mainstream research has effectively divorced the poetics, art, and sociality of *tekhnē* from the *logos* of object making and use. Practice (or agency) theory is fundamentally about subjects, intersubjectivity, and corporeal social engagement. It promises much in the way of bringing into view the human face of technology, past and present. This does not require forsaking attention to material matters; in fact, it demands their close scrutiny. To interject an explicit concern with social interaction, contexts and ways of learning, the sensuality of doing, meaning, politics, and value into the study of ancient technologies of survival and adaptation can only make our understandings richer, more nuanced, and more satisfactory in explanatory power. To take the "babble of technological voices" as a serious anthropological dynamic in the past requires a more human-focused lens than we have been using. I have tried, in this chapter, to articulate the contours of such a perspective.

On its own, however, a practice framework is only a partial corrective. We also need to rethink our analytic methodologies and how they can be modified to further these ends. It is to the question of operationalizing these concepts in materials research that I now turn.

6

Engendering the *Chaîne Opératoire*: Methodological Considerations

The previous chapter introduced the conceptual framework of the *chaîne opératoire*, exploring the unfolding relationship between the corporeal and social body of technicians and the sequential processing and use of the material world. This chapter takes up the *chaîne opératoire* again, this time discussing its value as a materials research tool, or analytic methodology, especially useful for detailing artifact life-histories. To this point I have kept my discussion of technology purposefully general, to help keep the reader's attention focused on the anthropological dynamic of social agency in the everyday practice of object making and use. Such a discussion, while hopefully compelling, cannot help but suffer from a lack of detailed discussion of material and social particulars that are time and space sensitive. Yet, as I have now argued, it is the *specifics* of these productive contexts that grounds the sensual and embodied nature of technological practices and links them to social agency, historical contingency, and social reproduction. What this chapter promotes is the view that the detailed materials analysis of artifact life-histories should be undertaken not only to identify and describe decision-making sequences of artifact making, use, and repair activities, but also to understand the social contexts and organizational dynamics structuring and giving meaning to them.

Importantly, for a vast number of archaeologists (myself included), we have no written texts or historical records with which to "flesh out" the material and social nature of past technologies. Similarly, many of us are not able to put much faith in the use of direct historical analogy. To those of us working in the "deep" past, the material traces constituting the archaeological record become a major source of data for the study of ancient technology. It is for these reasons (among others) that the analytic methods of *chaîne opératoire* research were developed first by researchers working on the Middle and Upper Palaeolithic. When broken stones and bones are all one has to work with, archaeologists are wonderfully clever at making sound inferences from their detailed study. But the same should be true for *all* archaeologists, even those working in historical periods with written texts of many sorts at their disposal. There are important anthropological questions that only detailed materials analysis can answer.

All the same, just because most of us necessarily start with the static vagaries of the archaeological record does not mean that their empirically measurable and invariant physical properties were more determinant of ancient technological practice than non-preservable social and symbolic factors. Such a stance is teleological. The extent to which social practices as well as ideological and symbolic constructs constrain practical decisions about resource exploitation and fabrication strategies, in formal and functional designs, and in the organization and mediation of labor practices has been demonstrated time and time again (synthesis in chapters 4 and 5). To slip conceptually from the factual necessity of working with tangible artifacts to the materialist claim that objective conditions such as resource availability or artifacts physics were the (likely) primary determinants of technological practice – or worse, that only when these more knowable factors are known can we move on to the more social side of the equation – is to succumb to the fallacy of misplaced concreteness (chapters 2 and 3). Indeed, to believe that technology preserves better than beliefs or social practices because stone tools and ceramic cooking pots constitute so much of the archaeological record is to accept as unproblematic the view that technology is the hard, utilitarian, and functional "side" of social life. I challenged this view in chapters 1 and 2, and offered what I hope is a more anthropological perspective in chapters 3–5. Taken together, the conceptual framework and analytic methods of *chaîne opératoire* research can be valuable for bringing to light the social and symbolic processes "hidden" within ancient material remains.

The first part of this chapter discusses the analytic techniques of *chaîne opératoire* as a research strategy particularly useful for identifying and describing in extraordinary empirical detail the physical sequences of technical stages (and their alternatives) by which classes of artifacts were manufactured, used, and variously repaired. Throughout, I continue to stress that material sequences of manufacture and use are social practices undertaken in peopled contexts and conducted by the hands of individual agents connected to the body politic. I believe this explicitly social spin on *chaîne opératoire* research, while not (yet) in the mainstream, can do much to broaden the uses to which such empirical research is currently put. The second half of this chapter offers a few brief examples and a sustained case study of how *chaîne opératoire* analysis can be employed to address questions of social agency, the latter based on my own research on the Late Magdalenian in the eastern French Pyrénées. I present this case study not as a methodological "road map" that will work for everyone interested in the social agency of ancient technological practice. Instead, it is offered as one example of how detailed materials analysis can help elucidate the social dynamics of ancient technology. It is my hope that the reader takes what they can from such an example, then modifies it to suit their particular research interests.

Two Caveats

Two qualifications are needed before discussing *chaîne opératoire* as a research strategy for the empirical study of ancient technology. The first is to make an important distinction between research methods and a research methodology; the second concerns the specific goal of this chapter in terms of laying out a model research methodology capable of covering any and all questions about the social agency of past technologies.

It is important, first, to distinguish between analytic *methods* (such as microscopic use-wear analysis, replicative studies, exploratory data analysis, typological seriations, refitting, GIS, and so forth) and a research *methodology* (which is a suite of particularly chosen methods combined for a specific research problem; distinction in Harding 1987). Analytic methods common to practically all archaeological research can be combined in any number of creative ways to produce significantly different research methodologies, each designed for the particular questions at hand and the interpretive or explanatory interests of the researcher. Using this distinction, *chaîne opératoire* is an analytic method that subsumes within it ancillary research techniques, most especially use-wear analysis, refitting, and replication. By itself, however, *chaîne opératoire* research methods are of limited value for the question of social agency. However, it is precisely because *chaîne opératoire* is also a conceptual framework for phenomenologically linking material and social reproduction (as discussed in chapter 5) that its analytic methods can help address questions of technology and social agency.

What *chaîne opératoire* research provides are detailed empirical observations about sequential procedures of artifact manufacture and use, and in this it has much in common with the American tradition known as behavioral chain or life-history analysis (most notably in Schiffer 1975b, 1992a; Schiffer and Skibo 1997; see also Bleed n.d.), as well as activity analysis (Dantzig 1963; Koopsman 1951; von Neumann 1945; elaboration in Roux and Matarasso 1999).[1] How those observations are employed to enrich understandings of the social dynamics of such gestural practices requires an anthropological conceptual framework, such as the one outlined in chapters 4 and 5. It is for these reasons that I privileged a discussion of this conceptual framework before considering its efficacy as an analytic research tool. One's conceptual framework must be articulated *before* pulling together a research methodology that depends heavily on *chaîne opératoire* or similar analysis. Otherwise, the documentation of data can succumb to the worst of empirically driven descriptive study, which is antithetical to the agendas of processualists, behaviorists, and post-processualists alike (Pelegrin 1990: 119).

Second, it is also necessary to resist the temptation of thinking there is a single best *chaîne opératoire* methodology that can work for all times, places, and material situations. Given what the first five chapters of this book have argued, there can be no one umbrella-like methodology for the study of technology and social agency able to suit all such practices across the vast expanses of time and space (more generally, see Wobst 1997; for a contrary position, see Schiffer 1992a; Skibo and Schiffer 1997, in press). How can we expect an empirical study of Harappan specialized bead production to employ the same research methodology and focus on the same material or social constraints and possibilities as those appropriate for a technical study of earthen mounds in the American mid-continent? Nor should either research project blindly follow the same methodological strategy I developed to study the social agency of Late Ice Age organic technology in the eastern French Pyrénées (discussed below). Not only are the social, organizational, and material practices decidedly different; so too are the research communities and what they want to understand. Each has their own intellectual history of research, expectations about how research should proceed, standards by which to assess findings and interpretations, and so forth. For these reasons, the methodology of *chaîne opératoire* research must be modified to fit the interests of the research community as well as the material nature of the technology in question. That said, however, there is much useful information that *chaîne opératoire* research can provide about the sequential processing and use of material culture that can elucidate the question of prehistoric technology and social agency.

The *Chaîne Opératoire* as an Analytic Research Methodology

What *chaîne opératoire* research provides is extraordinarily detailed and quantifiable data on artifact "life-histories," on sequential technical operations of raw material transformation, on by-products, on the relationship between design, raw material, and end product, and especially on problem-solving aspects of artifact production, use, and repair (Pelegrin et al. 1988). *Chaîne opératoire* research provides data on shared and contested community, regional, cultural, and even species-wide technical practices as well as their on-the-ground variants. It can identify not only the technical stigmata of fabrication sequences still observable on artifacts, but even those obliterated by subsequent modification, use, or repair (the latter most often inferred through replication, experimentation, and ethnoarchaeological study). As I show below, by making sense of the morass of debitage, refurbished, and discarded artifacts recovered from ancient living floors, *chaîne opératoire* research allows researchers to move beyond sterile questions of typology, function, and even the style–function debate, to explore their social underpinnings (as specifically argued in Dietler and Herbich 1998; Geneste 1988; Schlanger 1996).

As an analytic focus, knowing the step-by-step physical actions and material procedures by which ancient technicians procured, prepared, modified, altered, shaped, used, repaired, reworked, recycled, and ultimately discarded their material culture, tells the researcher an enormous amount: about technical stocks of knowledge and alternative technical strategies practiced to achieve a desired end, about levels of skill, competence, and *savoir-faire*, about the constraints and possibilities inherent in the chemical, mechanical, or other physical properties of the materials being worked, and especially about individual and group (even species-level) problem-solving strategies, cognitive capabilities, "world views," value judgments, intentions and shortcomings (Karlin and Julien 1994; Pelegrin et al. 1988; Schlanger 1994, 1996). Most importantly, *chaîne opératoire* research allows archaeologists to understand the *intersections* between these phenomena, rather than treating them as discrete entities.

The goal, of course, is to understand these social, material, and symbolic factors as cross-cutting currents played out in the day-to-day production and use of the material world by technical agents, not to divide them heuristically from one other for analytic ease, nor even for the sake of determining primary from secondary performance characteristics (after use of these terms in Schiffer and Skibo 1997). As I have now argued, even the most unequivocal constraints of physics, mechanics, and chemistry are worked through, worked out, and made salient through individual and collective labor constituted by the social body of tradition and agency (as shown so well in Gosselain 1998; Lechtman 1977). All technical strategies, from those most seemingly constrained by the real world to those presumably symbolic, non-functional, and gratuitous *together* constitute the package of operational chains of actions, decisions, judgments, and gestures constituting a community's technical repertoire. Because most researchers employing the French tradition of *chaîne opératoire* research define technology "as socialized action on matter, techniques can be apprehended through three orders of facts:

suites of gestures and operations (technical processes), objects (means of action on matter), and specific knowledge (*connaissances*)" (Lemonnier 1980: 1, quoted in Schlanger 1994: 145).

And while the stated goal of *chaîne opératoire* research is to delineate the manufacturing process from beginning to end (Cresswell 1983; Delaporte 1991; Sellet 1993), I maintain that such physical activities are always and everywhere socially embedded. An artifact's "life," therefore, and the gestures through which it comes into being and is used, has a social as much as a material beginning. As Gosden (1994: 185) puts it: "artefacts are not simply raw material for classification [by archaeologists] or evidence of production, but can show how streams of activity are embedded socially and the relations set up through these activity streams" (a point similarly argued by Schiffer 1975b, 1992c). Although *chaîne opératoire* analysis necessarily starts with the tangible remains of the archaeological record, it does not follow that understanding object life-histories through empirical research must remain focused on material factors alone.

So much has been written on the analytic methods of *chaîne opératoire* research that it might seem superfluous to reiterate these points here. However, little has actually been written in English on the explicitly *social* framework that underwrites it and which can lead to its being a problem-oriented research strategy (*sensu* methodology) rather than simply about data-driven research and description. Because of this anthropological lacuna, it is all too easy to confuse *chaîne opératoire* analysis with other, seemingly similar analytic projects employed to identify and describe the empirical life-histories of artifacts.[2] Does it make a difference to materials analysis to have such a social framework in hand undertaking laboratory and field study? Based on personal experience, my answer is a resounding yes. The reason it matters goes to the heart of what Redman (1973, 1987, 1991) and other processualists have been arguing for more than twenty years: the necessity of having a conceptual framework and specific research question before collecting data.

When grounded in social theory, such as that first articulated by Mauss (1935) and brought up to date through an explicit concern with agency and practice (chapter 5), *chaîne opératoire* research provides an enormous amount of empirical observation regarding the sequential activities of ancient materials processing. But which of these data are relevant to questions of social agency? It is necessary to consider this issue *before* one undertakes analysis, not after. This is not the same as saying that one must know in advance which particular material variables or patterns signify a particular sort of agentive practice and proceed to seek them out in order to confirm some hypothesis (for as I argued in chapter 5, this is not the best way to think about agency).

Rather, before one decides to concentrate on some suite of quantifiable and empirical attributes such as edge angles, thermal properties of clay, distance from source materials to their place of transformation, or the tensile strengths of bone and antler, it is necessary to consider *why* such variables would have anything to do with the question of technology and social agency and in what social and productive/use contexts. It is necessary to ask why a certain set of material attributes studied at particularly chosen analytic scales are relevant to mainly non-discursive social practices and the embodiment and negotiation of personhood and communal affiliation in the productive arena, and the answer cannot simply be because such attributes are measurable and time-honored. *Chaîne opératoire* research garners an extraordinary amount of observable and quantifiable data, but not all of it is relevant to the question of technology and agency.

Following gestures flake by flake
(but don't forget what that hand is connected to!)

Among the especially useful ancillary analytic techniques making up the now standard *chaîne opératoire* methodology are refitting studies, and perhaps no better exemplar of the pay-off from such laborious and time-consuming work can be offered than the collaborative effort of N. Pigeot, C. Karlin, S. Ploux, M. Olive and their colleagues working on the lithic and faunal assemblages from several Late Magdalenian (ca. 12,000 yBP) open-air sites in the Paris Basin (namely, Etiolles, Marsangy, Pincevent, and Verberie; figure 6.1).[3] While these regionally connected sites show an extraordinary degree of spatial integrity in the preservation and distribution of artifact remains, it is the detailed refitting studies of lithic and faunal debitage combined with microscopic use-wear analysis, replication, and experimentation that has enabled this team to identify the shared repertoire of strategies of artifact making and use as well as the variants these late Ice Age technicians practiced as they encountered and resolved material problems on a day-to-day basis. Such research has been able to trace both lithic and faunal artifact movement around the site by tracking their individual life-histories (something admittedly more difficult, but not impossible, to accomplish at disturbed sites; Dobres 1996b). As a result, by "following the gestures flake by flake" (Schlanger 1996: 248), they have identified spatial patterns in technological practices suggestive of inter-relationships between what they identify as hierarchically structured family units (especially see English summaries in Audouze 1987; Audouze and Enloe 1991; see also David and Enloe 1993; David et al. 1994; Karlin et al. 1992; Olive and Pigeot 1992; Pigeot 1987, 1990).

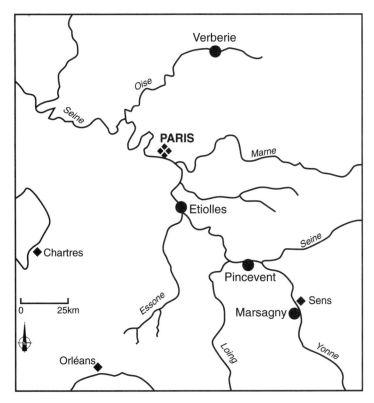

Figure 6.1   Map of the Paris Basin, with Magdalenian sites mentioned in the text.

"Following the gestures flake by flake" through a combination of *chaîne opératoire* methods has brought to light the technical routines of lithic blade production, use, refurbishment, and discard practiced in one small region of the Paris Basin, and have been used to model the socially grounded rules of technical practice. Those practices, which have a strong spatial component, include mundane and practical procedures having to do with choice of raw material, strategies of cortical flake removal, platform preparation, techniques of secondary and tertiary flaking, the striking of pre-formed blades, their finishing retouch, use, breakage, repair, and ultimate discard. Similar patterns have been found for dismemberment activities and the spatial distribution of reindeer remains between and among hearths (especially David and Enloe 1992; Enloe 1992; Enloe et al. 1994). More anthropologically relevant than these descriptive observations, "following gestures flake by flake" through detailed *chaîne opératoire* research has permitted the delineation of different levels of gestural skill, practical knowledge, and competence in working lithics, which are empirically betrayed by the physical stigmata of different approaches, successes, and/or failures of platform preparation and rejuvenation, crest production, the discard or continued use of worn-out cores, and so forth (more discussion, below).

For all their micro-scale variability, those mundane and practical actions were also and at the same time necessarily and decidedly social in both outward (gestural) expression and in the context of their enactment. They unfolded and were expressed through the physical bodies of technicians working in close proximity to each other around a number of discrete hearths and tent-like structures, such that the discursive and non-discursive nature of their interpersonal relationships both gave meaning to and helped materially shape those technical routines. Taken together, it has even been possible to reconstruct something of the interpersonal (and purportedly gendered) nature of these gestures and actions through the variable patterning of operational chains of blade production, use, repair, and discard, their spatial distribution around the site, and the varying levels of competence and skill with which they were accomplished (discussed below). But, interesting as these findings are, as currently formulated they are not (yet) about social agency, for physical activity and action are not, to my way of thinking, synonymous with agency.

Recent *chaîne opératoire* studies, by the French in particular, have begun to concentrate on more accurate and standardized systems for recording technical observations and how to diagram their sequences and variants, whether based in archaeological, ethnoarchaeological, or experimental study (especially chapters in Balfet 1991a). As well, there has been increased interest in understanding the overlaps of intersecting operational chains in order to understand how they impinge upon or augment each other when people are working in multiple materials and making and using different sorts of objects at the same time (for example, Dobres 1996a; Keeley 1987; a brief example is offered below; see also figure 5.1). It is important to realize, however, that while *chaîne opératoire* research can provide enormous empirical detail about artifact processing, such tangible data do *not* signify the "organization" of a technological system (*sensu* Sellet 1993: 106; also Andrefsky 1994; Nelson 1991). The organization of a technology depends on social labor, social relations of production, value systems, and the social negotiation of these phenomena in everyday practice and over the long term (Cobb 1997), and empirical descriptions of material *chaînes opératoires* do not automatically establish these social dynamics.

I maintain that what is still needed is to "engender" the *chaîne opératoire*.

Engendering the chaîne opératoire

To promote an agency perspective on prehistoric technology, I have found it especially useful to think about *chaînes opératoires* as engendered practices. "To engender," of course, brings to mind the inherently gendered nature of all human technologies (admitting, of course, a host of other overlapping social identities also caught in this web). As I discussed in previous chapters, gender embodies one's material experiences in the world such that engendered personhood becomes ideologically and practically associated with particular making and use activities (Lesick 1996). Engendering the *chaîne opératoire*, then, gives conceptual prominence to the unfolding dialectic – the *bringing forth* in tandem – of gendered social agents and their material culture through technological practice. Engendering *chaînes opératoires* brings to mind the embodied processes by which technological practices and objects are simultaneously personalized and conceptually objectified, or externalized, beyond the corporeal body of individual technicians.

To engender *chaîne opératoire* research is to resist artifact fetishism while conducting detailed materials analysis, and to avoid the fallacy of misplaced concreteness and the interpretive erasure of agents and agency from such analyses; to engender the *chaîne opératoire* is to keep focused on the question of social relations, interpersonal and other phenomenological scales of agency, as well as the process of affirming, contesting, and negotiating social values, rules, and tradition during the most mundane of technical activities; to engender the *chaîne opératoire* is to remember its social and corporeal basis and to recognize the socially constituted nature of embodied technological practice, no matter how simple or complex; finally, to engender the *chaîne opératoire* is to reconnect the heart and soul of technological practice to the hands making and working the material world in socially meaningful settings framed by tradition, history, and environment.

On normativism

As Bleed (1991, n.d.) and Edmonds (1990) have rightly noted, what the French have done with *chaîne opératoire* research that constitutes such an important epistemological breakthrough in ancient technology studies is blend extraordinarily rigorous empirical observation and quantification with a structuralist epistemology. *Chaîne opératoire* research uncovers the underlying *syntax* and logic of operational sequences, technical gestures, and material judgments, and it is this explicitly structuralist foundation that permits one to move beyond observable patterns of work chains and knowledgeable procedures and talk about underlying rules, templates, and world views (on a structural and linguistic basis for technology studies, see Johnson 1993; Lechtman 1977, 1984a; Lemonnier 1989a; essays in Renfrew and Zubrow 1994; Schlanger 1991; Wynn 1985). As I argued in chapters 4 and 5, object making and use are meaningful on a discursive, but especially on a non-discursive, level. Thus, whether the specific interest is in the operational chains producing Acheulean or Levallois flakes (Boëda et al. 1990), Aurignacian ivory beads (R. White 1989), Magdalenian bladelets (Inizan 1991), or present-day ceramics (Gosselain 1994, 1998), a dedicated application of a *chaîne opératoire* research strategy empirically identifies "reference routines stored in the brain" (Gowlett 1990: 85, figure 2) and materialized through bodily gestures.

In reviewing the ideas of Leroi-Gourhan (1943, 1945), who actually coined the term *chaîne opératoire*, Cresswell (1990: 46) notes that "the association of an agent and tool becomes a gesture and an action and results in a product in a technological relationship." However, it was Leroi-Gourhan's mentor, Mauss (1935), who showed how such technological practices served as "collective representations," or cultural ontologies and right-minded ways of acting that were reaffirmed through everyday gestural habits and technical routines (Dobres 1999b; Edmonds 1990; Lemonnier 1980, 1989a; Schlanger 1990, 1994, 1998). In all of this, however, normative conceptions of cultural and technical practice loom problematically large (Dietler and Herbich 1998; Dobres in press-b; Dobres and Hoffman 1994, 1999a), though this should come as no surprise, given that Mauss' teacher was none other than Durkheim.

Similarly, in contemporary archaeological practice the diagrammatic models used to illustrate material *chaînes opératoires*, whether in the form of artifact life sequences (figure 6.2a) or flow charts (figure 6.2b), typically summarize the linearity of technical schemas and actions (Karlin et al. 1991: 106), not every variant practiced. Although such a representational choice is understandable, it nonetheless obscures on-the-ground variability and deviation from that so-called norm, because such summaries are intended as heuristic, generalized models representing the cognitive maps and systems of knowledge that guide(d) on-the-ground technical gestures and actions.[4] While most researchers recognize that linear *chaîne opératoire* diagrams "provide no more than a descriptive summary of the very complex processes involved in even the simplest skilled routine" (Gowlett 1990: 86), they can easily lead to an overemphasis on abstract, normative practices (Vidale 1989), and through such means contribute to the erasure of the agents and the mindful communities of practice through which such routines played out.

In combining the structuralist underpinnings of the concept of *chaîne opératoire* with linear diagrams, one often gets the sense that prehistoric technicians had no minds of their own and were nothing more than technical robots following preordained rules. This need not be the case, however, and depending on the persuasions of the analyst and their particular research questions, *chaîne opératoire* findings (and diagrams) can emphasize normative technical practices and decisions, their variants, and/or their interrelationships (exemplary in this regard, see van der Leeuw 1993, 1994: 138–9; van der Leeuw et al. 1991; I discuss my own work below). Indeed, what rigorous *chaîne opératoire* research allows is an understanding of precisely when, how, and to what extent a technical procedure was faithfully practiced and when, how, and to what extent technicians deviated from it in a particular manner. To be able to identify, then juxtapose, the gestural traces of norms and variants in ancient technical practice through the study of materials as diverse as lithic debitage, glass beads, gold statuary, ivory figurines, metal slag, and clay pots is what makes the analytic methods of *chaîne opératoire* research so useful to archaeological inquiry.

More troubling than the overemphasis on linearity and norms, however, is that practitioners of *chaîne opératoire* research tend to highlight analytic scales beyond the lived experiences of the technical agents doing the work, often by generalizing the procedural strategy or template for making *classes of artifacts*: flakes, blades, beads, figurines, harpoons, pots, and so forth. Granted, many studies work to identify cross-cutting and site-specific *chaînes opératoires*, but for historical (and heuristic) reasons they often adhere to a typological or functional orientation (Boj et al. 1993; Dietler and Herbich 1998; Dobres 1995a, in press-b). To consider gestures and operational sequences in terms of social interaction (rather than object making and use) is thought of by some as wallowing in the vagaries of individual hands, a phenomenological scale which is said to bear neither on explanations of species-wide technical behaviors, nor on the hows and whys of wholesale and long-term change in technological repertoires (A. Gallay 1992; A. Goodyear, personal communication, 1998; M. B. Schiffer, personal communication, 1998).

While I think this claim unwarranted and based on a misunderstanding of what detailed *chaîne opératoire* research can accomplish, it is nonetheless clear that, for all their detail, the pictorial diagrams representing ancient operational work chains typically fail to provide any sense of the interactive social milieu in which certain sequential technical operations did (or did not) occur (figure 6.3). Yet this combined material, social, and embodied context is the only way to understand

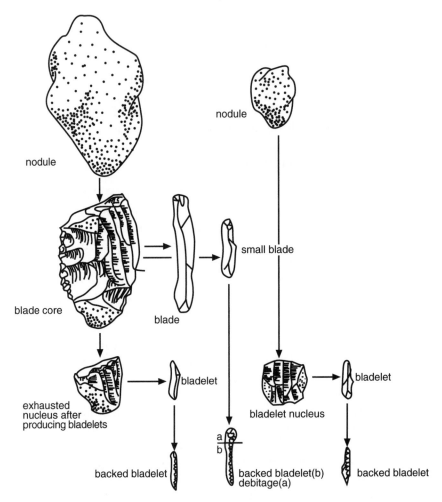

Figure 6.2a   Diagrammatic model illustrating a lithic *chaîne opératoire* using artifact images.
Source: Karlin et al. 1991, p. 107, figure 2

the dialectical unfolding of technique and technician in prehistory (Dietler and Herbich 1998: 239; Dobres 1999b). That the contingencies of agency, interaction, and mediation are not readily incorporated into *chaîne opératoire* diagrams points to an inherent limitation with the sometimes overly reductive nature of data-driven *chaîne opératoire* research and the normativism underlying the concept. As I argue next, however, by engendering the *chaîne opératoire* by keeping one's "eye" on the social agency of technological practice and resisting both artifact fetishism and the oppressive normativism of a structuralist ontology, it is possible to employ a *chaîne opératoire* methodology to identify and

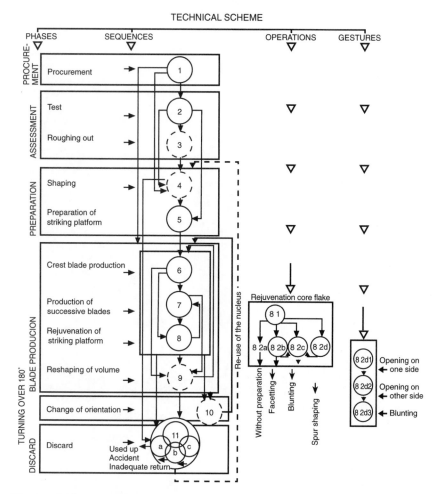

Figure 6.2b Diagrammatic model illustrating a lithic *chaîne opératoire* using a schematic flow chart.
Source: Karlin and Julien 1994, p. 155, figure 15.1

juxtapose shared norms and procedures (structures) against their practice, negotiation, and/or contestation (agency) in everyday arenas of material culture production and use.

Beyond templates: the social milieu as an embodied structure for chaînes opératoires

While the use of highly detailed and quantifiable observations about technical work chains to suggest the underlying cognitive rules and

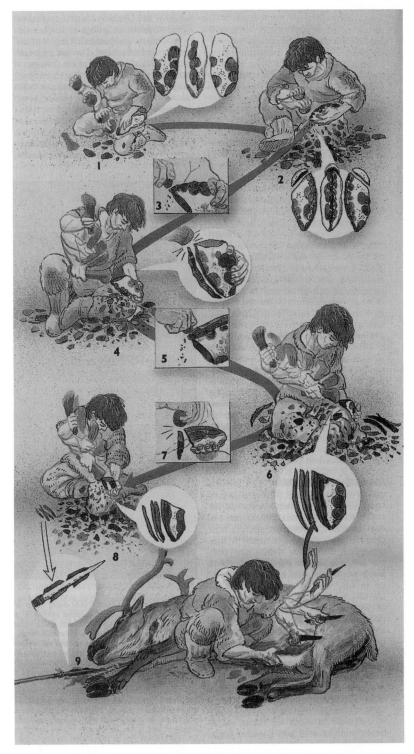

Figure 6.3 "Peopled" reconstruction of a lithic *chaîne opératoire* for reindeer-carcass processing. Note: all steps are undertaken by one worker (compare with figure 1.3).
Source: Karlin et al. 1992, p. 1110; artist: Gilles Tosello

learned dispositions structuring technological actions breaks the strictures that Hawkes (1954) and others once placed on what was and was not knowable about the past, glossing variability for the sake of the general *is* problematic, especially given the topic of this book. Once we accept that technology is an engendered, meaningful, social, lived, and corporeal experience of making and remaking the world and oneself through material means, then the question of "veering off the template" becomes important, even at the scale of mundane operational sequences that effect routine artifact manufacture and repair (Dobres in press-b). Enacting procedural chains of technical operations and gestures through learned dispositions is a "context specific [and] mediated understanding of how to proceed under particular conditions" (Edmonds 1990: 56). That is, while one may bring to their work a predetermined ideal of what they should, can, or must do and in what order, situational contingencies (both social and material) necessarily crop up to challenge and thwart even the best of intentions and the most faithful of techno-robots. As well, no matter what their intentions, technicians are never uniform in their abilities to pull off such procedures. Thus skill, talent, and *savoir-faire* play a large part in how faithfully, how variously, or how badly a particular work chain is effected.

In order to inquire into the social agency of ancient technological practice, empirical data on both normative procedures and their on-the-ground variants are required. How widely shared was some sequential strategy for the production, use, and repair of different classes of artifacts? How much variability was "tolerated," favored, or discouraged? Was variability confined to some classes of artifacts and not others, or to the use of some raw materials and not others? Was variability practiced more often at only particular stages of artifact production, and was it materially or socially strait-jacketed at others? Was it expressed overtly, or was it of a more covert and tacit nature? At what phenomenological scale(s) was technical *habitus* shared, and at what scales or in what contexts was difference indulged, and how did the one play off the other? Were technical stocks of knowledge shared widely, or restricted in some way? How widely known and practiced were techniques to circumvent the physical, chemical, and mechanical properties of the materials being modified? And at what phenomenological scale(s) were technical decisions made: by the group, by a restricted few, by each individual? These are the kinds of questions that detailed information on ancient *chaînes opératoires* can help answer when pursued within an agency-oriented research agenda (Dobres and Hoffman 1994; for example, see Sinclair in press; Wobst in press).

As Cresswell (1972) suggested more than two decades ago, variations within a normative set of technical procedures typically occur in one of three (interconnected) realms of social practice: in creating social relationships, in reflecting and reaffirming them, and in "everyday life" (also Cresswell 1990). His argument was that the phenomenological scale of everyday life was not only the scale at which culture was made and remade through a web of meaningful and material practices; everyday life was also a likely stimulus to macro-scale technological innovation (see also van der Leeuw 1993; van der Leeuw and Papousek 1992; the relationship of the everyday to wholesale cultural dynamics was more fully discussed in the preceding chapter). Norms and difference need to be understood as interrelated sociotechnical practices, and the analysis of artifact *chaînes opératoires* is an excellent place to begin researching such dynamics. Indeed, when technology is understood in light of the premises previously discussed, it is impossible for the minds and hands of individual technicians to be "heuristically" detached from the social body in which particular *chaînes opératoires* were practiced. It is for these reasons that regardless of how overt or covert the gestures, and no matter how discursive or routinized the activities, technical strategies and all their subtle variations constitute the "babble of technological voices" (Dobres 1999b: 136–7). It becomes an empirical question, then, whether variability identified in a repertoire of normative technical practices constituted nothing more than the idiosyncratic "noise" of individual workers or something more socially meaningful.

On variability around the template

Chaîne opératoire research is well suited to documenting and quantifying variability, deviations, and diversity – not just norms. Through detailed materials analysis, *chaîne opératoire* researchers are increasingly coming to understand that variations in how operational sequences are enacted are as likely to be sensitive to the social nature of artifact production and use in particularly constituted settings as they are to the "vagaries" of individual hands. Differences in how technical procedures are followed (or not) can play out within a community of workers (Delagnes 1991; Dobres 1996a; Gosselain 1994, 1998), or between contemporaneous groups (Aita et al. 1991; Bar-Yosef 1991; Lemonnier 1986); they can occur in levels of gestural skill (Dobres 1995c; Graburn 1976; Ingold 1993c); and they may be expressed from one artifact to another across a single habitation site (Olive 1992; Olive and Pigeot 1992; Pigeot et al. 1991; Roux 1991), or on a regional basis. Obviously, variations in technique can be tracked over short and long temporal sequences, as well.

Technical strategies and their variants turn out to be especially sensitive to collective and contested attitudes and rules about the "right" and "wrong" way to do such things, by whom, and where (Balfet et al. 1991c; Dietler and Herbich 1998; Hosler 1996; Sassaman in press; discussion in chapter 4). But even where material conditions significantly constrain one's range of options at any given stage of production or use, this does not preclude those options being meaningful, social, political, and hence put to agentive ends. Moreover, understanding how and when technicians strayed from their procedural "center," under what circumstances, and in what specific ways, can help define the situational context that structured and enabled those activities and practices in the first place (Delaporte 1991: 29; Dobres 1996a).

The earlier discussion of variability in gestural competence and enactment in Magdalenian lithic tool making in the Paris Basin juxtaposed against my findings regarding bone and antler artifact making and use in the French Pyrénées (discussed below) makes a good case in point. While in the Paris Basin, *chaîne opératoire* research suggests that variability in acting out the Magdalenian regional template for lithic manufacture, use, and repair materialized according to seemingly uncontested levels of competence dictated by age (experience) and gender (social practice), my findings in the Pyrénées suggest a more conscious (albeit non-discursive) set of strategies of differentiation promoted through material means (elaborated below). There are many reasons for variability and sameness in how regional-, site-, material-, or class-specific technologies were practiced in the past (much less the present): while most likely have something to do with artifact physics and how individual skill and/or collective dispositions worked to circumvent (or make the best of) them, because they are necessarily played out in the social arena and through the hands of embodied and gendered technicians, those reasons had multiple layers and furthered several ends, simultaneously.

Chaînes Opératoires as Situated Practice

In this second section, I ground my previous discussion of the promises and pitfalls of *chaîne opératoire* research with three examples, in order to show how "following the gesture flake by flake" can permit inferences concerning the social agency of technological practice. First, I briefly consider novel applications of *chaîne opératoire* methods to Levallois knapping, then Late Upper Palaeolithic lithic and faunal processing technologies, then offer an extended example from my own materials research explicitly focused on the social agency of Late Magdalenian organic technologies. While I highlight examples with which I am most conversant and which have inspired my own materials research, I hope that one or the other will do the same for the reader.

Recall that what are at issue in this chapter are analytic methods and research methodologies that, when explicitly underwritten by a practice framework and focus on social agency, can be adapted to suit the needs of innumerable technology studies. It must also be understood that while my first two examples are chosen for their effectiveness in materializing the abstract points under discussion, the original work did not have any specific interest in the question of social agency as I have been discussing it in these pages.

Levallois flint knapping: beyond templates and "hard-wiring"

Schlanger's (1994, 1996) detailed research on Levallois *chaînes opératoires* explores the cognitive, practical, and variable dimensions of Neandertal lithic core reduction strategies in terms of gestural skill and technique, practical knowledge, and even intentions, considering these in light of their evolutionary implications. Through a novel and explicit blending of Piagetian structuralism with Mauss' notion of the *enchaînement organique*, he has reevaluated the long-held position that Levallois reflects the cognitive upper limits of Neandertal stone-tool making capabilities (but also see S. Kuhn 1995). That standardized procedural template notwithstanding, his painstaking analysis of the step-by-step gestures taken to reduce "Marjorie's core," recovered from the 250,000-year-old "Site C" in the Maastricht-Belvédère gravel quarry (Netherlands), demonstrates that there was significant latitude in how Neandertal technicians produced those tell-tale flakes.

Building on a rich body of previous Levallois research, Schlanger notes that patterned variability obtained not only in the overall treatment of a core and the differently shaped end (flake) products struck from it, but also within the set of interrelated factors determining the nature of the striking surface and the angle of the striking platform (particularly, location, depth, and incidence of point of impact; see Schlanger 1996: figure 2), which together constitute an integrated "ensemble" (ibid.: 242). How the striking surface was prepared in advance of flake removal, particularly in creating distal and lateral convexities, is another locus wherein variable skill, know how, experience (and intention?) was materially expressed by individual technicians. In turn, at each sequential stage of flake removal, more platform preparation, another flake removal (and so on), there were possible variations on the theme, notably whether the knapper struck preformed flakes consistently from one area of the core (unipolar), alternated between two opposite striking platforms (bipolar), or struck from three different locales on the core (centripetal; ibid.: figure 3). Through his detailed *chaîne opératoire* analyses, Schlanger has been able to delineate variable treatments of the core itself, especially in terms of how it may have been rejuvenated to create still more striking platforms (and thus more flakes using unipolar, bipolar, and/or centripetal techniques).

In terms of Marjorie's core, Schlanger found a coherent and overall pattern in the variable use of two distinctly different knapping strategies, which consisted of "a series of non-Levallois flakes (generally smaller, with fewer dorsal scars, simple dorsal patterns, and unfaceted butts) . . . followed by either one or two Levallois flakes" (1996: 241)." Interestingly, as the core was reduced through sequential knapping incidents, the size of the flakes remained constant (ibid.: 243), suggesting neither a one-to-one nor a deterministic relationship between core size (a physical property) and flake product (the result of technique). Whoever struck flakes from Marjorie's core alternated between two perpendicularly oriented axes and preferred distally convex platforms, and through such means integrated "activities on the striking surface and the striking platform into an 'ensemble'" (ibid.: 246) that had both internal consistency but also some variability.

Among other things, these findings suggest that during Levallois work chains (at least those pursued at Maastricht-Belvédère), Neandertals were not so much techno-robots faithful to (or at the mercy of) their hard-wiring, but rather differently experienced interpreters of contingent factors of raw material intersecting with intention, design, knowledge, and skill, during implementation. As Schlanger (1996: 248) puts it, flake production (at least on Marjorie's core) was a "situated action" that was both "fluid and at the same time structuring," evidencing both normative practices and individual variations within them. What this research demonstrates is that by seeking out empirical data on both widely practiced norms and their local (even artifact-specific) variants, and specifically understanding these as the "interplay of thought and action" (ibid.: 239), we can comprehend the most mundane and everyday of material technologies in terms of thinking, knowing, feeling, and understanding technicians – even Neandertals.

All the same, what I find curiously missing from this clever and detailed application of a *chaîne opératoire* methodology to an understanding of hominid tool-making some 250,000 years ago is a framework for putting these observations into some sort of meaningful, interactive, socially constituted setting. One comes away from this study imagining only disembodied hands grasping at cores and skillfully going about a very material business. And while Schlanger is astute to argue the inseparability of doing and thinking, and of intention and contingency (Schlanger 1996: 248), it is nonetheless difficult to connect those busy, skillful, and knowledgeable hands to the corporeal (Neandertal) body, much less to the social body in which his or her flaking activities unfolded at Site C. Thus, in this study, we thus see both the analytic power of, and the conceptual limitations, with pursuing a materially (rather than engendered) use of a *chaîne opératoire* methodology. As it stands, this insightful study does not help us understand the social conditions within which Neandertal technicians negotiated between material contingency and individual intentions, skills, and, knowledge, how such tricks of the trade were learned and passed on from generation to generation, nor how such gestural actions of coordinated hands and minds contributed to the technician's place in their social collective; yet such questions are not outside the realm of legitimate inquiry.[5]

Back to blade production in the Paris Basin

As I mentioned earlier, the application of a clever *chaîne opératoire* research methodology has enabled an exceptionally detailed under-standing of Late Magdalenian lithic (and faunal processing) technol-ogy in the Paris Basin. Variability practiced around the regionally standard sequence of blade manufacture has been identified at several operational stages, and in combination with intrasite spatial distribu-tion patterns of lithic debitage has been used to infer something of the likely age and gender-based organization of those activities from site to site (notably, Balfet 1991b; Chauchat 1991; Karlin and Julien 1994; Karlin and Pigeot 1989; Pelegrin 1990; Perlès 1992; Pigeot 1988, 1990; Pigeot et al. 1991; Ploux 1991; Roux 1991). At Etiolles in particular, researchers argue that age-based cognitive and motor skills intersected with the "psychosocial" dynamics of parent–child inter-action and apprenticeship during the everyday production, use, and repair of macro-, average-sized, and micro-blades.

For example, by carefully following the gestures flake by flake at Etiolles, Olive and Pigeot (1992) have painstakingly tracked the individual life-histories of numerous cores and supports as they were moved between the contemporaneous locales of U5 and P15 (figures 6.4a and 6.4b). Their research has also been able to delineate the specific level of skill, knowledge, and technical precision with which these cores were worked during their "nomadic life" around the site. Combined, these observations have permitted an extraordinarily per-sonalized and phenomenological account of core treatment, primary, secondary, and tertiary flake removal, platform and crest preparation, blade production, retouch, and so forth. What allows this team to suggest a combined age- and gender-based structure for these activ-ities (figure 6.4c) playing out within what they theorize is a single corporate (family) unit in the vicinity of U5 and P15, are technical stigmata attesting to different levels of familiarity and skill at preparing platforms and blade crests, striking pre-formed blades, as well as knowing when a core was spent (though in at least one instance a discarded core was subsequently picked up and re-used – badly).

Their *chaîne opératoire* methodology has allowed not simply the tracking of the spatial life-histories of raw materials from resources to cores, flakes, blades, and waste, but also the reasonable association of these practices with differently situated technicians interacting with each other while taking care of business. According to Karlin et al. (1992), these data suggest that skill and need combined in three different social "packages." The most expert hands were those of adult men, who skillfully prepared platforms and crests and struck a number of uniformly shaped and oftentimes unusually large blades from single cores. Adult women most likely produced the more expedient (and less uniform) blades struck by less-than-expert hands. And children ("apprentices") made obviously unskillful attempts to re-use spent cores by literally whacking away at them after taking them away from the center of the corporate unit (additional explication in Karlin and Julien 1994).[6] While one should certainly question the proposed attribution of gender to these material traces of technological practice, which uncritically depends on Testart's (1982, 1986) problematic theory of "natural" gendered divisions of labor among hunter-gatherers, such interpersonal interpretations based on rigorous (some might say overly detailed) materials analysis shows especially well the promise such research holds for technology studies more generally.

And at nearby Verberie, Enloe (1992) and his colleagues (David and Enloe 1992, 1993; Enloe et al. 1994) have taken *chaîne opératoire* research into yet another realm, by refitting dismembered reindeer skeletons across the site to suggest something of the intrafamilial relationships and food-sharing practices among these nomadic hunter-gatherers. Aided by spatial distribution analyses and replicative experiments (and supplemented by ethnoarchaeological analogy), the detailed refitting of hundreds of faunal remains and thousands of pieces of lithic debitage, discarded blades, and exhausted cores has helped flesh out the interpersonal social dynamics among mothers, fathers, children and extended family units as mediated and reaffirmed through the most mundane activities of everyday material production.

Yet even this remarkable work falls short of an agency understanding, because the focus of attention is squarely on tool making and use and butchering activities, rather than on social agents mediating their relationships through such activities. I maintain that there is a significant interpretive difference in the way prehistoric technology is understood when research focuses attention, first, on material making

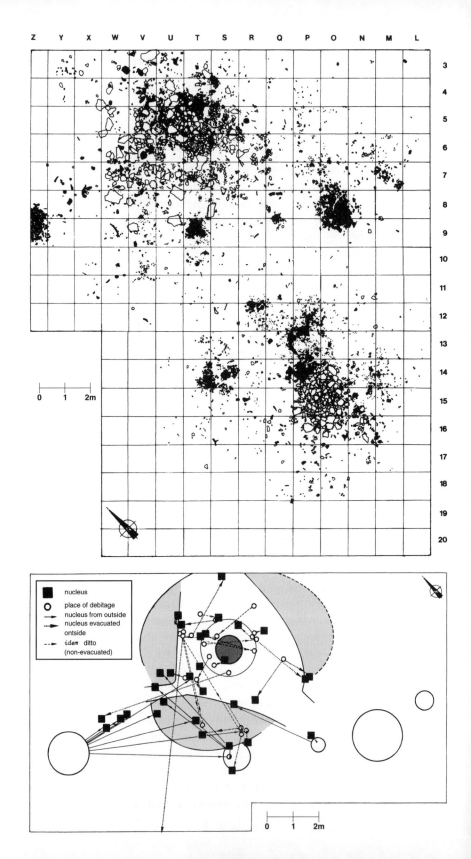

nucleus

place of debitage

nucleus from outside

nucleus evacuated
ontside

idem ditto
(non-evacuated)

Figure 6.4a (opposite, top)   Spatial distribution of lithic remains at Etiolles, units U5 (top) and P15 (bottom).
Source: Pigeot 1987, Plan 1
Figure 6.4b (opposite, bottom)   Map tracing movement of nuclei in and around unit U5 during lithic *chaînes opératoires* (Etiolles).
Source: Pigeot 1987, Plan 12 (modified)
Figure 6.4c (above)   "Peopled" reconstruction ("a socioeconomic model") of lithic technological activities in and around unit U5 (Etiolles).
Source: Olive and Pigeot 1992, p. 175, figure 2; artist: Gilles Tosello

and use activities and only adds agents later on, compared to research that makes social relationships the focus of materials analysis. By situating empirically grounded *chaîne opératoire* research within a social agency perspective it is possible to link on-the-ground material practices to the dynamic processes of personhood and even politics, both covert and overt, rather than attributing (gendered or age-specific) identities as an afterthought.

An Extended Case Study

It now makes sense to offer a more extended case study to show how questions about prehistoric social agency can affect *chaîne opératoire* research, rather than leave the discussion with the claim that these analytic methods can help address questions concerning the agency of prehistoric technology. In essence, there is a hermeneutic spiral operating: while the first section of this chapter concentrated on how analytic methods packaged within a carefully chosen research methodology can provide data that inform theory, here I discuss how theory informs one's research methodology and choice of specific analytic methods for data acquisition. In my own case, theory related to social agency and practice came before I realized that the analytic methods of *chaîne opératoire* research could be of assistance once appropriately configured to suit my interests in understanding the intersubjective nature of technological practice (rather than the making and use of artifacts *per se*). My purpose is to demonstrate the efficacy of taking people, social relations, meaning, and agency seriously in research on prehistoric technology and to show that it *does* matter to materials research, whether pursued with a *chaîne opératoire* methodology or some other life-history approach.

Of course, one must necessarily tailor their choice of analytic strategies to the history of their particular research question (which may be very unlike mine), the state of that art (which may be superior), as well as the material contours of that prehistory and technology. That said, I begin with some background on the state of materials research on the Upper Palaeolithic in southwestern Europe (though I restrict myself to one particular archaeological culture, the Magdalenian). I follow this with an extended discussion to show how taking the question of social agency seriously in technological research not only affects the analytic and physical scales at which *chaîne opératoire* research is conducted, but also how empirical observations can be obtained that advance those interests.

Materials research on the Magdalenian: typology gives way to functionalism

Once called the Golden Age of Prehistory because of its cultural and artistic developments, The Magdalenian (ca. 15,000–10,500 yBP; hereafter TM), has captured the minds and imagination of Francophile prehistorians for well over a century. The conventional model of TM has changed surprisingly little since the late 1880s, and it is still characterized as the Reindeer Age because of the predominance of this species in thickly stratified cave deposits across southwestern Europe. The Magdalenian is still thought of as an "Eskimo way of life" (Sollas 1911; but also see Binford 1978, 1980), characterized by nomadic hunter-gatherers in tune with the seasonal movements of migratory reindeer, by the practice of a primitive religion dominated by animistic art, totemism, and shamanism (Clottes and Lewis-Williams 1996;

Reinach 1903), and by a veritable explosion in lithic and organic technological activities (see summaries as diverse as Bahn 1984; Breuil 1912; Clottes 1989; de Mortillet 1869; Méroc 1953; Peyrony 1950). Throughout most of France during this 4,500-year period, and in the French Midi-Pyrénées in particular, the overall resource base remained rich and diverse, and there is broad consensus that TM is a period of cultural stability compared to preceding and subsequent culture phases. Especially in the French Pyrénées, Clottes (1989: 286) argues that there is far more regional variation *within* TM (for example, between the Paris Basin and the French Pyrénées, or between either region and Germany) than there is temporal variation between its earlier and later phases (also Straus 1996). Based on a century-old typological way of studying artifacts, most researchers argue that, on a regional basis, different so-called ethnic groups of Magdalenians lived apart from one another, though they sometimes exchanged source-specific objects over long distances, or intruded into one another's territories with artifact "styles" originating elsewhere (Audouze 1992: 345; Bahn 1982; Clottes 1989; Straus 1990–1: 19).

As had their nineteenth-century predecessors, mid-twentieth-century and French-trained archaeologists favored typologically oriented studies, and worked to identify the typical and the average in typologically discrete artifact classes from region to region and through time. In doing so, they tended to see the unusual as indicating the presence of some other group from somewhere else simply practicing their own variant of TM (especially Bordes 1961, 1972; Robert et al. 1953; but also more recently Clottes and Rouzaud 1983). As once practiced by generations of European-trained archaeologists, the general goal of Culture History research was to identify, describe, then compare temporal trends by determining regional norms "built up" from site-specific finds. With time, the goal was to develop even larger-scale spatiotemporal models of entire culture complexes, such as The Magdalenian. This Culture History emphasis on building up regional-scale spatiotemporal frameworks from site-specific findings is in no way unique to French researchers studying the Upper Palaeolithic. Indeed, the goal of tracking both regional and extraregional culture complexes through typological studies characterizes the explicit goal of most early and mid-century New and Old World archaeologists alike (Trigger 1989). It is precisely because of the normative interest in time-space systematics through an almost exclusive focus on artifact typology that *intra*regional variability was not taken as an important research question (discussion in G. A. Clark 1991: 84–5; S. Kuhn 1991: 248–9; Sackett 1981, 1991). It is important to note here how a particular theoretical framework (normativism) structured a particular way of dealing with the archaeological record (highlighting regional and extraregional scales of assemblage variability), which combined to structure a particular choice of analytic methodologies (namely, artifact typologies and time-space systematics).

In contrast, first-generation Anglo-American processualists became interested in developing causal accounts for the most ubiquitous and recurrent patterning of material culture in terms of an adaptationist, or functionalist, paradigm (namely, L. R. Binford 1968c; S. R. Binford and L. R. Binford 1968; J. G. D. Clark 1953; Clarke 1968; Higgs 1972). According to this "new" view of the past, temporal and/or spatial variability in artifact patterning, either within or beyond circumscribed geographic regions, was best explained as functionally specific behavioral adaptations to particular material (environmental) conditions. The introduction of so-called man-land studies to the European Palaeolithic constituted a major shift in how researchers thought about and studied the archaeological record (see personal reflections in G. A. Clark 1991; Straus 1991a). Curiously, however, this new way of studying the Palaeolithic provided a different reason to *still* focus on regional-scale variability, not because of "ethnicity" but because the region was the logical scale at which to model the adaptations of ancient hunter-gatherer settlement systems. The study of regional-scale variability made sense precisely because people "differentially participate in culture" (L. R. Binford 1965) and, for mobile hunter-gatherers in particular, no single site could possibly represent the entirety of their adaptations (also Clarke 1972). Although this explicit focus on the functional aspects of the variability of material culture, especially in technological endeavors, is surely one of the most significant contributions the functionalist paradigm made to archaeology, an adaptationist and homeostatic view of culture nonetheless emphasizes regional norms more than site-level variability (Dobres in press-b).

Thus, while typology-minded culture historians put site-specific patterns of artifact variability to use in describing regional (ethnic) Magdalenian lifeways and occasional intrusions from outsiders; function-minded processualists looked at individual sites as little more than differentiated points on the ground where varied subsistence strategies making up the regional settlement system were logistically situated. In both cases, however, "the region" was both the physical and phenomenological scale at which site-specific variability was explained or described. Site-specific finds were clearly necessary to further these different explanatory goals: for typologists, they were useful in describing the variety of things people did within their ethnic territories (and for determining local chronostratigraphic sequences), while for functionalists, site-specific patterns were necessary to model regional subsistence behaviors. In both cases, however, site-specific variability, especially in technological attributes, was seen as a means to an end rather than meaningful in its own right.

Contemporary materials research a soufflé *of typology and functionalism*

In the past two decades, French and Anglo-American trained archaeologists have forged a paradigmatic compromise. Today most research centers on the question of regional-scale settlement systems, subsistence practices, resource exploitation, and group mobility within and between regions through the study of the spatial distribution of sites and functionally specific activities across the landscape as well as activity-areas within sites. In the Paris Basin and the Dordogne (farther south), this focus on regional-scale settlement systems overlays, rather than replaces, a century's emphasis on typological studies, and is the result of the infusion of Leroi-Gourhan's work in the Paris Basin (for example, Leroi-Gourhan and Brézillion 1972) with L. R. Binford's (1977, 1978, 1980, 1983) ethnoarchaeological studies of logistical and collector subsistence strategies (see history in Audouze 1988b; Lemonnier 1992b).

Unfortunately, on the French side of the Pyrénées an explicit interest in subsistence and settlement has not developed at the same pace (Dobres in press-b), with the notable exceptions of Bahn (1977, 1984), Sieveking (1976), and Straus (1986, 1990–1, 1991b, 1992). Here, archaeological research is still primarily descriptive, focused separately on: (1) empirically rigorous typology-based technology (and art) studies; (2) identifying and describing various hunting techniques; (3) identifying seasons(s) of occupation from detailed pollen and faunal studies; and (4) delineating site-types (details in Dobres 1995c). It is within this antecedent research context that I have developed an alternative methodology for *chaîne opératoire* research explicitly driven by questions about the social agency of Magdalenian technicians.

In the French Pyrénées, contemporary research on the seasonal use of the landscape and its resources, and how these (actually) map out at the scale of individual sites, is conducted in order to identify variability in hunting strategies, to specify activities conducted from one site to another, to characterize intrasite activity areas, and to detail organic and lithic *chaînes opératoires*. Importantly, the focus here is not on sites as meaningful locales where people interacted with each other while going about their daily tasks, but as geographically distributed points on the land. The analytic focus only "dips" down to site-specific material patterning in order to "build up" regional generalizations. In all of this, *chaîne opératoire* research has figured prominently, and it is in large measure due to typologically-oriented technology studies that functionalist questions about widely shared and seemingly uncontested operational procedures for Magdalenian material action have been identified.

What difference does agency make? Some methodological effects

Matters of phenomenology and scale

Proposals of macro-scale explanatory models of artifact patterning in terms of regional adaptations to the environment and fluctuating availability of resources has never made it necessary or behaviorally relevant to think about material variability in terms of interpersonal social dynamics, nor to see interacting social agents as the explanatory culprits (Brumfiel 1991; Cowgill 1993; Dobres and Hoffman 1994, 1999a; Hodder 1986; Dobres and Robb in press-b; Wobst in press). And while palaeoeconomic research has long been dedicated to understanding not only behavioral norms but also functional variability around them, it is surprising that there has been so little explicit concern with variability at micro-analytic scales, such as "the site." Recall that, to date, research has focused primarily on *regional-scale variability* and that *chaîne opératoire* research has been *class-specific* – for example, with separate studies of harpoons, spear throwers, needles, and the like. In the process, material attributes that might pattern out at the physical scale of the site have been not been considered in terms of the people who produced them, but in terms of something else: functional variants of a regional adaptive system, ethnic variants of traditional lifeways, class-specific operational templates, and so forth.

In contrast, because a practice framework is premised on the idea that the interpersonal nature of social relationships matters to the shape, success, longevity, and failure of ancient lifeways and material behaviors, the phenomenological scale(s) at which social agents interacted with each other while taking care of material matters is particularly relevant. *The site* was the phenomenological scale at which its occupants gave meaning to their lives through their corporeal, material, and socially constituted technical activities. From this perspective, (technological) research must worry about variability practiced within a regional system and ask, in particular, what it implies about the dialectic of agency and structure being negotiated through intersubjective technological activities from one site of interaction to another (Dobres 1995c; Dobres and Hoffman 1994). Because I am interested to understand the unfolding nature of Magdalenian social interaction during artifact manufacture, use, repair, and discard activities, it makes analytic sense to focus on the physical scale experienced by the agents themselves while occupied with these tasks. Thus, in developing a specific *chaîne opératoire* methodology to further to my interest in Magdalenian technical agency, "the site" is an especially meaningful analytic scale at which material patterning could be linked to social practice.[7]

In tandem with my analytic focus on the site for what it suggests about the nature of interpersonal social relations mediated through material labor is another methodological implication: because people usually engage in more than one activity at a time, artifact analysis should grapple with multiple and overlapping technological endeavors and not separate them "by type" for heuristic convenience. Thus, I not only changed my analytic sightline from the region to the site (though I say more about this below), I also shifted from a traditional concern with class-specific artifact *chaînes* to the study of composite assemblages, a strategy I irreverently call my Humpty Dumpty methodology, because of its concern with integrated assemblages rather than specific artifact classes.

In sum, the centerpiece of my practice-oriented *chaîne opératoire* methodology highlights the site because that is where Magdalenian people interacted with each other while going about their daily chores, and it works with composite assemblages because during TM (as almost any other time, I suspect) people were involved in more than one activity at a time.[8]

Confusing things considerably: multiple axes and cross-cutting analytic categories

Just how much artifact function and physical properties structured a technicians' choice of raw materials, aspects of artifact design, techniques of fabrication, use and breakage patterns, as well as repair has long been of concern to *chaîne opératoire* research on the worked organic material culture of the Upper Palaeolithic. These issues are relevant to my interest in agency; thus to ferret out patterns that could inform on these concerns my methodology involves the recording of standard observations along a number of different axes: raw material, artifact morphology, class-specific work chains, use and breakage patterns, as well as details of repair and recycling strategies (the reader is referred to figure 6.5 for the following discussion). The attributes that obtain when investigated along these different axes are easily recorded at the analytic scale of the site and in no way contradict a focus on composite assemblages, for matters of raw material, form, function, and repair were surely routine concerns of Magdalenian technician-agents. When they are juxtaposed against each other, variability within and among

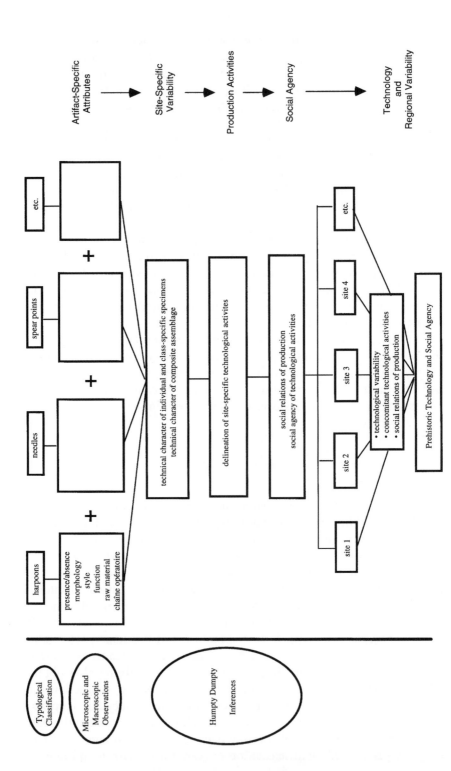

Figure 6.5 An agency-oriented research design based on *chaîne opératoire* research.

such axial patterns should inform the specific interests of a practice-oriented study at least as much as one dedicated to temporal, typological, or functional concerns.

However, because a practice framework starts with the premise that Magdalenian technicians brought to their tasks a preexisting familiarity with differences and similarities in the physical and functional properties of bone and antler, as well as stocks of knowledge and possibly different standards about when and how to work, repair, or recycle them, it is worth investigating patterns that might *cross-cut* artifact-specific classes. In other words, it is important to understand not just class-specific norms of standard and variable operations for making, using, or repairing harpoons, spear points, and needles, but how knowledge and skills applied to the making, use, or repair of one artifact type were or were not transferred to others, and under what circumstances. For this reason it is necessary to work *against* the traditional typological orientation so long the mainstay of Palaeolithic technology studies, and this is precisely what a focus on composite assemblages permits.

Thus, in addition to the simple claim that Magdalenian hunter-gatherer technicians probably did more than one technological activity at a time, I assume that individual technicians were likely to have made more than one class of objects. That is, each technician was likely to have made most of the everyday objects with which they gathered, hunted, fished, and so forth rather than there being "dedicated specialists" separately making then exchanging with their neighbors harpoons for spear points and needles for awls. Both working premises suggest the value of investigating possible cross-cutting fabrication, use, and repair techniques applied across artifact types, while at the same time recording attributes by artifact type. My intent here is not to try to identify the stigmata of individual hands from specimen to specimen, although that is a direction some *chaîne opératoire* research is now taking. Rather, to understand the agentive application of knowledge and skill to a variety of overlapping work habits involved in the making and use of multiple artifact types from site to site, it is worth investigating whether similar physical parts of different classes of objects made and used at individual sites were treated similarly (suggesting that such knowledge and techniques were not class specific but informed by other parameters such as intended function, morphology, or "tradition").

For example, were harpoon and spear points treated similarly (because of a generally similar function)? Were their bases made similarly (because of the necessity of hafting both classes of weapons to a shaft)? Or were they treated differently (and if so, why)? If similar parts of different artifact types are treated similarly, what does this suggest about the transfer of knowledge across technological activities at the sites where they took place? If similar parts are treated differently, what does this suggest about the rule-bound nature of class-specific artifact production, use, and repair from site to site? Similarly, were the points on spears and needles fabricated and/or repaired in the same manner (because of a generally similar function or template regarding the "right" way to make points)? Or were the everyday rules of production and repair different for each type of artifact? As well, were the eyes of needles made in the same way as holes pierced into horse teeth, or did the extremely different nature of the raw material or size of the objects being worked override any other factors? As interesting as these questions are, another of equal relevance to a practice framework is: Where, if any, was the variability or deviation in the way these strategies were practiced from site to site?

To evaluate whether technical treatment, knowledge, and skill did or did not vary across or within artifact categories and in what specific ways, I simply divide each specimen in a given assemblage into three physical segments (proximal, mesial, and distal) and record information on each (figure 6.6). This strategy proves especially useful in that it allows me to record technical observations on broken portions of arti-

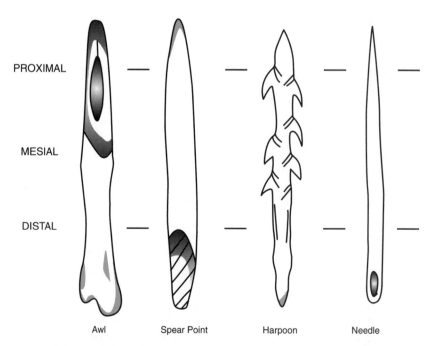

PROXIMAL

MESIAL

DISTAL

Awl   Spear Point   Harpoon   Needle

Figure 6.6 Division of type-specific artifacts into similar morphological zones for comparative purposes (artifacts not drawn to scale).

facts (thus increasing my sample size significantly), rather than simply characterize the nature of the break itself. This partitive approach to the study of artifact *chaînes opératoires* is not only amenable to a focus on site and composite assemblage, which is the centerpiece of my overall methodology, but also to the juxtaposition of norms and variability in technological practices as they unfolded throughout the region, as the reader will see below.

In sum, to obtain data relevant to the question of practice and agency in organic technological endeavors by Magdalenian technicians, I explore multiple axes (notably those concerning choice of raw material, artifact morphology, function, and strategies of repair), at multiple physical scales (microscopic and macroscopic; parts of objects and entire specimens; individual artifacts and composite assemblages), while investigating and recording standard observations on attributes that both uphold and cross-cut traditional analytical categories. This juxtaposition of different physical scales, axes, and categories allows me to obtain a wide variety of comparative observations: (1) on a composite assemblage as an integrated "whole"; (2) on morphologically similar segments of typologically different sorts of objects; (3) on differences in the technical treatment of similarly used artifacts; (4) on similarities in technical treatments of differently used objects; (5) on the handling of specific raw materials (specifically, bone, antler, ivory, teeth); and finally, (6) on all these patterns on a comparative, *inter*assemblage basis (discussed next). All said, this rather unwieldy approach to collecting data on site-specific *chaînes opératoires* requires that I record observations on some ninety specific attributes per specimen.

Beyond the site: back to issues of phenomenology and scale

While I especially emphasize the site as the phenomenological scale of social interaction most directly relevant to understanding the unfolding strategies and everyday routines of Magdalenian technicians, I also recognize that they "differentially participated in culture" (after L. R. Binford 1965). In particular, these were highly mobile foragers, who moved about and variously exploited the many river valleys and foothills making up the eastern Midi-Pyrénées (figure 6.7). Thus, while the site is the critically important phenomenological unit of analysis for my practice-oriented methodology (and not simply one of several physical scales at which to look for patterns), it is also necessary to compare and contrast observations across the region as a whole, for these agents played out their lives not at one site but in the course of daily, seasonally, and yearly movements around the region (and quite likely beyond it, as well).

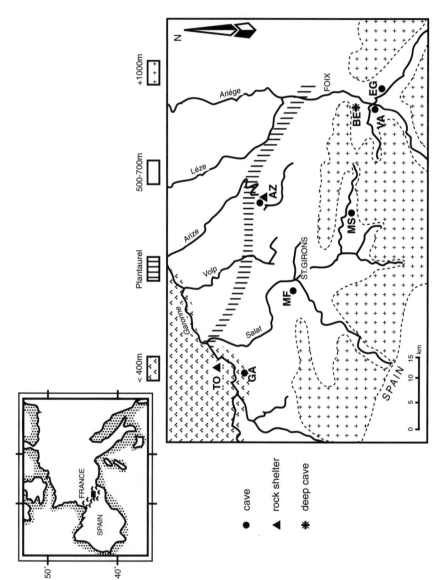

Figure 6.7 Map of the eastern French Midi-Pyrénées, with Magdalenian sites mentioned in the text (AZ: Mas d'Azil; BE: Bédeilhac; EG: Les Eglises; GA: Spugo de Ganties; MF: Montfort; MS: Massat; VA: La Vache).

Because my research design favors studying artifact *chaînes opératoires* at multiple physical scales and along cross-cutting analytic axes, it is a simple task to add yet one more physical scale to the fold, and juxtapose site-specific patterns to understand regional-scale norms and variability in technological practices. Thus, "the region" is not inconsequential to a practice-oriented study, for that would somehow (incorrectly) imply that any phenomenological scale "above" the individual is irrelevant, which is simply not true. As I stressed in chapter 5 (and will again in the following chapter), agency unfolds at multiple phenomenological scales, and concerns communities and groups as much as the individuals who constitute them. Thus, I find it worthwhile investigating (rather than assuming) just how widely shared TM technological template for organic material culture was, and in what particulars and under what contexts technicians deviated from it. Importantly, the intent here is not to generalize about a regional template for making, using, and repair harpoons, spear points, and needles "built up" from site- or typologically-specific findings; instead, it is to better understand the operative body of knowledge, skills, and gestural actions technicians variously expressed as they moved about the region, undertaking different sorts of technological activities from site to site and variously interacting with each other in the process.

Artifact assemblages: a link between individual technical gestures and the social body

As I previously explained, my empirical object of study is site-specific composite assemblages. By making the *assemblage* the object of study (and not separate classes of artifacts), and by investigating attribute patterning in more than one class of artifacts at a time, I am able to counter the conventional piecemeal approach to TM (and archaeological research, more generally) that effectively ignores the phenomenological reality of the technicians undertaking these activities in socially constituted contexts. The main objectives of this Humpty Dumpty methodology are: (1) to counter typological research that unnaturally segments the material remains of past webs of technological actions into heuristically discrete physical units that never get put back together; (2) to better discern empirical variability at multiple physical scales and analytic axes; but most importantly, (3) to organize findings in a way relevant to the agency questions driving this research – the nature of people's materially mediated interaction with each other that promoted (or hindered) personhood and political interests.

It should be clear by now that because my *subject* matter is people, social agency, and the question of social interaction within communities of workers making, using, and repairing material culture while mediating social relations, I treat my *object* matter differently from researchers whose interest is regional resource procurement strategies or settlement systems. It only makes sense to do so.

The methodology I have developed for seeking out, recording, and analyzing empirical observations from site to site allows me to ask not only about the regional template for making, using, and repairing everyday implements; it simultaneously permits me to investigate just how faithfully and how well (or how badly) Magdalenian technicians followed their own rules. Because the explicit goal is to make sense of the attribute patterns discerned as technical strategies mediating social interaction, I have chosen analytic methods, scales, and attributes with those dynamics in mind.

Some results

I do not wish to try the reader's patience by overemphasizing this one case study. But in order to demonstrate by example how making social agency one's explicit research question affects not only one's analytic methodology but also what can be learned as a result, I briefly describe a few of my own findings and show how they link to the question at hand. Six classes of formal artifacts made from antler and bone are ubiquitous at Magdalenian occupation sites throughout the Pyrénées: harpoons, needles, spear points, half-rounded rods, awls, and polishers (my study also investigated waste/debitage materials for what they could suggest about the nature and intensity of on-site production, use, and repair activities; details in Dobres 1995c, 1996a). In terms of site-specific patterns, it is striking to note both the variety of ways that single classes of artifacts were treated at the same site, and how variously technical treatments were practiced across the region as a whole.

For example, at Mas d'Azil I discerned two distinct techniques for creating needle eyes: one was a circular/piercing motion, the other involved cutting and scraping (figure 6.8). At Montfort, in contrast, two other techniques were practiced: an alternating rotational form of piercing, and a simple, straightforward form of pressure from a sharply pointed stone implement (without subsequent cutting and scraping). In contrast to these two patterns, at Bédeilhac technicians employed one of each of the techniques practiced at Mas d'Azil and Montfort (here they preferred either cutting and scraping or alternating rotation). At Spugo de Ganties all four techniques were in practice. By themselves, there is nothing remarkable about these empirical observations: they simply suggest that across the region there was more than one way to make needle eyes.

	CIRCULAR	CUT/SCRAPE	ALTERNATING ROTATION	PRESSURE
Mas d'Azil	+	+		
Bédeilhac		+	+	
Les Eglises	+	+	+	+
Spugo de Ganties	+	+		
Montfort			+	+

Figure 6.8   Variable techniques of needle-eye fabrication.

In terms of the morphology of antler point bases, Magdalenian *sagaies* are typically shaped in one of two ways: single-beveled and double-beveled bases (figure 6.9). Only at Les Eglises and La Tourasse did I find the same percentage of single- and double-beveled bases, an almost 50-50 presence of both forms in each assemblage. At all other sites, a somewhat different ratio obtained, with Mas d'Azil having more than 80 percent single-bevels and La Vache having almost the same percentage of double-bevels. Along yet another axis, the morphology of harpoon barbs, no two sites had anywhere close to the same pattern in terms of whether barbs ran down only one side of the shaft, ran down both sides symmetrically, or down both sides but with the barbs placed asymmetrically (figure 6.10).

As to which artifact classes were deemed worth repairing and how much labor Magdalenian technicians devoted to such efforts, yet again a fascinating pattern emerged. Spear points (*sagaies*) were by far the single artifact class most often subjected to repair; of the six sites where such repair was undertaken, four (or 66 percent) dedicated between three-quarters and all of the efforts to repairing spear points – except at La Vache, where three-quarters of all repair was done to harpoons. However, when I looked closely at which morphological parts of specimens were subject to repair (and therefore which part was broken during use), no two sites showed similar patterns. Variable breakage patterns (to points, shafts, or bases) suggest different patterns of use even within a single site, and this is marked in my findings (figure 6.11). Similarly, on-site decisions as to whether a break was worth repairing followed no overarching template: at Bédeilhac and Les Eglises, repair is almost evenly spread between shafts and bases (imply-

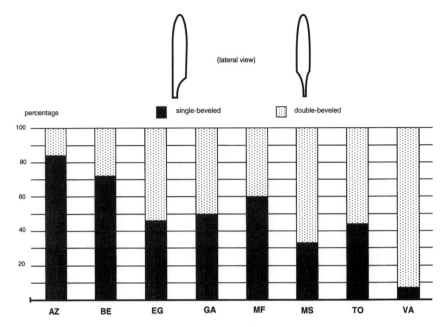

Figure 6.9 Intersite distribution of spear-point (*sagaie*) bases. Note, in particular, that EG (Les Eglises) and VA (La Vache) are similar upland sites used for the special purpose of hunting ibex, yet they have notably different proportions of single- and double-beveled forms (AZ: Mas d'Azil; BE: Bédeilhac; EG: Les Eglises; GA: Spugo de Ganties; MF: Montfort; MS: Massat; VA: La Vache).

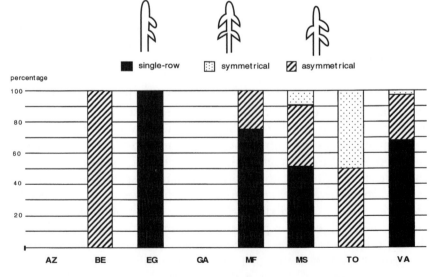

Figure 6.10 Intersite distribution of harpoon barbs. Note that no two sites approximate the same pattern (AZ: Mas d'Azil; BE: Bédeilhac; EG: Les Eglises; GA: Spugo de Ganties; MF: Montfort; MS: Massat; VA: La Vache).

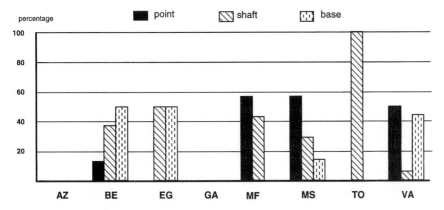

Figure 6.11   Intersite distribution of spear-point (*sagaie*) repair by artifact segment. Note that no two sites approximate the same pattern (AZ: Mas d'Azil; BE: Bédeilhac; EG: Les Eglises; GA: Spugo de Ganties; MF: Montfort; MS: Massat; VA: La Vache).

ing similar uses leading to breakage, as well); at Montfort and Massat points were most often broken and repaired; at La Vache repair was made almost exclusively to points and bases; while at La Tourasse 100 percent of all repair was to shafts.

What begins to emerge from these brief examples is empirical evidence attesting to the context-specific nature of artifact manufacture, use, and repair activities. When I compared site-specific findings along numerous axes one overarching pattern emerged: at no two sites did technicians blindly follow similar rules of procedure. Along every measure of technical activity I studied (save one, raw material), I found evidence not of a pan-Magdalenian template of what to do, how to do it, and when, but rather a situated application of knowledge and skill. But there is still more to be said about the contextual structure of Magdalenian technological practice. In terms of non-quantifiable data, I discerned site-specific applications of special kinds of knowledge and skill (or lack of it) variously applied to harpoon and spear-point bases and the eyes of needles (details in Dobres 1995a). In particular, while spear points and harpoons are the two most ubiquitous artifact types found throughout the region, the way they were handled at La Vache is striking (Dobres 1996a, 1999b). Here, not only were the bases of both classes subjected to special treatment (figure 6.12) in the form of a series of small depressions on the ventral surface for improved hafting (and this is found at no other site in the study) (Dobres 1995a); I also found that numerous harpoons and points were repaired over and over again, to the point that some were actually worked to a nub. And at Mas d'Azil, I found a significantly large

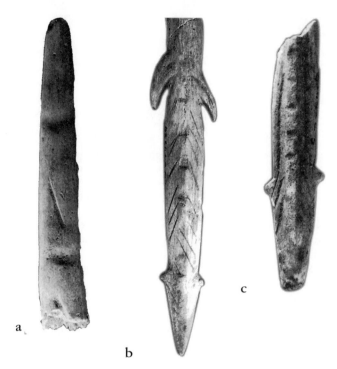

Figure 6.12   Antler spear point (*sagaie*) and harpoons (b,c) from La Vache showing hafting depressions unique to this site (not to scale).
Source: Author's photographs

number of repaired needle eyes; yet while a few were remade with a sure and steady hand, several betrayed the inexperience (or infirmity) of someone incapable of what to others was perhaps a simple task (figure 6.13).

In addition to these patterns pertaining to how artifacts were treated from site to site during manufacture, use, and repair, by considering each composite assemblage as a whole I was able to investigate the range of activities undertaken at each site and the intensity with which they were practiced (details in Dobres 1995c, 1996a). A number of particularly interesting findings in this regard concern La Vache and Les Eglises, which are similarly defined on the basis of their material culture and faunal assemblages as special-purpose, upland, ibex-hunting sites. However, as figure 6.14 shows, when these sites are compared on the basis of the overall "character" of their composite assemblage they are extremely different, both in the two measures used to assess the nature of production taking place (presence of blanks/preforms, and evidence of repair), and those used to assess the intensity with which such activities were pursued (suggested by the number

Figure 6.13 Inferior-quality needle-eye manufacture, Mas d'Azil.
Source: Author's photograph

of separate treatments given to each artifact, and evidence of final
sanding/polishing).[9]

Just beyond empirical data lie both habitus *and social agency*

Just as knowing the procedural template of a technological system is
necessary to identifying and explaining in human terms the variability practiced within it, knowing the extent to which technical practices vary around shared dispositions helps understand just how
constraining or liberating some template was. I have made use of
Bourdieu's (1977: 78) idea that *habitus* is "the generative principle of
regulated improvisations," in order to understand the extent to which
Magdalenian technicians deviated from their traditional routines of
organic artifact production and use, and to try to understand why and
under what circumstances they did so. My findings (only a few of which
are described above) juxtaposed artifact, class-specific, and assemblage-
wide patterns with those at ever-increasing physical scales, in order
to link the making and remaking of everyday material culture with
the making and remaking of social identities negotiated from site to
site. Importantly, *chaîne opératoire* research permits me to delineate the
specific social and material contexts of production, or situated structures, within which these diverse technical gestures and decisions

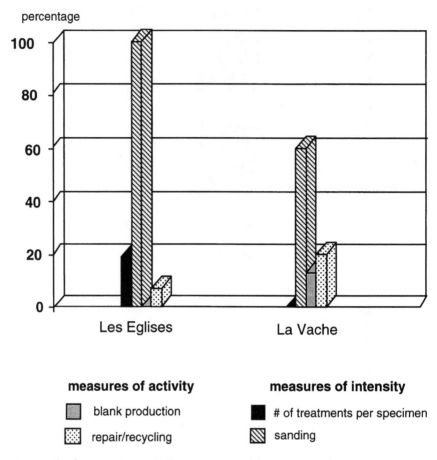

percentage

measures of activity

▨ blank production

▦ repair/recycling

measures of intensity

■ # of treatments per specimen

▧ sanding

Figure 6.14   Extremely different technical "character" of the composite organic assemblages from Les Eglises and La Vache, two similar upland sites used for specialized ibex hunting.

played out during face-to-face interaction. These contexts involved not only what specific making and use activities were unfolding, but also the intensity which they took place (Dobres 1996a).

Chaîne opératoire research has, thus, let me identify individual dispositions in technological practice and understand them as they unfolded in their original (prehistoric) social field. Such non-discursive social strategies advanced through technical labor were situated precisely at the dialectic center of an ever-contested relationship between (Magdalenian) structure and agency. In a similar vein, Dietler's and Herbich's (1998) ethnoarchaeological research on the Luo of western

Kenya also merges *chaîne opératoire* research with Bourdieu's concept of *habitus*. Their point of departure in making sense of standardized ("Luo") ceramic production routines and their variants is to note that "potters share a set of learned dispositions that guide their perceptions of an acceptable range of variation in choices at the different stages of the *chaîne opératoire*" (ibid.: 250). How faithfully these procedures are followed, and under what circumstances and in what ways technicians deviate from them, "is a function of the personal transformation of *habitus* through practice responding to certain demands of social relations" (ibid.: 253). In other words, templates shared by the community are played out through the learned hands of individuals situated *within* streams of ongoing social relations and traditional ways of working the world, not outside them.

I want to understand the material contours of Magdalenian organic technology as a form of social engagement and investigate how such interaction was advanced through material means. Did it operate on a discursive level or was it more non-discursive and habitual? As a form of social communication, was technique overt and aggrandizing or was it rather covert and tacit? Or, did these Magdalenian communities of technicians get along through some combination of these several strategies? These are not questions typically asked through traditional materials research, because until now they have not been considered behaviorally relevant; from an agency perspective, however, they are exceedingly so. Fortunately, the analytic methods of *chaîne opératoire* research are well suited to addressing them in ways that are simultaneously rigorous, materially grounded, and anthropologically relevant. With my Humpty Dumpty methodology I have, indeed, been able to identify in certain stages of production, at certain sites, and on certain classes of artifacts a revealing amount of context-specific variability in technical matters of choice, design, and implementation; variability that I believe goes to the heart of the agency dynamics by which these people negotiated their social relations of production while undertaking the most mundane of everyday activities. Thus, rather than collecting a morass of seemingly trivial data on the idiosyncratic "noise" of unidentifiable technical agents making harpoons, needles, and spear points slightly differently from each other at eight separate sites across their ethnic region, I provided myself with relevant empirical observations and a means for seeking patterns related to the mediation of everyday life through material means.

As presupposed by theory, the phenomenological scale at which I have found variability wavering around the norm was "the site." As I described above, variability is not class-specific nor can it be explained in terms of artifact use or even site function.[10] Had the choice of technical operations been structured by form, artifact physics, or function

I would have seen such evidence *in spite of* my focus on the site and composite assemblages. But across the landscape, technical strategies for making, using, and especially repairing, recycling, and finally discarding artifacts was *not* structured by blind submission to tradition, nor was it dictated by typology, the objective "limits" of raw material, nor even functional need. To me, this implies that for TM (in the Pyrénées at least), culture-bound technical rules of procedure and comportment were little more than guidelines (fuller elaboration in Dobres 1995a, 1995c, 1999b). Why people made the specific choices they did at different sites where many of the same activities were pursued is a fascinating anthropological question. As well, how these choices and strategies promoted self/Other/worldly knowledge, personhood, and related matters can be investigated precisely because data were collected at scales relevant to those phenomena. Given my specific reasons for collecting and organizing empirical data as I did, I did not have to assert or rationalize *post hoc* why a particular technique for preparing weapon bases for hafting, incising needle eyes, or repairing the broken bases of harpoons was chosen at site *x* but not site *y*. I was not left to simply speculate whether such actions were conscious or not. Nor did I have to bracket off as a less knowable, second-order phenomenon the socially constituted reasons why gestural skill and know how were only sometimes displayed in the specific ways they were.

Because agency theory informed my choice of research methodology, I had reasons already spelled out why these data at these scales were relevant to the question of technology and social agency. This does not mean that I predicted what the patterns might be, nor did I anticipate specifically what they would suggest about the social underpinnings of Magdalenian technology.[11] Indeed, as with most *chaîne opératoire* research, identifying material patterns was an inductive exercise. The deductive part was suggesting which physical and phenomenological scale could help me the most (the site and composite assemblages) and why. Indeed, had I found that technical strategies of transformative action on matter were bound to specific types of artifacts, constrained by the mechanical nature of the raw materials they worked, or dictated by practical function, I would have seen this "in spite" of my desire to see otherwise. I might have been led, furthermore, to conclude that the regional procedural template was not subject to much manipulation, and that within this top-down system technical agents had little room to maneuver.

Instead, where I found people veering off their template in all manner of directions, which is exactly what they did, was in the context of face-to-face interaction. More telling still, the material manner in which their technical *habitus* intersected with context, structure, and tradition was decidedly non-discursive. That is, Magdalenian technicians appear to have displayed their differently learned skills of the trade, betrayed their incompetence, and tried out new or unusual techniques in rather subtle and covert ways; not in overt or gratuitous displays of self-promotion. In simple gestures for cutting barbs, resharpening points, repairing broken bases, and incising new needle eyes these agents effected multiple ends, both material and social. And the particular sequences and options they knew about and variously practiced during material transformation, those minute hows and whens of artifact production, allowed for subtle social transformations, such as the making of skilled women and men and the unmaking of the more elderly craftspeople who could no longer pull off what was expected of them.

Conclusions

I suggested earlier that analytic methods packaged within a carefully chosen research methodology could provide data which inform theory, just as theory informs the research methodology and choice of specific analytic methods chosen for data acquisition. Had I not specifically sought to identify variability around the Magdalenian norm of organic technological practice through the ancillary methods of *chaîne opératoire* research modified to suit my needs, I could not have identified the material parameters of Magdalenian social agency in everyday artifact production and use. And had I not been concerned to identify what those norms were, again with the help of my modified *chaîne opératoire* methodology, I could not have understood how Magdalenian technical gestures were not as much constrained by the objective material world and tradition as much as enabled by a world that was socially mediated. The hermeneutic spiral between theory and data acquisition advanced through a *chaîne opératoire* methodology, between particular research interests and rigorous materials analysis, and between well-reasoned deductions and sound interpretive inferences shows that one need not consider the social agency of prehistoric technology as some second-order phenomenon sensitive to structure but not actually shaping it.

As *both* an analytic methodology and a conceptual framework for studying ancient technology, the study of sequential operational gestures, procedures, and judgments can bring to light material patterns capable of informing on what I think really counts about prehistoric technology: social relations of production, meaningful interaction, and an embodied being-in-the-world form of existence. The *chaîne opératoire* is many things: for technicians, it is a set of organizing principles and practical logic for transforming raw materials into cultural products; it is a blueprint that can be modified to suit material and social interests simultaneously; it is a model of the world and how it should be worked. For technology researchers, it is an analytic methodology for rigorous materials research; and, above all, it is a conceptual framework for linking the static material traces of ancient technique, gestures, knowledge, values, judgment, and skill to the socially constituted technicians who practiced them.

Chaînes opératoires were not a procedural strait-jacket that unthinking and unfeeling technicians blindly followed. Rather, they were guidelines for how to proceed; guidelines that under specific conditions might or might not be followed. How people gave meaning to their lives and negotiated their way in the world are questions that empirical research on prehistoric technology can address with more analytic confidence and theoretical rigor than it has done to date. When the study of artifact life-histories is pursued to elucidate the agency of social life-histories, researchers have at their disposal a vast array of exacting and precise analytic techniques. The trick is to not succumb to the fallacy of misplaced concreteness and let material *chaîne opératoire* research strait-jacket one's imagination and vision.

Chapters 4 and 5 argued that through the "biography of things," objects, techniques of fabrication and use, and even practical design choices are part of a larger web of meanings, political strategies, social proscriptions, and ways of seeing and acting properly in the world. Why is it so hard to entertain these issues as a legitimate *starting point* for materials analysis, when ethnographic, ethnoarchaeological, and even historic technology studies show this is the case? Why do we take for granted that the best, or only, place to start inquiry is with that small part of an ancient technology preserved in material traces, leaving the social dynamics to some later point in time? The brief historiography of Magdalenian research outlined above shows all too well that causal accounts to explain artifact variability take different forms, depending on the theoretical persuasions of the analyst and how they are taught to think about, see, and study such things (Trigger 1989; Dobres in press-b).

As chapter 2 showed, we can trace archaeology's instrumentalist approach to the scientific study of natural, human, and even social phenomena back to Enlightenment ideals and concepts. This framework makes a problematic distinction

> between [analytical] disengagement and objectification, on one hand, and a kind of power or control on the other; between this and the ideal of a correct procedure, a proper way of assembling and constructing our thoughts, which defines rationality; and lastly between rationality and

the attaining of knowledge. These connections have become so strong in certain departments of modern culture that they might seem the only possible construals. (C. Taylor 1989: 163)

But as Berger (1973), Forge (1970), and others have shown, although seemingly self-evident, "learning to see" any empirical phenomenon is a *learned* disposition that takes a lot of practice. Importantly, once you learn to see from a particular vantage point, it is often difficult to see any other way (Dobres in press-b).

If we are disposed to see ancient technology as first and foremost about practical, material, and objective matters, then we investigate material remains with these concerns in our mind's eye. If we see technology as an ongoing process of social existence and verb of interaction between and among people and the things they make and use, then we need to investigate attributes, employ analytic scales, and develop ways of organizing data that pertain to these subjective matters. In this chapter I have offered only one sustained example for how one might go about this, based on my experiences studying Magdalenian technology. I hope, however, that within this example the reader finds fodder for their own interest in technologies as if people mattered.

7

A Future for Technology's Pasts

to begin always anew, to make, to reconstruct, and to not spoil, to refuse to
bureaucratize the mind, to understand and to live life as a process – live to
become . . .

(Paulo Friere, quoted in hooks 1994: v)

The end of the twentieth century is an exciting time for technology
studies, but not because the "Y2K problem" has come and gone. It is
exciting because we have at our disposal more than one robust conceptual framework and analytic methodology with which to highlight
any of a number of human dynamics expressed during the production
and use of the material world. As we turn the millennial corner our
options are many, especially in archaeology. But as Charles (1992: 905)
perceptively notes:

> Theories, reconstructions, and explanations can only serve to illuminate
> portions of [the] past; it is too much to expect that one theory or recon-
> struction or one explanation will be sufficient. The task of the archaeo-
> logist then becomes, not choosing the best single model, but finding
> the several frameworks that increase our understanding of events and
> processes in the past.

In this book I have been outlining a practice framework that is explicitly devoted to recentering human subjects at the very heart and soul
of object making and use.

A momentum is building across the social sciences seeking to reclaim
and privilege the subject in relation to the object, and exploring new
(and even some old) ways of understanding their inseparability. In intellectual paradigms as diverse as nuclear genetics, evolutionary ecology,
and feminist theory, ontologies and premises are coming under deliber-
ate and well-intentioned scrutiny. Such reflection is creating the necessary room within which to identify and explore alternatives. In so doing,
the veil of obfuscation mystifying long-held truisms is being lifted from

claims about what can and cannot be known, what is and is not a legitimate line of inquiry, and what are and are not important phenomena, past and present. In the midst of all this, an interdisciplinary dialogue among technology researchers from contemporary culture studies, history, and philosophy, to sociology, anthropology, and archaeology has set the stage for new conceptual, analytical, and interpretive possibilities. In archaeology, especially, the fractious eighties are thankfully behind us and the oftentimes destructive processual/post-processual debate replaced by concerted attempts to find common ground, or at least let sleeping dogs lie.

As an archaeologist, what I find especially compelling about this movement to reclaim the subject is the practically across-the-board interest in agency, in social relations of production, in meaning making, and in how the very process of living in the everyday world becomes – and became – the edifice upon which both social institutions and culture change depend. By recentering the subject at the very heart of technology, there turns out to be a surprising resonance between at least some interests shared by processualists, behaviorists, and post-processualists. At the same time, our analytic methods for researching ancient technologies are also at their peak, not only because of the vast array of gizmos, gadgets, instruments, and measuring devices now in our laboratory tool kit, but also because of the anthropological uses to which they are being put: to study the evolution of cognition, symbolism, and the process of external objectification so central to the human condition; to discover the operative world views and non-discursive rules underlying the most mundane of ancient artifact making and use; to identify bodies of ancient technoscientific, and hence sociopolitical, knowledge; and to recognize the physical traces of ancient technical gestures as non-discursive strategies of compliance, contestation, and challenge to the social order.

It is clear that a focus on technological practice and agency is not a hindrance to macro-scale questions long of interest to much of the archaeological community. Indeed, from evolutionary ecology to feminist theory there is a new concern to understand the relationship between micro and macro, between agency and structure, between stability and change, and between thinking, doing, and feeling. Fortunately, it is no longer the case that we must choose between either wallowing in the idiosyncratic and particularistic noise of the "little people" of prehistory or researching macro-scale processual dynamics. We are now beginning to understand these extremes as part of the same process that must, in fact, be studied in concert. Thus, just as we can study the most minute traces of artifact debitage and breakage patterns to understand evolutionary changes in a species' cognitive abilities and gestural strategies of artifact manufacture and use, we can also investigate long-term macro-scale change in complex technologies to understand changing conceptions and conditions of self and personhood.

This book is dedicated to outlining the contours of a conceptual framework useful for taking up many of the issues and problems that archaeologists now find compelling. Eminently compatible and helpful in researching the many questions concerning technology, my perspective weaves together three strands of thought: (1) the embodied and sensual experience of technological practice as a meaningful and uniquely human form of involvement in the world (following Heidegger); (2) the metaphorical and literal resonance between material production and social reproduction embodied during *chaînes opératoires* and habitual routines of everyday practice (following Mauss); (3) the centrality of technicians and social agency in creating the structures that promote cultural stability and the processes of culture change (following practice theory). Whether one's interest is in Oldowan chopping tools or the bifacial symmetry of the Acheulean handaxe; the cognitive and gestural implications of Levallois reduction strategies or the overlap in material and symbolic domains of Upper Palaeolithic art and technology; the material transformation of clays to ceramics and ores to metals or the domestication of wheat, barley, corn, and cattle; the construction of pyramids, henges, and burial mounds or mass-produced clay pipes and iron shackles – in all of these cases the dialectic of production, reproduction, embodied engagement, agency, and structuration are central. As widely different as they are in time, place, and material and social contingency, the one thing that makes these technologies similar is that they are nothing without agents, be they early hominids or yesterday's slave traders. Social relations of production, systems of meaning and value, knowledge about how the world works, and artifacts, all come into existence and make their mark on the world through the mindful labor of socially engaged agents. And it is human agents and their webs of social relations and values that create not only culture but also culture change.

In saying this, I do not contest the claim that technology was, and is, absolutely central to the evolutionary success of the hominid lineage and to what it means to be human. But by redefining technology as a verb of embodied engagement and social interaction engendered and made meaningful within ongoing streams of tradition and contestation, and by placing special focus on the agents and agency of technological practice, it becomes a little easier (perhaps) to study the material traces of ancient technology without succumbing to the fallacy of misplaced concreteness; that is, without letting the physical part of ancient technology which fortuitously preserves in the present not only stand for the whole, but conflate with the process in question. At the same time, I admit it also becomes a little harder (perhaps) to know how to make sense of material traces as but one *part* of ancient *tekhnē*, the whole of which was always and necessarily more than the flakes, the tools, the debitage, the use-wear stigmata, the labor units, and the measurable efficiency of resource utilization.

A relational and practice-centered view of human (and hominid) technologies requires, first, a rethinking of what constitutes technology, and second, a reconsideration of what one is studying through the medium of material patterns and empirical traces. This is no easy task, and the previous chapters have only begun to identify what is required to move such inquiry forward. It is also clear that there are no across-the-board answers to these questions, nor a formulaic package of methods and material correlates that can work for all the world's technologies: it depends on the what the researcher wants to understand in particular (and this may not be consistent even within a research community); it depends upon the materiality and sociality of the technology in question; and it depends on the analytic means deemed appropriate for the task. The one thing it does *not* depend upon, in my view, is an inferential ladder of epistemological limitations linked to the nature of the archaeological record.

Embodied *Chaînes*, Being, and Agency: Enrolling Technicians in Society

What I want to understand about the social relations structuring the material contours of Magdalenian organic technology is not necessarily what another researcher may want to comprehend about Moche metallurgy, Chacoan architecture, Hopewell burial mounds, Zimbabwe iron working, Chalcolithic weaponry, the Harappan bead trade, Solutrean lithics, or the mass-production of British and Chinese ceramics, for that matter. In chapters 4 and 5, I paid special attention to the sensual experience of technological practice as an embodied way of being in the world that engenders self, Other, and worldly knowledge that can be put to ends quite different from the material practicalities at hand. It may seem, to some, that I have overemphasized the individual body in all of this. If I have, it is because in so much of current research the agent is practically erased from consideration as the essential element that makes technologies work and makes them culturally salient.

The individual body is, however, socialized to its very core; and just as one never has a direct and existential experience with things-in-themselves to which they "apply" meaning, there is also no such thing as a free-willed, self-referential agent able to divorce themselves from, or exist outside, the sociopolitical structures and symbolic constructs in which they exist. As Moore (1994: 74) puts it in a slightly different context: "meaning does not inhere in symbols, but must be invested in and interpreted from symbols by acting social beings. Interpretation is the product of a series of associations, convergences and condensations established through praxis." Simply put, the sense and sensibility of the technicians' body does not come from symbolic constructs above and outside it, but from how they are put into motion through practice. In the case of technology, engaged physical practice is socially constituted and therefore necessarily involves society at each stage of transformation.

The phenomenological dialectic of internalized self and externalized "member of society" is much the same slippery dynamic as that forever unfolding between agents and structures. The technician's body is simultaneously personal and social and always in the process of becoming rather than existing ready-made. Individuals intuit, construct, and project who and what they are out of a murky experiential arena in which their sentient, socialized bodies are grounded in the "real" and sensual world of technological practices while, simultaneously, they make that world meaningful through constructs and symbolic frames not necessarily their own. This suggests that self identity can never be an existence or an experience separate from group identity. Both develop in concert, from the ways the corporeal body enscripts and contests external categories and representations generated and expected by others (J. Chapman 1996, in press; Miller 1985). It is for these several reasons that the personal is necessarily social, the individual body forever part of the body politic, and the operational gestures of a single technician's hands always tied to collective representations. It is also why the concept "technical agent" can be an individual worker, a collective group, or both.

What this means for archaeological studies of technology is that within a given set of historical circumstances *bodies matter*, whether one focuses on the work of an individual technician (as did Schlanger in his study of "Marjorie's core"), a community of technicians working individually but in shared communities of practice (as in my research on the Magdalenian), or an hierarchically organized multitiered industrial system (such as those studied by historians, ethnographers, and the occasional ethnoarchaeologist; for example, see studies of contemporary engineering and computer-based technologies in Aronson in press; Engeström and Middleton 1998; Suchman in press).

These same dynamics operate and the same principles can still guide inquiry, even if one's interest is in the macro-communal dynamics of so-called specialized or complex technologies. Whether constructing a mound, henge, or pueblo, sailing a ship or designing and building a bridge, or mass-producing ceramics, metals, beads, or cloth for exchange, when the individual body works in concert with others in some collectively (even hierarchically) organized enterprise in which they are but a cog in the wheel, that body is being *enrolled* into that mindful practice in such a way that its identity as member-of-the-group may conflate with or even override internalized notions of personhood. Such a "fractal" or "distributed" concept of personhood (Strathern 1988; Wagner 1991) suggests that in some instances these embodied and transformative experiences, which are simultaneously subjective and objectified, may conflict with each other, as DuBois (1994: 5 [orig. 1903]) understood in his profound analysis of what he called African-American double-consciousness; of being "an American, a negro; two souls, two thoughts, two unreconciled strivings; two warring ideals in one dark body, whose dogged strength alone keeps it from being torn asunder."

An important question which the study of ancient craft and specialized technologies can address through a practice framework, then, is how and to what extent the phenomenological experience of collective work promoted (or depended upon) changing notions of personhood. R. White (for example, 1989, 1993) has actually opened the evolutionary door to such inquiry with his detailed study of Upper Palaeolithic (Aurignacian) ivory bead making on an extraordinary material scale, yet for the apparent adornment of only a few members of "special" standing in the community. While his research has focused on the evolution of self-expression and the historical shift from achieved to ascribed social status, the relationship of the individual (decorated body) embodied within larger and objectifying communal structures and constructs can be situated in a practice framework. Yet "it does not require sophisticated theorizing to recognize that every social being has a life of such multiplicity and that every social context creates such shifting between foreground and background" (Ortner 1995: 184). With this argument, then, it is not necessarily an either/or phenomenon (self or self-at-the-mercy-of-constructs), but rather one of ongoing dialogue, conversation, or possibly argument (Ledermann 1990). Thus, rather than think of identity as a fixed existence, or mantle one "wears" in public, a practice framework highlights the dynamic of becoming as simultaneously internalized and externalized, and as sensually experienced while also being objectified.

We must, however, be especially careful not to universalize western notions of self-identity as a unitary, ego-centered entity individuated through conscious distanciation and separation (as object relations theory and methodological individualism argue). "Indigenous or local concepts of the self vary in the way in which they conceptualize the relationship between self and non-self, the degree to which mind (if it exists at all) is separated from body, and the manner in which agency and motivation are conceptualized as arising internally or externally to the self" (Moore 1994: 31; also Ridington 1988). At the same time, however, even though not all societies define the individual as a rational and autonomous agent of its own making, "this does not mean that individuals do not exist or that people's actions are not evaluated in terms of an individual life trajectory or career" (Moore 1994: 33). As I have argued all along, the complex linkages between self and group through the structuration process, or more specifically between personhood, agency, corporate rules, expectations, and symbolic representations, are necessarily interwoven through the medium of socially constituted technological practices. Importantly, these multiple and overlapping dynamics are not easy to tease apart, nor do I think they should be.

Archaeological implications

In cultures where we see material evidence of hierarchically organized, large-scale technologies producing material surplus, where craft laborers plied their trade through finely honed skills and special access to the knowledge and means of production not accessible to all, and where their work separated them (socially and physically) from other members of the community (thereby setting in motion new relationships with their fellow workers), we can ask about how one's proscribed social role as a particular category of technician might have, in fact, defined and necessarily circumscribed their phenomenological sense of self (after Kopytoff 1990). Did incipient craft specialization and the particular configuration of labor practices create new social categories of persons defined by their differential contribution to material production (such as skilled "craftsperson" or unskilled "laborer")? In turn, did this process override and possibly denigrate other identities (such as father, wife, son, or daughter-in-law)? Or, did changing social relations set the stage for different technical and material configurations of artifact production and new forms of collective representations? And did these, in turn, promote and legitimate both specialized technologies and increasingly differentiated statuses, rights, privileges, and duties for the workers involved? And how did this transformation unfold? Was it discursive, or did it catch technical agents off-guard? Was it contested, or did those involved promote and embrace these new opportunities? And among the community most directly affected, how much contestation and compliance took place?

However one asks these questions, the point is that everyday technological practice and cultural representations intersected *in* and played out *on* the bodies of those involved. Philosophers and historians have shown that the materiality of particular technological practices (be they the factory line, virtual reality, or so-called time-saving domestic devices such as washing machines and microwaves) create unique relationships with their makers and users. While these studies have highlighted the alienating nature of these experiences in industrial contexts, technicians and consumers in other contexts, doing other sorts of material activities, and engaging in other sorts of social relations, engender wholly different experiences with the things they make and use. Clearly, the material and physical nature of the technology in question plays a role in shaping and engendering these experiences, but it is not through them alone that meaning is made (Dobres in press-a). When considered in light of the *chaîne opératoire*, however, detailed evidence of the physical configuration and "demands" of particular material practices provide not only material clues for investigating these questions, but also the links between them and their social milieu(s).

Thus, whether the operational sequences of technological production are studied at the micro-scale of individual artifacts made by individual hands, or at the macro-scale of nested operations conducted by different technical communities (perhaps in different physical locations), these transformative stages are still linked together through the mindful bodies that undertake them. How were the miners of ore in underground caverns constituted and defined by the physical nature of their work in relation to those who processed it in workshops, to those who then molded or hammered the metals into culturally valued objects through special skills and knowledge on which their own identity depended, and to those who then traded the end products for prestige, political gain, or economic benefit? How did the physical act and outcome of contributing one's personal labor to the sequential and communal construction of a mound or pueblo contribute to wholesale social reproduction, to corporate identity, and to personhood? These questions, I maintain, are central and necessary to understanding how artifacts were designed, made, used, and given value within a particular set of material and social conditions. They are neither of second-order importance nor are they unknowable. The agency implicated here was both individual and corporate, and the structures simultaneously social, symbolic, and material. What wove them into a single (complex) whole was practice.

Ethnographic grounding

To this point I have alluded to some of the more negative distancing and hierarchical aspects of self/group identity simultaneously forged and contested during technological practices. There is yet another relationship to consider, however. Subjective and objectified identities and the allegiances and relationships they promote or deny during corporate technological activities may, in some instances, actually promote and reaffirm each other, rather than sublimate one over the others. This is precisely what Pfaffenberger's (1999) analysis of Triobrand yam storage houses (*bwaymas*) shows: the communal forms of labor called upon (or more colloquially, required) to execute the sequential stages of building construction helps *enroll* individual agents into a corporate entity known as the chief's male relatives-in-law. In so doing, that community is reaffirmed and privileged as a collective body, and therefore *an* agent, having a specific obligatory, power, and hierarchical relationship with the chief and a particular place in society.

At the same time, the individual bodies physically, socially, and symbolically enrolled into this collective by virtue of the physical demands of *bwayma* construction allow individual agents to comprehend their personal place in the Triobrand scheme of things, thereby reaffirming and giving concrete expression to what Malinowski called their social template. As Pfaffenberger (1999: 149) explains it: "various individuals and groups brought into the fabrication process are already committed to the basic belief structure that underlies the activity, know what is expected of them and accept their obligation, and possess at least some sort of conception of what they are supposed to do." Their personal and physical involvement "pre-energizes" those templates, thus giving them corporeal, meaningful expression. Fundamental virtues by which Triobrand Islanders judge both themselves and their objects – qualities of lightness, emptiness, heaviness, and anchoring – become incorporated into one's physical sense of the world and their place in it through the specific ways individual labor is physically enrolled into the collective making of *bwaymas* (Pfaffenberger in press; after Munn 1974, 1986). This is precisely the point Heidegger makes on an abstract level.

Even from the chief's point of view (which Pfaffenberger does not elaborate), his very identity as chief is also simultaneously personal and political, individual and social, agent of his own interests while also subject to the overarching ontological structures within which Triobrand society operates. However, while in the Triobrand case the chief may not contribute his own physical labor to making or filling a *bwayma* with yams, he is nonetheless affiliated with that technology (by demanding it) and engenders part of his identity by virtue of the product that results. In other sorts of collectively organized technologies (in the past), those in charge of production may indeed have physically enrolled themselves in the sequential activities unfolding about them, and through such physically engaged means legitimated their identity(ies). If we are to understand the lived practices by which the "big men" and elites of the past were able to convince technicians to enroll themselves into collaborative work efforts without overt coercion, then a relational, embodied, and practice framework is called for (see, for example, A. Joyce in press).

Summary

Whether in the nature of a dialogue, conversation, or argument, the dialectic of self and its overlapping identities can be explored for many of the specialized and corporate-level (complex) technologies long of interest to archaeologists. The trick is to keep one's conceptual and interpretive eye on the embodied arena of social interaction, rather than material life-histories, labor measurements, or product output. Of course, the organizational and physical nature of these technologies will not necessarily call forth the same dynamics that Pfaffenberger identifies in the Triobrand case. But a fundamental quality of all such technologies is the interplay of individual bodies enrolled into collective enterprises of which they are not necessarily masters and mistresses, but through which fundamental social and economic relationships of power and meaning are constructed, reaffirmed, and contested.

A unifying and vibrant dialectic results from the fractal process of categorizing persons and displaying or contesting them during technological performance (after J. Chapman in press; Kopytoff 1990). But I maintain that, for archaeology, it is not necessary to know the specific virtues and sensibilities at stake prior to inquiry. These may be inferred through the structural underpinnings of *chaîne opératoire* analysis, as suggested, for example, in Lechtman (1977, 1984a; see chapters 4–6). Thus, one can (and should!) study material attributes, spatial arrangements, and evidence of variability and norms in gestural repertoires, skills, and the sharing (or hoarding) of knowledge in order to identify patterning suggestive of these intangible but fundamental structures. And while such studies may never yield "insider" (emic) details about the specific meanings or values at stake (as ethnographic research can), their structure and how they were realized and/or contested in practice can certainly be ascertained. In this regard, it may be more interesting to ask of the past *how* meaning was made, rather than *what* those meanings might have been (Conkey 1995, 1996; Dobres in press-a).

Thus, even when the technology under investigation is one in which a number of separate communities contributed their collective labor at different operational stages of design and implementation, analyses that investigate sequential operations engendered by the physical acts of particularly enrolled technicians are creating the inferential links between material production and social reproduction on personal, corporate, bodily, and institutional levels. The size of the technology is not the only important issue here; what matters more is how technicians engaged with each other in structures not of their choosing and beyond their full comprehension or control, but which they made meaningful nonetheless. Whether the technology was complex or simple, produced great quantities or a mere handful of objects, involved large numbers of workers enrolling at different production stages or just a few individuals sitting around a campfire, agency theory can help us understand these dynamics at whatever scales they occurred.

When undertaken with the analytic methodology of *chaîne opératoire* research, a practice framework can help us understand the technology–society equation in ways fundamentally different from those we have thus far utilized. When applied to the question of prehistoric technology, a practice framework allows us to begin prying open the black box too long encasing the artifice of embodied, interacting agents, and to think (indeed, see) beyond those heuristic and self-defeating dichotomies – process/product, subject/object, material/social, individual/society – so long constraining our understandings and our research methodologies.

Looking Back, Thinking Ahead

Of sense, sensibility, practice, and products (with apologies to Jane Austen)

The extended argument in this book started out in an admittedly negative vein, with what I see as dreadfully wrong, indeed perverted, about much of contemporary technology studies in archaeology. If I have convinced the reader that the prehistoric version of the Protestant Work Ethic is the most bizarre simulacrum ever projected on the past, then I have provided a conceptual wedge with which to think about ancient technologies differently and, I hope, more subjectively. What makes technology such an important and universal form of human involvement with the world is that its reach is far and wide, enfolding into agents' everyday practices their most fundamental cultural epistemologies, desires, needs, rules, and contests. Technology was both the medium and outcome of intended actions and unintended consequences, of knowing agents and structured collectives, and it was a mindful practice through which subject, object, and culture making happened in concert. Technological engagement is one of the most fundamental of human experiences, and to study technology is to seek out the heart and soul of culture. In both cases, the phenomenological experience of the individual tied to the body politic looms large, and agency theory is well positioned to inform on this dynamic in prehistory as well as the present.

To study technologies of times and circumstances vastly different from our own and to try and comprehend them in terms less blatantly shaped by the technocratic present, I have brought together ideas that make intuitive and interpretive sense, though they may seem foreign or inappropriate for archaeology: an explicit concern with technological practice as embodied in the thoughtful conduit of the technician's corporeal and political body; an interpretive and methodological interest in understanding the unfolding of such meaningful and relational practices through the gestural sequences of object making and use; and a recognition that the most mundane and non-discursive of physical activities contribute to macro-scale cultural institutions, systems of representation, traditions, and long-term culture change. To paraphrase Gosden (1994: 192), an approach to technology that starts with the multifaceted phenomenon of embodied practice centralizes a crucial archaeological (indeed anthropological) problem: to understand the two-sided world experienced by ancient technicians who made and remade culture on a day-to-day basis; who transformed themselves, their objects, and their institutions through physical gestures of artifact making and use; and, who blurred material production and social reproduction through the simplest of technical acts.

Heidegger's being-in-the-world is an especially worthwhile concept with which to start thinking about ancient technologies as embodied social practice, because it links phenomenological bodies to time, space, the material world, tradition, and social relations. Mauss' concern with the engendered and embodied nature of *chaînes opératoires* puts these elements into a hermeneutic spiral of personal, symbolic, and institutional transformations in particular material settings. And practice theory provides an especially robust and human-centered underpinning for such emphases, because it, too, focuses on bodies linked to time, space, the material world, tradition as well as contestation, and social relations. Thus, while physical sequences and traces of artifact design, production, morphology, and use are the necessary analytic starting point for archaeologists, the *conceptual* starting point must be on social relations, the question of agency, and practice. Or, to borrow a brilliant turn of phrase from Gell (1998: 7), what I believe should constitute an anthropology of prehistoric technology is "social relations in the vicinity of objects mediating social agency." This way of putting things highlights social agency and social interactions mediated, promoted, or hindered during the making and use of material culture, but the focus is squarely centered on social agency and mindful communities of practice rather than on the material mediators. This perspective (and the theory and premises on which it rests) is fundamentally different from the study of people–artifact relations and activities.

It is noteworthy that the term by which analysts often describe sequential artifact making and use – "stages" – suggests (no doubt unintentionally) a performative metaphor. "Stages" captures well not only the sequential and transformative operations of object making and use. It also provides a processual link to personal and societal transformations advanced through such means. It also implies that technical gestures and transformative actions are undertaken in intersubjective settings where they are enacted, and therefore subject to being (mis)read, (over)interpreted, and (mis)judged by other "actors" likewise engaged. As Schlanger (1998: 200) notes, "to follow the trajectory of transformations involved in all technical acts is to gain entry into a process of ongoing construction, mediation, and reconstruction involving material, social and symbolic elements." The phrase "sequential stages of operations," or *chaînes opératoires* (or life-histories, for that matter), provides our concept of technology with a relational and social spin. In so doing, it necessitates the study of subjects and intersubjective relations through the medium of objects, not the study of the objectified world increasingly mastered (or mistressed) by a technology held in the hand.

Importantly, technologies are not abstract systems of symbolic representations, as a world-view approach sometimes claims. Rather, *technologies are dispositional practices* that set in motion and materialize such representations. Principles, economic systems, representations, and institutions mean nothing (in fact, cannot even exist) until they are mobilized in the course of social interaction (Gell 1998: 4). That is why, for all the conceptual advances a world-view approach has contributed to technology studies in the past two decades, they still fail to explain adequately the overall system and specific practices and meanings subsumed within it (Dobres and Hoffman 1994, 1999a). The reason they fail is because they unduly focus on reified systems of meanings and rules floating in the stratosphere of Culture rather than on how such sensibilities are habitually engendered (and possibly transformed) through the everyday practices and interactions of socially circumscribed technicians.

Among the several implications of a subject-centered and relational view of technology is that it brings ideational factors down the earth while simultaneously raising so-called technomic factors to the level of meaningful experience. In so doing, it permits not only the study of those systems as structures impinging on agents, but also enables us to explore how they changed over time without presuming some *deus ex machina* or extrasomatic causality. On the other side of the explanatory gulf, a practice framework equally resists explanations that devolve into accounts of self-serving big men (or women) and omniscient elites (J. E. Clark in press; Pauketat in press). *It is at the contentious intersection of systems of representation, enrolled labor, institutional demands, traditions, and a host of historical and material contingencies that the sensual, dispositional practices of agents and collectivities materialize and contest the world.* This is also the arena in which social agency is the "linchpin." Thus, a practice framework does not discount the material world – it has a healthy respect for it. It does not dismiss end products as irrelevant – it recognizes their power to bear and promote of a host of agency and institutional interests. Nor does a practice framework deny the significance of structures and tradition – it enrolls them as necessary partners in the whole of *tekhnē*.

The limits of modernity in the study of prehistoric technologies

While the search for material correlates of sociocultural processes has long been at the center of mainstream archaeological research, from a practice framework they would appear (to me) to be something of a dead end. Whether sought through replicative efforts in the lab or ethnoarchaeology undertaken in the field, the search to identify and delimit invariant material patterns that reflect different "kinds" of technical agency (such that when you delineate pattern x, y, or z you can rest assured it indicates process-type 1, 2, or 3) is something of a misguided venture. This is because technologies are fundamentally dependent on constitutional specifics, because agency is something all technicians and collaborative groups can and do enact (and thus it is not "only" found in circumstance a, b, or c), and because context is essential to understanding how people express agency while taking care of their technical business. To try and simplify the complex bundle of interrelated and overlapping factors contributing to some (technical) agency dynamic to reified fixed-state categories correlated to particular material fixed-state outcomes is to fix what is an essentially unfolding dynamic. In so doing, one loses sight of the very concept of technological agency and, by extension, the structuration process.

Whereas clay, stone, and bone resources have certain inviolate physical, mechanical, and chemical properties, human agents in their everyday involvement with the world do not. Ironically, then, employing a practice framework to study ancient technology promotes a more processual understanding than that long attempted by processualists, because of its unwavering emphasis on the *artificial* (that is, artifice) processes of being, doing, making, feeling, using, thinking, experiencing, and interacting. I use the gerund forms here because, whereas artifacts may exist in a fixed physical state (for a time, at least), agency expressed in the technological arena is a forever unfolding practice never fully completed – much like society.

Thus, while I have a healthy respect for experimental, replicative, and ethnoarchaeological research, and use it in my own work, and although there are many understandings they can provide there are many more they cannot. If such time-honored analyses are to be put in the service of understanding ancient technical agency, then the object of study must shift from the modern emphasis on artifacts and material patterns to the intangible arena of pre-modern intersubjectivity; that is, it must center on social relations in the vicinity of objects mediating social agency. This does not mean that I advocate dressing up in bear skins or togas and play-acting a prehistoric technology in order to miraculously transcend the ages and empathize with ancient object makers and users through "the same" direct experience of making and using they had. But it does suggest that we must not assume that, because in the present one thinks they are making direct contact with the technical sequential operations, they can, from these means, deduce the hows and whys of ancient technology as a meaningful experience embodied by individuals and collaborative groups.

As chapters 1 and 2 argued, we can never physically replicate the dynamic social conditions experienced by ancient artifact makers and users using partitive, instrumentalist methodologies, nor (if we could) can we somehow tease apart and analytically separate the nomothetic "part" from the contingent factors, then measure and quantify the former's contribution to the whole. As Escobar (1994: 214) reminds us: "modernity constitutes the 'background of understanding' . . . that inevitably shapes the discourses and practices generated by and around the new technologies [of Cyberspace and virtual reality]. This background has created an image of technology as a neutral tool for releasing nature's energy and augmenting human capacities to suit human purposes." Modernity did not exist in prehistory, through from the look of some of our explanatory models you might think otherwise. Thus, much as I believe that the concept of (prehistoric) technology needs a radical overhaul in order to disentangle it from modernity, I also believe that we must rethink the research methodologies and ontological and epistemological premises they rest upon, and develop alternative strategies better suited to the question of technology and social agency (after Wobst 1997).

Of great and small chaînes *of being: difficult implications*
for archaeology

The "technoscapes" created to represent the past look far too modern to be anything other than simulacra (after Escobar 1994). Because ancient technicians were in different relationships with their technologies than we are with ours, we must rethink from the ground up how to understand them in ways that do not unwittingly project modern discourse back in time. We must get past thinking about *Homo habilis* as *Homo (faber) technologicus*, just as must get past visually and conceptually defining *Homo erectus* as the savvy maker of the handaxe. Informed by a critical awareness of the conceptual and explanatory limitations embedded in the Standard View of technology, we can, I hope, begin to understand technological evolution as turning on changes in social relationships, cultural ontologies, and in how systems of representation were put into motion through the agency and sensual involvement of technicians being-in-the-(material)-world.

"One important difference between human and non-human primates concerns the extent to which objects per se become a focus of social interactions: such object-mediated interactions are especially characteristic of humans" (Vauclair and Anderson 1994). But it is not simply that objects are a central and necessary focus of human (and hominid) social interaction; rather, it is that social-symbolic-material concert, and the particular way material culture "interferes" in social life (Wobst in press), that makes a technology. This "mutual involvement" (Gosden 1994: 82–4) of body, mind, social, symbolic, and material structures is what makes the difference between sequences of technical operations in the course of object making and use and technologies as ways of being-in-the-world.

When considered through a practice framework, then, it would appear that as human social relationships changed, so too did the nature of their involvement with the material world – and not the other way around. In turn, this suggests that over the millennia, as hominids (then humans) increasingly objectified their sense of personhood and communal involvement, they increasingly objectified the material world around them. At the same time, however, particularly configured technological practices would have promoted social solidarity (and differentiation) in new and different ways. Objectification and socialization were thus part and parcel of the practice of the most ancient of *tekhnē*, and this is, to my way of thinking, substantively different from the sociality of animal (even chimpanzee) tool making and use (Dobres in press-a; also Gosden 1994: 166–76). But we cannot keep "moving the goal posts" (that is, changing the criteria and explanatory conditions) in the study of technological evolution so that any kind of hominid modification of the material world equates with the term "technology," thereby affording it a (pre)human status. From a practice perspective, it is social relations and mindful practices that matter to the question of technology and agency, not material transformation *per se*.

If we, thus, define technology as social engagement and meaning making through the medium of artifact making and use, then we may have to reconsider the unquestioned status of Oldowan (and even Acheulean) *as* a technology significantly different from the tool making and use now recorded for the animal world. I admit to being uneasy with this implication. But if it was a particular, new, and different configuration of social relationships that set in motion a substantively new relationship to stone, which in turn led to increasing dependence on such social and material relations as a species-wide behavior, then the *material act* of unifacial stone knapping is not the necessary or sufficient condition that made Oldowan a technology. That is, if social relations and mindful practices are what make technologies different from animal tool making and using activities, then we must hypothesize some shift in social relations that could have promoted and fostered not just the physical act of unifacial stone knapping but also its becoming an increasingly necessary means for creating, expressing, and mediating social relationships.

However, if we find it hard to imagine this being the case for *Homo habilis*, and if we cannot comfortably argue that something about their social relations "allowed for" unifacial stone flaking as a (r)evolutionary form of being-in-the-world, then Oldowan is not, after all, a (pre)human technology (though it is certainly intentional and patterned modification of the natural world into identifiable and useable tools). Can we hypothesize that such a fundamental shift in social relations and sensual perceptions are what led to the development of the Acheulean? These are the sort of hard questions a practice framework suggests we need to start asking, and I recognize that may make the reader uneasy, frustrated, even angry. Don't get me wrong: I think Oldowan *is* a technology following the definition promoted in these pages. But until we begin to explicitly consider the social relationships and nature of meaning making that enabled this wholly new approach to and experience of being-in-the-world, we have not rightly understood the real social significance of such a simple but (r)evolutionary material act.

A *future for technology's pasts*

How the dialectic agency and structure, of artifice and artifacts, and of subjects and objects unfolded in particular times and places is a question I think archaeologists interested in technology can address through rigorous materials research. Such dynamics are not beyond our means to comprehend, though the conceptual, analytic, and interpretive tools for doing so require serious revision. Rather than focusing on artifacts, extrasomatic means of adaptation, operational chains, or even systems of representation to understand how technologies enabled society and cultural evolution, a practice framework calls for research on the contested and negotiated nature of social relationships mediated during technological practice. This is a difficult task. To study the material remains of past dynamics without falling prey to the frames of meaning, discourses, and conditions of (post)modernity, while at the same time resisting both artifact fetishism and empiricism, is not easy. To add to our problems, we have an extremely long research and model-building legacy that unwittingly twists our best intentions at every turn. Whether pursued through an evolutionary, culture history, or neo-evolutionary paradigm, intersubjective relationships are too easily transformed into objective, measurable practices; agents become little more than calculators and unfeeling robots; pots and stone tools miraculously make themselves; and "the system" effectively seals shut that mystical black box from which change occasionally escapes, much like steam from a kettle (Dobres 1995d).

Because of the fundamentally different premises underwriting a practice framework, we cannot simply "add and stir" social agency, *habitus*, and the like into preexisting models of technology and technological evolution. Rather than enveloping ourselves in (material) technology and using it to master an externalized world, a practice perspective makes the internal and external world part of an irreducible dialectic engendered through the socially constituted and thoughtful body of its variously enrolled participants. Rather than study social aspects after the material factors are in hand, a practice perspective asserts their inseparability. Rather than assume that a rational *logos* underwrites all object making and use, a practice perspective rests on the premise that artifact making and use is a symbolically meaningful form of social engagement. As these different perspectives call upon different research strategies and forms of explanation, to simply tack the question of agency onto the Standard View only makes matters worse.

This book is intended as an extended conceptual argument designed to promote substantive change in the way we think about and study technology, past and present. I believe such shifts in thinking must come before the necessary shifts in conducting research differently, though I have explored one methodological possibility at length (chapter 6). In the final analysis, bringing ideas from philosophy, culture studies, and sociology into dialogue with agency theory and the interpretive concept and methodology of *chaîne opératoire* research, and applying them to the question of prehistoric technology, can accomplish several things. Certainly it can help promote a more subject-centered understanding of these ancient practices. But it can also substantially broaden these ideas by grounding them in the real, material practices of socially constituted technicians living in times and under circumstances unlike those with which these disciplines are familiar. It can also provide them a time-depth they never imagined worth their while.

The more we open up a conversation among the several disciplines interested in technology, the more we all benefit. Importantly, it is not just that archaeology has much to learn from these disciplines – we have much to offer as well. And the more "undisciplined" the study of technology becomes, the more rigorous, coherent, satisfactory, and human our understandings will become.

Notes

INTRODUCTION

1 Lewontin, R. C., "The Organism as Subject and Object of Evolution", James T. Penney Lecture in Biology, University of South Carolina, 9 February 1999.
2 Fausto-Sterling, A. "Beyond Nature/Nurture: Human Sexuality as a Developmental System", University Lecture, University of South Carolina, 9 April 1998.
3 In STS studies, much of this work comes under the rubric of an "actor-network" approach, first articulated in Callon (1980, 1986, 1994 [orig. 1987]), and Callon and Law (1989). A synthesis can be found in Pickering's (1995) brilliant introduction to *The Mangle of Practice: Time, Agency, and Science*.
4 I'm happy to think this statement will soon be out of date. For example, see what I hope are glimmers of the future in Barrett (1994), Barrett and Richards (forthcoming), Hamilakis et al. (forthcoming), R. A. Joyce (1998), and Meskell (1996, 1998).

1 OF BLACK BOXES AND MATTERS MATERIAL

1 Throughout the book I employ the term "prehistoric" in its broadest sense, to encompass the entire subject domain of interest in archaeology. Its usage is not intended to suggest some temporal marker (in the sense of pre-, proto-, or "true" history, where the written word is the point of reference). Rather, I use "prehistoric" to mean any and all human lifeways that archaeological inquiry takes as its subject matter (thus even historical and industrial archaeology, as well as ethnoarchaeology, are included under this umbrella term). I will qualify the term "prehistoric" more specifically as it becomes necessary. As the reader will see, I also make free use of contemporary material culture studies in building my argument.
2 Examples where archaeology has challenged the *status quo* include shifts in thinking about the nature and antiquity of humans in the early

nineteenth century (Daniel 1981: 48–55); recognition of the antiquity of humans in the New World (Daniel 1975: 275–6); the demise of the self-legitimating osteodontokeratic theory of human evolution (Dart 1949) through taphonomic study (Brain 1981); the revolution ^{14}C dating made to understanding the timing and pace of major cultural "revolutions" (Trigger 1989: 304–5).

3   A more detailed and historically grounded exploration of the interrelationship between specific research programs, models of ancient technologies, and technological change situated against the background of social, economic, technological, political, and ideological conditions in which they were framed remains, and sorely needs, to be written. Because I see this as a momentous task, I do not pretend to accomplish it in this one chapter. It is for this reason, however, that I take the broadest view possible of the past and current "state of things" in the study of prehistoric technology, rather than take on in detail any specific recent research program.

4   I could as easily have chosen to explore contemporary attitudes about technological skill and the prestige (or lack of it) *vis-à-vis* the categories of race, ethnicity, class, or age. That I here use gender as my exemplar should not be taken to mean that it is the only, nor even primary, phenomenon shaping and giving meaning to technologies, for clearly it is not. What is so difficult to understand in all its complexity are the ways multiple and overlapping kinds of social identities are inseparably connected to the economic, material, and political factors shaping technology (D. Mackenzie and Wajcman 1985).

5   I purposefully avoid use of third-person pronouns and active tenses here, see discussion below.

6   Unfortunately, many of the most pernicious premises and goals defining Bacon's late-seventeenth-century version of science, and its "handmaiden" technology, are alive and well in the twentieth-century metaphor of knowledge production as the forceful act of rape. Chapter 2 takes up in detail the problematic coupling of science, technology, knowledge, and gender ideologies.

7   The racial implications of some of these reconstructions have been considered briefly by Conkey with Williams (1991). More work needs to be done in this regard, to understand the intersection of contemporary notions about gender and race as related to research on, and pictorial reconstructions of, prehistoric technologies.

8   On museum collections and the representation of Others and objects contextualized within the obsessive voyeurism of colonialism and imperialism, see Boon (1991), Clifford (1988: 135–45), Haraway (1984–5), Karp and Lavine (1991), Price (1989), and Stocking (1985). I must here put aside consideration of so-called "living dioramas" of evolutionary survivals popular at World's Fairs between 1851 and 1916 (but see Benedict 1983; and especially Hinsley 1991).

9   On the concept of progress in Enlightenment science and politics, see Cassirer (1951) and Taylor (1989). On progress and nineteenth-century evolutionary theory, see Bowler (1989).

10   In keeping with the distinctions suggested by Lynch and Woolgar (1990), Suchman (1990), and Tibbetts (1988), we must be wary not to lump all visual depictions of scientific models together as signifying the same messages to the viewer. Drawings, graphs, diagrams, charts, paintings, photographs, museum dioramas (and now Cyberspace and holographic images) re-present and convey information differently, depending on the context in which the images are viewed and by whom. An especially compelling pictorial technique used in the *Time-Life* series, *The Emergence of Man*, was to combine an artist's drawing of life-like hominids superimposed on a photographed (and hence authentic) natural surrounding, such as a tundra or savannah. The effect is an eerie and almost realistic "caught in the act" photomontage (see figure 1.4), but it is still a simulacrum.

11   What remains to be considered in a proper historiography of archaeology and its study of prehistoric technology is the relationship between *natural history* museums, with their displays of evolutionary progress, and museums of *culture and technology*, with their displays of (western) industrial inventions. As Bennett (1995: 179) points out, "as the influence of evolutionary thought increased, museums came increasingly to embody and instantiate ideologies of progress." But human technological progress was not displayed in only one kind of museum. The calculated separation of displays of "high-end" (western) technologies of the mid- to late-nineteenth century (steam engines, perpetual motion machines, telegraphs, automobiles, etc.) from the "low-end" technologies of the primitive world need to be considered together. On the distinction here between evolution and history as separate theories to explain the human condition, see Ingold (1995).

12   Sources for this survey included: *Advances in Archaeological Method and Theory* (now the *Journal of Archaeological Method and Theory*), *Journal of Anthropological Archaeology*, *Current Anthropology*, *American Antiquity*, *Journal of Archaeological Science*, *North American Archaeologist*, *Lithic Technology*, *Quaternary Science Review*, *Scientific American*, *World Archaeology*, *Canadian Journal of Archaeology*, *Antiquity*, *Rock Art Research*, *l'Anthropologie*, *Bulletin de la Société Préhistorique Française*, *Association Française pour l'Avancement de Science*, *Gallia Préhistoire* (and its various supplements), *La Recherche*, *Bulletin de la Société Préhistorique de l'Ariège-Pyrénées*, *African Archaeological Review*, and the *South African Archaeological Bulletin*. I do not presume to have conducted a complete investigation of these journals, nor have I covered the entirety of the literature reporting late Pleistocene research around the world. There is be no doubt, however, as to the recurrent visual conventions employed to portray what the archaeological community takes as the fundamental object of study.

13   I admit to having recently used this convention (in Dobres in press-a). This admission does not, however, negate these criticisms.

14   As Spector (1993) and others have shown, of course, third-person accounts and objectified language characterize all archaeological writing, not just the topic of technology.

15 The conferences leading up to the articulation of the Midwestern Taxonomic Method, as well as the typological debate between Ford and Spaulding (e.g., J. Ford 1954; Spaulding 1953) can be read in this light (Trigger 1989). As I discuss in chapters 2 and 3, these concerns run parallel to the more general issue, around since at least the time of Descartes, regarding how the language of interpretation and representation necessarily underwrites scientific description (also Berger 1973; Cassirer 1970; Gooding 1990; Kemp 1990: 221–57; Lewis-Williams 1984, 1990; Preziosi 1989). On objectivity as a goal of scientific description, see Bud (1988) and Daston and Galison (1992).

16 White was, of course, not an archaeologist. He was, however, explicitly interested in the question of cultural evolution and argued strenuously for the study of its materialist basis. His theories and methodologies had a profound effect on more than one generation of American archaeologists (Schiffer 1992a: 130a; Trigger 1989).

17 The term "black box" means different things. In this book I use it as a material metaphor expressing the idea that social agency, meaning, and intersubjective relations have been effectively divorced from equal and simultaneous consideration with the material dimensions of ancient technological practice. For the meaning of the term as used in technology studies by historians, see Kline and Pinch (1996: ff. 12, 767).

18 Schick and Toth's use of the active voice is especially telling in this regard, for it implies that, in the end, humans *are* in control of, or at least actively create, this relationship.

19 Among the obvious limitations of this hyper-materialist view is the fact that *only* the physical object used in technological activities can be measured, thus restricting the definition of technology to tangible things (also Basalla 1988; Oswalt 1973).

20 On the one hand, it should not be necessary here to define technological determinism, given its common use in popular culture as well as academic discourse (Bimber 1994; Feenberg 1995: 5–6; Mitcham 1994: 60–1, 110–12). On the other hand, precisely because it is the view by which industrial societies understand and describe their world, it is necessary to consider the many meanings of the term. I deal with this at length in chapter 2, but for the present:

> technological determinism is the view that technological discoveries and applications occur according to their own inner necessity, from laws that govern the physical and biological world, and that they, in turn, unilaterally affect social reality. From the perspective of technological determinism, human beings have few alternatives in their response to technology besides enthusiastic or resigned acceptance. (Drygulski Wright 1987: 9)

21 Consider, for example, these excerpts taken from the Unabomber's "manifesto" (made accessible over the internet, 1996). I in no way align

myself with these views; I only use them to suggest what an extremist's view of technological determinism conflated with a romanticized view of the past can look like:

180. The technophiles are taking us all on an utterly reckless ride into the unknown. Many people understand something of what technological progress is doing to us yet take a passive attitude toward it because they think it is inevitable. But we (FC) don't think it is inevitable. . . .

184. . . . Nevertheless, getting rid of industrial society will accomplish a great deal. . . . Whatever kind of society may exist after the demise of the industrial system, it is certain that most people will live close to nature, because in the absence of advanced technology there is not [sic] other way that people CAN live. To feed themselves they must be peasants or herdsmen or fishermen or hunters, etc. And, generally speaking, local autonomy should tend to increase, because lack of advanced technology and rapid communications will limit the capacity of governments or other large organizations to control local communities.

198. . . . When primitive man needed food he knew how to find and prepare edible roots, how to track game and take it with homemade weapons. He knew how to protect himself from heat, cold, rain, dangerous animals, etc. But primitive man did relatively little damage to nature because the COLLECTIVE power of primitive society was negligible compared to the COLLECTIVE power of industrial society.

22 In the next chapter I argue that these (and related aspects) of technological determinism are mythic and ideological attitudes about reified relations in the modern world, rather than factual descriptions of those relations.

23 I admit to over-generalizing here in order to keep to the main point of discussion. For detailed overviews of stylistic studies of prehistoric technology, see Conkey and Hastorf (1990) and Hegmon (1992), among others. I return to this issue in chapter 4, where I discuss in detail Lechtman's (1977, 1984a) and Lemonnier's (1986, 1989a) arguments for their more integrated notions of "technological style" and "sociotechnical representations" (respectively).

24 Chapters 2 and 3 consider not only the philosophical and historical basis of technological determinism, but also of the epistemological foundations of this commonly held view, best captured in Whitehead's (1927: 73–86) term, the "fallacy of misplaced concreteness."

25 Ingold (1990a, 1995) makes a similar argument in his devastating critique of the use of (neo)evolutionary theory to explain culture change through the anthropomorphizing of natural selection, described as "acting on" (a passively conceptualized) culture.

26 For example, in Nazi Germany the ideas of archaeologist Gustaf Kossinna were used to assert both the biological superiority of the Aryan race and Germany's right to annex for the Third Reich adjacent territories originally colonized – during the Mesolithic – by "true" Germanic peoples (B. Arnold 1990; B. Arnold and Hassmann 1995; Trigger 1989: 166). To substantiate these assertions, technological traits were considered direct reflections not only of Aryan ethnic identity, but also of the Aryan biological capacity and character. Claims about the technical (i.e., evolutionary) sophistication of Nordic/Aryan peoples were, thus, substantiated in part through archaeology. As well, the colonialist context within which New and Old World archaeology was practiced in the mid to late nineteenth-century led to the denunciation, by white archaeologists, that technologically sophisticated earthen and stone structures could possibly be of indigenous construction (e.g., on the Moundbuilder controversy, see Trigger 1980; on the Great Zimbabwe, see Fagan 1981: 43–4; Trigger 1989: 130–5). Similarly, with appeal to (a supposed lack of) archaeological evidence, the minority-controlled apartheid government of South Africa tried to claim that when the Dutch first landed on the southwestern Cape in 1652 there was no significant indigenous presence and that they had every right to claim the land as their own. Earlier, white settlers and amateur archaeologists alike pointed to the deficient nature of indigenous technologies and material accomplishments "to depreciate African talents and past accomplishments and to justify their own domination of the country" (Trigger 1989: 134).

27 There is a striking parallel here to mid- and late-nineteenth-century Europe and America. Then, too, there was the disturbing realization that the dreams of technological progress sparked by the machine age had turned nightmarish, especially for the middle and poor classes (although the push toward ecological awareness was not as strong; but, see Melosi 1980). However, as in the twentieth century, commentary at that time challenged the supposedly civilizing and progressive effects of high technology (e.g., as passionately decried in Charles Dickens' *The Old Curiosity Shop* [1841] and *Hard Times* [1854]). This rude awakening epitomizes the most disconcerting aspects of technological determinism, which both periods have in common.

28 This calls to mind Ingold's (1995: 196–201) argument regarding neo-evolutionary theories on the structure of DNA. We think of DNA in terms of blueprints; that within our genetic structure are innate rules of conduct lying dormant but "ready to go" at the appropriate time and given the necessary stimulus. It is my guess that we implicitly think the same about cultural sub-systems. Each is thought to have its own internal mechanism and set of rules that await the necessary stimuli to spark them into action. The question of what goes on *inside* particular sub-systems is not, perhaps, as interesting (or knowable) as how the various sub-systems integrate to form a functional whole.

29 Not to mention the strikingly similar phrases describing eighteenth-century Man [*sic*] purportedly made by Benjamin Franklin and Thomas Carlyle (reported in Oakley 1959: 431).

2   DECONSTRUCTING THE BLACK BOX

1   This is the non-Aristotelian definition. Artistotle did distinguish con-templative and non-practical reasoning from productive action (Kroes 1998).

2   Traditional historiographies of archaeology – for example, those by Daniel (1975, 1981) and Willey and Sabloff (1974) – accept the aphor-ism that abstract scientific knowledge is (and was) built upon primitive technologies of trial-and-error, not only as a fact of human history but equally of the history of archaeology. The development of anthropolog-ical archaeology over the past 150 years has often been described as progress from (mere field) practice to (explanatory, scientific) reason, such that it was technical (practical) gadgetry that provided the driving force in the maturing of (abstract, pure) archaeological theory.

   For example, we are often told that it was the application of a pre-existing radiometric science and the (material) technology of ^{14}C dating to questions of chronological systematics that sounded the death knell of Culture History and the birth of New Archaeology (e.g., Barth 1950). What is often lost from these accounts extolling the high-tech virtuos-ity of archaeological research is the extent to which more basic "ways of seeing" (Berger 1973), asking questions, and studying the past were *already* in flux, due to fundamental conceptual and intellectual frustrations on the part of some of its practitioners (for example, see such complaints in Kluckhohn 1939, 1940; W. Taylor 1948; also Jennings 1986).

3   In terms of our tendency to anthropomorphize inert entities, the very saying "necessity is the mother of invention" should be recognized as the gendered reckoning of a bizarre kinship coupling Nature and technology in a generative relationship: a (female) Nature provides the circumstances in which a (male) technological response is generated, giving "birth" to what we call technological inventions (and, in time, Civilization).

4   I recognize that not everyone likes such a broad and seemingly all-encompassing definition of technology (in particular, Schiffer 1992b: 138). Nonetheless, it is a view that I think can be helpful in address-ing archaeological interests, and is the thesis developed in this book.

5   See Davis (1992) for an interesting discussion of the *logos* and *logoi* under-pinning archaeological reasoning.

6   In particular, E. F. Keller (1985: 33–65; 1992) has detailed the effect of Bacon's seventeenth-century "engendered" agenda for modern science. See Franklin (1995) for an excellent overview of the extent of andro-centrism in the contemporary practice of science and the social sciences. These issues are critical to a fuller understanding of the inseparability of gender ideologies, divisions of labor, and the values differently afforded scientists and technicians in contemporary society (also Gero 1985, 1991b). Unfortunately, it beyond the scope of this chapter (or even this book) to consider them as they deserve.

7   E. F. Keller is not the only philosopher of science to consider the Enlightenment dialectic of changing gender ideologies and the development of modern science, although her writings are by far the most powerful. For a consideration of the French version of this dialectic, see Bloch and Bloch (1980); on the specific dialectic of gender ideology in Enlightenment medicine and physiology, see Jordanova (1980, 1993).

8   Compare this to Kant's own view, discussed in chapter 3.

9   On this point, Descartes went so far as to suggest that his theory of knowledge, founded on disengaged reason, was necessary to establishing both free will and secular salvation: "Now freewill is in itself the noblest thing we can have because it makes us in a certain manner equal to God and exempts us from being his subjects. . . . From this it follows that nothing but freewill can produce our greatest contentments" (cited in C. Taylor 1989: 147). On the Enlightenment's zeal to substitute aesthetic and religious forms of knowledge (and, hence, salvation) with scientific reasoning and computational procedures, see Cassirer (1951) and Weber (1946).

10 On the meaning of the word "nature" for Enlightenment thinkers, see Becker (1932) and Cassirer (1951).

11 This use of the term "agency" reflects the eighteenth-century democratic ideology of free will and the agent's ability to remake themselves through methodical and disciplined action (C. Taylor 1989: 159). As such, it is the precursor to what becomes, by the mid-twentieth century, Methodological Individualism. This is *not* the meaning of agency I develop in chapter 5.

12 The relationship between modern conceptions of technology and science (as described here) and Judeo-Christian beliefs is as fascinating as it is complex. I must put it aside here, except for these few brief comments. For a lucid discussion of Judeo-Christian, Taoist, Buddhist, and Hindu beliefs as they intersect with concepts of modern technology, see Cox (1965) and Ferré (1995: 97–116).

13 See Mumford (1967: 263–83) on the place of earlier Benedictine monastic life in laying the groundwork for a regulated and disciplined work force keeping rhythmic time through the (newly invented) mechanized clock. He describes this newly emergent coupling of scientific reason, technological invention, and Salvation, thus:

> Yet the conception of new kinds of power-machine, which could be put together and made to work without magical hocus-pocus [i.e., alchemy] fascinated various minds from the thirteenth century on, notably Albertus Magnus, Roger Bacon, and Campanella – all, be it noted, monks. Dreams of horseless carriages, flying machines, apparatus for effecting instantaneous communication, or transmuting the elements, multiplied. (ibid.: 282)

On certain large-scale industrial technologies of social discipline in eighteenth- and nineteenth-century France, most especially the Panopticon, see Foucault (1977).

14 As early as 1819, the French prehistorian François Jouannet published a series of artifacts from the open-air site of Ecorne-Boeuf (Dordogne), describing them in a manner still common in archaeology technology studies. He provided a detailed morphological description of the archaeological materials and paid particular attention to physical techniques of manufacture. He even recognized that technical steps involved in the manufacture of stone tools (such as flaking before polishing) could be confused with morphology, something not fully appreciated in Palaeolithic studies until the work of Dibble (1987a, 1987b, 1988, 1990), more than a century and a half later.

15 In the following two chapters I draw on sociological and historiographical studies of science and technology, particularly those conducted in that wonderfully interdisciplinary arena called STS.

16 For example, in his plea for a "science of culture," consider the forced analogy that M. Harris (1968, 1979) makes over and over between physics and astronomy as the appropriate model for anthropology.

17 As feminist scholars of science have now demonstrated, this welcomed "unity" of brain and hand still had its limits. Apparently only rational and dispassionate brains should merge with trained hands to effectively produce objective understanding. Hands, *hearts*, and brains brought together to produce more empathic, hermeneutic, and interpretive scientific knowledge is still considered highly suspect (discussion in Lloyd 1996; Longino 1995; Rose 1987, 1994; more generally, see essays in Rabinow and Sullivan 1987; especially C. Taylor 1987).

18 I realize I am on shaky ground here and it is easy to misread what I am saying, for I do not mean to suggest that the "entire" research community is at fault, nor that we are all equally blind to the issues under discussion. Indeed, were I to "take on" specific researchers and tease apart what they actually say and do in this regard, I would be guilty of the sort of *ad hominem* attacks I find loathsome and a hindrance to the honest sharing of ideas. I maintain, however, that as a community, researchers dedicated to the study of ancient technologies unduly privilege material factors *over and above* social ones, for at least three standard reasons (discussed at length in chapter 1). First, we excavate empirical data – therefore we must necessarily start analyses with these physical objects. Second, artifacts inherently have a certain number of nomothetic physical properties – therefore the better we understand these the more we can understand their constraints and the degree of "leeway" available to their makers and users. And third, some things are simply more knowable than others – therefore we can know with some surety the physical properties of clay and its possibilities and limits much better than we can ever know what clay and objects made of clay meant to people long dead. What science worthy of its name would speculate on such matters without empirical proof? These arguments rest, in large measure, on a problematic assumption known as the "fallacy of misplaced concreteness" (discussed below).

19 It is very hard to resist the seductiveness of tangible artifactual remains, and of confusing them with the "whole" of ancient *tekhnē*. For example,

Schiffer (1992a: ix) is among the many to fall prey to its power when he claims that "the archaeological record most clearly documents changes in technological behavior". This position rests upon the implicit idea that technology is fundamentally and primary material. It is strikingly similar to Bailey's (1983: 5) claim that data on ancient subsistence behaviors are more easily accessible to the archaeologist than less tangible patterns of social organization and ideology (discussed in chapter 1). This book argues a wholly different stance.

3   PRYING OPEN THE BLACK BOX

1   As Kroes (1998: 284) points out, "a coherent field of research known as Philosophy of Technology does not yet exist." While it may be a "strongly fragmented field," I believe it has much to offer anthropologists and archaeologists, who are themselves rather fragmented these days. The reader may wish to consult Mitcham (1994), Mitcham and Mackey (1972), and Staudenmaier (1989) for starters on the diversity of ideas and perspectives in the philosophy of technology. For excellent general introductions, see Durbin (1983), Ferré (1995), and Mitcham (1980).

2   Although this is not the appropriate place to explore them, I find striking parallels between Dessauer's phenomenological argument about the experiential basis of knowledge and insight and contemporary feminist standpoint epistemologies (i.e., Belenkey et al. 1986; Gilligan 1982; Haraway 1988a; Harding 1987; Hartsock 1983; E. F. Keller 1987; Rose 1987, 1988).

3   In sociocultural anthropology, these ideas originate in large measure with Mauss (1935). As I discuss in the next chapter, recent ethnographic examples include (among others): Herbert (1993), Johnson (1993), C. M. Keller and J. D. Keller (1991), Lemonnier (1989a, 1990), Mahias (1993), McGhee (1977), Ridington (1982). In archaeology, see Lechtman (1977), Childs (1999), Childs and Killick (1993), Dobres (in press-a), Hosler (1988, 1994, 1996), Schlanger (1994), J. Thomas (1993), and Tilley (1994).

4   Mumford is a fascinating read. The megamachine was not defined as the material determinism of modern industrial instruments and machinery. It had to do with the basis of *all* oppressive and authoritarian technologies – a bureaucratic, regulatory, and rigidly hierarchical form of social organization. Importantly, Mumford saw the material technologies supporting the megamachine as the *outcome* of social organization, rather than the stimulus for them. Because Mumford saw such a regulated and authoritarian "psycho-social" form of social organization as the *precondition* for complex material technologies (e.g., Mumford 1967: 163), he pinpointed the origins of modern technocratic, bureaucratic, and authoritarian conditions sometime during, or just after, the Neolithic, when, with a new kind of larger-scale and collective form of

social organization, the "expansion of collective power" became possible (ibid.: 164). According to Mumford, it took a "mechanized man" (ibid.: 168) to create a mechanized world, and not the other way around (also Engels 1972 [orig. 1884]; Foucault 1977; Marx 1967 [orig. 1883]).

5 My discussion of Ortega y Gasset's work is based primarily on Mitcham (1994: 45–9, and 55–7).

6 For those wanting to situate Heidegger's ideas about technology and Being in their political context, Nazism, I recommend: Dreyfus and Hall (1992), Janicaud (1990), Karlsson (1997: 22–7), Krell (1993: 25–9), Lang (1996), Lyotard (1990), Rockmore (1995), Wolin (1991), and Young (1997), among others.

7 For critiques of subtle distinctions in Heidegger's view of contemporary *vs.* "traditional" technologies, see Feenberg (1995: 17–8) and Pippin (1995: 46–7); for other apparent inconsistencies, see Rockmore (1995) and Vogel (1995: 35).

8 Gosden (1994: 109–13) provides an excellent synthesis of Heidegger's views on the problem of modern *tekhnē-logos*. I do not rehearse the argument here because it is discussed in chapters 1 and 2.

9 Feminist historians of contemporary technologies have explored the realm of techno-politics most powerfully. Of special interest, here, see Cockburn (1985), essays in Corea (1987), Cowan (1979, 1985a, 1985b), essays in Drygulski Wright et al. (1987), essays in Kirkup and Smith Keller (1992), McGaw (1982, 1989, 1996), essays in Rothschild (1983), and Trescott (1979). I explore some of these insights in the next two chapters.

10 This particular idea becomes one of the central themes of chapters 4 and 5.

11 To be clear here, I am *not* suggesting that the archaeological record directly preserves traces of ancient values, politics, or knowledge. These were socially and historically constituted *processes* engaged in, advanced, and hindered during everyday technological practices.

12 I realize this suggestion may rub some readers the wrong way, and I do not mean to suggest that experimental archaeologists never work in conditions simulating the past. Nonetheless, because of the many controls researchers put on their experiments (precisely because they are set up as scientific experiments), they are not structuring their research to comprehend the *fullness* of the technological experience they are trying to replicate. As I have now suggested several times, because of the analytic prioritizing of material pragmatics over the supposedly less controllable ("we'll get to it later") social factors, most researchers believe this is the necessary first step in the right direction (e.g., Skibo 1999: 5).

13 In neither its conventional formulation nor as redefined here is technology synonymous with production. In anthropology and archaeology, production is used in a more general and systemic sense, linking craft-level manufacture and surplus with economics and social organization (e.g., Brumfiel and Earle 1987; Costin 1991). Although it may appear that this is what I am attempting to say about technology, there are significant differences (especially see chapters 4 and 5).

14 Clearly there are many ways to read into Marx's inconsistent phraseo-
logy what he saw as the cause underlying any mode of production. Some
prefer to read Marx as saying that "in the last analysis he saw material
conditions as explaining social systems and social change" (Bettinger
1991: 133; also Meillassoux 1972). In contrast, I follow Hindess and
Hirst (1975), Keenan (1981), and Saitta and Keene (1990) in arguing
that Marx saw social relations as dominant over and determinant to the
forces and means of production. By definition, human technologies
cannot stand outside the body politic nor can they exist without the
socially constituted and value-laden organization of labor.

15 According to L. Harris (1983), commodity fetishism, alienation, and the
segmentation of the capitalist production process into its component
parts is what accounts for the debates among Marxist scholars as to
"which part" of this dialectic (social relations of production, forces of
production, infrastructure, or superstructure) determines the others.

16 I have only planted the germ of this idea in this chapter. In the next, I
elaborate and substantiate it with concrete examples.

4   A SYNOPTIC APPROACH TO TECHNOLOGY

1 STS stands for any one of the following emphases: Science and Technology Studies; Studies of Technology and Society; Sociology of Technology and Science; but most often, Science, Technology, and Society.
It is an intellectual meeting ground for philosophers, historians, archaeologists, anthropologists, engineers, feminists, marxists, and assorted
others interested in understanding from a multidisciplinary perspective
the history and development of scientific and technological "progress"
(and/or failure) in historic and contemporary societies.

2 The web metaphor derives from two primary sources: first, Marx's (1967
[orig. 1883]) famous allusion to the spider's web as a way to characterize the relationship of productive labor and *praxis* to material conditions
and technology (discussion in R. McGuire 1992: 102–6); and, second,
Hughes (1979, 1983), who builds on Marx's insights. Other theorists
who develop the idea that technology is a web weaving people and
things together include: Ingold (1988a), Johnson (1993), Lemonnier
(1986, 1989b, 1993c), Mauss (1935), and Simondon (1958).

3 For example, to suggest that technical choice comes from the mind and
is subsequently expressed in a physical act is as mistaken as to hold that
materials "suggest" certain options that a technician does or does not
act upon. It is the *inseparable* dialectic, or hermeneutic, of mind and
hand, and of thinking and doing, that is of interest here.

4 Among the many attempts to identify cognitive aspects structuring
ancient techniques and artifact forms, especially in lithic artifacts are:
Alimen and Goustard (1962), Gowlett (1984), Mithen (1990, 1996),
Pelegrin (1985, 1990, 1991), Pigeot (1990), various essays in Renfrew
and Zubrow (1994), and Wynn (1985, 1989). This body of literature
grows daily.

5   Equally compelling case studies that offer the same basic conclusion can be found in recent studies of contemporary, historic, and archaeological African iron technology, especially: Barndon (1996), Childs (1986, 1999), Childs and Killick (1993), Gordon and Killick (1993), Goucher and Herbert (1996), Herbert (1993), Schmidt (1996, 1998).

6   The concept of "stocks of knowledge" related to tacit routines of experientially based knowledge derives from Schütz (1962: 3–47; discussion in I. Cohen 1987). This is a pre-Giddens/Bourdieu sociological consideration of the relationship between everyday practice, agency, and social structures. Pálsson and Helgason (1999) have recently put the two concepts together in a most exciting way. See discussion in chapter 5.

7   Schiffer (personal communication, April 1999) clarifies this point as follows: from a behaviorist point of view, "techno-science inheres in technology, while "modern" science exists outside as an etic frame of reference."

8   Chapter 5 provides a lengthy discussion of the political dimensions of technical agency. In this chapter I concentrate on the ways in which normative social values and attitudes embedded and expressed in technologies and technical choices intertwine to become influential – that is, political.

9   See note 1 (above).

10 An important proviso is necessary: I am being careful here not to say that technologies "have" politics in the sense that technologies can ever act as autonomous and self-interested "agents" (after Winner 1986a; but see Illich 1973; Kranzberg 1980; Pippin 1995 for just such a view). Until the word "technology" immediately and always conjures up in the reader's mind the sociality, values, and politics of material making and using, I do not want to anthropomorphize the impact of technologies "on" people. Put another way, technologies can be political *only* when people practice them in ways that influence others. Without social agents, technologies are mute, apolitical, inert; in fact, they don't exist. While technology can have political aspects and "qualities," this can happen only in the context of social labor, social values, social usage, social proscriptions, and so forth.

11 On how this anti-technic view has been anachronistically retrodicted into the deep past, see Dobres (1995c: 54–7, 110–16, though it is briefly discussed in chapter 1).

12 Exemplary cases can be found in such edited volumes as: Drygulski Wright et al. (1987), Kirkup and Smith Keller (1992), D. MacKenzie and J. Wajcman (1985), Rothschild (1983), as well as the 1997 issue of *Technology and Culture* 38(1), which is devoted exclusively to "Gender Analysis and the History of Technology."

13 Chapter 5 concentrates on the agency "side" of these structural dynamics, as well as on their recursivity.

14 I do not mean to suggest that there have never been such considerations. Notable (rare) examples include: Cross (1990, 1993), Gibson (1982), Perlès (1989), Sassaman (1997); see overview in Dobres and Hoffman (1994). Most researchers, however, are careful to avoid the term

"politics" (or even "agency") as being somehow incompatible with the notion of egalitarian hunter-gatherers (Dobres in press-a; Wobst in press). For example, in the otherwise fascinating work on the social organization of late Pleistocene lithic technology at the open-air site of Etiolles (Paris Basin), Pigeot (1990) and Karlin and Pigeot (1989) have suggested that a family-based system of apprenticeship operated, but without any political under- (or over-) tones (discussion in chapters 5 and 6).

15   Note that these are material attributes of technologies and do not include the social relations accounting for their invention and/or widespread acceptance.

16   Another reason for the unwitting avoidance of the potentially political aspects of (Pleistocene) gatherer-hunter technologies (art or otherwise) lies with the scale(s) at which we comprehend and try to make sense of their material innovations and technological practices (Dobres and Hoffman 1994; Marquardt 1992). I take up the issue of interpretive, analytical, and phenomenological scales in the study and interpretation of prehistoric technology in chapters 5–7.

5   SOCIAL AGENCY AND PRACTICE

1   Chapter 6 again takes up the issue of scale.

2   Important exceptions to this harsh critique, several of which are discussed below, include Dietler and Herbich (1998), Ingold (1993a, 1993b), C. M. Keller and J. D. Keller (1996), Pálsson (1994), Schlanger (1990, 1996), and van der Leeuw et al. (1991).

3   Throughout this chapter I use the terms "practice" and "agency" somewhat interchangeably. While one could say that agency is instantiated through practice, one cannot reduce the concept of practice to activities (see also the discussion of *praxis* in chapter 3).

4   Notable works include: Barrett (1994), Bell (1992), Byers (1991, 1992), Dietler and Herbich (1998), Dobres and Robb (in press-a), Duke (1991), Halperin (1994), Hodder (1987b, 1992), Johnson (1989), Kirk (1991), Lewis-Williams (1997), Saitta (1994), Shanks and Tilley (1987a, 1987b), J. Thomas (1996b), Tilley (1982, 1994).

5   The following discussion explicates my understanding of these concepts as they relate to technology. As Sewell (1992) cautions, however, these terms are notoriously difficult to pin down, not only because theorists do not necessarily agree on a single fixed meaning for each, but also because the dynamics they concern are themselves rather "slippery."

6   This hyper-functionalist view is most evident in the neo-evolutionary writings of L. White (1959), Service (1962, 1975), Sahlins (1968), Fried (1967), and Friedman and Rowlands (1978). It can also be linked to the earlier Formalist sociological theories of institutions (and Methodological Individualism) found in Durkheim (e.g., 1933 [orig. 1893]) and Parsons (1949). Giddens (1979) and Ortner (1984) review with clarity these theories and the reasons for their explicit rejection by those articulating agency perspectives.

7   While ideologies and politics may not, themselves, be physical, they clearly have material referents. Sewell (1992) characterizes structures as rules, resources, principles, "memory traces," and schemas (knowledge).

8   The argument that one cannot "excavate" agency parallels the idea that one cannot "excavate" gender in the material remains of the archaeological record (Dobres 1995e). Both agency and gender, among many other social phenomena, are ongoing dynamic processes, not static entities preserved in the ground. If archaeological research is focused on studying transformative dynamic processes (be they about agency, gender, or culture change, for that matter), one excavates static material traces of past actions. Their patterning, in turn, become the material media with which infer the ancient dynamic in question. It is the same distinction as that between excavating faunal remains and using them to infer subsistence strategies, or surveying sites and plotting them on a map to infer a settlement system. In each case, the process of interest is not preserved directly. It is an inferential "leap" beyond material traces, to patterns, and ultimately to explanation or interpretation.

9   *Praxis* is an exceedingly important concept to both marxist and agency theory (chapter 3). See, in particular, R. McGuire (1992) and Tilley (1982).

10 As I begin to discuss below and develop in the next chapter, the archaeological record *does* provide material evidence capable of helping us understand the embodied nature of technology and agency: these data are the same empirically observable patterns of technical attributes long studied for other (processual or behavioral) interests.

11 One notable legacy stemming from this interest in the social control of the body as it moves through temporal and physical sequences is Foucault's (1977, 1978) work on bodily discipline.

12 But see Lemonnier (e.g., 1986, 1989b, 1993a) for a more faithful adherence to Mauss' ideas. Trained in the French legacy of symbolism and structuralism (from Durkheim to Mauss to Lévi-Strauss to Leroi-Gourhan), Lemonnier's (1989a, 1990, 1992a) work shows how operational sequences of artifact production and use are structured by social relations and symbolic systems of cultural logic, which he calls "social representations." For example, he argues that variation in the choice of technical procedures "often designates different social realities" (Lemonnier 1986: 155; 1993a; see also Suchman in press). Thus, Lemonnier's orientation has much in common with the symbolic, or "world view," approach discussed in chapter 4. But the question of agency and practice is not something he has explored.

13 Of course, not all technological activities during the Magdalenian were undertaken in intersubjective ("public") arenas. Material evidence, both in mundane utilitarian matters as well as some art production, indicates that sometimes individuals actually worked alone. Even in these situations, however, individual workers were still tied to the social body, though not, perhaps, under the watchful and knowing eye of their neighbors (Dobres in press-a).

6   ENGENDERING THE *CHAÎNE OPÉRATOIRE*

1   I refer the reader to the original authors for important distinctions between *chaîne opératoire*, behavioral chain, and activity analysis. My intent here is to discuss and elaborate the specific methods and overall methodology of *chaîne opératoire* research for the question of technology and social agency. I find this analytic methodology preferable precisely because it is underwritten by a robust conceptual framework well-suited to the questions asked from a practice framework (as explained in chapter 5).

2   For example, behavioral chain analysis as developed by Schiffer (1975b; further elaborated in 1992a, and especially 1992c; also Skibo and Schiffer 1987, 1997, in press). Bleed (n.d.) also discusses a similar research agenda by Japanese archaeologists, who (much like their American and French counterparts) have learned to document ancient artifact life-histories by combining empirical observation with refitting studies, replication, and experimentation.

3   Notable among these are: Audouze (1985, 1988a), Enloe (1992), Enloe et al. (1994), Karlin and Pigeot (1989), Olive (1992), Olive and Pigeot (1992), Olive et al. (1991), Pigeot (1987), and Schmider (1993).

4   This is, of course, no different from the problematic level of generality proffered at the expense of specificity in graphic models of cultures as systems (figure 1.7).

5   I intentionally side-step all discussion regarding the degree of anatomically modern cognitive and social "humanness" in *Homo sapiens neandertalensis*. I am here only interested in discussing this study for what it shows about the efficacy of "following gestures flake by flake" through the methods of *chaîne opératoire* research.

6   By the time of this 1994 publication, the specific gender attributions proposed in earlier publications were being downplayed (e.g., see pages 162–3).

7   It is worth reiterating at this point how different my emphasis on people interacting *with each other* during technological activities is from, in particular, Schiffer's "artifact-based" theory (of communication) that uses activities as the basic unit of analysis (clearly spelled out in Schiffer 1999; Schiffer with Miller 1999).

8   Note here, that the explicit conceptual emphasis is on human interaction rather than on artifacts or activities (as favored, for example, by Schiffer 1999; Schiffer with Miller 1999).

9   To make this case effectively in my dissertation, I compared and contrasted the technological character of every organic assemblage in the study (see figure 5.1). Here I am only highlighting one such comparison, to make my methodological point.

10 For example, both La Vache and Les Eglises are specialized ibex-hunting sites, yet the data show that their occupants took very different approaches to the handling of organic artifacts (primarily weaponry) throughout their life-cycle, as described above (figure 6.14).

11   Truth be told, what I had originally hoped I might find by way of material patterning (that would have allowed me to make the particular interpretation I wanted), never came to pass. I did not find the patterns I expected, nor could I make the anticipated claims I wanted. If this is an example of material data constraining interpretation such that one cannot say "anything they want" of the past through the study of the archaeological record (*sensu* Wylie 1992b; example in Brumfiel 1996), so be it.

References

Abbott, C. 1881. *Primitive Industry*. Salem, Mass.: Bates.

Abrams, P. 1982. *Historical Sociology*. Ithaca, N.Y.: Cornell University Press.

Adams, M. J. 1971. Work Patterns and Symbolic Structures in a Village Culture, East Sumba, Indonesia. *Southeast Asia* 1:321–34.

——— 1973. Structural Aspects of a Village Art. *American Anthropologist* 75:265–79.

Adkins, L., and Adkins, R. 1989. *Archaeological Illustration*. Cambridge: Cambridge University Press.

Aita, Y.; Kato, M.; and Yamanaka, I. 1991. "Le remontage des pièces lithiques: une illustration des différentes techniques du paléolithique supérieur au Japon," in *25 ans d'études technologiques en préhistoire: bilan et perspectives*. Edited by C. Perlès, pp. 255–62. Juan-les-Pins: Editions APDCA.

Aldenderfer, M. 1993. Ritual, Hierarchy, and Change in Foraging Societies. *Journal of Anthropological Archaeology* 12(1):1–40.

Alimen, M.-H., and Goustard, M. 1962. Le développement de l'intelligence et des structures paléo-biopsychologiques. *Bulletin de la Société Préhistorique Française* 59:389–406.

Allain, J., and Rigaud, A. 1986. Décor et fonction: quelques exemples tirés du Magdalénien. *l'Anthropologie* 90(4):713–38.

Alpers, S. 1991. "The Museum as a Way of Seeing," in *Exhibiting Cultures: The Poetics and Politics of Museum Displays*. Edited by I. Karp and S. Lavine, pp. 25–32. Washington, D.C.: Smithsonian Institution Press.

Ameriks, K. 1995. "Immanuel Kant," in *The Cambridge Dictionary of Philosophy*. Edited by R. Audi, pp. 398–404. Cambridge: Cambridge University Press.

Andrefsky, W., Jr. 1994. Raw-material Availability and the Organization of Technology. *American Antiquity* 59(1):21–34.

Appadurai, A. Editor. 1986. *The Social Life of Things*. New York: Cambridge University Press.

Archer, M. S. 1988. *Culture and Agency: The Place of Culture in Social Theory*. Cambridge: Cambridge University Press.

——— 1995. *Realist Social Theory: The Morphogenetic Approach*. Cambridge: Cambridge University Press.

Arnold, B. 1990. The Past as Propaganda: Totalitarian Archaeology in Nazi Germany. *Antiquity* 62(244):464–78.

Arnold, B., and Hassmann, H. 1995. "Archaeology in Nazi Germany: The Legacy of the Faustian Bargain," in *Nationalism, Politics, and the Practice of Archaeology*. Edited by P. L. Kohl and C. Fawcett, pp. 70–81. Cambridge: Cambridge University Press.

Arnold, J. E. 1993. Labor and the Rise of Complex Hunter-Gatherers. *Journal of Anthropological Archaeology* 12:75–119.

—— 1995. Transportation Innovation and Social Complexity among Maritime Hunter-Gatherer Societies. *American Anthropologist* 97(4):734–47.

Aronson, M., in press. "Fashioning a Foundation for Studying Practice in Technology-creating Organizations," in *Explorations in the Anthropology of Technology*. Edited by M. B. Schiffer. Albuquerque: University of New Mexico Press.

Asher, R. 1987. "Introduction," in *Women, Work and Technology: Transformations*. Edited by B. D. Wright et al., pp. 25–32. Ann Arbor: University of Michigan.

Ashton, N. 1985. Style et fonction dans le Moustérien Française. *Bulletin de la Société Préhistoric Française* 82(4):112–15.

Audouze, F. 1985. "L'apport des sols d'habitat à l'étude de l'outillage lithique," in *La signification culturelle des industries lithiques*. Edited by M. Otte, pp. 57–68. Oxford: BAR International Series no. 239.

—— 1987. "The Paris Basin in Magdalenian Times," in *The Pleistocene Old World: Regional Perspectives*. Edited by O. Soffer, pp. 183–200. New York and London: Plenum Press.

—— 1988a. Les activités de boucherie à Verberie. *Technologie Préhistorique* 25:97–111.

—— 1988b. Des modèles et des faits: les modèles de A. Leroi-Gourhan et de L. Binford confrontés aux résultats récents. *Bulletin de la Société Préhistorique Française* 85:343–52.

—— 1992. "L'occupation Magdalénienne du bassin Parisien," in *Le peuplement Magdalénien: paléogéographie physique et humaine*. Edited by J.-P. Rigaud, H. Laville, and B. Vandermeersch, pp. 345–56. Paris: Editions du Comité des Travaux Historiques et Scientifiques.

Audouze, F., and Enloe, J. G. 1991. "Subsistence Strategies and Economy in the Magdalenian of the Paris Basin," in *The Late Glacial in North-West Europe: Human Adaptation and Environmental Change at the End of the Pleistocene*. Edited by R. Barton, A. Roberts, and D. Roe, pp. 63–71. Council for British Archaeology; CBA Research Report 77.

Audouze, F., and Leroi-Gourhan, A. 1981. France: A Continental Insularity. *World Archaeology* 13(2):170–89.

Auel, J. 1980. *The Clan of the Cave Bear: A Novel*. New York: Crown Publishers.

Augusta, J., and Burian, Z. 1960. *Prehistoric Man*. London: P. Hamlyn.

Bahn, P. 1977. Seasonal Migration in Southwest France during the Late Glacial Period. *Journal of Archaeological Science* 4(3):245–57.

—— 1982. Inter-site and Inter-regional Links during the Upper Palaeolithic: The Pyrenean Evidence. *Oxford Journal of Archaeology* 1(3):247–68.

—— 1984. *Pyrenean Prehistory: A Palaeoeconomic Survey of the French Sites*. Wiltshire, UK: Aris & Phillips Ltd.

Baigire, B. Editor. 1996. *Picturing Knowledge: Historical and Philosophical Problems Concerning the Use of Art in Science.* Toronto: University of Toronto Press.

Bailey, G. 1983. "Hunter-Gatherer Behaviour in Prehistory: Problems and Perspectives," in *Hunter-Gatherer Economy in Prehistory: A European Perspective.* Edited by G. Bailey, pp. 1–10. Cambridge: Cambridge University Press.

Baker, E. F. 1964. *Technology and Women's Work.* New York: Columbia University Press.

Balbus, I. D. 1994. "The Missing Dimension: Self-reflexivity and the 'New Sensibility'," in *Marcuse: From the New Left to the Next Left.* Edited by J. Bokina and T. J. Lukes, pp. 106–17. Lawrence: University Press of Kansas.

Balfet, H. Editor. 1991a. *Observer l'action technique: des chaînes opératoires, pour quoi faire?* Paris: CNRS.

—— 1991b. "Chaîne opératoire et organisation sociale du travail: quatre exemples de façonnage de poterie au Maghreb," in *Observer l'action technique: des chaînes opératoires, pour quoi faire?* Edited by H. Balfet, pp. 87–96. Paris: CNRS.

Balfet, H. et al. 1991c. "Incident et maîtrise technique dans les chaînes opératoires," in *Observer l'action technique: des chaînes opératoires, pour quoi faire?* Edited by H. Balfet, pp. 179–87. Paris: CNRS.

Bann, S. 1988. "'Views of the Past' – Reflections on the Treatment of Historical Objects and Museums in History," in *Picturing Power: Visual Depictions and Social Relations.* Edited by G. Fyfe and J. Law, pp. 15–64. London: Routledge.

Barbour, I. 1980. *Technology, Environment, and Human Values.* New York: Praeger.

Barham, L. 1992. Let's Walk before We Run: An Appraisal of Historical Materialist Approaches to the Later Stone Age. *South African Archaeological Bulletin* 47:44–51.

Barndon, R. 1996. "Fipa Ironworking and Its Technological Style," in *The Culture and Technology of African Iron Production.* Edited by P. Schmidt, pp. 58–73. Gainesville: University Press of Florida.

Baron, A. 1987. "Contested Terrain Revisited: Technology and Gender Definitions of Work in the Printing Industry, 1850–1920," in *Women, Work, and Technology: Transformations.* Edited by B. Drygulski Wright M. Marx Ferree, G. Mellow et al., pp. 58–83. Ann Arbor: University of Michigan.

Barrett, J. C. 1994. *Fragments from Antiquity: An Archaeology of Social Life in Britain, 2900–1200 BC.* Oxford: Blackwell.

—— in press. "A Thesis on Agency," in *Agency in Archaeology.* Edited by M-A. Dobres and J. E. Robb. London: Routledge.

Barrett, J. C., and Richards, C. Editors. forthcoming. *Bodies Encountered: Archaeological and Cultural Studies of Embodiment.* London: Routledge.

Barth, F. 1950. Ecologic Adaptation and Cultural Change in Archaeology. *American Antiquity* 15(4):338–9.

Bar-Yosef, O. 1991. "The search for lithic variability among Levantine epipalaeolithic industries," in *25 ans d'etudes technologiques en préhistoire: bilan et perspectives.* Edited by C. Perlès, pp. 319–35. Juan-les-Pins: Editions APDCA.

Basalla, G. 1988. *The Evolution of Technology.* Cambridge: Cambridge University Press.

Baudrillard, J. 1983. The Precession of Simulacra. *Art and Text* 11:3–47.

Becker, C. L. 1932. *The Heavenly City of the Eighteenth Century Philosophers.* New Haven, Conn.: Yale University Press.

Belenkey, M.; Clinchy, B.; Goldberger, N.; and Tarule, J. 1986. *Women's Ways of Knowing: The Development of Self, Voice, and Mind.* New York: Basic Books.

Bell, J. 1992. "On Capturing Agency in Theories about Prehistory," in *Representations in Archaeology.* Edited by J.-C. Gardin and C. Peebles, pp. 30–55. Bloomington: Indiana University Press.

Bender, B. 1985a. "Prehistoric Developments in the American Mid-continent and in Brittany, Northwest France," in *Prehistoric Hunter-Gatherers: The Emergence of Cultural Complexity.* Edited by T. D. Price and J. Brown, pp. 21–58. Orlando, Fla.: Academic Press.

—— 1985b. Emergent Tribal Formations in the American Mid-continent. *American Antiquity* 50(1):52–62.

Benedict, B. 1983. *The Anthropology of World Fairs: San Francisco's Panama Pacific International Exposition of 1915.* Berkeley, Cal.: Lowie Museum of Anthropology.

Bennett, T. 1995. *The Birth of the Museum: History, Theory, Politics.* London: Routledge.

Berger, J. 1973. *Ways of Seeing.* New York: Viking.

Bettinger, R. 1991. *Hunter-Gatherers: Archaeological and Evolutionary Theory.* New York: Plenum.

Bigelow, J. 1831. *Elements of Technology.* Boston: Hilliard, Gray, Little & Wilkins.

Bijker, W. E.; Hughes, T. P.; and Pinch, T. Editors. 1994 [orig. 1987]. *The Social Construction of Technological Systems: New Directions in the Sociology and History of Technology.* Cambridge, Mass.: MIT Press.

Bimber, B. 1994. "Three Faces of Technological Determinism," in *Does Technology Drive History? The Dilemma of Technological Determinism.* Edited by M. R. Smith and L. Marx, pp. 79–100. Cambridge, Mass.: MIT Press.

Binford, L. R. 1962. Archeology as Anthropology. *American Antiquity* 28(2):217–25.

—— 1964. A Consideration of Archeological Research Design. *American Antiquity* 29:425–41.

—— 1965. Archeological Systematics and the Study of Culture Process. *American Antiquity* 31(2):203–10.

—— 1966. A Preliminary Analysis of Functional Variability in the Mousterian of Levallois Facies. *American Anthropologist* 68:238–59.

—— 1968a. "Methodological Considerations of the Archeological Use of Ethnographic Data," in *Man the Hunter.* Edited by R. B. Lee and I. DeVore, pp. 268–73. Chicago: Aldine.

—— 1968b. "Archeological Perspectives," in *New Perspectives in Archeology.* Edited by S. R. Binford and L. R. Binford, pp. 5–33. Chicago: Aldine.

—— 1968c. Some Comments on Historical versus Processual Archeology. *Southwestern Journal of Anthropology* 24(3):267–75.

Binford, L. R. 1972. "Model Building-Paradigms, and the Current State of Paleolithic Research," in *An Archeological Perspective*. Edited by L. R. Binford, pp. 252–94. New York: Academic Press.

—— 1973. "Interassemblage Variability – the Mousterian and the 'Functional' Argument," in *Explanation of Culture Change: Models in Prehistory*. Edited by C. Renfrew, pp. 227–54. London: Duckworth.

—— 1977. "Forty-seven Trips: A Case Study in the Character of Archeological Formation Processes," in *Contributions to Anthropology: The Interior Peoples of Northern Alaska*. Mercury Series No. 49. Edited by E. Hall, pp. 299–351. Ottawa: National Museum of Man.

—— 1978. *Nunamiut Ethnoarcheology*. New York: Academic Press.

—— 1980. Willow Smoke and Dog's Tails: Hunter-Gatherer Settlement Systems and Archeological Site Formation. *American Antiquity* 45: 4–20.

—— 1981. Behavioral Archeology and the "Pompeii Premise". *Journal of Anthropological Research* 37(3):195–208.

—— 1983. *In Pursuit of the Past: Decoding the Archeological Record*. New York: Thames & Hudson.

Binford, S. R., and Binford, L. R. Editors. 1968. *New Perspectives in Archeology*. Chicago: Aldine.

Bleed, P. 1986. The Optimal Design of Hunting Weapons: Maintainability or Reliability? *American Antiquity* 51(4):737–47.

—— 1991. Operations Research and Archeology. *American Antiquity* 56(1):19–35.

—— in press. "Seeking the Limits of Style: Finding the Margins of the Matrix," in *Explorations in the Anthropology of Technology*. Edited by M. B. Schiffer. Albuquerque: University of New Mexico Press.

—— n.d. Trees or Chains, Links or Branches: Conceptual Alternatives for Considerations of Sequential Activites. Manuscript under review.

Bleed, P., and Bleed, A. 1987. Energetic Efficiency and Hand Tool Design: A Performance Comparison of Push and Pull Stroke Saws. *Journal of Anthropological Archaeology* 6:189–97.

Bleier, R. Editor. 1988. *Feminist Approaches to Science*. New York: Pergamon Press.

Bloch, M., and Bloch, J. 1980. "Women and the Dialectics of Nature in Eighteenth-century French Thought," in *Nature, Culture, and Gender*. Edited by R. MacCormack and M. Strathern, pp. 25–41. Cambridge: Cambridge University Press.

Bloom, A. Editor. 1968. *The Republic of Plato*. New York: Basic Books.

Bodenhorn, B. 1990. "I'm Not the Great Hunter, My Wife is": Iñupiat and Anthropological Models of Gender. *Inuit Studies* 14(1–2):55–74.

—— 1993. "Gendered Spaces, Public Places: Public and Private Revistited on the North Slope of Alaska," in *Landscape Politics and Perspectives*. Edited by B. Bender, pp. 169–204. Providence, R.I.: Berg.

Boëda, E.; Geneste, J.-M.; and Meignen, L. 1990. Identification des chaînes opératoires lithiques au paléolithique inférieur et moyen. *Paléo* 2:43–80.

Boj, I.; Carbonell, E; Ollé, A.; Sala, R.; and Vergés, J.-M. 1993. "Mise en contraste de l'efficacité d'une chaîne opératoire," in *Traces et fonction: les gestes retrouvées*, vol. 2. Edited by P. Anderson, S. Beyries, M. Otte, and H. Plisson, pp. 423–528. Liège: ERAUL No. 50, Université de Liège.

Boon, J. 1991. "Why Museums Make Me Sad," in *Exhibiting Cultures: The Poetics and Politics of Museum Displays.* Edited by I. Karp and S. Lavine, pp. 255–77. Washington, D.C.: Smithsonian Institution Press.

Bordes, F. 1961. Mousterian Cultures in France. *Science* 134:803–10.

—— 1968. *The Old Stone Age.* London: Weidenfeld & Nicolson.

—— 1969. Reflections on Typology and Techniques in the Paleolithic. Translated by J. Kelley and J. Cinq-Mars. *Arctic Anthropology* 6(1):1–29.

—— 1970. Réflections sur l'outil au paléolithique. *Bulletin de la Société Préhistorique Française* 67:199–202.

—— 1971. Physical Evolution and Technological Evolution in Man: A Parallelism. *World Archaeology* 3:1–5

—— 1972. *A Tale of Two Caves.* New York: Harper & Row.

—— 1981. *Typologie du paléolithique ancien et moyen.* Paris: CNRS.

Bordes, F., and de Sonneville-Bordes, D. 1970. The Significance of Variability in Paleolithic Assemblages. *World Archaeology* 2(1):61–73.

Borgmann, A. 1995 [orig. 1992]. "The Moral Significance of the Material Culture," in *Technology and the Politics of Knowledge.* Edited by A. Feenberg and A. Hannay, pp. 85–96. Bloomington: Indiana University Press.

Bourdieu, P. 1977. *Outline of a Theory of Practice.* Cambridge: Cambridge University Press.

—— 1984. *Distinction: A Social Critique of the Judgment of Taste.* Cambridge, Mass.: Harvard University Press.

—— 1990 [orig. 1980]. *The Logic of Practice.* Cambridge: Polity Press.

Bowden, M. 1991. *Pitt-Rivers: The Life and Archaeological Work of Lieutenant-General Augustus Henry Lane Fox Pitt Rivers, DCL, FRS, FSA.* Cambridge: Cambridge University Press.

Bowler, P. J. 1989. *The Invention of Progress: The Victorians and the Past.* Oxford: Basil Blackwell.

Boyd, R. and Richerson, P. 1985. *Culture and the Evolutionary Process.* Chicago: University of Chicago Press.

Brain, C. K. 1981. *The Hunters or the Hunted? An Introduction to African Cave Taphonomy.* Chicago: University of Chicago Press.

Breuil, H. 1912. Les subdivisions du paléolithique supérieur et leur signification. *Congrès d'Anthropologie et d'Archéologie* 1:165–238.

Brown, J. 1970. A Note on the Division of Labor by Sex. *American Anthropologist* 72:1073–8.

Brumbach, H. J., and Jarvenpa, R. 1994. "Woman the Hunter: Ethnoarchaeological Lessons from Chipewyan Life-cycle Dynamics," in *Women in Prehistory: North America and Mesoamerica.* Edited by C. Claassen and R. A. Joyce, pp. 17–32. Philadelphia: University of Pennsylvania Press.

—— 1997. Ethnoarchaeology of Subsistence Space and Gender: A Subarctic Dene Case. *American Antiquity* 62(3):414–36.

Brumfiel, E. M. 1991. Distinguished Lecture in Archeology: Breaking and Entering the Ecosystem: Gender, Class, and Faction Steal the Show. *American Anthropologist* 94(3):551–67.

—— 1996. The Quality of Tribute Cloth: The Place of Evidence in Archaeological Argument. *American Antiquity* 61(3):453–62.

Brumfiel, E. M., and Earle, T. K. Editors. 1987. *Specialization, Exchange and Complex Societies*. Cambridge: Cambridge University Press.

Bud, R. 1988. "The Myth and the Machine: Seeing Science through Museum Eyes," in *Picturing Power: Visual Depictions and Social Relations*. Edited by G. Fyfe and J. Law, pp. 134–59. London: Routledge.

Bunge, M. 1985. "Technology: From Engineering to Decision Theory," in *Treastise on Basic Philosophy*, vol. 7, *Epistemology and Methodology III: Philosophy of Science and Technology, Part 2, Life Science, Social Science, and Technology,* pp. 219–311. Boston: D. Reidel.

Butler, J. 1993. *Bodies that Matter: On the Discursive Limits of "Sex"*. New York: Routledge.

Butts, R. E. 1995. "Francis Bacon," in *The Cambridge Dictionary of Philosophy*. Edited by R. Audi, pp. 60–1. Cambridge: Cambridge University Press.

Butzer, K. 1971. *Environment and Archeology*. Chicago: Aldine.

Byers, A. M. 1991. Structure, Meaning, Action and Things: The Duality of Material Cultural Mediation. *Journal for the Theory of Social Behavior* 21(1):1–30.

—— 1992. The Action-constitutive Theory of Monuments and Things: A Strong Pragmatist Version. *Journal for the Theory of Social Behavior* 24(4):403–45.

Callon, M. 1980. "Struggles and Negotiations to Define What is Problematic and What is Not: The Sociologic of Translation," in *The Social Process of Scientific Investigation*, vol. 4. Edited by K. Knoww, R. Krohn, and R. D. Whitley, pp. 197–219. Dordrecht, Holland: D. Reidel.

—— 1986. "The Sociology of an Actor-Network: The Case of the Electric Vehicle," in *Mapping the Dynamics of Science and Technology: Sociology of Science in the Real World*. Edited by M. Callon, J. Law, and A. Rip, pp. 19–34. Basingstoke: Macmillan.

—— 1994 [orig. 1987]. "Society in the Making: The Study of Technology as a Tool for Sociological Analysis," in *The Social Construction of Technological Systems: New Directions in the Sociology and History of Technology*. Edited by W. E. Bijker, T. P. Hughes, and T. Pinch, pp. 83–103. Cambridge, Mass.: MIT Press.

Callon, M., and Law, J. 1989. On the Construction of Sociotechnical Networks: Content and Context Revisited. *Knowledge and Society* 9:57–83.

Camps-Fabrer, H. Editor. 1977. *Méthodologie appliquée à l'industrie de l'os préhistorique: deuxième colloque international sur l'industrie de l'os dans la préhistoire*. Paris: CNRS.

—— 1989. "L'industrie osseuse préhistorique et la chronologie," in *Le Temps de la Préhistoire*, vol. I. Edited by J.-P. Mohen, pp. 190–3. Baume-les-Dames: Société Préhistorique Française, Edition Archéologia.

Camps-Fabrer, H.; Burrelly, L.; and Nivelle, N. 1974. *Lexique des termes descriptifs de l'industrie de l'os*. Version No. 2. Aix-en-Provence: Université de Provence.

Carr, C. 1994. "A Unified Middle-Range Theory of Artifact Design," in *Style, Society and Person: Archaeological and Ethnological Perspectives*. Edited by C. Carr and J. E. Neitzel, pp. 171–258. New York: Plenum.

Carr, C., and Maslowski, R. F. 1994. "Cordage and Fabrics: Relating Form, Technology and Social Processes," in *Style, Society and Person: Archaeological and Ethnological Perspectives.* Edited by C. Carr and J. E. Neitzel, pp. 297–343. New York: Plenum.

Carr, C., and Neitzel, J. E. Editors. 1994. *Style, Society and Person: Archaeological and Ethnological Perspectives.* New York: Plenum.

Carr, E. H. 1961. *What is History?* New York: Vintage.

Carrier, J. 1992. Emerging Alienation in Production: A Maussian History. *Man* 27:539–58.

Carson, R. 1962. *Silent Spring.* New York: Fawcett Crest.

Cassirer, E. 1951 [orig. 1932]. *The Philosophy of the Enlightenment.* Princeton, N.J.: Princeton University Press.

——— 1970 [orig. 1944]. *An Essay on Man.* New Haven, Conn.: Yale University Press.

Chapman, J. 1996. Enchainment, Commodification, and Gender in the Balkan Copper Age. *Journal of European Archaeology* 4:203–42.

——— in press. "Tension at Funerals: Social Practices and the Subversion of Community Structure in Later Hungarian Prehistory," in *Agency in Archaeology.* Edited by M-A. Dobres and J. E. Robb. London: Routledge.

Chapman, W. 1985. "Arranging Ethnology: A. H. L. F. Pitt Rivers and the Typological Tradition," in *Objects and Others: Essays on Museums and Material Culture.* Edited by G. Stocking, Jr., pp. 15–48. Madison: University of Wisconsin Press.

Charles, D. K. 1992. Shading the Past: Models in Archeology. *American Anthropologist* 94(4):905–25.

Chase, A. K. 1989. "Domestication and Domiculture in Northern Australia: A Social Perspective," in *Foraging and Farming: The Evolution of Plant Domestication.* Edited by D. Harris and G. Hillman, pp. 42–54. London: Unwin Hyman.

Chauchat, C. 1991. "L'approche technologique dans une étude régionale: Le Paijanien de la côte du pérou," in *25 ans d'études technologiques en préhistoire: bilan et perspectives.* Edited by C. Perlès, pp. 263–273. Juan-les-Pins: Editions APDCA.

Childe, V. G. 1936. *Man Makes Himself.* London: Watts.

——— 1956. *Society and Knowledge.* New York: Harper Brothers.

Childs, S. T. 1986. *Style in Technology: A View of African Early Iron Age Iron Smelting Through its Refractory Ceramics.* Unpublished Ph.D. dissertation, Boston University.

——— 1999. "'After All, a Hoe Bought a Wife': The Social Dimensions of Ironworking Among the Toro of East Africa," in *The Social Dynamics of Technology: Practice, Politics, and World Views.* Edited by M-A. Dobres and C. R. Hoffman, pp. 23–45. Washington, D.C.: Smithsonian Institution Press.

Childs, T., and Killick, D. 1993. Indigenous African Metallurgy: Nature and Culture. *Annual Review of Anthropology* 22:317–37.

Christian, J., and Gardner, P. 1977. *The Individual in Northern Dene Thought and Communication: A Study on Sharing and Diversity.* National Museum of Man Mercury Series, No. 35. National Museum of Canada, Ottawa.

Clairborne, R. 1973. *The Emergence of Man: The First Americans.* New York: Time-Life Books.

Clark, G. A. 1991. "A Paradigm is Like an Onion: Reflections on my Biases," in *Perspectives on the Past: Theoretical Biases in Mediterranean Hunter-Gatherer Research.* Edited by G. A. Clark, pp. 79–108. Philadelphia: University of Pennsylvania.

Clark, J. E. 1986. "From Mountains to Molehills: A Critical Review of Teotihuacan's Obsidian Industry," in *Economic Aspects of Prehispanic Highland Mexico.* Edited by B. Isaac, pp. 23–74. Research in Economic Anthropology, Supplement 2. Greenwich, Conn.: JAI Press.

—— in press. "Agency and Hereditary Inequality in Early Mesoamerica: The Search for a Lost Cause," in *Agency in Archaeology.* Edited by M-A. Dobres and J. E. Robb. London: Routledge.

Clark, J. G. D. 1953. "The Economic Approach to Prehistory," Reprinted in *Contemporary Archaeology: A Guide to Theory and Contributions.* Edited by M. P. Leone, pp. 62–77. Carbondale: Southern Illinois University Press.

Clarke, D. L. 1968. *Analytical Archaeology.* London: Methuen.

—— Editor. 1972. *Models in Archaeology.* London: Methuen.

—— 1973. Archaeology: The Loss of Innocence. *Antiquity* 47(185):6–18.

Clifford, J. 1988. *The Predicament of Culture.* Cambridge, Mass.: Harvard University Press.

Close, A. 1978. The Identification of Style in Lithic Artifacts. *World Archaeology* 10(2):223–37.

Clottes, J. 1989. "Le Magdalénien des Pyrénées," in *Le Magdalénien en Europe: la structuration du Magdalénien.* Edited by J.-P. Rigaud, pp. 281–360. Liège: ERAUL No. 38, Université de Liège.

Clottes, J., and Lewis-Williams, J. D. 1996. *Les chamanes de la préhistoire.* Paris: Seuil.

Clottes, J., and Rouzaud, F. 1983. La caverne des Eglises à Ussat (Ariège): fouilles 1964–1977. *Bulletin de la Société Préhistorique Ariège-Pyrénées* 38:23–81.

Cobb, C. R. 1993. Archaeological Approaches to the Political Economy of Nonstratified Societies. *Archaeological Method and Theory* 3:43–100.

—— 1997. Lithic's Labor Lost: Rethinking the Organization of Technology. Paper presented at the Annual Meetings of the Society for American Archaeology, Nashville, Tenn.

Cockburn, C. 1985. "The Material of Male Power," in *The Social Shaping of Technology: How the Refrigerator Got its Hum.* Edited by D. MacKenzie and J. Wajcman, pp. 125–46. Milton Keynes: Open University Press.

Cohen, I. 1987. "Structuration Theory and Social *Praxis,*" in *Social Theory Today.* Edited by A. Giddens and J. H. Turner, pp. 273–308. Stanford, Cal.: Stanford University Press.

Cohen, J. 1955. Technology and Philosophy. *Colorado Quarterly* 3(4):409–20.

Collingwood, R. G. 1946. *The Idea of History.* Oxford: Oxford University Press.

Colton, H. S., and Hargrave, L. L. 1937. *Handbook of Northern Arizona Pottery Wares.* Flagstaff: Museum of Northern Arizona, Bulletin No. 11.

Conkey, M. W. 1986. Some Thoughts on Origins Research in Archaeology. Paper presented at the Annual Meetings of the Society for American Archaeology, New Orleans, La.

—— 1990. "Experimenting with Style in Archaeology: Some Historical and Theoretical Issues," in *The Uses of Style in Archaeology*. Edited by M. W. Conkey and C. Hastorf, pp. 5–17. Cambridge: Cambridge University Press.

—— 1991. "Contexts of Action, Contexts for Power: Material Culture and Gender in the Magdalenian," in *Engendering Archaeology: Women and Prehistory*. Edited by J. M. Gero and M. W. Conkey, pp. 57–92. Oxford: Basil Blackwell.

—— 1993. "Humans as Materialists and Symbolists: Image-making in the Upper Palaeolithic of Europe," in *Origins of Humans and Humanness*. Edited by T. Rasmussen, pp. 95–118. Boston and London: Jones & Bartlett.

—— 1995. "Making Things Meaningful: Approaches to the Interpretation of the Ice Age Imagery of Europe," in *Meaning in the Visual Arts: Views from the Outside. A Centennial Commemoration of Erwin Panofsky*. Edited by I. Lavin, pp. 49–64. Princeton, N.J.: Institute for Advanced Study, Princeton University Press.

—— 1996. "Paleovisions: Interpreting the Imagery of Ice Age Europe," in *The Art of Interpreting*. Edited by S. Scott, pp. 11–29. Papers in Art History, Vol. IX. University Park, Pa.: Pennsylvania State University.

—— 1997. "Mobilizing Ideologies: Palaeolithic 'Art,' Gender Trouble, and Thinking about Alternatives," in *Women in Human Origins*. Edited by L. Hager, pp. 172–207. London: Routledge.

—— in press. *Paleovisions: Interpretation and the Imagery of Ice Age Europe.* Berkeley: University of California Press.

Conkey, M. W., and Hastorf, C. Editors. 1990. *The Uses of Style in Archaeology*. Cambridge: Cambridge University Press.

Conkey, M. W., with Williams, S. 1991. "Original Narratives: The Political Economy of Gender in Archaeology," in *Gender at the Crossroads of Knowledge: Feminist Anthropology in the Post-modern Era*. Edited by M. di Leonardo, pp. 102–39. Berkeley: University of California Press.

Constable, G. 1973. *The Emergence of Man: The Neanderthals.* New York: Time-Life Books.

Corea, G. Editor. 1987. *Man-made Women: How the New Reproductive Technologies Affect Women*. Bloomington: Indiana University Press.

Costin, C. L. 1991. Craft Specialization: Issues in Defining, Documenting, and Explaining the Organization of Production. *Archaeological Method and Theory* 3:1–56.

—— 1996. "Exploring the Relationship between Gender and Craft in Complex Societies: Methodological and Theoretical Issues of Gender Attribution," in *Gender and Archaeology*. Edited by R. P. Wright, pp. 111–37. Philadelphia: University of Pennsylvania Press.

Cowan, R. S. 1979. From Virginia Dare to Virginia Slims: Womanhood and Technology in American Life. *Technology and Culture* 20:51–63.

—— 1983. *More Work for Mothers: The Ironies of Household Technology from the Hearth to the Microwave.* New York: Basic Books.

Cowan, R. S. 1985a. "The Industrial Revolution at Home," in *The Social Shaping of Technology: How the Refrigerator Got its Hum*. Edited by D. MacKenzie and J. Wajcman, pp. 181–201. Milton Keynes: Open University Press.

——1985b. How the Refrigerator Got its Hum," in *The Social Shaping of Technology: How the Refrigerator Got its Hum*. Edited by D. MacKenzie and J. Wajcman, pp. 202–18. Milton Keynes: Open University Press.

——1994. "The Consumption Junction: A Proposal for Research Strategies in the Sociology of Technology," in *The Social Construction of Technological Systems*. Edited by W. E. Bijker, T. P. Hughes, and T. Pinch, pp. 261–80. Cambridge, Mass.: MIT Press.

——1996. Technology is to Science as Female is to Male: Musings on the History and Character of our Discipline. *Technology and Culture* 37(3):572–82.

Cowgill, G. L. 1993. Distinguished Lecture in Archeology: Beyond Criticizing New Archeology. *American Anthropologist* 95(3):551–73.

——in press. "Agents, Contexts, and Interests," in *Agency in Archaeology*. Edited by M-A. Dobres and J. E. Robb. London: Routledge.

Cox, H. 1965. *The Secular City: Secularization and Urbanization in Theological Perspective*. New York: Macmillan.

Crabtree, D. 1966. A Stoneworker's Approach to Analyzing and Replicating the Lindenmeier Folsom. *Tebiwa* 9:3–39.

——1968. Mesoamerican Polyhedral Cores and Prismatic Blades. *American Antiquity* 33(4):446–78.

Crespi, F. 1994. "Hermeneutics and the Theory of Social Action," in *Agency and Structure: Reorienting Social Theory*. Edited by P. Sztompka, pp. 125–42. Yuerdon, Switzerland: Gordon & Breach.

Cresswell, R. 1972. "Les trois sources d'une technologie nouvelle," in *Langues et techniques, nature et société*, Tome II: *approche ethnologie, approche naturaliste*. Edited by J. Thomas and L. Bernot, pp. 21–7. Paris: Klincksieck.

——1983. Transferts de techniques et chaînes opératoires. *Techniques et Culture* 2:145–64.

——1990. "A New Technology" Revisited. *Archaeological Review from Cambridge* 9(1):39–54.

——1993. "Of Mills and Waterwheels: The Hidden Parameters of Technological Choice," in *Technological Choices: Transformation in Material Cultures since the Neolithic*. Edited by P. Lemonnier, pp. 181–213. London: Routledge.

Cross, J. R. 1990. Specialized Production in Non-stratified Society: An Example from the Late Archaic in the Northeast. Ph.D. dissertation, University of Massachusetts at Amherst.

——1993. Craft Specialization in Nonstratified Societies. *Research in Economic Anthropology* 14:61–84.

Csikszentmihalyi, M., and Rochberg-Halton, E. Editors. 1981. *The Meaning of Things: Domestic Symbols and the Self*. Cambridge: Cambridge University Press.

Csordas, T. Editor. 1994a. *Embodiment and Experience: The Existential Ground of Culture and Self*. Cambridge: Cambridge University Press.

——1994b. "Introduction: The Body as Representation and Being-in-the-World," in *Embodiment and Experience: The Existential Ground of Culture and*

Self. Edited by T. Csordas, pp. 1–24. Cambridge: Cambridge University Press.

Cutliffe, S. 1995. Review of "Handbook of Science and Technology Studies" Edited by Jasanoff, Markle, Petersen, and Pinch; Sage Publications. *Technology and Culture* 36(4):1013–20.

Dahlberg, F. Editor. 1981. *Woman the Gatherer.* New Haven, Conn.: Yale University Press.

Daniel, G. 1963. *The Idea of Prehistory.* Cleveland, Ohio: World Publishing Co.

—— 1967. *The Origins and Growth of Archaeology.* Harmondsworth: Penguin.

—— 1975. *A Hundred and Fifty Years of Archaeology.* London: Duckworth.

—— 1981. *A Short History of Archaeology.* London: Thames & Hudson.

Dantzig, G. B. 1963. *Linear Programming and Extensions.* Princeton, N.J.: Princeton University Press.

Dart, R. 1949. The Bone-bludgeon Hunting Technology of *Australopithecus. South African Journal of Science* 2:150–2.

Daston, L., and Galison, P. 1992. The Image of Objectivity. *Representations* 40:81–128.

David, F., and Enloe, J. G. 1992. Chasse saisonnière des Magdaléniens du bassin Parisien. *Bulletin et Mémoire de la Société d'Anthropologie de Paris* n.s. 4(3–4):167–74.

—— 1993. "L'exploitation des animaux sauvages de la fin du Paléolithique moyen au Magdalénien," in *Exploitation des animaux sauvages à travers le temps.* Edited by J. Desse and F. Audouin, pp. 29–47. Juan-les-Pins: Editions APDCA.

David, S.; Séara, F.; and Thevenin, A. 1994. Territoires Magdaléniens: occupation et exploitation de l'espace à la fin du paléolithique supérieur dans l'est de la France. *l'Anthropologie* 98(4):666–73.

Davidson, I., and Nobel, W. 1993. "Tools and Language in Human Evolution," in *Tools, Language and Cognition in Human Evolution.* Edited by K. R. Gibson and T. Ingold, pp. 363–88. Cambridge: Cambridge University Press.

Davis, W. 1992. The Deconstruction of Intentionality in Archaeology. *Antiquity* 66:334–47.

Dawson, J. 1887. *Fossil Men and their Modern Representatives: An Attempt to Illustrate the Characters and Conditions of Pre-historic Men in Europe by Those of the American Races.* London: Hodder & Stoughton.

de Certeau, M. 1984. *The Practice of Everyday Life.* Berkeley: University of California Press.

de Lauretis, T. 1987. *Technologies of Gender: Essays on Theory, Film, and Fiction.* Bloomington: Indiana University Press.

de Mortillet, G. 1869. Essai d'une classification des cavernes et des stations sous abris, fondée sur les produits de l'industrie humaine. *Matériaux pour l'histoire primitive* 5(2nd series):172–9.

—— 1890. *Origines de la chasse, de la pêche, et de l'agriculture.* Paris: Le Crosnier et Babé.

de Sonneville-Bordes, D., and Perrot, J. 1954–6. Lexique typologie du paléolithique supérieur. *Bulletin de la Société Préhistorique Française* 51:327–35; 52:76–9; 53:408–12; 53:547–59.

Deetz, J. 1972. "Archaeology as Social Science," in *Contemporary Archaeology: A Guide to Theory and Contributions.* Edited by M. P. Leone, pp. 108–17. Carbondale: Southern Illinois University.

—— 1977. *In Small Things Forgotten: The Archaeology of Early North American Life.* New York: Doubleday.

Delagnes, A. 1991. "Mise en évidence de deux conceptions différentes de la production lithique au paléolithique moyen," in *25 ans d'études technologiques en préhistoire: bilan et perspectives.* Edited by C. Perlès, pp. 125–37. Juan-les-Pins: Editions APDCA.

Delaporte, Y. 1991. "Le concept de variante dans l'analyse des chaînes opératoires," in *Observer l'action technique: des chaînes opératoires, pour quoi faire?* Edited by H. Balfet, pp. 27–30. Paris: CNRS.

Desrosiers, S. 1991. "Sur le concept de chaîne opératoire," in *Observer l'action technique: des chaînes opératoires, pour quoi faire?* Edited by H. Balfet, pp. 21–5. Paris: CNRS.

Dewey, J. 1960 [orig. 1929]. *The Quest for Certainty.* New York: Paragon.

Diamond, J. 1988. The Last First Contacts. *Natural History* 97(8):28–31.

Dibble, H. 1987a. The Interpretation of Middle Palaeolithic Scraper Morphology. *American Antiquity* 52(1):109–17.

—— 1987b. "Reduction Sequences in the Manufacture of Mousterian Implements of France," in *The Pleistocene Old World: Regional Perspectives.* Edited by O. Soffer, pp. 33–45. New York: Plenum.

—— 1988. "Typological Aspects of Reduction and Intensity of Utilization of Lithic Resources in the French Mousterian," in *Upper Pleistocene Prehistory of Western Eurasia.* Edited by H. Dibble and A. Montet-White, pp. 181–97. Philadelphia: University Museum, University of Pennsylvania.

—— 1989. "The Implications of Stone Tool Types for the Presence of Language during the Lower and Middle Palaeolithic," in *The Human Revolution: Behavioural and Biological Perspectives on the Origin of Modern Humans.* Edited by P. Mellars and C. Stringer, pp. 415–32. Edinburgh: Edinburgh University Press.

—— 1990. A New Synthesis of Middle Palaeolithic Variability. *American Antiquity* 53(3):480–99.

Dickens, D. 1983. "The Critical Project of Jürgen Habermas," in *Changing Social Science: Critical Theory and Other Critical Perspectives.* Edited by D. Sabia, Jr. and J. Wallulis, pp. 131–55. Albany: State University of New York.

Dickens, P. 1996. *Reconstructing Nature: Alienation, Emancipation, and the Divison of Labour.* London: Routledge.

Dietler, M., and Herbich, I. 1998. "*Habitus*, Techniques, Style: An Integrated Aproach to the Social Understanding of Material Culture and Boundaries," in *The Archaeology of Social Boundaries.* Edited by M. T. Stark, pp. 232–63. Washington, D.C.: Smithsonian Institution Press.

Dobres, M-A. 1992. Re-presentations of Palaeolithic Visual Imagery: Simulacra and their Alternatives. *Kroeber Anthropological Society Papers* 73–4:1–25.

—— 1995a. Gender and Prehistoric Technology: On the Social Agency of Technical Strategies. *World Archaeology* 27(1):25–49.

—— 1995b. Prehistoric Cyborgs!? Or, How to Weave Ancient Technosocial Webs in the Present. Paper presented at the Annual Meetings of the American Anthropological Association, Washington, D.C.

—— 1995c. Gender in the Making: Late Magdalenian Social Relations of Production in the French Midi-Pyrénées. Ph.D. dissertation, Department of Anthropology, University of California at Berkeley. University Microfilms, Ann Arbor, Mich.

—— 1995d. Of Paradigms Lost and Found: Archaeology and Prehistoric Technology, Sleepwalking through the Past. Paper presented at the Annual Meetings of the Society for American Archaeology, Minneapolis, Minn.

—— 1995e. "Beyond Gender Attribution: Some Methodological Issues for Engendering the Past," in *Gendered Archaeology*. Edited by J. Balme and W. Beck, pp. 51–66. ANH Publications, Research School of Pacific Studies, Research Papers in Archaeology and Natural History, No. 26. Canberra: Australian National University.

—— 1996a. Variabilité des activités Magdaléniennes en Ariège et en Haute-Garonne, d'après les chaînes opératoires dans l'outillage osseux. *Bulletin de la Société Préhistorique Ariège-Pyrénées* LI:149–94.

—— 1996b. "Early Thoughts on Technology and 'Cultural Complexity': Peopling the Relationship," in *Debating Complexity*. Edited by D. Meyer and P. Dawson, pp. 224–40. Proceedings of the 26th Annual Chacmool Conference. Calgary, Canada: Archaeological Association of the University of Calgary.

—— 1999a. Grammar 101: Of Subjects, Objects, Verbs, and Nouns in the Study of Technological Complexity. Paper presented at the Annual Meetings of the Society for American Archaeology, Chicago, Ill.

—— 1999b. "Technology's Links and *Chaînes*: The Processual Unfolding of Technique and Technician," in *The Social Dynamics of Technology: Practice, Politics, and World Views*. Edited by M-A. Dobres and C. R. Hoffman, pp. 124–46. Washington, D.C.: Smithsonian Institution Press.

—— in press-a. "Meaning in the Making: Agency and the Social Embodiment of Technology and Art," in *Explorations in the Anthropology of Technology*. Edited by M. B. Schiffer. Albuquerque: University of New Mexico Press.

—— in press-b. "Of Paradigms and Ways of Seeing: Artifact Variability as if People Mattered," in *Material Meanings: Critical Approaches to the Interpretation of Material Culture*. Edited by E. Chilton, pp. 7–23. Salt Lake City: University of Utah Press.

Dobres, M-A., and Hoffman, C. R. 1994. Social Agency and the Dynamics of Prehistoric Technology. *Journal of Archaeological Method and Theory* 1(3):211–58.

—— 1999a. "Introduction: A Context for the Present and Future of Technology Studies," in *The Social Dynamics of Technology: Practice, Politics, and World Views*. Edited by M-A. Dobres and C. R. Hoffman, pp. 1–19. Washington, D.C.: Smithsonian Institution Press.

—— Editors. 1999b. *The Social Dynamics of Technology: Practice, Politics, and World Views*. Washington, D.C.: Smithsonian Institution Press.

Dobres, M-A., and Robb, J. E. Editors. in press-a. *Agency in Archaeology*. London: Routledge.

Dobres, M-A., and Robb, J. E. in press-b. "Agency in Archaeology: Paradigm or Platitude?" in *Agency in Archaeology*. Edited by M-A. Dobres and J. E. Robb. London: Routledge.

Dreyfus, H., and Hall, H. Editors. 1992. *Heidegger: A Critical Reader*. Oxford: Blackwell.

Drygulski Wright, B. 1987. "Introduction," in *Women, Work, and Technology: Transformations*. Edited by B. Drygulski Wright, M. Marx Ferree, G. Mellow et al., pp. 1–22. Ann Arbor: University of Michigan.

Drygulski Wright, B.; Marx Ferree, M.; Mellow, G. et al. Editors. 1987. *Women, Work, and Technology: Transformations*. Ann Arbor: University of Michigan.

DuBois, W. E. B. 1994 [orig. 1903]. *The Soul of Black Folk*. New York: Gramercy Books.

Duke, P. 1991. *Points in Time: Structure and Event in a Late Northern Plains Hunting Society*. Niwot: University of Colorado Press.

Dumouchel, P. 1995 [orig. 1992]. "Gilbert Simondon's Plea for a Philosophy of Technology," in *Technology and the Politics of Knowledge*. Edited by A. Feenberg and A. Hannay, pp. 255–71. Bloomington: Indiana University Press.

Dunnell, R. 1982. Science, Social Science, and Common Sense: The Agonizing Dilemma of Modern Archaeology. *Journal of Anthropological Research* 38:1–23.

Durbin, P. 1972. Technology and Values: A Philosopher's Perspective. *Technology and Culture* 13(4):556–76.

——— 1978. Toward a Social Philosophy of Technology. *Research in Philosophy of Technology* 1:67–97.

——— 1983. "Introduction: Some Questions for Philosophy of Technology," in *Philosophy and Technology*. Edited by P. Durbin and F. Rapp, pp. 1–14. Boston Studies in the Philosophy of Science, vol. 80. Dordrecht, Holland: D. Reidel.

——— 1992. *Social Responsiblity in Science, Technology, and Medicine*. Bethlehem, Pa.: Lehigh University Press.

Durkheim, E. 1933 [orig. 1893]. *Division of Labor in Society*. New York: Macmillan.

Dworkin, R. M. 1986. *The Law's Empire*. Cambridge, Mass.: Belknap Press.

Eagleton, T. 1983. *Literary Theory: An Introduction*. Minneapolis: University of Minnesota Press.

Edey, M. 1972. *The Emergence of Man: The Missing Link*. New York: Time-Life Books.

Edmonds, M. 1990. Description, Understanding, and the *Chaîne Opératoire*. *Archaeological Review from Cambridge* 9(1):55–70.

Elkins, J. 1996. On the Impossibility of Close Reading. The Case of Alexander Marshack. *Current Anthropology* 37:185–201.

Ellul, J. 1954. *La Technique, ou l'enjeu de siècle*. Paris: Colin.

——— 1980. "The Ethics of Nonpower," in *Ethics in an Age of Pervasive Technology*. Edited by M. Kranzberg, pp. 204–12. Boulder, Col.: Westview Press.

——— 1989 [orig. 1983]. The Search for Ethics in a Technicist Society. *Research in Philosophy and Technology* 9:23–36.

Engels, F. 1972 [orig. 1884]. *The Origin of the Family, Private Property, and the State*. New York: International Publishers.

Engeström, Y., and Middleton, D. 1998. "Introduction: Studying Work as Mindful Practice," in *Cognition and Communication at Work*. Edited by Y. Engeström and D. Middleton, pp. 1–14. Cambridge: Cambridge University Press.

Enloe, J. G. 1992. "Le partage de la nourriture à partir des témoins archéologiques: une application ethnoarchéologique," in *Ethnoarchéologie: justification, problèmes, limites*. Edited by A. Gallay, F. Audouze, and V. Roux, pp. 307–23. Juan-les-Pins: Editions APDCA.

Enloe, J. G.; David, F.; and Hare, T. 1994. Patterns of Faunal Processing at Section 27 of Pincevent: The Use of Spatial Analysis and Ethnoarchaeological Data in the Interpretation of Archaeological Site Structure. *Journal of Anthropological Archaeology* 13(2):105–24.

Escobar, A. 1994. Welcome to Cyberia: Notes on the Anthropology of Cyberculture. *Current Anthropology* 35(3):211–31.

Fabian, J. 1983. *Time and the Other: How Anthropology Makes its Object*. New York: Columbia University Press.

Fagan, B. 1981. "Two Hundred and Four Years of African Archaeology," in *Antiquity and Man: Essays in Honour of Glyn Daniel*. Edited by J. D. Evans, B. Cutliffe, and C. Renfrew, pp. 42–51. London: Thames & Hudson.

Fedigan, L. 1986. The Changing Role of Women in Models of Human Evolution. *Annual Review of Anthropology* 15:25–66.

Feenberg, A. 1995 [orig. 1992]. "Subversive Rationalization: Technology, Power, and Democracy," in *Technology and the Politics of Knowledge*. Edited by A. Feenberg and A. Hannay, pp. 3–22. Bloomington: Indiana University Press.

Feenberg, A., and Hannay, A. Editors. 1995 [orig. 1992]. *Technology and the Politics of Knowledge*. Bloomington: Indiana University Press.

Ferguson, E. 1978. Elegant Inventions: The Artistic Component of Technology. *Technology and Culture* 19:450–60.

Ferré, F. 1995 [orig. 1988]. *Philosophy of Technology*. Athens: University of Georgia Press.

Fisher, H. 1983. *The Sex Contract: The Evolution of Human Behavior*. New York: Quill.

Flanagan, J. G. 1989. Hierarchy in Simple "Egalitarian" Societies. *Annual Review of Anthropology* 18:245–66.

Foley, R. 1987. Hominid Species and Stone Tool Assemblages: How are they Related? *Antiquity* 61(233):380–92.

Ford, J. 1954. On the Concept of Types. *American Anthropologist* 56:42–53.

Ford, R. 1973. "Archeology Serving Humanity," in *Research and Theory in Current Anthropology*. Edited by C. Redman, pp. 83–93. New York: John Wiley & Sons.

Forge, A. 1970. "Learning to See in New Guinea," in *Socialization: The Approach from Social Anthropology*. Edited by P. Mayer, pp. 269–91. London: Tavistock.

Foucault, M. 1977. *Discipline and Punish: The Birth of the Prison*. New York: Pantheon.

Foucault, M. 1978. *The History of Sexuality*, vol. 1: *An Introduction*. New York: Pantheon Books.

Franklin, S. 1995. Science as Culture, Cultures of Science. *Annual Review of Anthropology* 24:163–84.

Frazer, J. 1890. *The Golden Bough.* New York: Macmillan.

Fried, M. H. 1967. *The Evolution of Political Society.* New York: Random House.

Friedman, J., and Rowlands, M. J. 1978. *The Evolution of Social Systems.* London: Duckworth.

Frisch, M. 1957. *Homo Faber.* London: Abelard-Schuman.

Fritz, J. 1973. "Relevance, Archaeology, and Subsistence Theory," in *Research and Theory in Current Archaeology*. Edited by C. Redman, pp. 59–82. New York: John Wiley & Sons.

Fritz, J., and Plog, F. 1970. The Nature of Archeological Explanation. *American Antiquity* 35:405–12.

Fuller, B. 1963. *No More Secondhand God and Other Writings.* Garden City, N.Y.: Doubleday.

Fyfe, G., and Law, J. Editors. 1988. *Picturing Power: Visual Depictions and Social Relations.* London: Routledge.

Gallay, A. 1992. "On the Study of Habitat Structures: Reflections Concerning the Archaeology–Anthropology–Science Transition," in *Representations in Archaeology*. Edited by J.-C. Gardin and C. Peebles, pp. 107–21. Bloomington: Indiana University Press.

Gallay, J.-C. 1986. *L'Archéologie Demain.* Paris: Belfond.

Gamble, C. 1998. "Foreword," in *Ancestral Images: The Iconography of Human Origins*. By S. Moser, pp. ix–xxiv. Ithaca, N.Y.: Cornell University Press.

Game, A., and Pringle, R. 1984. *Gender at Work.* London: Pluto Press.

Garfinkel, H. 1984. *Studies in Ethnomethodology.* Cambridge: Polity Press.

Gatens, M. 1996. *Imaginary Bodies: Ethics, Power, and Corporeality.* London: Routledge.

Geertz, C. 1966. "Religion as a Cultural System," in *Anthropological Approaches to the Study of Religion*. Edited by M. Banton, pp. 1–46. London: Tavistock.

——— 1973a. "Thick Description: Toward an Interpretive Theory of Culture," in *The Interpretation of Culture*, pp. 3–30. New York: Basic Books.

——— 1973b. *The Interpretation of Culture.* New York: Basic Books.

Gell, A. 1998. *Art and Agency: An Anthropological Theory.* Oxford: Clarendon Press.

Geneste, J.-M. 1988. "Systèmes d'approvisionnement en matières premières au paléolithique moyen et au paléolithique supérieur d'Aquitaine," in *L'Homme de Néandertal*, vol. VIII: *La mutation*. Edited by J. K. Kozlowski, pp. 61–70. Liège: ERAUL No. 35, Université de Liège.

Geras, N. 1983. "Fetishism," in *A Dictionary of Marxist Thought*. Edited by T. Bottomore, L. Harris, V. G. Kiernan, and R. Miliband, pp. 165–6. Cambridge, Mass.: Harvard University Press.

Gero, J. M. 1985. Socio-politics and the Woman-at-Home Ideology. *American Antiquity* 50:342–50.

——— 1991a. "Genderlithics: Women's Roles in Stone Tool Production," in

Engendering Archaeology: Women and Prehistory. Edited by J. M. Gero and M. W. Conkey, pp. 163–93. Oxford: Basil Blackwell.

—— 1991b. "Gender Divisions of Labor in the Construction of Archaeological Knowledge," in *The Archaeology of Gender.* Edited by D. Walde and N. Willows, pp. 96–102. Proceedings of the 22nd Annual Chacmool Conference. Calgary, Canada: Archaeological Association of the University of Calgary.

Gibson, E. 1982. Upper Palaeolithic Flintknapping Specialists? The Evidence from Corbiac, France. *Lithic Technology* 11(3):41–9.

Giddens, A. 1979. *Central Problems in Social Theory: Action, Structure, and Contradiction in Social Analysis.* Berkeley: University of California Press.

—— 1984. *The Constitution of Society: Outline of a Theory of Structuration.* Berkeley: University of California Press.

Gifford-Gonzalez, D. 1993a. You Can Hide but You Can't Run: Representations of Women's Work in Illustrations of Palaeolithic Life. *Visual Anthropology Review* 9(1):23–41.

—— 1993b. "Gaps in Ethnoarchaeological Analyses of Butchery: Is Gender an Issue?," in *Bones to Behavior: Ethnoarchaeological and Experimental Contributions to the Interpretation of Faunal Remains.* Edited by J. Hudson, pp. 181–99. Carbondale: Southern Illinois University Press.

Gilbert, G., and Mulkay, M. 1984. *Opening Pandora's Box: A Sociological Analysis of Scientists' Discourse.* Cambridge: Cambridge University Press.

Gilligan, C. 1982. *In a Different Voice.* Cambridge, Mass.: Harvard University Press.

Glassie, H. 1975. *Folk Housing in Middle Virginia.* Knoxville: University of Tennessee Press.

Golinski, J. 1991. "Newtonianism," in *The Blackwell Companion to the Enlightenment.* Edited by J. W. Yolton, R. Porter, P. Rogers, and B. M. Stafford, pp. 367–9. Oxford: Blackwell.

Gooding, D. 1990. *Experiment and the Making of Meaning: Human Agency in Scientific Observation and Experiment.* Dordrecht, Holland: Kluwer.

Gordon, K. 1995. Exhibition Review: Hall of Human Biology and Evolution, American Museum of Natural History (New York City). *Museum Anthropology* 19(1):57–60.

Gordon, R. B., and Killick, D. 1993. Adaptation of Technology to Culture and Environment: Bloomery Iron Smelting in America and Africa. *Technique and Culture* 34(2):243–70.

Gosden, C. 1994. *Social Being and Time.* Oxford: Blackwell.

Gosselain, O. P. 1994. "Skimming through Potters' Agendas: An Ethnoarchaeological Study of Clay Selection Strategies in Cameroon," in *Society, Culture, and Technology in Africa.* Edited by S. T. Childs, pp. 99–107. MASCA Research Papers in Science and Archaeology, Supplement to vol. 11. Philadelphia: University of Pennsylvania.

—— 1998. "Social and Technical Identity in a Clay Crystal Ball," in *The Archaeology of Social Boundaries.* Edited by M. T. Stark, pp. 78–106. Washington, D.C.: Smithsonian Institution Press.

Goucher, C., and Herbert, E. W. 1996. "The Blooms of Banjeli: Technology and Gender in West African Iron Making," in *The Culture and Technology of African Iron Production.* Edited by P. Schmidt, pp. 40–57. Gainesville: University Press of Florida.

Gould, R. 1980. *Living Archaeology.* Cambridge: Cambridge University Press.

Gowlett, J. A. J. 1984. *Ascent to Civilization.* New York: Alfred A. Knopf.

——1990. Technology, Skill and the Psychosocial Sector in the Long Term of Human Evolution. *Archaeological Review from Cambridge* 9(1):82–103.

Graburn, N. 1976. "Introduction: Art of the Fourth World," in *Ethnic and Tourist Arts: Cultural Expressions from the Fourth World.* Edited by N. Graburn, pp. 1–22. Berkeley: University of California Press.

Grosz, E. 1989. *Sexual Subversions.* London: Allen & Unwin.

Habermas, J. 1970. "Technology and Science as 'Ideology'," in *Toward a Rational Society: Student Protest, Science, and Politics*, pp. 81–122. Boston: Beacon Press.

Halberstram, M. 1999. *Totalitarianism and the Modern Conception of Politics.* New Haven, Conn.: Yale University Press.

Halperin, R. H. 1994. *Cultural Economies Past and Present.* Austin: University of Texas Press.

Hamilakis, Y.; Pluciennik, M.; and Tarlow, S. Editors. forthcoming. *Thinking through the Body.*

Haraway, D. 1984–5. Teddy Bear Patriarchy: Taxidermy in the Garden of Eden, 1908–1936. *Social Text* 11:20–64.

——1988a. Situated Knowledges: The Science Question in Feminism as a Site of Discourse on the Privilege of Partial Perspective. *Feminist Studies* 14(3):575–99.

——1988b. "Primatology is Politics by Other Means," in *Feminist Approaches to Science.* Edited by R. Bleier, pp. 77–118. New York: Pergamon.

——1989. *Primate Visions: Gender, Race and Nature in the World of Modern Science.* New York: Routledge.

——1991. "A Cyborg Manifesto: Science, Technology, and Socialist-Feminism in the Late Twentieth Century," in *Simians, Cyborgs, and Women: The Reinvention of Nature*, pp. 149–81. New York: Routledge.

Harding, S. 1987. The Method Question. *Hypatia* 2(3):19–35.

Harding, S., and Hintikka, M. B. Editors. 1983. *Discovering Reality: Feminist Perspectives on Epistemology, Metaphysics, Methodology, and Philosophy of Science.* Dordrecht, Holland: D. Reidel.

Harris, L. 1983. "Forces and Relations of Production," in *A Dictionary of Marxist Thought.* Edited by T. Bottomore, L. Harris, V. G. Kiernan, and R. Miliband, pp. 178–80. Cambridge, Mass.: Harvard University Press.

Harris, M. 1968. *The Rise of Anthropological Theory.* New York: Thomas Y. Crowell.

——1979. *Cultural Materialism: The Struggle for a Science of Culture.* New York: Vintage Books.

Hartsock, N. 1983. "Feminist Standpoint: Developing the Ground for a Specifically Feminist Historical Materialism," in *Discovering Reality: Femi-*

nist Perspectives on Epistemology, Metaphysics, Methodology, and Philosophy of Science. Edited by S. Harding and M. B. Hintikka, pp. 283–310. Dordrecht, Holland: D. Reidel.

Hastorf, C. 1991. "Gender, Space, and Food in Prehistory," in *Engendering Archaeology: Women and Prehistory.* Edited by J. M. Gero and M. W. Conkey, pp. 132–59. Oxford: Basil Blackwell.

Hawkes, C. 1954. Archaeological Theory and Method: Some Suggestions from the Old World. *American Anthropologist* 56:155–68.

Hayden, B. 1993. *Archaeology: The Science of Once and Future Things.* New York: W. H. Freeman.

——— 1994. "Competition, Labor, and Complex Hunter-Gatherers," in *Key Issues in Hunter-Gatherer Research.* Edited by E. Burch, Jr. and L. Ellanna, pp. 223–39. Providence, R.I.: Berg.

——— 1995a. "The Emergence of Prestige Technologies and Pottery," in *The Emergence of Pottery Production: Technology and Innovation in Ancient Societies.* Edited by W. Barnett and J. Hoopes, pp. 257–65. Washington, D.C.: Smithsonian Institution Press.

——— 1995b. "Pathways to Power: Principles for Creating Socioeconomic Inequalities," in *Foundations of Social Inequality.* Edited by T. D. Price and G. Feinman, pp. 15–86. New York: Plenum.

——— 1998. Practical and Prestige Technologies: The Evolution of Material Systems. *Journal of Archaeological Method and Theory* 5(1):1–55.

Hegmon, M. 1992. Archaeological Research on Style. *Annual Review of Anthropology* 21:517–36.

Heidegger, M. 1962 [orig. 1926]. *Being and Time.* Oxford: Basil Blackwell.

——— 1967 [orig. 1962]. "Modern Science, Metaphysics, and Mathematics," in *What is a Thing?* Translated by W. B. Barton, Jr. and V. Deutsch. Chicago: Henry Regnery Co. [Reprinted in *Martin Heidegger Basic Writings* (1993), edited by D. F. Krell, pp. 268–305; New York: Harper Collins].

——— 1977. *The Question Concerning Technology and Other Essays.* New York: Garland Publishers.

Heizer, R. 1966. Ancient Heavy Transport, Methods, and Achievments. *Science* 153:821–30.

Herbert, E. W. 1993. *Iron, Gender, and Power: Rituals of Transformation in African Societies.* Bloomington: Indiana University Press.

Heritage, J. 1987. "Ethnomethodology," in *Social Theory Today.* Edited by A. Giddens and J. H. Turner, pp. 224–72. Stanford, Cal.: Stanford University Press.

Hickman, L. 1990. *John Dewey's Pragmatic Technology.* Bloomington: Indiana University Press.

Higgs, E. Editor. 1972. *Papers in Economic Prehistory.* Cambridge: Cambridge University Press.

Hindess, B., and Hirst, P. 1975. *Pre-capitalist Modes of Production.* London: Routledge & Kegan Paul.

Hinsley, C. 1991. "The World as Marketplace: Commodification of the Exotic at the World's Columbian Exposition, Chicago, 1893," in *Exhibiting Cultures: The Poetics and Politics of Museum Displays.* Edited by I. Karp and S. Lavine, pp. 344–65. Washington, D.C.: Smithsonian Institution Press.

Hodder, I. Editor. 1982a. *Symbols in Action: Ethnoarchaeological Studies of Material Culture.* Cambridge: Cambridge University Press.

——Editor. 1982b. *Symbolic and Structural Archaeology.* Cambridge: Cambridge University Press.

——1986. *Reading the Past.* Cambridge: Cambridge University Press.

——Editor. 1987a. *The Archaeology of Contextual Meanings.* Cambridge: Cambridge University Press.

——1987b. "The Contribution of the Long-Term," in *Archaeology as Long-Term History.* Edited by I. Hodder, pp. 1–8. Cambridge: Cambridge University Press.

——1992. *Theory and Practice in Archaeology.* London: Routledge.

——in press. "The Agent and the Individual: Diverging Approaches towards Agency in Archaeology," in *Agency in Archaeology.* Edited by M-A. Dobres and J. E. Robb. London: Routledge.

Honigmann, J. 1981. "West Main Cree," in *Handbook of North Americans: Subarctic.* vol. 6. Edited by J. Helm, pp. 217–30. Washington, D.C.: Smithsonian.

hooks, b. 1994. *Teaching to Transgress: Education as the Practice of Freedom.* New York: Routledge.

Hosler, D. 1988. Ancient West Mexican Metallurgy: South and Central American Origins and West Mexican Transformations. *American Anthropologist* 90:832–55.

——1994. *The Sounds and Colors of Power: The Sacred Metallurgical Technology of Ancient West Mexico.* Cambridge, Mass.: MIT Press.

——1996. Technical Choices, Social Categories and Meaning among the Andean Potters of Las Animas. *Journal of Material Culture* 1(1):63–92.

Howell, F. C. 1965. *The Emergence of Man: Early Man.* New York: Time-Life Books.

Hubbard, R. 1982. "Have Only Men Evolved?" in *Biological Woman – The Convenient Myth.* Edited by R. Hubbard, M. S. Henifin, and B. Fried, pp. 17–46. Cambridge, Mass.: Schenkman.

Hughes, T. P. 1979. The Electrification of America: The System Builders. *Technology and Culture* 20(1):124–62.

——1983. *Networks of Power: Electric Supply Systems in the US, England, and Germany, 1880–1930.* Baltimore, Md.: Johns Hopkins University Press.

Ihde, D. 1983a. "The Historical-Ontological Priority of Technology over Science," in *Philosophy and Technology.* Edited by P. Durbin and F. Rapp, pp. 235–52. Boston Studies in the Philosophy of Science, vol. 80. Dordrecht, Holland: D. Reidel.

——1983b. *Existential Technics.* Albany: State University of New York.

——1986. *Consequences of Phenomenology.* Albany: State University of New York.

——1990. *Technology and the Lifeworld: From Garden to Earth.* Bloomington: Indiana University Press.

Illich, I. 1973. *Tools for Conviviality.* New York: Harper & Row.

Ingold, T. 1988a. Tools, Minds, and Machines: An Excursion in the Philosophy of Technology. *Techniques et Culture* 12:151–76.

—— 1988b. Comment to Testart. *Current Anthropology* 29(1):14–15.

—— 1990a. An Anthropologist Looks at Biology. *Man* 25:208–29.

—— 1990b. Society, Nature, and the Concept of Technology. *Archaeological Review from Cambridge* 9(1):5–17.

—— 1991. "Notes on a Foraging Mode of Production," in *Hunters and Gatherers 1: History, Evolution and Social Change*. Edited by T. Ingold, D. Riches, and J. Woodburn, pp. 269–85. New York: Berg.

—— 1993a. "Tool-use, Sociality and Intelligence," in *Tools, Language, and Cognition in Human Evolution*. Edited by K. R. Gibson and T. Ingold, pp. 429–45. Cambridge: Cambridge University Press.

—— 1993b. "Technology, Language, and Intelligence: A Reconsideration of Basic Concepts," in *Tools, Language, and Cognition in Human Evolution*. Edited by K. R. Gibson and T. Ingold, pp. 449–72. Cambridge: Cambridge University Press.

—— 1993c. "The Reindeerman's Lasso," in *Technological Choices: Transformation in Material Cultures since the Neolithic*. Edited by P. Lemonnier, pp. 108–25. London: Routledge.

—— 1995. "People Like Us": The Concept of the Anatomically Modern Human. *Cultural Dynamics* 7(2):187–214.

—— 1999. "Foreword," in *The Social Dynamics of Technology: Practice, Politics, and World Views*. Edited by M-A. Dobres and C. R. Hoffman, pp. ix–xiii. Washington, D.C.: Smithsonian Institution Press.

Inizan, M.-L. 1991. "Le débitage par pression: des choix culturels," in *25 ans d'études technologiques en préhistoire: bilan et perspectives*. Edited by C. Perlès, pp. 367–77. Juan-les-Pins: Editions APDCA.

James, W., and Allen, N. J. Editors. 1998. *Marcel Mauss: A Centenary Tribute*. New York: Berghahn Books.

Janicaud, D. 1990. *L'ombre de cette pensée: Heidegger et la question politique*. Grenoble: Jérôme Millon.

Janich, P. 1978. "Physics: Natural Science or Technology?" in *The Dynamics of Science and Technology*. Edited by R. Krohn, E. T. Layton, and P. Weingart, pp. 3–27. Dordrecht, Holland: D. Reidel.

Jarvenpa, R., and Brumbach, H. J. 1995. Ethnoarchaeology and Gender: Chipewyan Women as Hunters. *Research in Economic Anthropology* 16:39–82.

Jennings, J. 1986. "American Archaeology, 1930–1985," in *American Archaeology Past and Future*. Edited by D. Meltzer, D. Fowler, and J. Sabloff, pp. 53–62. Washington, D.C.: Smithsonian Institution Press.

Jochim, M. A. 1981. *Strategies for Survival: Cultural Behavior in an Ecological Context*. New York: Academic Press.

—— 1983. "Palaeolithic Cave Art in Ecological Perspective," in *Hunter-Gatherer Economy in Prehistory: A European Perspective*. Edited by G. Bailey, pp. 212–19. Cambridge: Cambridge University Press.

Johnson, M. 1989. Conceptions of Agency in Archaeological Interpretation. *Journal of Anthropological Archaeology* 8(2):189–211.

—— 1993. *Housing Culture: Traditional Architecture in an English Landscape*. Washington, D.C.: Smithsonian Institution Press.

Jonas, H. 1984. *The Imperative of Responsiblity: In Search of an Ethics for the Technological Age*. Chicago: University of Chicago Press.

Jordanova, L. 1980. "Natural Facts: A Historical Perspective on Science and Sexuality," in *Nature, Culture, and Gender*. Edited by R. MacCormack and M. Strathern, pp. 42–69. Cambridge: Cambridge University Press.

——1993. Gender and the Historiography of Science. *British Journal for the History of Science* 26:469–83.

Jouannet, F. 1819. Antiquités Gauloises. *Calendrier de la Dordogne* 1819:3–12.

Joyce, A. in press. "The Founding of Monte Albán: Propositions and Social Practices," in *Agency in Archaeology*. Edited by M-A. Dobres and J. E. Robb. London: Routledge.

Joyce, R. A. 1998. Performing the Body in Pre-Hispanic Central America. *RES* 33:147–65.

Kant, I. 1996 [orig. 1781 and 1787]. *Critique of Pure Reason*. Indianapolis, Ind.: Hackett Publishing Co., Inc.

Karlin, C.; Bodu, P.; and Pelegrin, J. 1991. "Processus techniques et chaîne opératoires: comment les préhistoriens s'appropient un concept élaboré par le ethnologues," in *Observer l'action technique: des chaînes opératoires, pour quoi faire?* Edited by H. Belfet, pp. 101–17. Paris: CNRS.

Karlin, C., and Julien, M. 1994. "Prehistoric Technology: A Cognitive Science," in *The Ancient Mind: Elements of Cognitive Archaeology*. Edited by C. Renfrew and E. B. W. Zubrow, pp. 152–64. Cambridge: Cambridge University Press.

Karlin, C., and Pigeot, N. 1989. L'apprentissage de la taille du silex. *Le Courrier du CNRS: Dossiers Scientifiques* 73:10–12.

Karlin, C.; Pigeot, N.; and Ploux, S. 1992. L'ethnologie préhistorique. *La Recherche* 247:1106–16.

Karlsson, H. 1997. *Being and Post-processual Archaeological Thinking: Reflections upon Post-processual Archaeologies and Anthropocentrism*. Göteborg, Sweden: Gotarc Serie C, Arkeologiska Skrifter No. 15, Department of Archaeology, Göteborg University.

Karp, I. 1991. "Culture and Representation," in *Exhibiting Cultures: The Poetics and Politics of Museum Displays*. Edited by I. Karp and S. Lavine, pp. 11–24. Washington, D.C.: Smithsonian Institution Press.

Karp, I., and Lavine, S. Editors. 1991. *Exhibiting Cultures: The Poetics and Politics of Museum Displays*. Washington, D.C.: Smithsonian Institution Press.

Kaufmann, W. 1974. *Nietzsche: Philosopher, Psychologist, Anti-Christ*. Princeton, N.J.: Princeton University Press.

Keeley, L. 1987. "Hafting and 'Retooling' at Verberie," in *La main et l'outil: manches et emmanchements préhistoriques*. Edited by D. Stordeur, pp. 89–96. Lyon: Maison de l'Orient.

Keenan, J. 1981. "The Concept of the Mode of Production in Hunter-Gatherer Societies," in *The Anthropology of Pre-capitalist Societies*. Edited by J. Kahn and J. Llobera, pp. 2–21. London: Macmillan Press Ltd.

Keene, A. S. 1991. "Cohesion and Contradiction in the Communal Mode of Production: The Lessons of the Kibbutz," in *Between Bands and States*. Edited by S. A. Gregg, pp. 376–94. Carbondale: Southern Illinois University Press.

——1993. "Stories We Tell: Gatherer Hunters as Ideology," in *Ela' Qua: Essays in Honor of Richard Woodbury*. Edited by D. Krass, R. Thomas, and

J. Cole, pp. 62–74. Research Report No. 28; Department of Anthropology. Amherst: University of Massachusetts.

Kegan Gardiner, J. 1995. "Introduction," in *Provoking Agents: Gender and Agency in Theory and Practice.* Edited by J. Kegan Gardiner, pp. 1–20. Urbana: University of Illinois Press.

Kehoe, A. 1992. "The Paradigmatic Vision of Archaeology: Archaeology as a Bourgeoise Science," in *Rediscovering our Past: Essays on the History of American Archaeology.* Edited by J. Reyman, pp. 3–14. Hampshire, England: Avebury.

———1998. *The Land of Prehistory: A Critical History of American Archaeology.* New York: Routledge.

Keightly, D. 1987. Archaeology and Mentality: The Making of China. *Representations* 18:91–128.

Keller, C. M., and Keller, J. D. 1991. *Thinking and Acting with Iron.* Urbana-Champaign: University of Illinois: Beckman Institute for Advanced Science and Technology.

———1996. *Cognition and Tool Use: The Blacksmith at Work.* Cambridge: Cambridge University Press.

Keller, E. F. 1982. Feminism and Science. *Signs* 7(3):589–602.

———1983. *A Feeling for the Organism.* New York: W. H. Freeman.

———1985. *Reflections on Gender and Science.* New Haven, Conn.: Yale University Press.

———1987. "Gender and Science," in *Discovering Reality: Feminist Perspectives on Epistemology, Metaphysics, Methodology, and Philosophy of Science.* Edited by S. Harding and M. B. Hintikka, pp. 187–205. Dordrecht, Holland: D. Reidel.

———1992. *Secrets of Life, Secrets of Death: Essays on Language, Gender, and Science.* New York: Routledge.

Kelley, J., and Hanen, M. 1988. *Archaeology and the Methodology of Science.* Albuquerque: University of New Mexico Press.

Kemp, M. 1990. *The Science of Art: Optical Themes in Western Art From Brunelleschi to Seurat.* New Haven, Conn.: Yale University Press.

Kevles, D., and Hood, L. Editors. 1992. *The Code of Codes: Scientific and Social Issues in the Human Genome Project.* Cambridge, Mass.: Harvard University Press.

King, T. 1978. "Don't That Beat the Band? Nonegalitarian Political Organization in Prehistoric Central California," in *Social Archeology: Beyond Subsistence and Dating.* Edited by C. E. Redman, M. J. Berman, E. Curtin, W. Langhorne, Jr., N. Versaggi, and J. Wanser, pp. 225–48. New York: Academic Press.

Kirk, T. 1991. "Structure, Agency, and Power Relations 'Chez les Derniers Chasseurs-Cueilleurs" of Northwestern France,' in *Processual and Post-processual Archaeologies: Multiple Ways of Knowing the Past.* Edited by R. Preucel, pp. 108–25. Carbondale: Center for Archaeological Investigation, Occasional Paper No. 10. Southern Illinois University Press.

Kirkup, G., and Smith Keller, L. Editors. 1992. *Inventing Women: Science, Technology, and Gender.* Cambridge: Polity Press and Open University.

Kitching, G. 1988. *Karl Marx and the Philosophy of Praxis.* London: Routledge.

Kline, R., and Pinch, T. 1997. Users as Agents of Technological Change: The Social Construction of the Automobile in the Rural United States. *Technology and Culture* 37(4):763–95.

Kluckhohn, C. 1939. The Place of Theory in Anthropological Studies. *Philosophy of Science* 6:328–44.

——— 1940. "The Conceptual Structure of Middle American Studies," in *The Maya and their Neighbors.* Edited by C. L. Hays and A. Tozzer, pp. 41–51. New York: Appleton-Century.

Koopsman, T. C. Editor. 1951. *Activity Analysis of Production and Allocation.* Monograph No. 13 of the Cowles Foundation. New York: John Wiley.

Kopytoff, I. 1986. "The Cultural Biography of Things: Commodization as a Process," in *The Social Life of Things.* Edited by A. Appadurai, pp. 64–91. New York: Cambridge University Press.

——— 1990. "Women's Roles and Existential Identities," in *Beyond the Second Sex: New Directions in the Anthropology of Gender.* Edited by P. R. Sanday and R. G. Goodenough, pp. 75–98. Philadelphia: University of Pennsylvania Press.

Kranzberg, M. Editor. 1980. *Ethics in an Age of Pervasive Technology.* Boulder, Col.: Westview Press.

Krell, D. F. 1993. "General Introduction: The Question of Being," in *Martin Heidegger: Basic Writings.* Edited by D. F. Krell, pp. 3–35. San Francisco: Harper Collins Publishers.

Kroes, P. 1998. "Philosophy of Technology," in *Routledge Encyclopedia of Philosophy.* Edited by E. Craig, pp. 284–8. London: Routledge.

Kuhn, S. 1991. "New Problems, Old Glasses: Methodological Implications of an Evolutionary Paradigm for the Study of Palaeolithic Technologies," in *Perspectives on the Past: Theoretical Biases in Mediterranean Hunter-Gatherer Research.* Edited by G. A. Clark, pp. 242–57. Philadelphia: University of Pennsylvania.

——— 1995. *Mousterian Lithic Technology.* Princeton, N.J.: Princeton University Press.

Kuhn, T. 1970. *The Structure of Scientific Revolutions.* Chicago: University of Chicago Press.

——— 1977. *The Essential Tension: Selected Studies in Scientific Traditions and Change.* Chicago: University of Chicago Press.

Kus, S. 1986. The Power of Origins. Paper presented at the Annual Meetings of the Society for American Archaeology, New Orleans, La.

Lakoff, G. 1987. *Women, Fire, and Dangerous Things: What Categories Reveal about the Mind.* Chicago: University of Chicago Press.

——— 1989. How Metaphors Shape our Lives. *East Bay Express* 11:16.

Lakoff, G., and Johnson, M. 1980. *Metaphors We Live By.* Chicago Press: University of Chicago Press.

Laming-Emperaire, A. 1964. *Origines de l'archéologie préhistorique en France.* Paris: Editions A. et J. Picard et Cie.

Landau, M. 1984. Human Evolution as Narrative. *American Scientist* 72:262–8.

——— 1991. *Narratives of Human Evolution.* New Haven, Conn.: Yale University Press.

Lang, B. 1996. *Heidegger's Silence.* Ithaca, N.Y.: Cornell University Press.

Laqueur, T. 1990. *Making Sex: Body and Gender from the Greeks to Freud.* Cambridge, Mass.: Harvard University Press.

Latour, B. 1987. *Science in Action: How to Follow Scientists and Engineers through Society.* Cambridge, Mass.: Harvard University Press.

——— 1991. "Technology is Society Made Durable," in *A Sociology of Monsters: Essays on Power, Technology, and Domination.* Edited by J. Law, pp. 103–31. New York: Routledge.

——— 1992. "Where are the Missing Masses? The Sociology of a Few Mundane Artifacts," in *Shaping Techology/Building Society.* Edited by W. E. Bijker and J. Law, pp. 225–58. Cambridge, Mass.: MIT Press.

——— 1993. *We Have Never Been Modern.* Cambridge, Mass.: Harvard University Press.

Latour, B., and Woolgar, S. Editors. 1986. *Laboratory Life: The Construction of Scientific Facts.* Princeton, NJ: Princeton University Press.

Lave, J., and Wenger, E. 1991. *Situated Learning: Legitimate Peripheral Participation.* Cambridge: Cambridge University Press.

Law, J. Editor. 1991. *A Sociology of Monsters: Essays on Power, Technology, and Domination.* New York: Routledge.

Law, J., and Whittaker, J. 1988. "In the Art of Representation: Notes on the Politics of Visualization," in *Picturing Power: Visual Depictions and Social Relations.* Edited by G. Fyfe and J. Law, pp. 160–83. London: Routledge.

Layton, E., Jr. 1974. Technology as Knowledge. *Technology and Culture* 15:31–41.

Leach, E. 1973. "Concluding Address," in *Explanation of Culture Change: Models in Prehistory.* Edited by C. Renfrew, pp. 761–71. London: Duckworth.

Leacock, E., and Lee, R. B. 1982. "Introduction," in *Politics and History in Band Societies.* Edited by E. Leacock and R. B. Lee, pp. 1–20. Cambridge: Cambridge University Press; Paris: Editions de la Maison des Sciences de l'Homme.

Lechtman, H. 1977. "Style in Technology: Some Early Thoughts," in *Material Culture: Styles, Organization, and Dynamics of Technology.* Edited by H. Lechtman and R. S. Merrill, pp. 3–20. St. Paul, Minnesota: American Ethnological Society.

——— 1984a. Andean Value Systems and the Development of Prehistoric Metallurgy. *Technology and Culture* 25(1):1–36.

——— 1984b. Pre-Columbian Surface Metallurgy. *Scientific American* 250:56–63.

——— 1993. "Technologies of Power: The Andean Case," in *Configurations of Power in Complex Societies.* Edited by J. Henderson and P. Netherly, pp. 244–80. Ithaca, N.Y.: Cornell University Press.

Lechtman, H., and Steinberg, A. 1979. "The History of Technology: An Anthropological Perspective," in *History and Philosophy of Technology.* Edited by G. Bugliarello and D. B. Doner, pp. 135–60. Urbana: University of Illinois Press.

Ledermann, R. 1990. "Contested Order: Gender and Society in the Southern New Guinea Highlands," in *Beyond the Second Sex: New Directions in the Analysis of Gender*. Edited by P. R. Sanday and R. G. Goodenough, pp. 45–73. Philadelphia: University of Pennsylvania Press.

Lee, R. B. 1982. "Politics Sexual and Non-Sexual in an Egalitarian Society," in *Politics and History in Band Societies*. Edited by E. Leacock and R. B. Lee, pp. 37–59. Cambridge: Cambridge University Press; Paris: Editions de la Maison des Sciences de l'Homme.

Lee Bartky, S. 1995. "Agency: What's the Problem?" in *Provoking Agents: Gender and Agency in Theory and Practice*. Edited by J. Kegan Gardiner, pp. 178–93. Urbana: University of Illinois Press.

Lemonnier, P. 1980. *Les salines de l'ouest – logique technique, logique sociale*. Paris: Maison des Sciences de l'Homme.

——1986. The Study of Material Culture Today: Towards an Anthropology of Technical Systems. *Journal of Anthropological Archaeology* 5:147–86.

——1989a. "Bark Capes, Arrowheads, and Concorde: On Social Representations of Technology," in *The Meaning of Things: Material Culture and Symbolic Expression*. Edited by I. Hodder, pp. 156–71. London: Unwin Hyman.

——1989b. Towards an Anthropology of Technology. *Man* 24:526–7.

——1990. Topsy Turvy Techniques: Remarks on the Social Representation of Techniques. *Archaeological Review from Cambridge* 9(1):27–37.

——1992a. *Elements for an Anthropology of Technology*. Anthropological Papers, No. 88. Museum of Anthropology. Ann Arbor: University of Michigan.

——1992b. Leroi-Gourhan: ethnologue des techniques. *Les Nouvelles de l'Archéologie* 48–9:13–17.

——1993a. "Introduction," in *Technological Choices: Transformation in Material Cultures since the Neolithic*. Edited by P. Lemonnier, pp. 1–35. London: Routledge.

——1993b. "Pigs as Ordinary Wealth: Technical Logic, Exchange, and Leadership in New Guinea," in *Technological Choices: Transformation in Material Cultures since the Neolithic*. Edited by P. Lemonnier, pp. 126–56. London: Routledge.

——Editor. 1993c. *Technological Choices: Transformation in Material Cultures since the Neolithic*. London: Routledge.

Leone, M. P. 1982. Some Opinions about Recovering Mind. *American Anthropologist* 47:742–60.

Leroi-Gourhan, A. 1943. *Evolution et techniques: l'homme et la matière*. Paris: Albin Michel.

——1945. *Evolution et techniques: milieu et techniques*. Paris: Albin Michel.

——1958. Repartition et groupement des animaux dans l'art pariétal paléolithique. *Bulletin de la Société Préhistorique Française* 55:515–27.

——1964a. *Le geste et la parole II: la mémoire et les rythmes*. Paris: Albin Michel.

——1964b. *Le geste et la parole I: technique et langage*. Paris: Albin Michel.

——1965. *Préhistoire de l'art occidental*. Paris: Louis Mazenod.

Leroi-Gourhan, A., and Brézillion, M. 1972. *Fouilles de Pincevent, essai d'analyse ethnographique d'un habitat Magdalénien.* VII Supplément à Gallia Préhistoire. Paris: CNRS.

Lesick, K. S. 1996. "Re-engendering Gender: Some Theoretical and Methodological Concerns on a Burgeoning Archaeological Pursuit," in *Invisible People and Processes: Writing Gender and Children into European Archaeology.* Edited by J. Moore and E. Scott, pp. 31–41. Leicester: Leicester University Press.

Lévi-Strauss, C. 1963. *Structural Anthropology.* New York: Basic Books.

Levins, R., and Lewontin, R. C. 1985. *The Dialectical Biologist.* Cambridge, Mass.: Harvard University Press.

Lewis-Williams, J. D. 1984. The Empiricist Impasse in Southern African Rock Art. *South African Archaeological Bulletin* 39:58–66.

——— 1987. A Dream of Eland: An Unexplored Component of San Shamanism and Rock Art. *World Archaeology* 19(2):165–77.

——— 1990. Documentation, Analysis, and Interpretation: Dilemmas in Rock Art Research. *South African Archaeological Bulletin* 45:126–36.

——— 1992. Ethnographic Evidence Related to "Trance" and "Shamans" among Northern and Southern Bushmen. *South African Archaeological Bulletin* 47:56–60.

——— 1995. Modelling the Production and Consumption of Rock Art. *South African Archaeological Bulletin* 50:143–54.

——— 1997. Agency, Art, and Altered States of Consciousness: A Motif in French (Quercy) Upper Palaeolithic Parietal Art. *Antiquity* 71:810–30.

Lloyd, E. A. 1996. "Science and Anti-science: Objectivity and its Real Enemies," in *Feminism, Science, and the Philosophy of Science.* Edited by L. H. Nelson and J. Nelson, pp. 217–59. Dordrecht, Holland: Kluwer.

Longino, H. 1993. Feminist Standpoint Theory and the Problems of Knowledge. *Signs* 19(1):201–12.

——— 1995. "To See Feelingly: Reason, Passion, and Dialogue in Feminist Philosophy," in *Feminisms in the Academy.* Edited by D. Stanton and A. Stewart, pp. 19–45. Ann Arbor: University of Michigan Press.

Lubbock, J. 1865. *Pre-historic Times as Illustrated by Ancient Remains and the Manners and Customs of Modern Savages.* London: William & Norgate.

Lynch, M., and Woolgar, S. 1990. "Introduction: Sociological Orientations to Representational Practice in Science," in *Representation in Scientific Practice.* Edited by M. Lynch and S. Woolgar, pp. 1–18. Cambridge, Mass.: MIT Press.

Lyotard, J.-F. 1990 [orig. 1988]. *Heidegger and "The Jews".* Minneapolis: University of Minnesota Press.

McGaw, J. A. 1982. Women and the History of American Technology. *Signs* 9(2):798–828.

——— 1989. "No Passive Victims, No Separate Spheres: A Feminist Perspective on Technology's History," in *In Context.* Research in Technology Studies, vol. 1. Edited by R. Cutliffe and S. Post, pp. 172–91. Bethlehem, Pa.: Lehigh University Press.

——— 1996. "Reconceiving Technology: Why Feminine Technologies Matter," in *Gender and Archaeology.* Edited by R. P. Wright, pp. 52–75. Philadelphia: University of Pennsylvania Press.

McGhee, R. 1977. Ivory for the Sea Woman: The Symbolic Attributes of a Prehistoric Technology. *Canadian Journal of Archaeology* 1:141–9.

McGuire, K. R., and Hildebrandt, W. R. 1994. The Possibilities of Women and Men: Gender and the California Milling Stone Horizon. *Journal of California and Great Basin Anthropology* 16(1):41–59.

McGuire, R. 1992. *A Marxist Archaeology.* San Diego, Cal.: Academic Press.

McGuire, R., and Schiffer, M. B. 1983. A Theory of Architectural Design. *Journal of Anthropological Archaeology* 2:277–303.

MacKenzie, D. 1984. Marx and the Machine. *Technology and Culture* 25:473–502.

MacKenzie, D., and Wajcman, J. 1985. "Introductory Essay," in *The Social Shaping of Technology: How the Refrigerator Got its Hum.* Edited by D. MacKenzie and J. Wajcman, pp. 2–25. Milton Keynes: Open University Press.

MacKenzie, M. A. 1991. *Androgynous Objects: String Bags and Gender in Central New Guinea.* Chur, Switzerland: Harwood Academic Publishers.

MacWhite, E. 1956. On the Interpretation of Archeological Evidence in Historical and Sociological Terms. *American Anthropologist* 58:3–25.

Mahias, M.-C. 1989. Les mots et les actes: allumer le feu, baratter, question de texte, et d'ensemble technique. *Techniques et Culture* 14:157–76.

—— 1993. "Pottery Technique in India," in *Technological Choices: Transformation in Material Cultures since the Neolithic.* Edited by P. Lemonnier, pp. 157–80. London: Routledge.

Malinowski, B. 1939. The Group and the Individual in Functional Analysis. *American Journal of Sociology* 44:938–64.

—— 1948. "Magic, Science, and Religion," in *Magic, Science, and Religion and Other Essays.* Edited by P. Redfield, pp. 17–36. Boston: Beacon Press.

Manolakakis, L. 1994. La production des outils en silex dans les sociétés hiérarchisées de l'Enéolithique en Bulgaire: évolution, traditions culturelles et organisation sociale. Doctorat, Université de Paris I, Panthéon Sorbonne.

Marcuse, H. 1964. *One-dimensional Man.* Boston: Beacon Press.

—— 1968. "Industrialization and Capitalism in the Work of Max Weber," in *Negations: Essays in Critical Theory*, pp. 201–26. Boston: Beacon Press.

Marquardt, W. H. 1992. Dialectical Archaeology. *Archaeological Method and Theory* 4:101–40.

Martin, H. 1910. La percussion osseuse et les esquilles qui en dérivent: expérimentation. *Bulletin de la Société Préhistorique Française* 7:299–304.

Marx, K. 1963 [orig. 1869]. *The Eighteenth Brumaire of Louis Bonaparte.* New York: International Publishers.

—— 1967 [orig. 1883]. *Capital I: A Critical Analysis of Capitalist Production.* New York: International Publishers.

Marx, K., and Engels, F. 1970. *The German Ideology.* New York: International Publishers.

Mauss, M. 1924. *The Gift.* New York: W. W. Norton.

—— 1935. Les techniques du corps. *Journal de Psychologie* 32:271–93. [Reprinted in: *Sociologie et Anthropologie* (1950), pp. 365–86. Paris, Presses Universitaires de France; and in *Sociology and Psychology: Essays of Marcel*

Mauss (1979), Translated by B. Brewster, pp. 97–123. London: Routledge & Kegan Paul.]

—— 1969a [orig. 1927]. Division et proportions des divisions de la sociologie. *Année Sociologique* n.s. 2. [*Reprinted in Oeuvres*, vol. III: *Cohésion sociale et divisions de la sociologie* (1969), Presented by V. Karady, pp. 178–245. Paris: Editions de Minuit.]

—— 1969b [orig. 1934]. Fragment d'un plan descriptif de la sociologie. *Année Sociologique* n.s. 2. [Reprinted in *Oeuvres*, vol. III: *Cohésion sociale et divisions de la sociologie* (1969), Presented by V. Karady, pp. 303–54. Paris: Editions de Minuit.]

Meggers, B. 1960. "The Law of Cultural Evolution as a Practical Research Tool," in *Essays in the Science of Culture*. Edited by G. Dole and R. Carneiro, pp. 302–16. New York: Crowell.

Meillassoux, C. 1972. From Reproduction to Production: A Marxist Approach to Economic Anthropology. *Economy and Society* 1(1):93–105.

Melosi, M. Editor. 1980. *Pollution and Reform in American Cities, 1870–1930*. Austin: University of Texas Press.

Merchant, C. 1980. *The Death of Nature: Women, Ecology and the Scientific Revolution*. San Francisco: Harper & Row.

—— 1983. "Mining the Earth's Womb," in *Machina Ex Dea: Feminist Perspectives on Technology*. Edited by J. Rothschild, pp. 99–117. New York: Pergamon.

Méroc, L. 1953. La conquête des Pyrénées par l'homme. *Premier Congrès International de Spéléologie*. Paris IV(4):35–53.

Meskell, L. M. 1996. The Somatisation of Archaeology: Institution, Discourses, Corporeality. *Norwegian Archaeological Review* 29(1):1–16.

—— 1998. "The Irresistible Body and the Seduction of Archaeology," in *Changing Bodies, Changing Meanings: Studies on the Human Body in Antiquity*. Edited by D. Montserrat, pp. 139–61. London: Routledge.

Miller, D. 1985. *Artefacts as Categories: A Study of Ceramic Variability in Central India*. Cambridge: Cambridge University Press.

—— 1987. *Material Culture and Mass Consumption*. Oxford: Blackwell.

—— Editor. 1998. *Material Culture: Why Some Things Matter*. Chicago: University of Chicago Press.

Miller, D., and Tilley, C. Editors. 1984. *Ideology, Power, and Prehistory*. Cambridge: Cambridge University Press.

—— 1996. Editorial. *Journal of Material Culture* 1(1):5–14.

Mitcham, C. 1980. "The Philosophy of Technology," in *A Guide to the Culture of Science, Technology, and Medicine*. Edited by P. Durbin, pp. 282–363. New York: Free Press.

—— 1994. *Thinking through Technology: The Path between Engineering and Philosophy*. Chicago: University of Chicago Press.

Mitcham, C., and Mackey, R. Editors. 1972. *Philosophy of Technology: Readings in the Philosophical Problems of Technology*. New York: Free Press.

Mithen, S. 1990. *Thoughtful Foragers: A Study of Prehistoric Decision Making*. Cambridge: Cambridge University Press.

—— 1996. *The Prehistory of the Mind: The Cognitive Origins of Art, Religion, and Science*. London: Thames & Hudson.

Molyneaux, B. L. Editor. 1997. *The Cultural Life of Images: Visual Representation in Archaeology.* London: Routledge.

Moore, H. L. 1986. *Space, Text, and Gender: An Anthropological Study of the Marakwet of Kenya.* Cambridge: Cambridge University Press.

——1994. *A Passion for Difference.* Oxford: Polity Press.

Morrow, C. 1987. "Blades and Cobden Chert: A Technological Argument for their Role as Markers of Regional Identification during the Hopewell Period in Illinois," in *The Organization of Core Technology.* Edited by J. Johnson and C. Morrow, pp. 119–50. Boulder, Col.: Westview Press.

Morton, J. 1988. Comment to Testart. *Current Anthropology* 29(1):18–20.

Moser, S. 1992. The Visual Language of Archaeology: A Case Study of the Neanderthals. *Antiquity* 66:831–44.

——1993a. "Gender Stereotyping in Pictorial Reconstructions of Human Origins," in *Women in Archaeology: A Feminist Critique.* Occasional Papers in Prehistory, No. 23. Edited by H. du Cros and L. Smith, pp. 75–93. Department of Prehistory, Research School of Pacific Studies. Canberra: Australian National University.

——1993b. Picturing the Prehistoric. *Metascience* 4:58–67.

——1996. "Visual Representation in Archaeology: Depicting the Missing-link in Human Origins," in *Picturing Knowledge: Historical and Philosophical Problems Concerning the Use of Art in Science.* Edited by B. Baigire, pp. 184–214. Toronto: University of Toronto Press.

——1998. *Ancestral Images: The Iconography of Human Origins.* Ithaca, N.Y.: Cornell University Press.

Moser, S., and Gamble, C. 1997. "Revolutionary Images: The Iconic Vocabulary for Presenting Human Antiquity," in *The Cultural Life of Images: Visual Representation in Archaeology.* Edited by B. L. Molyneaux, pp. 184–212. London: Routledge.

Mumford, L. 1934. *Technics and Civilization.* New York: Harcourt Brace.

——1952. *Art and Technics.* New York: Columbia University Press.

——1964. Authoritarian and Democratic Technics. *Technology and Culture* 5(1):1–8.

——1967. *Technics and Human Development: The Myth of the Machine*, vol. I. New York: Harcourt Brace Jovanovich.

Munn, N. D. 1974. Spatiotemporal Transformations of Gawa Canoes. *Journal de la Société des Océanistes* 33:39–52.

——1986. *The Fame of Gawa: A Symbolic Study of Value Transformation in a Massim (Papua New Guinesa) Society.* Cambridge: Cambridge University Press.

Murray, P. 1982. The Frankfurt School Critique of Technology. *Research in Philosophy and Technology* 5:223–48.

Myers, G. 1990. "Every Picture Tells a Story: Illustrations in E. O. Wilson's *Sociobiology*," in *Representation in Scientific Practice.* Edited by M. Lynch and S. Woolgar, pp. 231–65. Cambridge, Mass.: MIT Press.

Nagel, E. 1961. *The Structure of Science: Problems in the Logic of Scientific Explanation.* New York: Harcourt, Brace, & World.

Nance, J. 1975. *The Gentle Tasaday: A Stone Age People in the Philippine Rain Forest.* New York: Harcourt Brace Jovanovich.

——— 1982. *Lobo of the Tasaday: A Stone Age Boy Meets the Modern World.* New York: Pantheon.

Nelson, M. C. 1991. The Study of Technological Organization. *Archaeological Method and Theory* 3:57–100.

Oakley, K. 1959. Tools Makyth Man. *Smithsonian Report for 1958*:431–45.

O'Brien, M. 1981. *The Politics of Reproduction.* Boston: Routledge & Kegan Paul.

Olive, M. 1992. En marge des unités d'habitations d'Etiolles: les foyers d'activité satellites. *Gallia Préhistoire* 34:85–140.

Olive, M., and Pigeot, N. 1992. "Les tailleurs de silex Magdaléniens d'Etiolles: vers l'identification d'une organisation sociale complexe?" in *La pierre préhistorique.* Edited by M. Menu and P. Walter, pp. 173–85. Paris: Laboratoire de Recherche des Musées de France.

Olive, M.; Pigeot, N.; and Taborin, Y. 1991. *Il y a 13,000 ans à Etiolles.* Paris: Argenton-sur-Creuse.

Ortner, S. B. 1984. Theory in Anthropology since the Sixties. *Comparative Studies in Society and History* 26(1):126–66.

——— 1995. Resistance and the Problem of Ethnographic Refusal. *Comparative Study of Society and History* 37(1):173–93.

Osborn, H. F. 1915. *Men of the Old Stone Age: Their Environment, Life, and Art.* New York: Charles Scribner's & Sons.

Oswalt, W. 1973. *Habitat and Technology: The Evolution of Hunting.* New York: Holt, Rinehart, & Winston.

——— (with the assistance of G. Mann and L. Satterthwait). 1976. *An Anthropological Analysis of Food-getting Technology.* New York: John Wiley & Sons.

Oudemans, C. W. 1996. Heidegger and Archaeology. *Archaeological Dialogues* 3(1):29–33.

Pacey, A. 1983. *The Culture of Technology.* Cambridge, Mass.: MIT Press.

Pálsson, G. 1994. Enskilment at Sea. *Man* 29:901–27.

Pálsson, G., and Helgason, A. 1999. Schooling and Skipperhood: The Development of Dexterity. *American Anthropologist* 100(4):908–23.

Parkington, J., and Smith, A. 1986. Guest Editorial. *South African Archaeological Bulletin* 41(144):1–2.

Parsons, T. 1949 [orig. 1937]. *The Structure of Social Action.* New York: The Free Press of Glencoe.

Pauketat, T. R. in press. "The Tragedy of the Commoners," in *Agency in Archaeology.* Edited by M-A. Dobres and J. E. Robb. London: Routledge.

Pelegrin, J. 1985. "Reflexion sur le comportement technique," in *La signification culturelle des industries lithiques.* Edited by M. Otte, pp. 72–82. BAR International Series No. 239.

——— 1990. Prehistoric Lithic Technology: Some Aspects of Research. *Archaeological Review from Cambridge* 9(1):116–25.

——— 1991. Les savoir-faires: une très longue histoire. *Terrain* (March). 106–13.

Pelegrin, J.; Karlin, C.; and Bodu, P. 1988. "'Chaînes opératoires': un outil pour le préhistorien," in *Technologie préhistorique.* Edited by J. Tixier, pp. 55–62. Notes et Monographies Techniques, No. 25. Paris: CNRS.

Perlès, C. 1989. *From Stone Procurement to Neolithic Society.* Indiana University, Department of Anthropology: The David Skomp Distinguished Lecture in Anthropology.

—— 1992. "In Search of Lithic Strategies: A Cognitive Approach to Prehistoric Chipped Stone Assemblages," in *Representations in Archaeology.* Edited by J.-C. Gardin and C. Peebles, pp. 223–47. Bloomington: Indiana University Press.

Petroski, H. 1994. Men and Women of Progress. *American Scientist* 82(3):216–19.

Petrovic, G. 1983a. "Alienation," in *A Dictionary of Marxist Thought.* Edited by T. Bottomore, L. Harris, V. G. Kiernan, and R. Miliband, pp. 9–15. Cambridge, Mass.: Harvard University Press.

—— 1983b. "Reification," in *A Dictionary of Marxist Thought.* Edited by T. Bottomore, L. Harris, V. G. Kiernan, and R. Miliband, pp. 411–13. Cambridge, Mass.: Harvard University Press.

—— 1983c. "Praxis," in *A Dictionary of Marxist Thought.* Edited by T. Bottomore, L. Harris, V. G. Kiernan, and R. Miliband, pp. 384–9. Cambridge, Mass.: Harvard University Press.

Peyrony, D. 1950. Passage du paléolithique au mésolithique dans la sud-ouest Européen: Magdalénien final et Azilien ancien. *Congrès Préhistorique de France* XIIIeme session:536–41.

Pfaffenberger, B. 1988. Fetishized Objects and Humanized Nature: Towards an Anthropology of Technology. *Man* 23:236–52.

—— 1992. Social Anthropology of Technology. *Annual Review of Anthropology* 21:491–516.

—— 1999. "Worlds in the Making: Technological Activities and the Construction of Intersubjective Meaning," in *The Social Dynamics of Technology: Practice, Politics, and World Views.* Edited by M-A. Dobres and C. R. Hoffman, pp. 147–64. Washington, D.C.: Smithsonian Institution Press.

—— in press. "Making People: Applications of 'Virtual Reality' in Non-Western Technology," in *Explorations in the Anthropology of Technology.* Edited by M. B. Schiffer. Albuquerque: University of New Mexico Press.

Pickering, A. 1995. *The Mangle of Practice: Time, Agency, and Science.* Chicago: University of Chicago Press.

Piette, E. 1892. Phases successives de la civilisation pendant l'âge du renne dans le midi de la France et notamment sue la rive gauche de l'Arise (Grotte du Mas d'Azil). *Congrès de l'Association Française pour l'Avancement des Sciences* 21:649–54.

—— 1895. Hiatus et lacune: vestiges de la période de transition dans la grotte du Mas d'Azil. *Bulletin de la Société d'Anthropologie de Paris* VI(4):235–67.

Pigeot, N. 1987. *Magdaléniens d'Etiolles: débitage et organisation sociale.* XXV Supplément à Gallia Préhistoire. Paris: CNRS.

—— 1988. "Apprendre à débiter des lames: un cas d'education technique chez des Magdaléniens d'Etiolles," in *Technologie préhistorique.* Edited by J. Tixier, pp. 63–70. Notes et Monographies No. 25. Paris: CNRS.

—— 1990. Technical and Social Actors: Flintknapping Specialists at Magdalenian Etiolles. *Archaeological Review from Cambridge* 9(1):126–41.

Pigeot, N.; Phillippe, M.; Licon, G. L.; and Morgenstern, M. 1991. "Systèmes techniques et essai de technologie culturelle à Etiolles: nouvelles perspectives," in *25 ans d'études technologiques en préhistoire: bilan et perspectives*. Edited by C. Perlès, pp. 169–85. Juan-les-Pins: Editions APDCA.

Piggott, S. 1978. *Antiquity Depicted: Aspects of Archaeological Illustration*. London: Thames & Hudson.

Pippin, R. 1995 [orig. 1993]. "On the Notion of Technology as Ideology," in *Technology and the Politics of Knowledge*. Edited by A. Feenberg and A. Hannay, pp. 43–61. Bloomington: Indiana University Press.

Pitt, J. 1990. "The Autonomy of Technology," in *From Artifact to Habitat: Studies in the Critical Engagement of Technology*. Edited by G. Ormiston, pp. 117–31. Bethlehem, Pa.: Lehigh University Press.

Pitt-Rivers, A. H. L. F. 1874. "Principles of Classification," in *The Evolution of Culture and Other Essays*. Edited by J. Meyer, pp. 1–19. Oxford: Clarendon Press.

—— 1875. "The Evolution of Culture," in *The Evolution of Culture and Other Essays*. Edited by J. Meyer, pp. 20–44. Oxford: Clarendon Press.

—— 1891. Typological Museums, as Exemplified by the Pitt-Rivers Museum at Oxford and his Provincial Museums at Farnham, Dorset. *Journal of the Society of the Arts* 40:115–22.

Plog, F. 1973. "Diachronic Anthropology," in *Research and Theory in Current Archaeology*. Edited by C. Redman, pp. 181–98. New York: John Wiley & Sons.

Ploux, S. 1991. "Technologie, technicité, techniciens: méthode de déterminations d'auteurs et comportements techniques individuels," in *25 ans d'études technologiques en préhistoire: bilan et perspectives*. Edited by C. Perlès, pp. 206–14. Juan-les-Pins: Editions APDCA.

Pollock, G. 1987. "What's Wrong with Images of Women?" in *Looking On: Images of Femininity in the Visual Arts and Media*. Edited by R. Betterton, pp. 40–8. New York: Pandora.

Polt, R. 1999. *Heidegger: An Introduction*. Ithaca, N.Y.: Cornell University Press.

Preziosi, D. 1989. *Rethinking Art History: Meditation on a Coy Science*. New Haven, Conn.: Yale University Press.

Price, S. 1989. *Primitive Art in Civilized Places*. Chicago: University of Chicago Press.

Prideaux, T. 1973. *The Emergence of Man: Cro-Magnon Man*. New York: Time-Life Books.

Pringle, H. 1998. New Women of the Ice Age. *Discover* 19(4):62–9.

Pye, D. 1964. *The Nature of Design*. New York: Van Nostrand Reinhold.

Rabinow, P., and Sullivan, W. Editors. 1987. *Interpretive Social Science: A Second Look*. Berkeley: University of California Press.

Redman, C. 1973. Multistage Fieldwork and Analytical Techniques. *American Antiquity* 38:61–79.

—— 1977. "The 'Analytical Individual' and Prehistoric Style Variability," in *The Individual in Prehistory: Studies of Variability in Style in Prehistoric Technologies*. Edited by J. Hill and J. Gunn, pp. 41–53. New York: Academic Press.

Redman, C. 1987. Surface Collection, Sampling, and Research Design: A Retrospective. *American Antiquity* 52(2):249–65.

—— 1991. Distinguished Lecture in Archeology: In Defense of the Seventies – the Adolescence of New Archeology. *American Anthropologist* 93(2):295–307.

Reinach, S. 1903. L'art et la magie: à propos des peintures et des gravures de l'âge du renne. *L'Anthropologie* 14:257–66.

Renfrew, C., and Zubrow, E. B. W. Editors. 1994. *The Ancient Mind: Elements of Cognitive Archaeology.* Cambridge: Cambridge University Press.

Reynolds, P. C. 1993. "The Complementation Theory of Language and Tool Use," in *Tools, Language, and Cognition in Human Evolution.* Edited by K. R. Gibson and T. Ingold, pp. 407–28. Cambridge: Cambridge University Press.

Rice, P. 1981. The Evolution of Specialized Pottery Production. *Current Anthropology* 22(3):219–40.

Ricoeur, P. 1971. The Model of the Text: Meaningful Action Considered as Text. *Social Research* 38(3):529–62.

Ridington, R. 1982. Technology, World View, and Adaptive Strategy in a Northern Hunting Society. *Canadian Review of Society and Anthropology* 19(4):469–81.

—— 1983. From Artifice to Artifact: Stages in the Industrialization of a Northern Hunting People. *Journal of Canadian Studies* 18(3):55–66.

—— 1988. Knowledge, Power, and the Individual in Subarctic Hunting Societies. *American Anthropologist* 90:98–110.

—— 1999. "Dogs, Snares and Cartridge Belts: The Poetics of a Northern Athapaskan Narrative Technology," in *The Social Dynamics of Technology: Practice, Politics, and World Views.* Edited by M-A. Dobres and C. R. Hoffman, pp. 167–85. Washington, D.C.: Smithsonian Institution Press.

Robb, J. E. 1999. "Secret Agents: Culture, Economy and Social Reproduction," in *Material Symbols: Culture and Economy in Prehistory.* Edited by J. E. Robb, pp. 3–14. Center for Archaeological Investigations, Occasional Paper No. 26. Carbondale: Southern Illinois University Press.

Robert, R.; Malvesin-Fabre, M.; and Nougier, L.-R. 1953. Sur l'existence possible d'une école d'art dans le Magdalénien Pyrénéen. *Bulletin Archéologique du Comité des Travaux Historiques et Scientifiques* 1953:187–93.

Rockmore, T. 1995 [orig. 1992]. "Heidegger on Technology and Democracy," in *Technology and the Politics of Knowledge.* Edited by A. Feenberg and A. Hannay, pp. 128–44. Bloomington: Indiana University Press.

Rosaldo, R. 1989. Imperialist Nostalgia. *Representations* 26:107–22.

Rose, H. 1987. "Hand, Brain, and Heart: A Feminist Epistemology for the Natural Sciences," in *Sex and Scientific Inquiry.* Edited by S. Harding and J. F. O'Barr, pp. 265–82. Chicago: University of Chicago Press.

—— 1988. "Beyond Masculinist Realities: A Feminist Epistemology for the Sciences," in *Feminist Approaches to Science.* Edited by R. Bleier, pp. 57–76. New York: Pergamon Press.

—— 1994. *Love, Power, and Knowledge: Towards a Feminist Transformation of the Sciences.* Bloomington: Indiana University Press.

Rosenberg, N. 1985. *Inside the Black Box: Technology and Economics.* Cambridge: Cambridge University Press.

Ross, D. 1991. *The Origins of American Social Sciences.* Cambridge: Cambridge University Press.

Rothenberg, D. 1993. *Hand's End: Technology and the Limits of Nature.* Berkeley: University of California Press.

Rothschild, J. Editor. 1983. *Machina ex Dea: Feminist Perspectives on Technology.* New York: Pergamon Press.

Roux, V. 1991. "Peut-on interpréter les activités lithiques préhistoriques en termes de durée d'apprentissage? Apport de l'ethnologie et de la psychologie aux études technologiques," in *25 ans d'études technologiques en préhistoire: bilan et perspectives.* Edited by C. Perlès, pp. 47–56. Juan-les-Pins: Editions APDCA.

Roux, V., and Matarasso, P. 1999. "Crafts and the Evolution of Complex Societies: New Methodologies for Modeling the Organization of Production and an Harappan Example," in *The Social Dynamics of Technology: Practice, Politics, and World Views.* Edited by M-A. Dobres and C. R. Hoffman, pp. 46–70. Washington, D.C.: Smithsonian Institution Press.

Roux, V., and Pelegrin, J. 1989. Taille des perles et spécialisation artisinale: enquête ethnoarchéologique dans le Gujarat. *Techniques et Cultures* 14:23–49.

Roux, V. with Corbetta, D. 1989. *The Potter's Wheel: Craft Specialization and Technical Competence.* New Delhi: IBH Publishing.

Rudwick, M. 1976. The Emergence of a Visual Language for Geological Science, 1760–1840. *History of Science* 14:149–95.

—— 1992. *Scenes from Deep Time.* Chicago: University of Chicago Press.

Ryan, M. 1981. *Cradle of the Middle Class: The Family in Oneida County, New York, 1790–1865.* Cambridge: Cambridge University Press.

Sabia, D., Jr., and Wallulis, J. Editors. 1983. *Changing Social Science.* Albany: State University of New York Press.

Sabloff, J., and Willey, G. 1967. The Collapse of Maya Civilization in the Southern Lowlands: A Consideration of History and Process. *Southwestern Journal of Anthropology* 23:311–36.

Sackett, J. 1981. "From de Mortillet to Bordes: A Century of Palaeolithic Research," in *Toward a History of Archaeology.* Edited by O. Klindt-Jensen and G. Daniel, pp. 85–99. London: Thames & Hudson.

—— 1991. "Straight Archaeology French Style: The Phylogenetic Paradigm in Historic Perspective," in *Perspectives on the Past: Theoretical Biases in Mediterranean Hunter-Gatherer Research.* Edited by G. A. Clark, pp. 109–39. Philadelphia: University of Pennsylvania.

Sahlins, M. 1968. *Tribesmen.* Englewood Cliffs, N.J.: Prentice-Hall.

—— 1976. *Culture and Practical Reason.* Chicago: University of Chicago Press.

Saitta, D. J. 1994. Agency, Class, and Archaeological Interpretation. *Journal of Anthropological Archaeology* 13(3):201–27.

Saitta, D. J., and Keene, A. S. 1990. "Politics and Surplus Flow in

Prehistoric Communal Societies," in *The Evolution of Political Systems: Sociopolitics in Small-scale Sedentary Societies.* Edited by S. Upham, pp. 203–24. Cambridge: Cambridge University Press.

Sassaman, K. E. 1997. Acquiring Stone, Acquiring Power. Paper presented at the Annual Meetings of the Society for American Archaeology, Nashville, Tenn.

—— in press. "Agents of Change in Hunter-Gatherer Technology," in *Agency in Archaeology.* Edited by M-A. Dobres and J. E. Robb. London: Routledge.

Sawicki, J. 1991. *Disciplining Foucault.* New York: Routledge.

Schick, K., and Toth, N. 1993. *Making Silent Stones Speak: Human Evolution and the Dawn of Technology.* New York: Simon & Schuster.

Schiebinger, L. 1993. *Nature's Body: Gender in the Making of Modern Science.* Boston: Beacon Press.

Schiffer, M. B. 1972. Archeological Context and Systemic Context. *American Antiquity* 37:156–65.

—— 1975a. Archeology as a Behavioral Science. *American Anthropologist* 77:836–48.

—— 1975b. Behavioral Chain Analysis: Activities, Organization, and the Use of Space. *Fieldiana* 65:103–74.

—— 1976. *Behavioral Archeology.* New York: Academic Press.

—— 1991. *The Portable Radio in American Life.* Tucson: University of Arizona Press.

—— 1992a. *Technological Perspectives on Behavioral Change.* Tucson: University of Arizona Press.

—— 1992b. "Technology and Society," in *Technological Perspectives on Behavioral Change,* pp. 130–41. Tucson: University of Arizona Press.

—— 1992c. "A Framework for the Analysis of Activity Change," in *Technological Perspectives on Behavioral Change,* pp. 77–93. Tucson: University of Arizona Press.

—— 1994. Review of Lemonnnier's *Elements for an Anthropology of Technology. American Anthropologist* 96:202–3.

—— 1999. "A Behavioral Theory of Meaning," in *Pottery and People.* Edited by J. M. Skibo and G. M. Feinman, pp. 199–217. Salt Lake City: University of Utah Press.

Schiffer, M. B., and Skibo, J. M. 1987. Theory and Experiment in the Study of Technological Change. *Current Anthropology* 28(5):595–622.

—— 1997. The Explanation of Artifact Variability. *American Antiquity* 62(1):25–50.

Schiffer, M. B., with Miller, A. R. 1999. *The Material Life of Human Beings: Artifacts, Behavior, and Communication.* London: Routledge.

Schlanger, N. 1990. Techniques as Human Action. *Archaeological Review from Cambridge* 9(1):18–26.

—— 1991. Le fait technique total: la raison pratique et les raisons de la pratique dans l'oeuvre de Marcel Mauss. *Terrain* 1991:114–30.

—— 1994. "Mindful Technology: Unleashing the *Chaîne Opératoire* for an Archaeology of Mind," in *The Ancient Mind: Elements of Cognitive Archaeology.* Edited by C. Renfrew and E. B. W. Zubrow, pp. 143–51. Cambridge: Cambridge University Press.

—— 1996. Understanding Levallois: Lithic Technology and Cognitive Archaeology. *Cambridge Archaeological Journal* 6(2):231–54.

—— 1998. "The Study of Techniques as an Ideological Challenge: Technology, Nation, and Humanity in the Work of Marcel Mauss," in *Marcel Mauss: A Centenary Tribute*. Edited by W. James and N. J. Allen, pp. 192–212. New York: Berghahn Books.

Schmider, B. Editor. 1993. *Marsangy: un campement des derniers chasseurs Magdaléniens sur les bords de l'Yonne*. Liège: ERAUL No. 55, Université de Liège.

Schmidt, P. 1996. "Cultural Representations in African Iron Production," in *The Culture and Technology of African Iron Working*. Edited by P. Schmidt, pp. 1–28. Gainesville: University Press of Florida.

—— 1998. "Reading Gender in the Ancient Iron Technology of Africa," in *Gender in African Prehistory*. Edited by S. Kent, pp. 139–77. Walnut Creek, Cal.: Alta Mira Press.

Schopenhauer, A. 1958 [orig. 1818]. *The World as Will and Representation*, vol. I. New York: Dover Publishers, Inc.

Schrire, C. 1995. *Digging through Darkness: Chronicles of an Archaeologist*. Charlottesville: University of Virginia Press.

Schütz, A. 1962. *The Problem of Social Reality*, vol. 1, edited by M. Nathanson. The Hague: Martinus Nijhoff.

Scott, J. W. 1990. Review of *Heroes of Their Own Lives* (by L. Gordon). *Signs* 15(4):848–53.

Sellet, F. 1993. *Chaîne Opératoire:* The Concept and its Applications. *Lithic Technology* 18(1 and 2):106–12.

Service, E. 1962. *Primitive Social Organization: An Evolutionary Approach*. New York: Random House.

—— 1975. *The Origins of the State and Civilization: The Process of Cultural Evolution*. New York: Norton.

Sewell, W. H., Jr. 1992. A Theory of Structure: Duality, Agency, and Transformation. *American Journal of Sociology* 98(1):1–29.

Shanks, M., and McGuire, R. 1996. The Craft of Archaeology. *American Antiquity* 61(1):75–88.

Shanks, M., and Tilley, C. 1987a. *Re-constructing Archaeology*. Cambridge: Cambridge University Press.

—— 1987b. *Social Theory and Archaeology*. Albuquerque: University of New Mexico Press.

Sharp, H. S. 1991. "Dry Meat and Gender: The Absence of Chipewyan Ritual for the Regulation of Hunting and Animal Numbers," in *Hunters and Gatherers 2: Property, Power, and Ideology*. Edited by T. Ingold, D. Riches, and J. Woodburn, pp. 183–91. New York: Berg.

Sharp, L. 1952. Steel Axes for Stone-Age Australians. *Human Organization* 11:17–22.

Shilling, C. 1993. *The Body and Social Theory*. London: Sage.

Shostak, M. 1981. *Nisa: The Life and Words of a !Kung Woman*. Cambridge, Mass.: Harvard University Press.

Shott, M. 1986. Technological Organization and Settlement Mobility: An Ethnographic Excavation. *Journal of Anthropological Research* 42(1):15–51.

Sieveking, A. 1976. "Settlement Patterns in the Later Magdalenian in the Central Pyrenees," in *Problems in Economic and Social Archaeology*. Edited by G. de G. Sieveking, I. Longworth, and K. Wilson, pp. 583–603. London: Duckworth.

Silberbauer, G. 1982. "Political Process in G/wi Bands," in *Politics and History in Band Societies*. Edited by E. Leacock and R. B. Lee, pp. 23–35. Cambridge: Cambridge University Press; Paris: Editions de la Maison des Sciences de l'Homme.

Sillar, B. 1996. The Dead and the Drying. *Journal of Material Culture* 1(3):259–89.

Silverblatt, I. 1988. Women in States. *Annual Review of Anthropology* 17:427–60.

Simondon, G. 1958. *Du mode d'existence des objets techniques*. Paris: Aubier.

Sinclair, A. G. in press. "Constellations of Knowledge: Human Agency, Symbolism, and Material Affordance in Lithic Technology," in *Agency in Archaeology*. Edited by M-A. Dobres and J. E. Robb. London: Routledge.

Skibo, J. M. 1999. "Pottery and People," in *Pottery and People*. Edited by J. M. Skibo and G. M. Feinman, pp. 1–8. Salt Lake City: University of Utah Press.

Skibo, J. M., and Schiffer, M. B. in press. "Understanding Artifact Variability and Change: A Behavioral Framework," in *Explorations in the Anthropology of Technology*. Edited by M. B. Schiffer. Albuquerque: University of New Mexico Press.

Slocum, S. 1975. "Woman the Gatherer: Male Bias in Anthropology," in *Toward an Anthropology of Women*. Edited by R. R. Rapp, pp. 36–50. New York: Monthly Review Press.

Smith, C. S. 1970. Art, Technology, and Science: Notes on their Historical Interaction. *Technology and Culture* 11:493–549.

Smith, M. A. 1955. The Limitations of Inference in Archeology. *Archeological Newsletter* 6:3–7.

Sollas, E. 1911. *Ancient Hunters and their Modern Representatives*. London: Macmillan and Co.

Spaulding, A. 1953. Statistical Techniques for the Discovery of Artifact Types. *American Antiquity* 18(4):305–13.

Spector, J. 1993. *What this Awl Means: Feminist Archaeology at a Dakota Village*. St. Paul: Minnesota Historical Society Press.

Sperber, D. 1985. Anthropology and Psychology: Towards an Epidemiology of Representations. *Man* 20:73–89.

Squier, E., and Davis, E. 1848. *Ancient Monuments of the Mississippi Valley*. Washington, D.C.: Smithsonian Contributions to Knowledge, No. 1.

Srole, C. 1987. "'A Blessing to Mankind, and Especially to Womankind': The Typewriter and the Feminization of Clerical Work," in *Women, Work, and Technology: Transformations*. Edited by B. Drygulski Wright, M. Marx Ferree, G. Mellow et al., pp. 84–100. Ann Arbor: University of Michigan.

Stafford, B. 1991. *Body Criticism: Imagining the Unseen in Enlightment Art and Medicine*. Cambridge, Mass.: MIT Press.

Stanworth, M. Editor. 1987. *Reproductive Technologies: Gender, Motherhood, and Medicine*. Minneapolis: University of Minnesota Press.

Staudenmaier, J. 1989 [orig. 1985]. *Technology's Storytellers: Reweaving the Human Fabric.* Cambridge, Mass.: MIT Press.

Steiner, G. 1971. *In Bluebeard's Castle: Some Notes towards the Redefinition of Culture.* New Haven, Conn.: Yale University Press.

Steward, J. 1949. Cultural Causality and Law: A Trial Formulation of Early Civilization. *American Anthropologist* 51:1–27.

——1955. *Theory of Culture Change: The Methodology of Multilinear Evolution.* Urbana: University of Illinois Press.

Stocking, G., Jr. 1968. *Race, Culture, and Evolution: Essays in the History of Anthropology.* New York: Free Press.

——Editor. 1985. *Objects and Others: Essays on Museums and Material Culture.* Madison: University of Wisconsin Press.

——1987. *Victorian Anthropology.* New York: Free Press.

——Editor. 1991. *Colonial Situations: Essays on the Contextualization of Ethnographic Knowledge.* Madison: University of Wisconsin Press.

Stoczkowski, W. 1994. *Anthropologie naïve, anthropologie savante: l'origine de l'homme, de l'imagination, et des idées reçues.* Paris: CNRS.

——1997. "The Painter and Prehistoric People: A 'Hypothesis on Canvas'," in *The Cultural Life of Images: Visual Representation in Archaeology.* Edited by B. L. Molyneaux, pp. 249–62. London: Routledge.

Strathern, M. 1988. *The Gender of the Gift: Problems with Women and Problems with Society in Melanesia.* Berkeley: University of California Press.

Straus, L. G. 1986. Late Würm Adaptive Systems in Cantabrian Spain: The Case of Eastern Asturias. *Journal of Anthropological Archaeology* 5:330–68.

——1990–1. An Essay at Synthesis: Tardiglacian Adaptive Systems in the Vasco-Cantabrian and Pyrenean Regions of S. W. Europe. *Kobie (Serie Paleoantropologia). Bilbao* 19:9–22.

——1991a. "Paradigm Found? A Research Agenda for Study of the Upper and Post-Palaeolithic in Southwest Europe," in *Perspectives on the Past: Theoretical Biases in Mediterranean Hunter-Gatherer Research.* Edited by G. A. Clark, pp. 56–78. Philadelphia: University of Pennsylvania.

——1991b. Epipalaeolithic and Mesolithic Adaptations in Cantabrian Spain and Pyrenees, France. *Journal of World Prehistory* 5(1):83–104.

——1992. *Iberia before the Iberians: The Stone Age Prehistory of Cantabrian Spain.* Albuquerque: University of New Mexico Press.

——1996. "The Archaeology of the Pleistocene-Holocene Transition in Southwest Europe," in *Humans at the End of the Ice Age.* Edited by L. G. Straus, B. V. Eriksen, J. M. Erlandson, and D. R. Yesner, pp. 83–99. New York: Plenum.

Suchman, L. 1990. "Representing Practice in Cognitive Science," in *Representation in Scientific Practice.* Edited by M. Lynch and S. Woolgar, pp. 301–21. Cambridge, Mass.: MIT Press.

——in press. "The Design and Use of Contemporary Artifacts," in *Explorations in the Anthropology of Technology.* Edited by M. B. Schiffer. Albuquerque: University of New Mexico Press.

Sztompka, P. 1991. *Society in Action.* Chicago: University of Chicago Press.

——1994a. "Society as Social Becoming: Beyond Individualism and Collectivism," in *Agency and Structure: Reorienting Social Theory.* Edited by P. Sztompka, pp. 251–82. Yverdon, Switzerland: Gordon & Breach.

Sztompka, P. 1994b. "Evolving Focus on Human Agency in Contemporary Social Theory," in *Agency and Structure: Reorienting Social Theory*. Edited by P. Sztompka, pp. 25–60. Yverdon, Switzerland: Gordon & Breach.

Tanner, N. 1976. Women in Evolution II: Innovation and Selection in Human Origins. *Signs* 1:585–608.

Tanner, N., and Zihlman, A. 1976. Women in Evolution I: Innovation and Selection in Human Origins. *Signs* 1(3):104–19.

Taylor, C. 1987. "Interpretation and the Sciences of Man," in *Interpretive Social Sciences: A Second Look*. Edited by P. Rabinow and W. Sullivan, pp. 33–81. Berkeley: University of California Press.

———1989. *Sources of the Self: The Making of the Modern Identity*. Cambridge, Mass.: Harvard University Press.

Taylor, W. 1948. *The Study of Archeology*. Carbondale: University of Southern Illinois Press.

Teilhart, J. 1978. The Equivocal Role of Women Artists in Non-literate Cultures. *Heresies* 1(4):96–102.

Terrell, J. 1990. Storytelling and Prehistory. *Archaeological Method and Theory* 2:1–29.

Testart, A. 1982. The Significance of Food Storage among Hunter-Gatherers: Residence Patterns, Populations Densities, and Social Inequalities. *Current Anthropology* 23(5):523–37.

———1986. *Essai sur les fondements de la division sexuelle du travail chez les chasseurs-cueilleurs*. Paris: CNRS and Editions de l'Ecole des Hautes Etudes en Sciences Sociales.

———1988. Some Major Problems in the Social Anthropology of Hunter-Gatherers. *Current Anthropology* 29(1):1–32.

Thomas, D. H. 1974. An Archeological Perspective on Shoshonean Bands. *American Anthropologist* 76:11–23.

Thomas, J. 1993. "The Hermeneutics of Megalithic Space," in *Interpretive Archaeology*. Edited by C. Tilley, pp. 73–97. Oxford: Berg.

———1996a. Précis of Time, Culture and Identity. *Archaeological Dialogues* 3(1):6–21.

———1996b. *Time, Culture and Identity*. Oxford: Blackwell.

Thompson, M. 1977. *General Pitt-Rivers: Evolution and Archaeology in the Nineteenth Century*. Bradford-on-Avon: Moonraker Press.

Tibbetts, P. 1988. Representation and the Realist–Constructionist Controversy. *Human Studies* 11(2–3):117–32.

Tilley, C. 1982. "Social Formation, Social Structures and Social Change," in *Symbolic and Structural Archaeology*. Edited by I. Hodder, pp. 26–38. Cambridge: Cambridge University Press.

———1994. *A Phenomenology of Landscape: Places, Paths, and Monuments*. Oxford: Berg.

Torrence, R. 1983. "Time Budgeting and Hunter-Gatherer Technology," in *Hunter-Gatherer Economy in Prehistory: A European Perspective*. Edited by G. Bailey, pp. 11–22. Cambridge: Cambridge University Press.

———1986. *Production and Exchange of Stone Tools: Prehistoric Obsidian in the Aegean*. Cambridge: Cambridge University Press.

Tosi, M. 1984. "The Notion of Craft Specialization and its Representation in the Archaeological Record of Early States in the Turanian Basin," in *Marxist Perspectives in Archaeology*. Edited by M. Spriggs, pp. 22–52. Cambridge: Cambridge University Press.

Toth, N.; Clark, J. D.; and Ligabue, G. 1992. The Last Stone Ax Makers. *Scientific American* 267(1):88–93.

Touraine, A. 1984. *Le retour de l'actor*. Paris: Faynard.

Trescott, M. Editor. 1979. *Dynamos and Virgins Revisited: Women and Technological Change in History*. Metuchen, N.J.: Scarecrow Press.

Trigger, B. 1980. Archaeology and the Image of the American Indian. *American Antiquity* 45(4):662–76.

———1984. Alternative Archaeologies: Nationalist, Colonialist, Imperialist. *Man* (n.s.) 19:355–70.

———1989. *A History of Archaeological Thought*. Cambridge: Cambridge University Press.

Tylor, E. B. 1873. *The Origins of Culture*. New York: Harper & Row.

———1878. *Researches into the Early History of Mankind and the Development of Civilisation*. London: John Murray.

Ucko, P. 1970. Penis Sheaths: A Comparative Study. The Curl Lecture. *Proceedings of the Royal Anthropological Institute for 1969*: 27–67.

Valenz, D. 1995. *The First Industrial Woman*. New York: Oxford University Press.

van der Leeuw, S. E. 1993. "Giving the Potter a Choice: Conceptual Aspects of Pottery Techniques," in *Technological Choices: Transformation in Material Cultures since the Neolithic*. Edited by P. Lemonnier, pp. 238–88. London: Routledge.

———1994. "Cognitive Aspects of 'Technique,'" in *The Ancient Mind: Elements of Cognitive Archaeology*. Edited by C. Renfrew and E. B. W. Zubrow, pp. 135–42. Cambridge: Cambridge University Press.

van der Leeuw, S. E., and Papousek, D. A. 1992. "Tradition and Innovation," in *Ethnoarchéologie: justification, problèmes, limites*. Edited by A. Gallay, F. Audouze, and V. Roux, pp. 135–58. Juan-les-Pins: APDCA.

van der Leeuw, S. E.; Papousek, D. A.; and Coudart, A. 1991. Technical Traditions and Unquestioned Assumptions: The Case of Pottery in Michoacan. *Techniques et Culture* 17–18:145–73.

Vauclair, J., and Anderson, J. 1994. Object Manipulation, Tool Use, and the Social Context in Human and Non-human Primates. *Techniques et Culture* 23–4:121–36.

Velson, J., and Clark, T. 1975. Transport of Stone Monuments to the La Venta and San Lorenzo Sites. *Contributions of the University of California Archaeological Research Facility* 24:1–39.

Vickers, B. 1991. "Francis Bacon," in *The Blackwell Companion to the Enlightenment*. Edited by J. W. Yolton, R. Porter, P. Rogers, and B. M. Stafford, pp. 50–2. Oxford: Blackwell.

Vidale, M. 1989. "Specialized Producers and Urban Elites: On the Role of Craft Industries in Mature Harappan Urban Contexts," in *Old Problems and New Perspectives in the Archaeology of South Asia*. Edited by J. M. Kenoyer, pp. 171–81. Madison: University of Wisconsin Press.

Vogel, S. 1995 [orig. 1991]. "New Science, New Nature: The Habermas–

Marcuse Debate Revisited," in *Technology and the Politics of Knowledge.* Edited by A. Feenberg and A. Hannay, pp. 23–42. Bloomington: Indiana University Press.

von Neumann, J. 1945. A Model of General Economic Equilibrium. *Review of Economic Studies* 13.

Wagner, R. 1991. "The Fractal Person," in *Big Men and Great Men: Personifications of Power in Melanesia.* Edited by M. Strathern and M. Godelier, pp. 159–73. Cambridge: Cambridge University Press.

Wajcman, J. 1996. [orig. 1991]. *Feminism Confronts Technology.* University Park: Pennsylvania State University Press.

Wallace, M. 1986. "Visiting the Past: History Museums in the United States," in *Presenting the Past: Essays on the History and the Public.* Edited by S. Porter Benson, S. Brier, and R. Rosenzweig, pp. 137–61. Philadelphia: Temple University Press.

Washburn, D. 1977. *A Symmetry Analysis of Upper Gila Area Ceramic Design.* Peabody Museum Papers, vol. 68. Cambridge, Mass.: Harvard University Press.

—— 1994. "Style, Perception, and Geometry," in *Style, Society, and Person: Archaeological and Ethnological Perspectives.* Edited by C. Carr and J. E. Neitzel, pp. 101–22. New York: Plenum.

Watson, P. J. 1991. "A Parochial Primer: The New Dissonance as Seen from the Midcontinental United States," in *Processual and Post-Processual Archaeologies: Multiple Ways of Knowing the Past.* Edited by R. Preucel, pp. 265–76. Center for Archaeological Investigation, Occasional Paper No. 10. Carbondale: Southern Illinois University Press.

Watson, P. J.; Le Blanc, S.; and Redman, C. 1971. *Explanation in Archeology: An Explicitly Scientific Approach.* New York: Columbia University Press.

Weber, M. 1946 [orig. 1915]. "Religious Rejections of the World and their Directions," in *From Max Weber: Essays in Sociology.* Edited by H. Gerth and C. W. Mills, pp. 323–59. New York: Oxford University Press.

Wenger, E. 1998. *Communities of Practice: Learning, Meaning, and Identity.* New York: Cambridge University Press.

Westfall, R. S. 1991. "Isaac Newton," in *The Blackwell Companion to the Enlightenment.* Edited by J. W. Yolton, R. Porter, P. Rogers, and B. M. Stafford, pp. 366–67. Oxford: Blackwell.

Westkott, M. 1979. Feminist Criticism of the Social Sciences. *Harvard Educational Review* 49:422–30.

White, L. 1959. *The Evolution of Culture: The Development of Civilization to the Fall of Rome.* New York: McGraw-Hill.

White, L., Jr. 1967. The Historical Roots of our Ecologic Crisis. *Science* 155:1203–7.

White, R. 1989. "Production Complexity and Standardization in Early Aurignacian Bead and Pendant Manufacture: Evolutionary Implications," in *The Human Revolution: Behavioural and Biological Perspectives in the Origins of Modern Humans.* Edited by P. Mellars and C. Stringer, pp. 366–90. Edinburgh: Edinburgh University Press.

—— 1992. Beyond Art: Towards an Understanding of the Origins of

Material Representation in Europe. *Annual Review of Anthropology* 21:537–64.

—— 1993. "Technological and Social Dimensions of 'Aurignacian-Age' Body Ornaments across Europe," in *Before Lascaux: The Complex Record of the Early Upper Palaeolithic*. Edited by H. Knecht, R. White, and A. Pike-Tay, pp. 277–99. Boca Raton, Fla.: CRC Press.

Whitehead, A. 1927. *Science and the Modern World*. New York: Macmillan.

Willey, G., and Sabloff, J. 1974. *A History of American Archaeology*. San Francisco: W. H. Freeman.

Williams, R. 1973. *The Country and the City*. New York: Chatto & Windus.

Winner, L. 1977. *Autonomous Technology: Technics-out-of-Control as a Theme in Political Thought*. Cambridge, Mass.: MIT Press.

—— 1983. "Technologies as Forms of Life," in *Epistemology, Methodology, and the Social Sciences*. Edited by R. Cohen and M. Wartofsky, pp. 249–63. Dordrecht, Holland: D. Reidel.

—— 1986a [orig. 1980]. "Do Artifacts Have Politics?," in *The Whale and the Reactor: A Search for the Limits in an Age of High Technology*, pp. 19–39. Chicago: University of Chicago Press.

—— 1986b. *The Whale and the Reactor: A Search for the Limits in an Age of High Technology*. Chicago: University of Chicago Press.

—— 1991. "Upon Opening the Black Box and Finding it Empty: Social Constructivism and the Philosophy of Technology," in *The Technology of Discovery and the Discovery of Technology*. Edited by J. Pitt and E. Lugo, pp. 503–19, Proceedings of the Sixth International Conference of the Society for Philosophy and Technology. Blacksburg: Virginia Polytechnic.

—— 1995 [orig. 1992]. "Citizen Virtues in a Technological Order," in *Technology and the Politics of Knowledge*. Edited by A. Feenberg and A. Hannay, pp. 65–84. Bloomington: Indiana University Press.

Winterhalder, B., and Smith, E. A. Editors. 1981. *Hunter-Gatherer Foraging Strategies: Ethnographic and Archeological Analysis*. Chicago: University of Chicago Press.

Wissler, C. 1923. *Man and Culture*. New York: Thomas Y. Crowell.

Wobst, H. M. 1997. "Towards an 'Appropriate Metrology' of Human Action in Archaeology," in *Time, Process, and Structured Transformation in Archaeology*. Edited by S. van der Leeuw and J. McGlade, pp. 426–48. London: Routledge.

—— in press. "Agency in (Spite of) Material Culture," in *Agency in Archaeology*. Edited by M-A. Dobres and J. E. Robb. London: Routledge.

Wolf, E. 1982. *Europe and the People without History*. Berkeley: University of California Press.

Wolf, M. 1974. "Chinese Women: Old Skills in a New Context," in *Women, Culture, and Society*. Edited by M. Z. Rosaldo and L. Lamphere, pp. 157–72. Stanford, Cal.: Stanford University Press.

Wolin, R. W. Editor. 1991. *The Heidegger Controversy: A Critical Reader*. New York: Columbia University Press.

Woolgar, S. 1990. "Time and Documents in Researcher Interaction: Some Ways of Making out What is Happening in Experimental Science," in

Representation in Scientific Practice. Edited by M. Lynch and S. Woolgar, pp. 123–52. Cambridge, Mass.: MIT Press.

Wright, J., and Mazel, A. 1987. Bastions of Ideology: The Depiction of Precolonial History in the Museums of Natal and KwaZulu. *South African Museum Arts Bulletin* 17(7–8):301–10.

—— 1991. Controlling the Past in the Museums of Natal and KwaZulu. *Critical Arts* 5(3):59–77.

Wright, R. P. 1991. "Women's Labor and Pottery Production in Prehistory," in *Engendering Archaeology: Women and Prehistory.* Edited by J. M. Gero and M. W. Conkey, pp. 194–223. Oxford: Basil Blackwell.

Wylie, A. 1985a. Putting Shakertown Back Together. *Journal of Anthropological Archaeology* 4:133–47.

—— 1985b. Between Philosophy and Archaeology. *American Antiquity* 50(2):478–90.

—— 1986. "Bootstrapping in the Un-natural Sciences: An Archaeological Case," in *Proceedings of the Philosophy of Science Association,* vol. 1. Edited by A. Fine and P. Machamer, pp. 314–22. East Lansing, Mich.: Philosophy of Science Association.

—— 1989. "Matters of Fact and Matters of Interest," in *Archaeological Approaches to Cultural Identity.* Edited by A. Shennan, pp. 94–109. London: Unwin Hyman.

—— 1992a. "On 'Heavily Decomposing Red Herrings': Scientific Method in Archaeology and the Ladening of Evidence with Theory," in *Metaarchaeology.* Edited by L. Embree, pp. 269–88. Dordrecht, Holland: Kluwer.

—— 1992b. The Interplay of Evidential Constraints and Political Interests: Recent Archaeological Research on Gender. *American Antiquity* 57(1):15–35.

—— 1996. "The Constitution of Archaeological Evidence: Gender, Politics, and Science," in *Disunity and Contextualism: New Directions in the Philosophy of Science Studies.* Edited by P. Galison and D. Stump, pp. 311–43. Stanford, Cal.: Stanford University Press.

—— 1997. The Engendering of Archaeology: Refiguring Feminist Science Studies. *Osiris* 12:80–99.

Wynn, T. 1985. Piaget, Stone Tools, and the Evolution of Human Intelligence. *World Archaeology* 17(1):32–43.

—— 1989. *The Evolution of Spatial Competence.* Illinois Studies in Anthropology, vol. 17. Urbana: University of Illinois Press.

Young, J. 1997. *Heidegger, Philosophy, Nazism.* Cambridge: Cambridge University Press.

Zimmerman, M. E. 1990. *Heidegger's Confrontation with Modernity: Technology, Politics, and Art.* Bloomington: Indiana University Press.

Index

35656417